NEW YORK REVIEW
CLASSICS

MEMOIRS FROM BEYOND THE GRAVE

FRANÇOIS-RENÉ DE CHATEAUBRIAND (1768–1848) was born in Saint-Malo, on the northern coast of Brittany, the youngest son of an aristocratic family. After an isolated adolescence, spent largely in his father's castle, he moved to Paris not long before the Revolution began. In 1791, he sailed for America but quickly returned to Europe, where he enrolled in the counterrevolutionary army, was wounded, and emigrated to England. The novellas *Atala* and *René*, published shortly after his return to France in 1800, made him a literary celebrity. Long recognized as one of the first French Romantics, Chateaubriand was also a historian, a diplomat, and a staunch defender of the freedom of the press. Today, he is best remembered for his posthumously published *Memoirs from Beyond the Grave*.

ALEX ANDRIESSE is a writer and translator. He lives in the Netherlands.

ANKA MUHLSTEIN was awarded the Prix Goncourt in 1996 for her biography of Astolphe de Custine and has twice received the History Prize of the French Academy. Her books include *Balzac's Omelette*, *Monsieur Proust's Library*, and, most recently, *The Pen and the Brush*.

MEMOIRS FROM BEYOND THE GRAVE

1768–1800

FRANÇOIS-RENÉ DE CHATEAUBRIAND

Translated from the French by
ALEX ANDRIESSE

Introduction by
ANKA MUHLSTEIN

NEW YORK REVIEW BOOKS

New York

THIS IS A NEW YORK REVIEW BOOK
PUBLISHED BY THE NEW YORK REVIEW OF BOOKS
435 Hudson Street, New York, NY 10014
www.nyrb.com

Library of Congress Cataloging-in-Publication Data
Names: Chateaubriand, François-René, vicomte de, 1768–1848 author. |
   Andriesse, Alex translator.
Title: Memoirs from beyond the grave : 1768–1800 / by François-René de
   Chateaubriand ; introduction by Anka Muhlstein ; translation by Alex
   Andriesse.
Description: New York : New York Review Books, 2018.
Identifiers: LCCN 2017025073 (print) | LCCN 2017028760 (ebook) | ISBN
   9781681371306 (epub) | ISBN 9781681371290 (alk. paper)
Subjects: LCSH: France—History—Consulate and First Empire, 1799–1815. |
   Napoleon I, Emperor of the French, 1769–1821—Contemporaries.
Classification: LCC DC255.C4 (ebook) | LCC DC255.C4 A3 2017 (print) |
   DDC 944.04—dc23
LC record available at https://lccn.loc.gov/2017025073

ISBN 978-1-68137-129-0
Available as an electronic book; ISBN 978-1-68137-130-6

Printed in the United States of America on acid-free paper.
10 9 8 7 6 5 4 3 2

CONTENTS

INTRODUCTION

BORN IN 1768 during the reign of Louis XV, François-René de Chateaubriand died in 1848, a few months after the revolution that drove Louis-Philippe from the throne and paved the way to the reign of Napoleon III. Thus did Chateaubriand straddle not only two centuries but also two worlds, that of the ancien régime and that of the modern era. He was brought up in the solitude of a medieval castle, nestled in the woods of Brittany, by a father whose nostalgia for feudal times was unremitting. At eighteen, he left his family home and enlisted as a sublieutenant in the royal army and was thrown into the vortex of the most turbulent period of French history, a span of time marked by the Revolution of 1789, the downfall of the monarchy and the execution of the king, the advent of Napoleon Bonaparte and the empire, the restoration of the Bourbon dynasty after the definite defeat of Napoleon by the powers that joined in the Holy Alliance, its overthrow by the Revolution of July 1830, the inauguration of Louis-Philippe and the establishment of the July monarchy, and finally the birth of the short-lived Second Republic.

How did Chateaubriand live through and adapt to these tumultuous times? The brutal scenes he witnessed in Paris during the first months of the Revolution shattered him, and realizing that he had to leave France, at least temporarily, he resolved to sail to America in the hope of finding the elusive Northwest Passage. Like so many others, he failed in this undertaking, but the voyage was otherwise rewarding. He discovered American democracy and, more important yet for his particular sensibility and sometimes frenzied imagination, the splendor of the wilderness of the New World. However, as soon as he heard the news of the arrest of Louis XVI at Varennes, he decided to cut his American sojourn short and return to France. There he joined the army loyal to the king, which was swiftly defeated by the revolutionary forces.

Sick and wounded, Chateaubriand took refuge in England where, like many of his compatriots, he made a meager living as a tutor and translator of French. All the while he was working on the novels that would make him famous.

Order was finally restored in France during the Consulate, and Chateaubriand concluded that it would be safe for him to return to Paris. His novels, *Atala* and *René*, brought him success and distinction and gave him reason to hope that Bonaparte would find an appropriate role for him in the new regime. But after a promising start, Chateaubriand broke with a government that was becoming more and more authoritarian, and spent the remaining years of Napoleonic rule writing and traveling. He wandered through Italy and Greece, reached Jerusalem, and came back to Paris through Spain. These journeys provided indispensable material for his later oeuvre.

Convinced that the Bourbon Restoration of 1815 would inaugurate a moderate and honorable regime, he agreed to join the new government. The publication of *The Genius of Christianity* had earned Chateaubriand a lasting reputation in influential Catholic circles. Louis XVIII, eager to have him on his side, named him Minister of State and later entrusted him with embassies in Berlin and London, but Chateaubriand did not have an easy rapport with the king's entourage. "This Janus, guardian of the past and obsessed by visions of the future . . . too lucid, too independent, not easily deceived"* was regarded with suspicion. His energetic defense of the freedom of the press finally made his resignation inevitable. The Bourbon dynasty, itself obsessed by the past, was fragile. Charles X, who succeeded his brother Louis XVIII in 1824, was ousted six years later by the Revolution of July 1830 and fled the country. Much to the disgust of

---

*Jean-Paul Clément in his introduction, Chateaubriand, *Mémoires d'outre-tombe*, vol. I (Gallimard: Paris, 1997), 36.

Chateaubriand, the king's cousin Louis-Philippe d'Orléans replaced
Charles on the throne. Chateaubriand, who remained faithful to the
legitimate branch of the Bourbons, retired from public life.

Chateaubriand was attached to the past and its centuries-old
traditions, but he was also a liberal, open to modernity: this is one
thing that sets him apart in the history of ideas. He had been repulsed
by the discourse and the violence of the French revolutionaries and
was deeply impressed by the powerful composure of George Washington, "the representative of the needs, ideas, intelligence, and opinions of his epoch." He had a vision of social transformation that did
not entail the obliteration of the past, and was proud to declare
himself "Bourboniste by honor, royalist by reason and republican by
inclination."

The *Memoirs from Beyond the Grave* cover a lifetime. Chateaubriand
claims to have begun them in 1811, but in fact the first passages of the
Memoirs were written as early as 1803 or 1804. The last corrections
were made in 1846. The history of the publication of the *Memoirs* is
complicated. Financially ruined by 1836, as his resignation from the
Chamber of Peers in protest against the regime of Louis-Philippe
entailed the loss of practically all his income, Chateaubriand agreed
to sell the rights to publication to a limited partnership that raised
sufficient funds to extend to him a down payment of 155,000 francs
along with the promise of an annuity of 12,000 francs for him and,
should she survive him, his wife. Chateaubriand had hoped to delay
publication for half a century after his death, but his new patrons,
unsurprisingly, had a different schedule in mind and he had to accept
a less distant date. In 1844, the society sold its rights to Émile de
Girardin, the director of the newspaper *La Presse*, who announced
that he would begin serializing the *Memoirs* as soon as Chateaubriand
died. Though indignant, Chateaubriand was powerless to alter Girardin's decision, so he set about enlarging and carefully revising his
memoirs as a whole. Unfortunately neither the newspaper editors
nor the first publishers took his changes into consideration. It was

only a century later, thanks to the Pléiade edition, that French readers gained access to the correct version of Chateaubriand's text.

The *Memoirs* did not enjoy an immediate success, but their appeal
grew in the years after publication. Baudelaire was one of Chateaubriand's first admirers and considered him "a master when it came
to language and style";* Proust recognized his debt to the "marvelous
and transcendent"† artist who was the first to recognize the power of
involuntary memory. Closer to us in time, General de Gaulle, after
his resignation in 1946, confessed: "I don't care about anything, I am
immersed in the *Memoirs from Beyond the Grave*."‡

The *Memoirs* are characterized by a striking freedom. Composed
as they were over an extensive period of time, they display an uncon-
ventional and distinctive sense of chronology. Chateaubriand does
not separate his life at the time he was writing from the period of the
past he is describing, nor does he hesitate to insert himself into his
narrative when the occasion arises. The result is a double strand: that
of the events he recalls and that of the moment of composition of the
narrative. "The changing forms of my life are thus intermingled," he
explained. "It has sometimes happened that, in my moments of prosperity, I have had to speak of times when I was poor, and in my days
of tribulation, to retrace days when I was happy." At one point, for
example, he humorously interrupts his story: in his capacity as an
ambassador, he has an urgent diplomatic question to take care of, and
he begs the reader to be patient. Indeed, Chateaubriand revels in a
certain insouciance, throughout his memoirs. "At the most critical
and decisive moments, he turns into a dreamer and starts talking to
swallows and crows in the trees along the road,"§ commented an irritated Sainte-Beuve.

*Baudelaire to Armand du Mesnil, February 9, 1861, in Charles Baudelaire, *Œuvres
complètes*, vol. II, edited by Claude Pichois (Paris: Gallimard, 1976), 152.
†Marcel Proust, "Chateaubriand," in *Contre Sainte-Beuve* (Paris: Gallimard, 1971),
652.
‡Quoted by Jean-Claude Berchet in the preface to Chateaubriand, *Mémoires
d'outre-tombe* (Paris: Garnier, 1989), 5.
§Sainte-Beuve, *Causeries du Lundi*, vol. II (Paris: Garnier Frères, 1852), 431.

Thus Chateaubriand will freely pass from pure reportage, for example in his closely observed description of Paris in the first months of the revolution, to introspective analyses; from historical or political considerations to lyrical evocations of nature; and from light anecdotes to carefully drawn portraits, even as he casually intersperses Greek and Latin quotations throughout. And yet for all this wide diversity, the work is meticulously constructed, which is one of the reasons why Chateaubriand was appalled at the prospect of serialization, since the cutting of the *Memoirs* into pieces was sure to obliterate the sense of the architecture of the whole. He may have never shrunk from a digression, but he adhered closely to the three-part plan of composition he announces at the beginning of his work, which corresponds to the principal stages of his career: soldier and traveler during the Revolution, writer during the empire, and political figure during the restoration.

From the beginning of the *Memoirs*, two passions emerge: for women and for politics. Though Chateaubriand observes a gentlemanly discretion, the scent of feminine presence permeates the text—from the imaginary enchantress of his adolescence to Juliette Récamier, who would become the object of his enduring adoration. And, in passing, a succession of graces is evoked: the young fisher-girl collecting tea leaves in Newfoundland; the light-footed Indian girls with "their long eyes half concealed beneath satin lids"; the modest Miss Ives who brightened his stay in England; the mercurial Delphine de Sabran of the long, blond tresses; the poignant consumptive Pauline de Beaumont, who joined him in Rome only to die in his arms; and many others who remained unnamed. The one woman who never appealed to his imagination or his senses was his wife. Unable to resist the entreaties of his mother and his sister, he had reluctantly married the eighteen-year-old Céleste de Lavigne on his return from America. The young couple was separated almost immediately by Chateaubriand's short stint in the army and long exile in England. They were reunited twelve years later. Though Chateaubriand paid homage to the moral qualities of his wife, their life together lacked warmth and liveliness. According to Victor Hugo, Madame de Chateaubriand was stiff, ugly, charitable without being kind, witty without being intelligent. Worse than anything else she bored her husband.

Chateaubriand had taken a devouring interest in politics ever since he witnessed, as a very young man, the first assemblies of the Breton noblemen asserting their independence. Somewhat later, his observation of political life in the United States and in Great Britain, and his relief at the quelling of the revolutionary fervor during the Consulate, confirmed him in the conviction that society was subject to change. Back in Paris in 1800, after his long stay in England, he rejoiced at the reuniting of families, the reopening of churches, the return of order even when it meant that an émigré might be seen chatting with the murderers of friends and family, and concluded: "A fact is a fact.... One has to take men as they are and not always see them as they are not and as they cannot be anymore."* It should be said, however, that though politics is one of the great subjects of the *Memoirs*, Chateaubriand himself never played an important political role. Nor for that matter does he pretend that he did. The charm and relevance of the *Memoirs* lie more in his constant introspection than in his scrutiny of the outside world. Chateaubriand once wrote: "It seemed to me that the apparent disorder that one finds [in my book] in revealing the inner state of a man is perhaps not without a certain charm."† The true subject of the work is a man speaking with himself.

One of the great difficulties, a difficulty admirably surmounted by Alex Andriesse, of translating the *Memoirs* is the wealth and the variety of Chateaubriand's language. He turns to archaic French in the pages on his childhood in the medieval atmosphere of Brittany; he grows technical in his description of Atlantic navigation; he produces sumptuous lyrical poetry when he evokes Niagara Falls or the melancholy of Roman ruins. He has a taste for the rare word and a

---

*Chateaubriand, "Réflexions politiques," in *Grands Ecrits Politiques*, vol. I (Paris: Imprimerie Nationale, 1993), 215.
†Berchet, 6.

passion for precision. He was himself very conscious of his gift for shifting from a classical register to boldly romantic forms of expression rendered in a language so free that to men of the previous generations it appeared barbarous. His extravagance was, he claimed, always tempered by his ability to "respect the ear."

Chateaubriand's style reflects, as he knew, the constant tug-of-war between past and present that inspired him in many ways. He knew better than to fight these contradictions. "Due to a bizarre fusion two men coexist in me, the man of the past and the man of today, and it happened that both the ancient French language and the modern one came to me naturally."*

The result is a glorious literary monument.

—ANKA MUHLSTEIN

---

*Draft of a preface to the *Memoirs*, quoted in Berchet, 48.

CHATEAUBRIAND IN AMERICA

A Translator's Note

"Dreaming is another world."

—Gérard de Nerval

WHY DID François-René de Chateaubriand go to America? If his *Mémoires d'outre-tombe* are to be believed, it was because he feared for his life. In 1789, two years before he journeyed across the Atlantic, he had seen the severed heads of Foulon and Bertier carried through the streets of Paris on pikes and then watched as the chaos mounted around him. "It was enough to bear an 'aristocratic' name to be exposed to persecution," he writes: "the more conscientious and moderate your opinions, the more suspect and prone to attack." By January 1791, the twenty-two-year-old chevalier had made up his mind to leave the turbulence of Paris for the coast of Brittany and set sail for the United States.

But he was not about to leave France without some ostensible purpose for his trip. That would have been out of keeping with his character, and if the Republican authorities came to think of him as an enemy of the state fleeing from justice, potentially dangerous. With the encouragement of his mentor, Malesherbes, he convinced himself that he was going to America not only to save his neck but to discover the Northwest Passage, the semilegendary sea route connecting the Atlantic with the Pacific—a plan hatched out of desperation and a child's fascination with tales of exotic adventures, guidebooks, and maps.

Whether Chateaubriand seriously imagined he could discover the Northwest Passage without any financial assistance or knowledge of

North American terrain is unclear. Leaving aside the horrors he had witnessed in Paris, he had little experience of the wider world. He was a Breton boy who'd grown up in Saint-Malo, a stony port town famous for its seagoing sons (Du Fresne, Jacques Cartier), and at the tender age of twenty-two, his proudest accomplishment was having placed a short poem in the *Almanach des Muses*, the appearance of which, he recalls in the *Memoirs*, "nearly killed me with hope and fear." It is just possible that such a person at such an age might really have believed that he alone could find what no earlier explorer had found.

In any event, Chateaubriand sailed for Baltimore from Saint-Malo in April 1791 aboard a two-masted vessel called the *Saint-Pierre*. After a series of stops in the Azores, on the island of Saint-Pierre, and along the Virginian coast, he arrived in Baltimore in July, traveled on to Philadelphia and New York City by stagecoach, up the Hudson to Albany by boat, and on horseback through the dense forests of New York State to Niagara Falls. Beyond this point, Chateaubriand's itinerary becomes hazy, as if clouded by the great falls' mist. According to the *Memoirs*, he went from Niagara to Lake Erie, from Lake Erie to Pittsburgh, from Pittsburgh to what today is Cairo, Illinois. Considering the limited velocity allowed by early American travel and the fact that Chateaubriand had fractured his arm by falling off a high rock while trying to get a better view of Niagara Falls, it would have required fantastic diligence to cover all this ground and still catch a ship back to France from Philadelphia in December, but I suppose it could be done. I don't suppose, however, that Chateaubriand could have gone on, as he claims, to follow the Natchez Trace down from Nashville before wending his way through Kentucky and Virginia, over the Appalachian Mountains, back to the mighty Delaware, all in the course of five late-eighteenth-century months. At some point, the journey he recounts is sublimed from the shifting sands of memory into the upper atmosphere of imagination.

It is not hard to comprehend why Chateaubriand felt free to bend the truth about his travels. When he visited America, he was younger than Shelley or Keats in their prime, and though he was nearer to thirty when he wrote about America in *Atala* and *René*, he was by then a starving exile in England, showing all the gruesome symptoms of advanced tuberculosis; he could have had no idea that he would survive, become famous, and then, in going on to write his autobiography, as Alfonso Reyes puts it, "be obliged to enlarge his journey immeasurably." Yet I suspect that this view of the matter is too rational, too close to the ground. I suspect that Chateaubriand conceived of America—as he conceived of his father's medieval castle in rural Brittany—as a land of dreams, a continent of solitude, a second space. This second space is essential to understanding Chateaubriand's writing.

The *Mémoires d'outre-tombe* are not exactly a historical document. They are a concoction of the imagination, a composite of memory and myth. Julien Gracq, in his book *Reading Writing* (1980), acknowledges this when he speaks of Chateaubriand's "mythomania," which is to say his tendency to mythologize experience, to heighten reality, to insert himself, Where's Waldo–like, into every conceivable historical tableau. Probably there is no clearer example of this tendency than the account Chateaubriand gives of his meeting with George Washington in Philadelphia—a meeting that in all likelihood never occurred. In July 1791, when Chateaubriand claims to have called on Washington, the president was laid up in bed, recovering from the recurrence of a carbuncle on his left buttock, and by all accounts was not seeing visitors.

Faced with this almost certainly fictitious episode, readers who value the *Memoirs* mainly for their historical insights are forced either to condemn the author as a self-aggrandizing liar or, as the biographer George Painter does in *Chateaubriand: The Longed-for Tempests, 1768–1793*, to set themselves the hopeless task of proving the veracity of Chateaubriand's inventions.* On the other hand, readers who come

---

*Painter is at pains to demonstrate that Chateaubriand did indeed meet Washington, just not in the month that he remembers having done so.

to the *Memoirs* as a work of literature seldom seem to care whether the interview with Washington ever took place. In the eyes of Gracq, the episode is proof only of Chateaubriand's raconteurial charm. "Even when he recounts his fake visit with Washington," Gracq says, "his mythomania always remains good-natured, a wink at the reader." Indeed, most of the *Memoirs*' finest French readers (Charles Baude-laire, Marcel Proust, Roland Barthes, Marc Fumaroli) have hardly paid the fake visit with Washington—or, for that matter, the fake voyage to the American South—any mind.

One could draw large conclusions from this divide between French and English reactions to Chateaubriand's fibbing and say that while the French are satisfied by a well-told tale, we Anglophones can't help but fact-check. Given a choice between beauty and truth, we prefer the truth, ideally unvarnished. Just consider the colorless titles the *Mémoires d'outre-tombe* have been given over the years by English publishers and translators: *Memoirs of Chateaubriand* (anonymous, 1849); *The Memoirs of Chateaubriand* (Robert Baldick, 1961); *The Memoirs of François René, Vicomte de Chateaubriand, Sometime Ambassador to England* (Alexander Teixeira de Mattos, 1902).* Every one of these titles suggests that the significance of the book lies in the author's pedigree or the conjuring power of his name. And in doing so they belie the very thing that distinguishes Chateaubriand's scribbling from the hundreds of other memoirs composed by his contemporaries: its artfulness, its architecture, its phrasal flair, all that the historian Philip Mansel calls "the seduction of its style."

My approach has been different. Although this is not a complete edition of the *Memoirs*, it does reproduce the first of the work's four parts, including the oft-omitted chapter headings and detailed dates of composition. As for the translation, it is, I recognize, imperfect and provisional—a failure in a sense. However, as I failed, I tried always to bear in mind that the work I was wrenching into English

---

*Baldick (or the people at Penguin Books) originally titled his abridged translation *The Memoirs of Chateaubriand*, although when Penguin reissued the book as a paperback in 2014, they also rebranded it: *Memoirs from Beyond the Tomb*.

was the work of a writer steeped in literary tradition. I hope that this is reflected in the prose itself, but it is on deliberate display in the notes at the end of the volume, where I have tried to give some sense of Chateaubriand's personal canon. This canon included not only the expected Greek, Latin, and French classics but the English, the Italian, the Portuguese, and the Persian, not to mention Jewish and Christian scripture, medieval lais, Breton proverbs, popular song lyrics, and Catholic hymns, all of which are incorporated into his gargantuan text.

Compiling notes is child's play, though, in comparison with trying to capture some reverberation of Chateaubriand's style in English. Because this style is stifled in earlier translations and abridgements, it may sometimes seem to echo later writers who followed after it. Thus, in my rendering, Chateaubriand may occasionally sound like Cioran (who called him "a sonorous Pascal"), or Baudelaire (who called him "one of the surest and rarest masters"), or Proust (who compared his distinctive sentences to the barn owl's distinctive cry), or Sebald (who so seamlessly integrated passages of the *Memoirs* into the penultimate chapter of *The Rings of Saturn*). It is not that I intended to echo the style of any of these writers, but that, in certain turns of phrase, certain attitudes, certain moods, all of their styles resemble one another. Chateaubriand is their precursor.

The *Memoirs from Beyond the Grave* have come to be considered a classic of French literature as much for the elegiac beauty of their language as for the way they capture an age. If they are the recollections of a sometime ambassador, a part-time politician, and a onetime celebrity, they are also the masterwork of an artist in consummate control of his prose. The person who writes that, on the day of his birth, his mother "inflicted" life on him, who makes up a meeting with George Washington and has the gall to declare that the first president "resembled his portraits," has picked up the plume for more complicated reasons than the urge to compose a record of his times. The seductiveness of the *Memoirs*' style—what Barthes calls the "vivid, sumptuous, desirable seal of Chateaubriand's writing"—makes questions of factual authenticity seem piddling. The voice of the *Memoirs* is the voice of the private man behind the public façade, the grown-up boy who left home out of fear and in search of the Northwest Passage, the death-haunted exile, the solitary writer at his desk at night, who knew that he had to imagine himself and his world into being, as if everywhere were America, a second space and a dominion of dreams.

—ALEX ANDRIESSE

MEMOIRS FROM BEYOND THE GRAVE

PREFACE

Paris, April 14, 1846;
Revised July 28, 1846

"as a cloud ... as the swift ships ... as a shadow"

—*Job*[1]

As IT IS impossible for me to predict the moment of my death, and at my age the days accorded a man are but days of grace, or rather days of rigor, I am going to offer a few words of explanation.

On September 4, I will have reached my seventy-eighth year. It is high time for me to leave a world that is fast leaving me and that I shall not mourn.

The same sad necessity which has always held its foot against my throat has forced me to sell these *Memoirs*. No one can know what I have suffered, having been obliged to pawn my tomb; but I owed this final sacrifice to my solemn promises and to the consistency of my conduct. It is perhaps cowardly of me, but I have regarded these *Memoirs* as private, and I would have liked not to part with them. My plan was to leave them to Madame de Chateaubriand, who could have sent them out into the world as she pleased, or else suppressed them. The latter seems more preferable to me than ever today.

Ah! if only, before leaving this world, I could have found someone trustworthy enough, someone rich enough to buy back the shares of the Society[2]—someone who would not, like them, be compelled to put my work to press the moment my death knell tolls! A few of the shareholders are my friends, it's true, and several others are kind people who have tried to be of use to me; but finally the shares may be sold; they may be transferred to third parties whom I do not know and whose family interests must come first. It is only natural that my life, so long as it continues, should be an importunity to them, or at least a bother. In short, if I were still master of these *Memoirs*, I would either keep the manuscript to myself or delay their publication until fifty years after my death.

These *Memoirs* have been composed at different dates and in different countries. For this reason, I have been obliged to add some prefatory passages which describe the places that I had before my eyes and the feelings that were in my heart when the thread of my narrative was resumed. The changing forms of my life are thus intermingled. It has sometimes happened that, in my moments of prosperity, I have had to speak of times when I was poor, and in my days of tribulation, to retrace days when I was happy. My childhood entering into my old age, the gravity of experience weighing on the lightness of youth, the rays of my sun mingling and merging together, from its dawn to its dusk, have produced in my stories a kind of confusion, or, if you will, a kind of ineffable unity. My cradle has something of the grave, my grave something of the cradle; my sufferings become pleasures, my pleasures pains, so that I no longer know, having just finished reading over these *Memoirs*, whether they are the product of a brown-haired youth or a head gray with age.

I cannot say whether this mixture, which anyhow I cannot remedy, will be pleasing or displeasing to the reader; it is the fruit of my ever-changing lot: the tempests have often left me with no writing table except the rock where I was shipwrecked.

Though I have been pressed to let some pieces of these *Memoirs* appear in my lifetime, I would prefer to speak from the depth of my coffin. My narrative will then be accompanied by those voices which have something sacred about them because they issue from the sepulcher. If I have suffered enough in this world to be a happy shade in the next, a ray from the Elysian Fields shall cast a protective light on these last pictures of mine. Life fitted me badly; death, perhaps, will suit me better.

These *Memoirs* have been my constant thought. Saint Bonaventure was granted heavenly sanction to go on writing his book after death: I cannot hope for such a favor, much as I would like to be resurrected one night, at the witching hour, to correct my proofs. Yet soon enough Eternity will have clapped its hands over my ears and, having joined the dusty family of the deaf, I will no longer hear anyone.

If one part of my work has been more captivating to me than others, it is that which concerns my youth—the obscurest corner of my life. There, I have had to reawaken a world known only to me; I found, as I wandered in that vanished company, nothing but memories and silence. Of all the people I have known, how many are still alive today?

On August 25, 1828, the inhabitants of Saint-Malo appealed to me, through their mayor, regarding a wet dock that they wanted to build in the harbor. I hastened to reply, asking only that, in an exchange of goodwill, I be granted a few feet of earth for my grave on Le Grand-Bé.* There were difficulties, owing to the opposition of military engineers, but finally, on October 27, 1831, I received a letter from the mayor, M. Hovius. He wrote to me:

> The resting place that you requested at the edge of the sea, a stone's throw from your birthplace, shall be prepared for you by the filial piety of the Maloans. But how sad it makes us to consider this task! May the monument stand empty a long time yet, though Honor and Glory outlive everything on earth!

I quote M. Hovius's words with gratitude. There is nothing excessive in them but the word *Glory*.

I shall go to rest then on the shore of the sea that I have loved. If I should die outside of France, I request that my body not be brought back to my native land until fifty years have elapsed since its first interment. Let my remains be spared a sacrilegious autopsy; let no one search my cold brain or my extinguished heart for the mystery

*A small island in Saint-Malo harbor.

of my being. Death does not reveal the secrets of life. A corpse travel-ing by post fills me with horror; but dry, white bones are easily transported. They will be less weary on that final voyage than when I dragged them over the earth, burdened with my troubles.[3]

BOOK ONE

I.

ORIGINS

La Vallée-aux-Loups, near Aulnay, October 4, 1811

FOUR YEARS ago now, on my return from the Holy Land, I bought a country house close to the hamlet of Aulnay, near Sceaux and Châtenay, hidden among the wooded hills. The area around the house is sandy, uneven—a sort of wild orchard with a gully and a grove of chestnuts at the far end. This narrow space seemed room enough to contain my long hopes; *spatio brevi spem longam reseces.*[1] The trees that I have planted here are thriving, though they are still so small that I give them shade when I stand between them and the sun. One day, they will give me shade: they will shelter me in my old age as I have sheltered them in their youth. I have chosen them, so far as I was able, from the many places I have wandered. They put me in mind of my travels, and nourish other illusions in the depths of my heart.

Should the Bourbons ever resume the throne, I would ask nothing more of them, in return for my loyalty, than to be made rich enough to buy the woodlands surrounding my estate. Ambition has taken hold of me; I would like to add a few acres to my walks. Knight-errant though I am, I have the sedentary tastes of a monk. Since I have lived in this place, I doubt whether I have set foot outside my enclosure more than three times. If my pines, my spruces, my larches, and my cedars live up to their promise, someday the Vallée-aux-Loups will be a veritable hermitage. And when Voltaire was born at Châtenay, on February 20, 1694, how did it look—this hillside where, in 1807, the author of *The Genius of Christianity* would come to retire?

The place pleases me. It has supplanted, in my mind, even my father's fields. I have paid for it with my dreams and my sleepless nights. It is to the great wilderness of Atala that I owe this little wilderness of Aulnay, and to create this refuge I did not, like the American settlers, have to scalp any Florida Indians. I am fond of my trees; I have read elegies, sonnets, and odes to them. There is not one of them that I haven't cared for with my own hands, that I haven't relieved of a worm attached to its roots or a caterpillar clinging to its leaves; I know all of them by their names, like children. They are my family—I have none other—and I hope to die among them.

Here, I wrote *The Martyrs*, the *Abencerages*, the *Itinerary*, and *Moïse*. Now what shall I do, these autumn evenings? This October 4, 1811, my saint's day and the anniversary of my entry into Jerusalem, tempts me to begin the story of my life. The man who gives France power over the world today only to trample her underfoot, this man whose genius I admire and whose despotism I abhor, this man encircles me with his tyranny as with a second solitude; but though he crushes the present, the past defies him, and I remain free in everything that preceded his glory.

Most of my feelings have hitherto stayed hidden in the depths of my soul or shown themselves in my work in the guise of imaginary beings. I still miss my chimeras today, but I shall not pursue them. I want to climb back up the slope of my better years. These pages shall be a funerary shrine raised to the light of my memories.

The circumstances of my father's birth and the trials of his early life gave him one of the gloomiest characters that there have ever been. No doubt, this character influenced my ideas by terrorizing my childhood, desolating my youth, and deciding the manner of my education.

I was born a gentleman. And I think I have profited from this accident of birth, for I have retained that very firm love of liberty which belongs principally to the aristocracy whose last hour has struck. Aristocracy has three successive ages: the age of superiority, the age of privilege, and the age of vanity. Once through with the first, it degenerates into the second, and dies out in the last.

One can find my family, if the fancy strikes him, in Moréri's dictionary, in the various histories of Brittany by d'Argentré, Dom Lobineau, and Dom Morice, in the *Histoire généalogique de plusieurs maisons illustres de Bretagne* by Father Dupaz, in Toussaint Saint-Luc, Le Borge, and finally in Father Anselme's *Histoire des Grands Officiers de la Couronne.**

The proofs of my lineage were made out by Chérin when my sister Lucile was admitted as a canoness to the Chapter of L'Argentière, before she went on to the Chapter of Remiremont; they were reproduced when I was presented to Louis XVI, again when I joined the Order of Malta, and once more when my brother was presented to that same unfortunate Louis XVI.

My family name was originally written *Brien*, then *Briant* and *Briand*, after the invasion of French spelling. Guillaume le Breton renders it *Castrum-Briani*. But there's not a name in France that lacks such variations. Who knows the correct spelling of Du Guesclin?

The Briens, at the beginning of the eleventh century, gave their name to an important castle in Brittany, and this castle became the seat of the Barony of Chateaubriand. Originally, the family coat of arms was a cluster of pinecones bearing the motto: *Je sème l'or.*[2] Then Geoffroy, Baron de Chateaubriand, went with Saint Louis to the Holy Land. Taken prisoner during the battle of Masura, he returned; his wife Sybille died of joy and shock at seeing him again. Saint Louis, as a reward for his services, granted him and his heirs, in exchange for their old coat of arms, a shield of gules[3] scattered with gold fleurs-de-lys. *Cui et ejus haeredibus*, attests a cartulary in the priory at Bérée, *sanctus Ludovicus tum Francorum rex, propter ejus probitatem in armis, flores lilii auri, loco pomorum pini auri, contulit.*[4]

Almost from the outset, the Chateaubriands diverged into three branches. The first, called the Barons de Chateaubriand, formed the stock of the other two and began in the year 1000 in the person of

---

*A summary of this genealogy can be found in the *Histoire généalogique et héraldique des Pairs de France, des grands dignitaires de la Couronne* by M. le Chevalier le Courcelles.

Thiern, the son of Brien and the grandson of Alain III, Count or Lord of Brittany. The second were named the Seigneurs de Roches Baritaut or the Seigneurs de Lion d'Angers. The third went under the title of the Sires de Beaufort.

When the Beaufort line died out in the person of Lady Renée, one Christophe II, who came from a collateral branch of the bloodline, inherited the Guérande estate in Morbihan. At that time, in the middle of the seventeenth century, there was widespread confusion in the order of nobility. Many names and titles had been usurped, so that Louis XIV called for an inquest, in order to restore each noble to his proper station. Christophe, having provided proof of his ancient noble extraction, was upheld in his right to arms and title by decree of the tribunal established at Rennes for the reformation of the Breton nobility. The decree, issued on September 16, 1669, reads as follows:

> Between the King's Attorney General and Monsieur Christophe de Chateaubriand, Sieur de la Guérande, the tribunal declares the aforesaid Christophe to be of ancient noble extraction, permits him to the rank of Chevalier, and confirms his right to bear arms of gules scattered with fleurs-de-lys without limit; and this after the production of his authentic claims thereto, from which it appears, etc., etc. The said judgment signed, *Malescot*.

This decree certifies that Christophe de Chateaubriand de la Guérande was directly descended from the Sires de Beaufort, who were themselves directly descended, as historical documents show, from the first Barons de Chateaubriand. The Chateaubriands of Villeneuve, du Plessis, and de Combourg[5] were thus younger branches of the Chateaubriands de la Guérande, through the lineage of Amaury, whose brother Michel was the son of this same Christophe de la Guérande whose noble extraction was confirmed by the decree of September 16, 1669, quoted above.

After my presentation to Louis XVI, my brother had the idea of augmenting my fortune as a younger son by securing me some of those ecclesiastical benefits called *bénéfices simples*. There was only one practicable way to go about this, since I was a layman and a soldier, and that was to make me a member of the Order of Malta. So it came about that my brother sent my proofs to Malta, and soon after presented a petition in my name to the Chapter of the Grand Priory of Aquitaine, held at Poitiers, requesting that commissioners be appointed to decide my urgent case.

M. Pontois was then the archivist, vice chancellor, and genealogist of the Order of Malta. The president, bailiff, and Grand Prior of Aquitaine was Louis-Joseph des Escotais, having with him the Bailiff of Freslon, the Chevalier de La Laurencie, the Chevalier de Murat, the Chevalier de Lanjamet, the Chevalier de La Bourdonnaye-Montluc, and the Chevalier du Bouetiez. My petition was reviewed from September 9 to 11, 1789. It was decided, in the words of my admission documents, that I merited "by more than one claim" the favor I requested and that "considerations of the greatest weight" made me worthy of the satisfaction I demanded.

And all this took place after the taking of the Bastille, on the eve of the events of October 6, 1789, and the transfer of the royal family to Paris! Only two months earlier, on August 7, the National Assembly had abolished all aristocratic titles! How was it that the Chevaliers and examiners of my proofs found that I merited "by more than one claim the favor I requested"—I, who was nothing but a puny sublieutenant in the infantry, unknown, without credit, without favor or fortune?

My brother's eldest son, the Comte Louis de Chateaubriand (I am adding this in 1831 to my original text, written in 1811), married Mademoiselle d'Orglandes, by whom he had five daughters and a son named Geoffroy. Louis's younger brother, Christian, the great-grandson and godson of M. de Malesherbes (to whom he bore a striking resemblance), served with distinction in Spain as a captain of the dragoons, in 1823.[6] He later became a Jesuit in Rome. The Jesuits alleviate the pains of solitude even as solitude passes from the earth.

Not long ago, Christian died in Chieri, near Turin. I am old and sick and should have gone before him, but his virtues called him to heaven before me: I still have a fair number of faults to lament.

In the division of the family patrimony, Christian received the estate of Malesherbes and Louis the estate of Combourg. Christian, who did not regard this equal allotment as lawful, wished, on leaving the world, to dispossess himself of the properties that did not belong to him and to bequeath them to his elder brother.

In light of my proofs, it would be no one's affair but mine, had I inherited my father and brother's infatuation, if I considered myself the scion of the ancient Dukes of Brittany, descended from Thiern, the grandson of Alain III.

Twice the Chateaubriands have mingled their blood with the blood of English sovereigns: Geoffroy IV de Chateaubriand took as his second wife Agnès de Laval, the granddaughter of the Comte d'Anjou and Matilda, the daughter of Henry I; Marguerite de Lusignan, the widow of the King of England and the granddaughter of Louis Le Gros, was married to Geoffroy V, the twelfth Baron de Chateaubriand. If we turn to the royal families of Spain, we discover another Brien, the younger brother of the ninth Baron de Chateaubriand, who married Jeanne, the daughter of Alphonso, the King of Aragon. If we turn yet again, to the great families of France, we find that Édouard de Rohan took as his wife Marguerite de Chateaubriand, and that one Croï married a Charlotte de Chateaubriand. Tinteniac, the victor in the *Combat des Trente*, and Du Guesclin, the Constable, might well have made alliances with any of the three branches of the family. Tiphaine du Guesclin, the granddaughter of the famous Constable Bertrand, ceded the estate of Plessis-Bertrand to Brien de Chateaubriand, her cousin and heir. Chateaubriands have signed their names as sureties on treaties between warring kings of France, for Clisson, and for the Baron de Vitré. The Dukes of Brittany used to send the Chateaubriands records of their proceedings. Chateaubriands became High Officers of the Crown and *illustrious* members of the Court of Nantes. They were charged with the duty of guarding their province against English attack. Brien I, the son of

Eudon, Comte de Penthièvre, took part in the Battle of Hastings. Guy de Chateaubriand was one of a number of lords that Arthur de Bretagne appointed to accompany his son when he served as ambassador to the Pope in 1309.

I would never come to an end if I were to complete this family history that I have merely wished here to outline in brief. But then, many today go to the other extreme. It has become commonplace to declare that one comes from "exploited laborers" or that one has the honor of being the son of a "man of the soil." But are these declarations of pride or philosophy? Are they not merely taking the side of the powerful? The marquis, comtes, and barons of the present age have neither privileges nor plows. Three-fourths of them are starving to death even as they go on gossiping behind each other's back, refusing to recognize each other, and mutually contesting their claims to noble birth. These nobles, denied even their own names, or permitted them only because they must be listed in an inventory—can they really inspire fear? For the rest, please pardon me for having been compelled to lower myself to such puerile recitations. My aim was to give some account of my father's ruling passion, a passion which formed the core drama of my youth. For my part, I neither glorify nor complain of the old society or the new one. If in the first I was the Chevalier or Vicomte de Chateaubriand, in the second I am François de Chateaubriand, and I prefer my name to my title.

Monsieur my father, like a medieval lord, would readily have called God "the Gentleman on high" and nicknamed Nicodemus (the Nicodemus of the Gospel) a "holy gentleman." But now, passing over my immediate progenitor, let us go from Christophe, the feudal lord of Guérande, and descend down the direct line of the Barons de Chateaubriand to me, François, the Lord, without vassals or money, of the Vallée-aux-Loups.

Looking back at the Chateaubriand family tree, composed of three branches, one observes that the first two stopped short, and that the third, the Sires de Beaufort, kept alive by Christophe's branch at La

Guérande, became impoverished. This was an inevitable result of the law of the land. Eldest sons, according to Breton custom, received two-thirds of the estate, while the others divided the remaining third among themselves. The decomposition of such puny portions occurred all the more rapidly when these younger sons married. As the same distribution of two-thirds and one-third was visited upon their children, the younger sons of younger sons soon came to dividing a pigeon, a hare, a duck pond, and a hunting hound among them, even as they continued to be "noble knights and puissant lords" of a dovecote, a toadhole, or a warren of rabbits. One finds a preponderance of these unfortunate cadets in old aristocratic families. Their lines persist for a generation or two, then vanish, as their children return one by one to the plow, or are absorbed into the laboring classes, without anyone knowing what became of them.

The head of my family in name and arms was, at the beginning of the eighteenth century, a man named Alexis de Chateaubriand, Lord of La Guérande. He was the son of Michel, the elder brother of Amaury and the son of Christophe, whose noble extraction from the Sires de Beaufort was confirmed by the decree quoted above. This Alexis de la Guérande was a widower and a committed souse. He passed his days carousing with his servants in complete disorder and used the finest family documents to seal his butter jars.

At the same time, there lived another Chateaubriand, named François, the son of Amaury. François, born February 19, 1683, owned the small domains of Les Touches and La Villeneuve. On August 27, 1713, he had married Pétronille-Claude Lamour, Lady of Lanjegu, by whom he had four sons: François-Henri, René (my father), Pierre, and Joseph. My grandfather, François, died March 28, 1729; but my grandmother I knew all through my childhood, when her lovely eyes still sparkled in the shadow of her years. She resided, after her husband's death, on the manor at La Villeneuve, near Dinan. Her entire fortune amounted to no more than 5,000 livres a year, of which her eldest son would take two thirds, leaving the last third to be divided among the younger three, from which sum the eldest would again deduct the praecipuum.

To crown her misfortunes, my grandmother found her every plan thwarted by the character of her sons. The eldest, François-Henri, to whom the magnificent estate of La Villeneuve devolved, refused to be married and became a priest; but instead of collecting the benefices which his name could have secured him, and with which he might have supported his brothers, out of pride and insouciance he asked for nothing. He buried himself in a country parish and became a rector, first of Saint-Launeuc and then of Merdrignac, in the diocese of Saint-Malo. He had a passion for poetry, I know, because I have looked over a good number of his verses. The merry temperament of this aristocratic sort of Rabelais, and the worship that this Christian priest dedicated to the pagan Muses, aroused no small curiosity. In the end, he gave away everything he had and died insolvent.

The youngest son, Joseph, went to Paris and immured himself in a library. Every year, he was sent his little parcel of 416 livres. Every year of his short life, on January 1, he wrote his mother a letter: the only sign that he ever gave of his existence. Otherwise, he lived unknown among his books, occupying himself with historical research. Singular fate! Here you have my two uncles, one a scholar and the other a poet. My elder brother used to write pleasant enough verse, and one of my sisters, Madame de Farcy, had a real talent for poetry. Another of my sisters, the Comtesse Lucile, a canoness, deserves to be remembered for a few of her admirable pages. And I have blackened plenty of paper myself. My brother perished on the scaffold, my two sisters departed their painful lives after many years spent languishing in prison, and my two uncles didn't leave enough to pay for the four planks of their coffins. As for myself, literature has caused me both joy and sorrow, and I don't despair, God willing, of dying in the poorhouse.

My grandmother, having exhausted her means of doing anything for her eldest and youngest sons, could do nothing for either René, my father, or Pierre, my uncle. This family, which had once "scattered gold," according to its motto, now looked out from its modest manor onto the rich abbeys it had founded and where its ancestors lay entombed. Chateaubriands had presided over the Estates of Brittany, signed treaties between sovereigns, and served as sureties to Clisson. Now they lacked enough credit to obtain a sublieutenancy for the heir to their name.

The only resource that remained to poor Breton nobles was the Royal Navy. The family tried turning this to my father's advantage. But first he would have to travel to Brest, pay for lodgings, hire instructors, buy uniforms, weapons, books, and mathematical instruments. How were these expenses to be defrayed? The commission sent to the Naval Minister never arrived, for want of a patron to demand its dispatch. And the Lady of Villeneuve fell sick with grief.

Then my father showed the first sign of that deep-seated decisiveness which I later knew so well. He was about fifteen years old. Seeing his mother's distress, he went to sit beside the bed where she lay and said to her, "I will no longer be a burden on you."

At this, my grandmother started to cry. (I heard my father tell this story twenty times at least.)

"René," she said, "what do you want to do? You must till your fields."

"They cannot keep us fed," he said. "Let me go."

"Very well," said my grandmother. "Go then, wherever God wills you go."

She embraced her child, sobbing. That same night, my father left his mother's farm and rode to Dinan, where one of our relatives gave him a letter of recommendation to take to a man in Saint-Malo. There, the orphaned adventurer embarked as a volunteer on an armed schooner, which set sail a few days later.

The tiny republic of Saint-Malo was then alone in defending the honor of the French flag at sea. The schooner joined the fleet that Cardinal Fleury was sending to aid Stanislaus, besieged at Danzig by the Russians. My father set foot ashore and found himself in the memorable battle of May 29, 1734, when fifteen hundred Frenchmen, commanded by the brave Breton de Bréhan, Comte de Plélo, fought 40,000 Muscovites, commanded by Munich. De Bréhan, a diplomat, a warrior, a poet, was killed. My father was wounded twice. He returned to France and set sail again. Shipwrecked on the coast of Spain, he was beaten and robbed by Galician bandits. He found passage on a ship in Bayonne and materialized once again beneath the paternal roof. By now his courage and clear thinking had garnered him a reputation. He sailed for the West Indies, grew rich in the colonies, and laid the foundations of a new family fortune.

My grandmother entrusted her son René with the fate of her son Pierre, M. de Chateaubriand du Plessis, whose child, Armand de Chateaubriand, was shot, at Bonaparte's command, on Good Friday, 1810. He was one of the last French gentlemen to die for the cause of the monarchy.* Although my father did take care of his brother, he had contracted, through long suffering, a rigidity of character which he would retain all his days. Virgil's *non ignara mali* does not always hold true.[7] Misfortune breeds severity as well as tenderness.

Monsieur de Chateaubriand was tall and lean; he had an aquiline nose, pale thin lips, and deep-set eyes that were small and sea-green, or glaucous, like the eyes of lions or ancient barbarians. I have never seen anyone with eyes such as his. When he was angered, the gleaming pupils seemed to detach themselves and strike you like bullets.

A single passion dominated my father, and that was his passion for the family name. His usual state of being was a profound sadness that deepened with age and a silence broken only by fits of anger. Miserly, in hopes of restoring his family to its former vigor; haughty with other gentlemen at the Estates of Brittany; harsh with his vassals in Combourg; taciturn, despotic, and menacing at home, to see him was to fear him. If he had lived until the Revolution, and if he had been younger, he would have played an important role, or he would have been slaughtered in his castle. He was certainly possessed of genius, and I have no doubt that, had he been a statesman or a general, he would have been an extraordinary man.

It was on returning from America that he thought to marry. Born September 23, 1718, he was thirty-five years old on July 3, 1753, when he wedded Apolline-Jeanne-Suzanne de Bedée, born April 7, 1726, the daughter of Messire Ange-Annibal, Comte de Bedée, Lord of La

---

*This was written in 1811. (Geneva, 1831)

Bouëtardais. He set up house with her in Saint-Malo, seven or eight leagues from the places where the two of them were born. From the windows of this house, the couple gazed out at the same horizon beneath which they had first entered the world.

My maternal grandmother, Marie-Anne de Ravenel de Boisteilleul, Dame de Bedée, born in Rennes on October 16, 1698, had been raised in Saint-Cyr, in the twilight years of Madame de Maintenon. Her education had been extended to her daughters. My mother, Apolline de Bedée, endowed with great wit and a prodigious imagination, was formed by reading Fénelon, Racine, and Madame de Sévigné. She was nourished on anecdotes of the Court of Louis XIV and knew all of Cyrus by heart. A small woman of large features, dark-haired and ugly, her elegant manners and lively disposition were at odds with my father's rigidity and calm. Loving society as much as he loved solitude, as exuberant and animated as he was expressionless and cold, she possessed no taste not antagonistic to the tastes of her husband. As time wore on, this constant contrariety made her melancholy, lighthearted and gay though she was. Obliged to hold her tongue when she would rather have spoken, she compensated herself with a sort of noisy sadness interspersed with sighs, the only sounds to interrupt the mute sadness of my father. In the realm of devotion, my mother was an angel.

2.

BIRTH OF MY BROTHERS AND SISTERS—I ENTER THE WORLD

La Vallée-aux-Loups, December 31, 1811

IN SAINT-MALO, my mother gave birth to a son who died in the cradle. He was named Geoffroy, like nearly all the eldest sons of my family. This boy was followed by another and by two girls, none of whom lived for more than a few months.

These four children died of an effusion of blood in the brain. At last, my mother brought into the world a third boy, named Jean-Baptiste. It was he who, by and by, would become the grandson-in-law of M. de Malesherbes. After Jean-Baptiste came four girls: Marie-Anne, Bénigne, Julie, and Lucile, all four of a rare beauty, and of whom only the two eldest survived the Revolution's storms. Beauty, a serious trifle, remains when all else has passed away. I was the last of these ten children. Probably my four sisters owed their existence to my father's desire to ensure his name by the birth of a second son. I resisted. I had an aversion to life.

My baptismal certificate reads as follows:

François-René de Chateaubriand, son of René de Chateaubriand and of Pauline-Jeanne-Suzanne de Bedée, his wife, born September 4, 1768, baptized the following day by us, Pierre-Henry Nouail, High Vicar to the Bishop of Saint-Malo. Serving as godfather was Jean-Baptiste de Chateaubriand, his brother, and as godmother, Françoise-Gertrude de Contades. Acting as signatories for the registry: Contades de Plouër, Jean-Baptiste

de Chateaubriand, Brignon de Chateaubriand, de Chateaubri-
and et Nouail, vicar-general.

One can see that I was mistaken in my earlier writings: I was born
September 4, not October 4, and my Christian names are François-
René, not François-*Auguste*.*

The house where my parents then lived stands in a gloomy, narrow
street of Saint-Malo called the rue des Juifs. It has since been transformed into an inn. The room where my mother gave birth overlooks
a bare stretch of the city walls, and through the windows of this room
one has a view of the sea outspread to the horizon and crashing on
the reefs. My godfather, as my baptismal certificate shows, was my
brother; my godmother, the Comtesse de Plouër, the daughter of
Marshal de Contades. I was nearly dead when I came into the world.
The booming of the waves, stirred up by one of those squalls that
herald the autumn equinox, drowned my cries. These details were
often repeated to me, and their sadness has never been effaced from
my memory. Not a day passes when, reflecting on what I have been,
I do not see in my mind's eye the rock where I was born, the room
where my mother inflicted life on me, the raging tempest that was
my first lullaby, the doomed brother who gave me a name that I have
almost always dragged through disaster. Heaven itself seemed to
arrange these circumstances to place in sight of my cradle an emblem
of my destinies.

---

* Twenty days before me, on August 15, 1768, on another island, at the other end of
France, a man was born who would put an end to the old society: Bonaparte.

3.

PLANCOUËT—VOWS—COMBOURG—MY FATHER'S
PLANS FOR MY EDUCATION—LA VILLENEUVE—
LUCILE—MESDEMOISELLES COUPPART—I AM A POOR
SCHOLAR

Vallée-aux-Loups, January 1812

ON LEAVING my mother's womb, I underwent my first exile: I was
relegated to Plancouët, a pretty village situated between Dinan, Saint-
Malo, and Lamballe. Close to this village, my mother's only brother,
the Comte de Bedée, had built the Château de Monchoix. My maternal grandmother's properties in the region extended to the market
town of Corseul: the *Curiosolites* of Caesar's *Commentaries*.[8] My
grandmother, who by then had been a widow for a long time, lived
with her sister, Mademoiselle de Boisteilleul, in a hamlet separated
from Plancouët by a bridge and called L'Abbaye, after its Benedictine
abbey, which was consecrated to Notre-Dame de Nazareth.

My wet nurse was found to be barren, and another poor Christian
took me to her breast. She vowed my soul to the patron of the hamlet, Notre-Dame de Nazareth, and promised that, in her honor, I
would wear blue and white until I reached the age of seven. I had
been alive no more than a few hours, and already the weight of time
was on my brow. Why was I not allowed to die? Somehow it entered
into God's plans to grant this obscure and innocent prayer and preserve a life that a vain reputation later threatened to overtake.

This Breton peasant's vow is no longer of our century; but it was
a touching thing, the intervention of a Mother on high, mediating
between a child and heaven, and sharing in the worries of a mother
on earth.

After three years, I was taken back to Saint-Malo. It had already
been seven years since my father, wishing to forge a new entry into

one of those places where his ancestors had lived and died, regained the estate of Combourg. Unable to negotiate for the lordship of Beaufort, which had passed to the family Goyon, or for the barony of Chateaubriand, which had fallen to the house of Condé, he set his sights on Combourg, a name that Froissart spells *Combour* and that several branches of my family had already possessed by marriage with the Coëtquens. Combourg defended Brittany against both the Normans and the English: it was built by Junken, Bishop of Dol, in 1016, although its tallest tower dates from 1100. The Marshal de Duras, who had acquired Combourg through his wife, Maclovie de Coëtquen, whose mother was a Chateaubriand, made the arrangements with my father. It was this same Marshal de Duras, acting as our kinsman, who would later present my brother and me to Louis XVI.

I was destined for the Royal Navy: estrangement from the Court came naturally to all Bretons, and particularly to my father. The aristocracy of the Estates of Brittany only served to fortify this feeling.

When I was brought back to Saint-Malo, my father was already in Combourg, my brother was at the Collège de Saint-Brieuc, and my four sisters were living with my mother. All the latter's affections were concentrated on her eldest son. This is not to say that she didn't cherish her other children, but she exhibited a blind preference for the young Comte de Combourg. As a boy, as a latecomer, and as *le chevalier* (so they called me), it's true that I had some privileges over my sisters. But for the most part I was left in the hands of servants. My mother, a woman of wit and virtue, was preoccupied by the demands of society and the duties of religion. The Comtesse de Plouër, my godmother, was her close companion; she also used to visit with relatives of Maupertuis and the Abbé Trublet. She loved people, gossip, and politics; and they played politics in Saint-Malo like the monks of Saba in the Ravine of Cedron.[9] She threw herself fervently into the La Chatolais affair.[10] But she brought home a shrewish temper, a distracted mind, and a parsimonious spirit which at first prevented us from recognizing her more admirable qualities. She was orderly, but her children were raised in disorder; she was generous, but she gave the impression of being a penny-pincher; she was gentle, but she was always scolding. If my father was the terror of the servants, my mother was the scourge.

Such were the dispositions of my parents, from which the first feelings of my life were born. I became attached to the woman who looked after me, an excellent creature called La Villeneuve, whose name I write now with a rush of gratitude and with tears in my eyes. La Villeneuve was a sort of superintendent of the household, always carrying me around in her arms, giving me treats on the sly, wiping away my tears, kissing me, putting me down in a corner, picking me up again, and muttering all the while: "This little one here won't be proud! He has a good heart! He doesn't snub the poor folk! Do you now, little one?" And she would stuff my mouth with wine and sugar.

My childish sympathies for La Villeneuve were soon surpassed by a worthier friendship.

Lucile, the fourth of my sisters, was two years older than I. She was a neglected youngest daughter, and her wardrobe consisted solely of her sisters' cast-off clothes. Imagine a thin little girl, too tall for her age, with gangling arms and a timid gaze, who speaks only with difficulty and cannot learn a thing; dress her in a borrowed frock a size too small for her; bind her chest in a piqué corset whose stays leave wounds in her sides; gird her neck in an iron collar with brown velvet trim; coil her hair atop her head and tuck it up beneath a black cloth toque, and you shall have some idea of the miserable creature who greeted me beneath my father's roof. No one could have suspected that this puny Lucile would one day be a woman of superior talent and beauty.

She was handed over to me like a plaything, but I did not at all abuse my power. Instead of making her bend to my will, I made myself her defender. Every morning, I was taken with her to the house of the Couppart sisters, two old hunchbacks dressed all in black, who taught children how to read. Lucile was very bad at reading: I was still worse. The sisters scolded her, I scratched at them, and great complaints were brought before my mother. I began to pass for a scapegrace, a rebel, a layabout, ultimately an ass. These ideas were soon entrenched in my parents' minds. My father said that all the

Chevaliers de Chateaubriand had been moochers, drunks, and brawlers. My mother sighed and grumbled at the sight of my filthy coat. Child though I was, I felt revolted by my father's remarks, and when my mother crowned her remonstrances by singing the praises of my brother, whom she called a Cato, a hero, I felt disposed to do every wicked thing that seemed expected of me.

My writing teacher, Monsieur Després, with his old-fashioned sailor's wig, was no more satisfied with me than my parents were. He made me copy interminably, after a sample of his own style, these two lines that I held in horror, though by no fault of the language itself:

> *C'est à vous mon esprit à qui je veux parler:*
> *Vous avez des défauts que je ne puis celer.*[11]

He would accompany his reprimands by hitting me in the neck with his fist and calling me a "lardhead." Did he mean to say a "hardhead"?* I don't know what a lardhead is, but I have always imagined it to be something terrifying.[12]

Saint-Malo is nothing but a rock. In former times, this rock stood in the middle of a salt marsh. Then, in 709, the seas erupted and deepened the bay: Saint-Malo became an island and Mont-Saint-Michel was set in its place among the waves. Today, the rock of Saint-Malo is kept on terra firma only by a causeway, poetically called "Le Sillon."[13] On one side, Le Sillon is assailed by the open sea; on the other, it is washed by the tides which turn there and run into the harbor. A tempest almost completely destroyed it in 1730. During the hours of low tide, the harbor dries out, and along the northern and eastern shoreline is a very fine sand beach. It is then possible to make a tour of my paternal nest. Near and far are scattered rocks, forts, and uninhabited islets: Fort-Royal, La Conchée, Cézembre, and Le Grand-Bé, where my grave will be. I have chosen well without knowing it, for *bé*, in Breton, means *tomb*.

At the end of Le Sillon, planted with a cross, is a sand dune called

---

*Ἀχώρ, *gourme*.

La Hoguette, which stands at the edge of the open sea. Atop this dune is an old gallows: as children, we used to play games of four corners among its posts, disputing possession with the shorebirds. It was never, however, without a certain sense of terror that we loitered in this spot.

Here, too, are the Miels, the dunes where the sheep once grazed; to the right are the meadows that lie below Paramé, the post-road to Saint-Servan, the new cemetery, a calvary cross, and the windmills on the dunes, which are like those windmills above Achilles' tomb at the mouth of the Hellespont.

4.

LIFE OF MY MATERNAL GRANDMOTHER AND HER SISTER AT PLANCOUËT—MY UNCLE, THE COMTE DE BEDÉE, AT MONCHOIX—THE LIFTING OF MY NURSE'S VOW

I REACHED my seventh year, and my mother took me to Plancouët to be released from my nurse's vow. We stayed there at my grandmother's. If I have ever known happiness, it was certainly in that house.

My grandmother lived on the rue du Hameau de L'Abbaye, in a house whose gardens wended down a series of terraces into a dell, at the bottom of which there was a spring encircled by willows. Madame de Bedée could no longer walk, but apart from that she suffered none of the inconveniences of her age. She was a charming old woman: stout, pale, neat, refined. She had beautiful, noble manners, and wore pleated dresses in the old style and a black lace cap that tied beneath the chin. Her wit was polished, her conversation grave, her tone serious. She was cared for by her sister, Mademoiselle de Boisteilleul, who resembled her in nothing except her generosity. Mademoiselle de Boisteilleul was a thin little person: playful, chatty, always bantering. She had been in love with a Comte de Trémignan, who had promised to marry her, but who had subsequently broken that promise. My aunt consoled herself by celebrating her love affair in song, for she was a poetess. I remember having many times heard her snuffling, with her spectacles on her nose and her hands busy embroidering some double ruffles for her sister, a ballad that began—

> A sparrowhawk loved a warbler
> And the warbler loved him too

—which always seemed to me a very unusual thing for a sparrowhawk to do. The song ended with this refrain:

> Oh, Trémignon, Trémignon,
> Does the story make you frown?
> Oh, Trémignon, Trémignon,
> A derry, derry down.

Strange how many things in the world end just like my aunt's love affair, with a *derry, derry down*!

My grandmother left the housekeeping to her sister. Every morning she dined at eleven, took a siesta, and woke again at one; she was then carried down the garden terraces to a spot beneath the willows by the spring, where she would knit, surrounded by her sister, her children, and her grandchildren. In those days, old age was a dignity; today it is a burden. At four, the servants carried my grandmother back up to her parlor; Pierre, the footman, brought in the card-table; Mademoiselle de Boisteilleul rapped on the chimneypiece with a pair of iron tongs, and a few moments later three other old maids came in from the neighboring house, in response to my great-aunt's call. These three sisters were called "the *desmoiselles* Vildéneux." Daughters of an impoverished gentleman, rather than dividing their meager inheritance, they had enjoyed it in common: they had never been apart from one another and never left their ancestral village. Since childhood, they had been close with my grandmother, they lived next door to her, and every day, at the established signal from the chimneypiece, they came to play quadrille with their friend. No sooner had the game got underway than the good ladies quarreled: it was the only event in their lives, the only moment when their moods soured. At eight o'clock, supper reestablished peace. Often my uncle de Bedée, together with his son and three daughters, sat down to supper with my grandmother. She would tell story after story from the old days, and my uncle, in his turn, would recount the Battle of Fontenoy, in which he had taken part, and then crown his boasting with a few rather frank anecdotes that made the chaste *desmoiselles* weak with laughter. At nine, when supper was over, the servants entered; we all of us got down on our knees, and Mademoiselle de Boisteilleul said the evening prayer aloud. By ten, everyone in the house was asleep, except my grandmother, whose maid went on reading to her in bed until one in the morning.

This society, which was the first I knew, was also the first to have disappeared from my sight. I saw death enter that dwelling of peace and benediction, and make of it a lonelier and lonelier place, closing one room after another that would never be opened again. I saw my grandmother forced to give up her quadrille, lacking her usual partners. I saw the number of her old friends dwindle, until the day came when my grandmother was the last to fall. She and her sister had sworn an oath that, as soon as one of them went, she would summon the other, and they kept their word. Madame de Bedée survived Mademoiselle de Boisteilleul by little more than a month. I am perhaps the only man in the world who knows that these people existed. Twenty times since then I have made the same observation; twenty times societies have formed and dissolved around me. This impossibility of duration and continuity in human relations, the profound forgetfulness that follows us wherever we go, the invincible silence that fills our graves and stretches from there to our homes, puts me constantly in mind of our inexorable isolation. Any hand will do to give us the last glass of water we will ever need, when we lie sweating on our deathbed. Only let it not be a hand that we love! For how, without despair, can we let go of a hand that we have covered with kisses, a hand that we would like to hold forever to our heart?

The Comte de Bedée's house was situated in a high and pleasant spot about a league from Plancouët. Everything about the place exuded joy: my uncle's good cheer was inexhaustible. He had three daughters, Caroline, Marie, Flore, and a son, the Comte de La Bouëtardais, a councilor in the Parliament, all of whom shared his lavish love of life. Cousins from the countryside flocked to Monchoix, where they played music, danced, hunted, and made merry from morning to night. My aunt, Madame de Bedée, seeing my uncle thus gaily squandering his capital and revenue, quite reasonably quarreled with him; but no one listened, and her low mood only lifted the high spirits of her family, especially since my aunt herself was subject to such a host of crazes: she always had a big snarly hunting dog that slept in her lap and a tamed wild boar that followed her from room to room, filling the château with its grunts. Whenever I went from my father's somber and silent house to this house of festivity and noise, it was as if I had stumbled into paradise. The contrast was all the more striking later, when my family had moved to the country. Going from Combourg to Monchoix was like going from a wilderness to a great city, from a medieval keep to the villa of a Roman prince.

On Ascension Day 1775, I set out from my grandmother's house for Notre-Dame de Nazareth with my mother, my aunt de Boisteilleul, my uncle de Bedée and his children, my nurse, and my foster brother. I wore a long white robe, white shoes, white gloves, a white hat, and a blue silk sash. We arrived at the Abbey at ten in the morning. The monastery, which stood by the roadside, was enaged by a quincunx of elms dating from the time of Jean V of Brittany. This quincunx led to the cemetery: a Christian could not reach the church except by crossing this region of headstones. It is through death that man enters into the presence of God.

Already the monks were in their stalls; the altar was lit by a multitude of candles; the lamps hung down from the various vaults: there are, in Gothic buildings, distances something like successive horizons. The mace-bearers came to meet me at the door and ceremoniously conducted me to the choir. Three chairs had been arranged there, and I took my place in the middle one; my nurse sat down on my left, my foster brother on my right.

The Mass began. At the offertory, the celebrant turned toward me and read the prayers. Then my white clothes were removed and hung as an *ex-voto* beneath a picture of the Virgin, and I was vested anew in a violet-colored frock. The prior delivered a speech on the efficacy of vows; he recalled the story of the Baron de Chateaubriand who had traveled to the Orient with Saint Louis, and told me that one day I too would perhaps visit, in Palestine, that Virgin of Nazareth to whom I owed my life by the intercession of a poor woman's prayers, which were always powerful to God. This monk, who recounted the history of my family to me, as Dante's grandfather recounted the history of his ancestors to him, might also, like Cacciaguida, have interwoven a prophecy of my exile:

> *Tu proverai sì come sa di sale*
> *Lo pane altrui, e com'è duro calle*
> *Lo scendere e il salir per l'atrui scale.*
>
> *E quel che più ti graverà le spalle,*
> *Sarà la compagnia malvagia e scempia,*
> *Con la qual tu cadrai in questa valle;*
>
> *Che tutta ingrata, tutta matta ed empia*
> *Si farà contra, a te; . . .*
> . . . .
> *Di sua bestialitate il suo processo*
> *Farà la prova: sì ch'a te fia bello*
> *Averti fatta parte per te stesso.*[14]

"You shall know the salty savor of other people's bread. You shall know how hard it is going up and down other people's stairs. And what will weigh still more heavily on your shoulders will be the terrible and senseless company into which you shall fall: all of them ingrates, mad, impious. They shall turn against you.... They shall prove their stupidity by their every action, so that you do well to form a party of yourself alone."

After hearing the Benedictine's exhortation, I always dreamed of a pilgrimage to Jerusalem, and in the end I made it.

I have been dedicated to religion; the garments of my innocence have rested on its altars; but it is not my clothing that should be hung there today, it is my miseries.

I was brought back to Saint-Malo. Saint-Malo is not the Aleth of the *Notitia Imperii*.[15] Aleth was better placed by the Romans on the outskirts of Saint-Servan, in the military port called Solidor at the mouth of the Rance. Across from Aleth was a rock, *est in conspectu Tenedos*,[16] not the refuge of the perfidious Greeks, but the hideaway of Aaron the Hermit, who, in the year 507, established a dwelling place on this island. It was the same year that Clovis triumphed over Alaric. One founded a tiny monastery, the other a great monarchy: two structures that have toppled just the same.

Malo, in Latin *Maclovius, Macutus, Machutes*, became the Bishop of Aleth in 541. He was drawn there by the fame of Aaron the Hermit, and after this saint died he built a monastic church *in praedio Machutis*.[17] The name Malo was extended to the island, and later to the town of Maclovium, or Maclopolis.

From Saint Malo, the first bishop of Aleth, to the blessed Jean named "de la Grille," who was canonized in 1140 and who built the cathedral, there were forty-five bishops. Jean de la Grille, seeing that Aleth was almost totally deserted, transferred the episcopal see from the old Roman town to the new Breton one spreading over Aaron's rock.

Saint-Malo had much to suffer in the wars waged between the French and English kings.

The Earl of Richmond, later Henry VII of England, with whom the tangles between the White Rose and the Red Rose came to an end, was imprisoned in Saint-Malo. The Duke of Brittany delivered him to Richard III's ambassadors, who were to take him to London to be killed. But he escaped these guards and took refuge in the cathedral: *Asylum quod in eâ urbe est inviolatissum*.[18] This right of asylum, or *minihi*,[19] dated back to the age of the Druids, the first priests of Aaron's isle.

A Bishop of Saint-Malo was one of the favorites (the other two were Arthur de Montauban and Jean Hingaut) who betrayed the ill-fated Gilles de Bretagne, whose story may be read in the *Histoire lamentable de Gilles, seigneur de Chateaubriand et de Chantocé, prince du sang de France et de Bretagne, étranglé en prison par les ministres du favori, le 24 avril 1450*.[20]

There was a handsome capitulation between Henri IV and

Saint-Malo. The city negotiated power with power, protected those who sought refuge within its walls, and remained free, by ordinance of Philibert de La Guiche, the Grandmaster of the French artillery, to cast one hundred cannonballs. No place more resembled Venice (excepting Venice's sunshine and its arts) in religion, riches, and maritime chivalry than this little republic of Saint-Malo. It backed Charles V's expedition to Africa and aided Louis XIII at La Rochelle. It flew its flag over every ocean and established trade with Moka, Surat, and Pondicherry. A company formed in its womb explored the South Seas.

As early as the reign of Henri IV, my native city distinguished itself by its devotion and loyalty to France. The English raided the harbor in 1693; on November 29 of that year, they bombarded it with their infernal machine, in the debris of which I often played with my friends. They bombarded it again in 1758.

The Maloans lent considerable sums to Louis XIV during the War of 1701. In recognition of this sacrifice, he confirmed their right to fortify themselves and ordered that the Royal Navy's flagship vessel be composed exclusively of sailors from Saint-Malo and its territories.

In 1771, the Maloans repeated their sacrifice and lent thirty million to Louis XV. During the Seven Years' War, in 1758, the famous Admiral Anson descended on Cancale and burned Saint-Servan. In the Château de Saint-Malo, La Chatolais wrote on linen with a toothpick dipped in water and soot those *Memoirs* which caused such a stir and which no one even remembers today. Events obscure events; inscriptions engraved over other inscriptions, they form pages in a history of palimpsests.

Saint-Malo once furnished the best sailors in our navy. One can see the extent of their role in a folio volume, published in 1682, under the title *Rôle général des officiers, mariniers, et matelots de Saint-Malo*. There is also a *Coutume de Saint-Malo*, printed in the collection of the *Coutumier général*.[21] The city archives are rich in charts useful to the study of maritime history and rights.

Saint-Malo is the birthplace of Jacques Cartier, the French Christopher Columbus, who discovered Canada. Its sailors have even journeyed west of America to the Îles Malouines that now bear their name.[22] Duguay-Trouin, one of the greatest seamen who have ever lived, was born here, and in my lifetime it has given France Surcouf. The celebrated governor of Île-de-France, Mahé de la Bourdonnais, was born in Saint-Malo, as were La Mettrie, Maupertuis, and that Abbé Trublet whom Voltaire mocked. All this is not bad for an enclosure smaller than the Tuileries garden.

Far ahead of these lesser literary lights of my birthplace stands the Abbé de Lamennais: Broussais also was born here, as was my noble friend the Comte de La Ferronnays.

Finally, in order to omit nothing, I should recall the mastiffs that formed the garrison of Saint-Malo. These were descended from those famous dogs raised among the regiments of the Gauls which, according to Strabo, charged in battle formation with their masters against the Romans. Albertus Magnus, a Dominican monk and a writer just as grave as the Greek geographer, recorded that in Saint-Malo "the protection of so important a place was entrusted each night to the loyalty of certain mastiffs that served as an effective and reliable patrol." In my day, they were condemned to death for having had the misfortune to snap unthinkingly at the legs of a gentleman, an incident that gave rise to the song "Bon Voyage." All the dogs are mocked; they are imprisoned as criminals; one of them refuses to take food from the hands of his weeping master, and the noble animal is left to die of hunger. Dogs, like men, are punished for their loyalty. Once the Capitol, like my Delos,[23] was also guarded by dogs, who did not bark when Scipio Africanus came to offer his prayers at dawn.[24]

Enclosed by walls of diverse epochs that are divided into the *great* and the *small*, and atop which the townspeople take their strolls, Saint-Malo is still defended by the castle I have already mentioned, and is further fortified by towers, bastions, and moats established by Duchesse Anne. Seen from without, this insular city looks like a granite citadel.

It is on the beach by the open sea, between the castle and the Fort-Royal, that the children congregate; it is there that I grew up, a companion of the winds and the waves. One of the first pleasures that I ever tasted was battling the storms, playing with the breakers that retreated before me or rushed after me along the shore. Another of my pastimes was building, from the gravelly sand of the beach, monuments that my playmates called "*fours*." Since those days, I have often seen castles built for eternity crumble more swiftly than my palaces of sand.

My fate having been irrevocably decided, I was abandoned to an idle childhood. A few notions of drawing, the English language, hydrography, and mathematics seemed more than enough education for a little boy destined in advance for the rough life of a sailor.

I was brought up at home, without any course of study. We were no longer living in the house where I was born. My mother now occupied the first floor of a building in the place Saint-Vincent, almost facing the gate that led to Le Sillon. The town urchins had become my closest friends. I filled the courtyard and the staircases with them, and I came to resemble them in everything. I picked up their language, their mannerisms, their looks. I dressed like them, unbuttoned and unwashed like them. My shirts hung down in rags, and I never had a pair of stockings that wasn't mostly holes. All day I limped around in wretched, worn-down shoes that slipped off with every step I took. I often lost my hat and sometimes my coat. My face was filthy, scratched, and bruised; my hands were black with dirt. My appearance was so strange that my mother, even in the midst of her anger, could not keep from laughing and crying out, "How ugly he is!"

Yet I loved and have always loved cleanliness, even elegance. At night, I tried to mend my ragged clothes. La Villeneuve and Lucile, in an effort to spare me my mother's reprovals and punishments, helped me repair my wardrobe; but their patchwork only made my apparel more bizarre. I was especially humiliated when I had to appear in tatters among children proud of their new coats and their finery.

My compatriots had something foreign about them, something Spanish. A few Maloan families had established themselves in Cádiz, and a few families from Cádiz had taken up residence in Saint-Malo. The insular setting, the causeway, the architecture, the houses, the water towers, and the granite walls of Saint-Malo gave it a close resemblance to Cádiz. When later I visited the latter city, on my return from the Orient, I was put in mind of the former.

Closed up in their city each night under the same lock and key, Maloans had become like members of a single family. Their mores were so artless that young women who sent away for ribbons and veils from Paris were considered "worldly" and shunned by their scandalized companions. Adultery was unthinkable. When one Comtesse d'Abbeville was suspected of infidelity, it resulted in a plaintive ballad that one sung while making the sign of the cross. The poet, however, faithful despite himself to the traditions of the troubadours, sided against the husband, and called him a "monstrous barbarian."

Certain days of the year, the inhabitants of the city and the surrounding country gathered together at fairs called "assemblies," held in the forts and on the islands around Saint-Malo. One went to them on foot when the water was low and in boats when the water was high. The multitude of sailors and peasants; the covered carts; the caravans of horses, donkeys, and mules; the competing merchants; the tents pitched along the shoreline; the processions of monks and confraternities wending their way through the crowd with their banners and crosses held high; the longboats coming and going by oar or by sail; the ships entering the harbor or anchored in the roadstead; the salvos of artillery and the swinging bells, all contributed their share of noise, motion, and variety to these gatherings.

I was the only witness to these festivities who did not share in the jubilation. I arrived at them with no money to buy toys or cakes. Avoiding the scorn that always attends hard luck, I sat far from the crowd, beside those pools of water that the sea sustains and renews in the hollows of the rocks. There, I amused myself by watching the puffins and the gulls at their flight; I gazed off into the bluish distances; I collected seashells; I closed my eyes and listened to the music of the waves among the reefs. In the evenings at home, I was not much happier. I abhorred certain dishes: I was forced to eat them. I used to implore the eyes of La France, who would skillfully relieve me of my plate the moment my father turned his head. As for the fire, the same austerity applied: I was not permitted even to approach the hearth. It is a long way from these strict parents to the child-spoilers of today.

But if I had sorrows that children now cannot imagine, I also had some pleasures of which the new breed knows nothing.

Gone are those rites of religion and family in which the whole country seemed to rejoice in the presence of its God. Christmas, New Year, Twelfth Night, Easter, Whitsunday, and Midsummer Day were days of plenty for me. Perhaps my native rock has worked upon my feelings and influenced my studies. As long ago as the year 1015, the Maloans made a vow to go help build "with their hands and their means" the belfries of the cathedral at Chartres. Have I not also worked with my hands to restore the fallen spire of the old Christian church?

"The sun," says Father Maunoir, "has never shone upon a place more steadfast and unwavering in its loyalty to the true faith than Brittany. For thirteen centuries, not one sacrilege has soiled the tongue which has served to spread the word of Jesus Christ; and the man has yet to be born who has heard a Breton-speaking Breton preach any but the Catholic religion."

On the feasts days that I have just recalled, I would be taken with my sisters to the shrines of the town, to the chapel of Saint Aaron and to the convent of La Victoire, where my ear was struck by the sweet voices of the unseen women: the harmonies of their canticles mingled with the booming of the waves. When, in wintertime, at the hour of the evening service, the cathedral filled with people; when the old sailors got down on their knees and the young women and their children read, by the light of little candles, from the book of hours; when the multitude, at the moment of benediction, repeated in chorus the "Tantum ergo"; when, in the silence between these songs, the Christmastime squalls beat against the basilica's stained-glass windows and shook the vaults of that nave which had once resounded with the manly voices of Jacques Cartier and Duguay-Trouin, I experienced an extraordinary religious feeling. I did not need Villeneuve to tell me to fold my hands or to call on God by all the names that my mother had taught me. I saw the heavens open and the angels offering up our incense and our prayers, and I bowed my head. It was not yet burdened with those troubles which weigh so horribly upon us that we are tempted never to lift our heads again, when we have bent down at the foot of the altar.

One sailor, on leaving these ceremonies, boarded his ship freshly fortified against the night; another came sailing into the harbor, navigating by the lighted dome of the church. Religion and danger were continually face to face, and their images presented themselves inseparably to my mind. No sooner was I born than I heard talk of death. In the evenings, a man went through the streets ringing a bell, calling Christians to pray for the soul of one of their drowned brethren. Nearly every year a boat sank before my very eyes, and even as I scampered along the beaches the sea rolled the corpses of foreign sailors at my feet. I knew that these men had died far from home. But Madame de Chateaubriand would say to me, as Saint Monica had once said to her son: *Nihil longe est a Deo.* "Nothing is far from God."[25] My education had been entrusted to Providence, and Providence did not spare me her lessons.

Having been vowed to the Virgin, I came to know and love my protectress, though at first I confused her with my guardian angel. Her image, which had cost the good Villeneuve half a sou, was affixed by four nails to the wall above my bed. I should have lived in the days when people still spoke to Mary aloud: "Sweet Lady of heaven and earth, mother of mercy, source of all that is good, who bore Jesus Christ in your precious womb, most sweet and beautiful Lady, I thank you and implore you."

The first thing that I learned by heart was a sailor's hymn that begins:

> *Je mets ma confiance,*
> *Vierge, en votre secours;*
> *Servez-moi de défense,*
> *Prenez soin de mes jours;*
> *Et quand ma dernière heure*
> *Viendra finir mon sort,*
> *Obtenez que je meure*
> *De la plus sainte mort.*[26]

I have since heard this hymn sung during a shipwreck. Even today, I recite these paltry rhymes with as much pleasure as the verses of Homer. A madonna fitted with a Gothic crown and dressed in a blue silk robe fringed with silver still inspires me with a deeper devotion than any virgin painted by Raphael.

If only that peaceful Star of the Seas could have calmed the turmoil of my life! But I was to be troubled even in my childhood. Like the Arab's date tree, my trunk had barely sprouted from the rock before it was battered by the wind.

5.

GESRIL—HERVINE MAGON—A FIGHT WITH TWO
CABIN BOYS

La Vallée-aux-Loups, June 1812

I HAVE said that my precocious revolt against Lucile's teachers gave
rise to my bad reputation. Now I shall tell how a friend completed it.

My uncle, M. de Chateaubriand du Plessis, also lived in Saint-Malo,
and, like his brother, he had four daughters and two sons. My cousins, Pierre and Armand, were at first my comrades; but Pierre went
off to become a page to the Queen, and Armand, destined for the
priesthood, was sent away to school. Years later, after leaving the
Queen's service, Pierre joined the navy and drowned off the coast of
Africa; Armand, after more than a decade cloistered in his school,
left France in 1790, served the whole length of the Emigration, made
a dozen intrepid voyages to the coast of Brittany in a rowboat, and
finally came to die for the King on the Plain of Grenelle, on Good
Friday, 1809, as I have already said, and as I shall say again when recounting his ruin.*

Deprived of the company of my two cousins, I replaced it with a
new acquaintance.

On the second floor of our building, there lived a gentleman named
Gesril who had one son and two daughters. This son had been brought
up quite differently than I had. He was a spoiled child, and whatever

---

*Armand left behind a son named Frédéric, for whom I secured a place in the
Guards of *Monsieur*, and who later entered a regiment of cuirassiers. In Nancy,
Frédéric married Mademoiselle de Gastaldi, by whom he had two sons, and thereafter retired from the service. Armand's elder sister is and for many years now has
been a Mother Superior in a Trappist convent. (Geneva, 1831)

he did was found charming. He liked nothing so much as to fight and above all to provoke quarrels of which he then made himself the arbiter. He was forever playing nasty tricks on the nurses when they took the children out for walks, and it was never long before these pranks, transformed into the blackest crimes, were the talk of the town. His father laughed at all of it. The naughtier Joson was, the more he was loved. This boy soon became my constant companion, and the ascendancy he gained over me was incredible. I learned something from this master, even though my character was entirely the opposite of his. I loved solitary games and looked for a quarrel with no one: Gesril was mad for the thrills of the crowd and exulted in boyish brawls. When some street urchin spoke to me, Gesril would ask, "You're going to *allow* that?"

At this, I would believe my honor compromised and hurl myself at the impudent one with no regard for his age or size. My friend applauded my courage, but he always remained a spectator of the scuffle and made no move to help me. Sometimes, he raised an army of all the little guttersnipes he met, divided his conscripts into two bands, and had us skirmish on the beach with stones.

Another game that Gesril devised was still more dangerous. When the sea was high and a tempest raging, the waves, churning against the foot of the castle on the side of the long beach, leapt to the level of the great towers. Twenty feet above the base of one of these towers was a granite parapet, narrow and slippery, which sloped down to the ravelin that defended the moat. The trick was to seize the instant between two waves and cross the perilous thing before the next wave broke and engulfed the tower. If you dared to look, you would see a mountain of water advancing toward you, roaring as it came, and you would know that if you hesitated even for a moment this water could either drag you away or crush you against the wall. Not one of us would refuse the challenge, though I saw some boys go pale before the attempt.

This penchant for pushing others into adventures of which he remained a spectator might lead one to think that Gesril would later show himself to be an ungenerous man. It was nevertheless he who, on a smaller stage, perhaps eclipsed the heroism of Regulus: he only lacked Rome and Livy to ensure his glory. He became an officer in the navy, and was taken prisoner at the Quiberon landing.[27] When the action was over and the English went on cannonading the Republican army, Gesril flung himself into the sea, swam out toward the ships, and shouted to the English to cease fire. He told them that the émigrés had suffered grave misfortune and had surrendered. The English sailors wanted to save him and threw him a rope, urging him to climb aboard. "I am a prisoner on parole!" he shouted from the water, and began swimming back to shore. He was shot with Sombreuil and his companions.

Gesril was my first friend. Both misjudged in our childhoods, we were bound together by an intuition of what we might one day become.

Two adventures brought an end to this first part of my story and produced a notable change in the method of my education.

One Sunday we were on the beach, at the "fantail" of the Porte Saint-Thomas along Le Sillon, where big stakes had been hammered into the sand to shield the walls against the surging sea. We often used to clamber atop these stakes to watch the first undulations of high tide flow beneath us. On this day, we took our places as usual, several little girls mixed in with the little boys. Of the boys, I took the post farthest out to sea, so that I had no one in front of me except a pretty little girl, named Hervine Magon, who was laughing with pleasure and at the same time crying with fear. Gesril took his post at the other end, nearest the town. The tide was coming in, the wind was picking up, and already the maids and servants were shouting: "Come down, Mademoiselle! Come down, Monsieur!" Gesril had been waiting for a big wave. The moment it rushed in between the piles, he pushed the child seated in front of him; this one tumbled onto the next one; that one onto another. The whole line was collapsing like a row of dominoes, but with each child held in place by his neighbor. There was only the little girl at the end of the line, onto whom I capsized, who had no one to lean on, and fell. The backswirl dragged her away. At once there were a thousand cries, and a horde of maids hitched up their skirts, waded into the sea, seized their little marmots, and boxed their ears. Hervine was fished out; but she insisted that François had pushed her down. The maids fell upon me, but I escaped them. I ran home and barricaded myself in the cellar, with the female army at my heels. Fortunately, my mother and father were out. La Villeneuve valiantly defended the door and slapped the enemy's vanguard. The real author of the trouble, Gesril, also lent his assistance. He scrambled up to his room and, with his two sisters, dumped jugfuls of water and baked apples through the windows on the assailants. They raised the siege at nightfall; but the news spread through town that the Chevalier de Chateaubriand, aged nine, was a cruel man, a mortal remnant of those pirates that Saint Aaron had purged from his rock.

Here is the other adventure:

I was going with Gesril to Saint-Servan, a suburb separated from Saint-Malo by the trading port. In order to get there at low tide, one crosses currents of water over narrow bridges built of flat stones which vanish when the tide comes in. The servants who accompanied us were lagging far behind, when, at the end of one of these bridges, we spotted two cabin boys coming our way. Gesril turned to me and said, "Are we going to let these fleabags pass?" And straightaway he shouted at them, "Into the water, ducklings!" But these ducklings, being cabin boys, did not see the joke and continued toward us. Gesril retreated. We took a position at the far end of the bridge and, grabbing up some pebbles, hurled them at the cabin boys' heads. They fell upon us, forced us to give ground, armed themselves with fistfuls of gravel, and drove us back to our reserve corps, which is to say our servants. I was not, like Horatius, wounded in the eye; but a stone had struck me so violently that my left ear, half detached, hung down on my shoulder.

I thought nothing of my injury, but only of returning home. When my friend returned from his escapades with a black eye and a torn coat, he was comforted, cuddled, coddled, and given a fresh change of clothes. Under similar circumstances, I was punished. The blow that I had received was dangerous, but nothing La France could say would persuade me to go home, so frightened was I by the thought of it. Instead, I went and hid on the second floor of the house with Gesril, who wrapped my head in a towel. The towel put him in a good mood. It reminded him of a mitre. He transformed me into a bishop and made me recite the High Mass with him and his sisters until suppertime. The pontiff was then obliged to go downstairs, his heart pounding. My father, though taken aback by my drained and blood-stained face, said not a word. My mother shrieked. La France pleaded my pitiful case and made excuses for me, but I was chided nonetheless. My ear was bandaged, and Monsieur and Madame de Chateaubriand resolved to separate me from Gesril at once.*

I believe that same year the Comte d'Artois came to Saint-Malo and was treated to the spectacle of a naval battle. Looking down from the bastion of the powder-magazine, I caught sight of the young prince in the crowd on the seashore. He was in his radiance, and I was in the shadows, but between us—what unknown workings of fate! Thus, unless my memory fails me, Saint-Malo has seen only two Kings of France: Charles IX and Charles X.

Here you have a picture of my earliest childhood. I do not know whether the harsh education I received is sound in principle, but it was adopted by my parents for no fixed reason and as a natural result of their temperaments. What is certain is that it made my ideas less similar to those of other men; what is still more certain is that it imprinted my feelings with a melancholy stamp—a melancholy born of habitual suffering in the years of weakness, recklessness, and joy.

Do you say that my upbringing must have led me to detest the authors of my early days? Not at all. The memory of their strictness is almost dear to me. I honor and esteem their good qualities. When my father died, my comrades in the Navarre Regiment bore witness

---

*I have already spoken of Gesril in my works. One of his sisters, Angélique Gesril de La Trochardais, wrote me in 1818 to ask me to obtain permission for her husband and her sister's husband to add the name "Gesril" to their surnames. My negotiations ran aground. (Geneva, 1831)

to my grief. To my mother, I owe the consolation of my life, since it was through her that I took my faith: I gathered the Christian truths that came from her lips, as Pierre de Langres studied at night in his church, by the light of the lamp that burned before the Blessed Sacrament. Would my mind have been better developed if I had been plunged into my studies earlier? I doubt it. The waves, the winds, and the solitude that served as my first masters were perhaps better suited to my native dispositions. Perhaps I owe these wild instructors some virtues that I would otherwise lack. The truth is that no system of education is in itself preferable to any other system. Do children love their parents more today, now that they address them as *tu* and no longer fear them? Gesril was spoiled in the same house where I was chastised, but we have both been honest men and respectful, loving sons. The things that you consider wicked may bring out your child's talents; the things that you find good may stifle them. God does well whatever He does. It is Providence that guides us when she destines us to play a role on the world's stage.

6.

NOTE FROM M. PASQUIER—DIEPPE—A CHANGE IN MY EDUCATION—SPRINGTIME IN BRITTANY —HISTORIC FOREST—PELAGIAN COUNTRY— THE MOON SETTING IN THE SEA

Dieppe, September 1812

ON SEPTEMBER 4, 1812, I received this note from M. Pasquier, the Prefect of Police:

> *The Prefect's Office*
> The Prefect of Police invites M. de Chateaubriand to call on him in his office, either at four o'clock in the afternoon today, or tomorrow at nine o'clock in the morning.

It was an order to leave Paris at once that M. the Prefect of Police wished to present me. That is why I have traveled to Dieppe, a place called Bertheville until four hundred years ago, when it was renamed after the English word *deep*, which means "a safe place to anchor." In 1788, I was garrisoned here with the second battalion of my regiment. To live in this town today, among the brick houses and the shops dealing in ivory, this town of clean streets and clear light, is to take refuge in my youth. When I went out for a walk yesterday, I stumbled on the ruins of the Château d'Arques and the thousand bits of rubble surrounding it. One must not forget that Dieppe was the birthplace of Duquesne. When I stay at home, I have a view of the sea. From the table where I sit, I contemplate the same waters that saw my birth and that wash the coasts of Great Britain, where I suffered such a long exile. My gaze soars over the waves that brought me to America, carried me back to Europe, and conveyed me to the shores of Africa and Asia. Here's to you, my sea, my cradle and my emblem! I wish to tell you the rest of my story. If I lie, your waves, which have commingled with my days, will accuse me of imposture in generations to come.

My mother had never given up her desire that I be given a classical education. She said that the sailor's life for which I was destined "would not be to my taste." It seemed to her a good thing, in any event, to prepare me for another career. Her piety led her to hope that I would decide on the Church. She therefore proposed to send me to a school where I could learn mathematics, drawing, fencing, and English; she did not mention Greek and Latin for fear of agitating my father; but she reckoned that I could be taught these languages in secret at first, and in the open once I had made some progress. My father agreed to the proposition, and it was decided that I should be sent to the Collège de Dol. The town of Dol was preferred because it lay on the road from Saint-Malo to Combourg.

During the very cold winter that preceded my first scholastic internment, our house in Saint-Malo caught fire. I was saved by my eldest sister, who carried me through the flames. M. de Chateaubriand, who had by then already withdrawn to his castle, summoned his wife to his side. It was settled that we would go to Combourg in the spring.

Spring, in Brittany, is milder than spring in Paris, and bursts into flower three weeks earlier. The five birds that herald its appearance— the swallow, the oriole, the cuckoo, the quail, and the nightingale— arrive with the breezes that refuge in the bays of the Armorican peninsula.[28] The earth is covered over with daisies, pansies, jonquils, daffodils, hyacinths, buttercups, and anemones, like the wastelands around San Giovanni of Laterano and the Holy Cross of Jerusalem in Rome. The clearings are feathered with tall and elegant ferns; the fields of gorse and broom blaze with flowers that one may take at first glance for golden butterflies. The hedges, along which strawberries, raspberries, and violets grow, are adorned with hawthorn, honeysuckle, and brambles whose brown, curving shoots burst forth with magnificent fruits and leaves. All the world teems with bees and birds;

hives and nests interrupt the child's every footstep. In certain sheltered spots, the myrtle and the rose-bay flourish in the open air, as in Greece; figs ripen, as in Provence; and every apple tree, bursting with carmine flowers, looks like the big bouquet of a village bride.

In the twelfth century, the cantons of Fougères, Rennes, Bécherel, Dinan, Saint-Malo, and Dol were occupied by the forest of Brécheliant, which served as the battleground of the Franks and the tribes of the Dommonée. Wace says that wild men were seen in this forest, as well as the spring of Barenton and a pond of gold.[29] A historical document of the fifteenth century, *Les Usements et Coutumes de la Fôret de Brécilien*, confirms the *Roman de Rou*. The forest, the *Usements* tells us, was once a large and spacious expanse: "There are four castles, a very large number of beautiful ponds, fine hunting grounds where no venal beasts or buzzing flies trouble the hunter, and there are two hundred tall forests and as many springs, including the spring of Belenton, beside which the knight Pontus defended his keep."

Today, the landscape still bears traces of its ancestry. Its wooded gorges, seen from a distance, have the look of wild forests, such as one finds in England. These woods were once the dwelling place of fairies, and you shall soon see that I myself encountered a sylph there. Thin, innavigable rivers water the narrow valleys, divided by heaths and holly holms. On the hillsides, one after another, are beacons, watchtowers, dolmens, Roman constructions, the ruins of medieval castles, and Renaissance bell towers; and all of this bordered by the sea. Pliny called Brittany a "Peninsula keeping watch over the Ocean."[30]

Between the sea and the land is a stretch of pelagian country where the frontiers of the two elements become indistinct. Skylarks from the fields fly with sealarks. The plow and the fishing boat, a stone's throw apart, furrow the land and the water alike. The sailor and the shepherd borrow from one another's tongues: the sailor says *the waves are flocking*, and the shepherd speaks of *fleets of sheep*. The multicolored sands, the variegated heaps of shells, the kelp, and the silvery fringe of foam rise up to the blond or green edges of the wheatfields. I forget now on which Mediterranean island I saw a bas-relief depicting the Nereids pinning scallops to the hem of Ceres's robe.

But what one must admire in Brittany is the moon rising over the land and setting in the sea.

The moon, established by God as governess of the deep, has her clouds, her mists, her rays, and her shadows, like the sun; and, like him, she does not retire alone. A procession of stars accompanies her. As she descends to the skyline of my native shore, her silence deepens and spreads over the sea; she sinks to the horizon, hovers upon it, and then, showing only half her face, drowses, bows her head, and disappears into the soft intumescence of the waves. The stars arrayed around their queen, before they follow in her wake, seem to pause a moment, as if suspended on the surface of the water. No sooner has the moon set than a breath from the open ocean extinguishes this mirror image of the constellations, as the torches are extinguished after a solemn rite.

7.

DEPARTURE FOR COMBOURG—DESCRIPTION OF
THE CASTLE

I WAS TO follow my sisters to Combourg: we set out in the first fortnight of May. At sunrise one morning we left Saint-Malo, my mother, my four sisters, and I, in an enormous old-fashioned Berlin with gilded panels, exterior footboards, and purple tassels hanging from the four corners of the carriage. Eight horses, bedecked like Spanish mules, with large bells draped around their necks and smaller ones fastened to their bridles, sporting many-colored housings and woolen fringe, dragged us on our way. While my mother sighed and my sisters chattered without pausing once for breath, I looked with both my eyes, I listened with both my ears, and I marveled at every turn of the wheel: the first step of a Wandering Jew who would never afterward manage to stop. Still, if a man only changed his place! But his life and his heart change too.

Our horses were rested in a fishing village on the beach at Cancale; then we crossed the marshes, through the feverish town of Dol, and, passing the door of the school to which I was soon to return, we plunged deeper and deeper into the inland country.

For ten mortal miles we saw nothing but uplands bordered by woods, fallow fields that had scarcely been cleared, rows of black wheat-stubble and indigent oats. Charcoal-burners led strings of scrawny ponies with tangled manes. Longhaired peasants in goatskin tunics drove emaciated oxen with shrill cries or trudged in the wake of heavy plows, like so many laboring fauns. At long last, we came to a valley, at the bottom of which, not far from a pond, there rose the single spire of a village church. The towers of a feudal castle loomed above a copse of trees lighted by the fires of the setting sun.

I had to stop myself just now. My heart was beating so hard that it shook the table on which I write these words. The memories reawakening in my brain overwhelm me with their number and their power; and yet what can they mean to the rest of the world?

At the foot of the hill, we forded a stream. After another half hour, we left the highway, and the carriage rolled along the edge of a quincunx into an avenue of trees whose branches interlaced over our heads. I can still remember the moment I entered under that shade and the dreadful joy that I felt there.

Leaving the darkness of the woods, we crossed a forecourt planted with walnut trees which led to the steward's house and the garden. From there, we went through a little gate into a grassy courtyard called the Green Court: to the right were a row of stables and a stand of chestnuts; to the left, another stand of chestnuts; and at the far end of the courtyard, which sloped almost imperceptibly upward, the castle stood between two clumps of trees. Its bleak and melancholy façade was dominated by a curtain-wall supporting a machicolated gallery, enameled and denticulated, that linked together two large towers of disparate age, height, girth, and material. These towers were topped with crenellations and surmounted by pointed roofs, like bonnets set upon Gothic crowns.

Barred windows were visible here and there in the bare walls. A large staircase of twenty-two steps, steep and wide, without banister or parapet, had been built over the filled-in moat where the drawbridge used to be. These stairs led up to the main door of the castle, carved into the middle of the curtain-wall. Over this door, the coat of arms of the "Seigneurs de Chateaubriand" hung between the fissures through which the arms and chains of the drawbridge once had passed.

The carriage stopped at the foot of the staircase, and my father came down the steps to meet us. The reunion of his family so softened his mood for the moment that he favored us with the most gracious expressions. We climbed the staircase and proceeded into an echoing anteroom with a high, ribbed ceiling, and from this anteroom onward into a small interior courtyard. From there, we entered the block that faced south over the pond and adjoined the two small towers. The castle, taken all together, had the shape of a four-wheeled chariot. We found ourselves on the ground floor, in a room formerly known as the "Salle des Gardes." There was a window at each end of this room and two more that had been carved into the side wall: in order to enlarge these windows, it had been necessary to chisel through eight or ten feet of stone. Two corridors that sloped gradually upward, like the corridor of the Great Pyramid, led from the far corners of the room to the two small towers, and a staircase, spiraling inside one of these towers, established relations between the Salle des Gardes and the upper story.

The block between the high tower and the fat tower, which faced north over the Green Court, consisted of a sort of dark, square dormitory that served as a kitchen; there was also an anteroom, a staircase, and a chapel. Above these rooms was the Salon des Archives, des Armoires, des Oiseaux, or des Chevaliers, so called because of its ceiling, which was covered with colorful escutcheons and painted birds. So deep were the narrow embrasures of its trefoiled windows that they formed closets bound by granite benches hewn into the walls. Add to all this, in various parts of the building, secret passageways and stairwells, dungeons and keeps, a labyrinth of covered and uncovered galleries, walled-up subterranean passages whose ramifications were unknown, and everywhere silence, darkness, and a face of stone—and there you have the Château de Combourg.

A supper served in the Salle des Gardes, which I ate without constraint, brought the first happy day of my life to a close. True happiness is cheap; if costly, it is not the real thing at all.

The next morning, the moment I opened my eyes, I went out to inspect the castle grounds and celebrate my accession to solitude. Seated on the diazoma of the staircase, facing northwest, I saw before me the Green Court, and beyond this court, a kitchen garden planted between two groves of trees. The one on the right (the quincunx by which we had arrived) was called the "Little Mall"; the other, on the left, the "Grand Mall." This latter grove consisted of a forest of oaks, beeches, sycamores, elms, and chestnuts. In her day, Madame de Sévigné was already praising these ancient trees for their shade: since then, one hundred and forty years had been added to their beauty.[31]

On the opposite side, to the south and east, the country presented an altogether different picture. Through the windows of the great hall, one could see the houses of Combourg, a pond, and on the causeway above this pond the highway to Rennes, a water mill, and a meadow covered with herds of cattle and separated from the pond by the road. At the edge of the meadow was a hamlet attached to a priory, founded in 1149 by Rivallon, Seigneur de Combourg, and inside which his mortuary statue lay peacefully asleep, supine, in knightly armor. Up from the pond and the priory the terrain steadily inclined, forming an amphitheater of trees above which the belfries of the village and the turrets of neighboring manors jutted into the sky. On a last plane of the horizon, to the southwest, were the silhouetted heights of Bécherel. A terrace bordered with large manicured boxwoods wrapped around the foot of the castle on this side, passed behind the stables, and descended, by various turnings, to join the water garden that gave onto the Grand Mall.

If, following this overlong description, a painter were to take his pencil in hand, would he produce a sketch in any way resembling my father's castle? I don't believe he would. Yet my memory beholds the place as though it were before my very eyes. Such is the weakness of words and the strength of memory in the face of material things. In beginning to speak of Combourg, I sing the first lines of a ballad that charms no one but me. Ah, well! Ask a goatherd in the Tyrol why he takes such delight in those three or four notes that he keeps repeating to his animals, those alpine melodies that cast echo after echo, re-sounding from one bank of a mountain stream to the other.

My first appearance at Combourg was of short duration. Two weeks had scarcely passed before I saw the arrival of the Abbé Porcher, the principal of the Collège de Dol. I was delivered into his hands, and I followed him in spite of my tears.

BOOK TWO

I.

COLLÈGE DE DOL—MATHEMATICS AND
LANGUAGES—TWO FEATURES OF MY MEMORY

Dieppe, September 1812;
Revised in June 1846

I WAS NOT entirely a stranger to Dol. My father was a canon there, as he was a descendant and representative of the house of Guillaume de Chateaubriand, Lord of Beaufort, who, in 1529, founded the first stall in the choir of the cathedral. The Bishop of Dol was M. de Hercé, a friend of my family and a prelate of quite moderate political views who, on his knees, crucifix in hand, was shot with his brother, the Abbé de Hercé, at Quiberon, in the Field of the Martyrs. On arriving at school, I was placed under the private guardianship of M. l'Abbé Leprince, who taught rhetoric and possessed a thorough knowledge of geometry. A witty man with a handsome face, a lover of the arts and a painter of fairly good portraits, he was charged with teaching me my Bézout.[1] The Abbé Égault, the master of the third-years, became my Latin instructor. So it was that I studied mathematics in my dormitory and Latin in the schoolroom.

It took some time for an owl of my species to accustom himself to the cage of a college and regulate his flight to the sound of school bells. I could find none of those ready friends that wealth allows you, for there was nothing to be gained from friendship with a poor scamp who didn't even have a weekly allowance. Still, I did not enroll myself in any clique, for I hate protectors. On the playing fields, I made no effort to lead others, but neither would I be led: I was unfit to be a tyrant or a slave, and so I have remained.

It soon happened, however, that I became the leader of a group; I would later exert a similar power over my regiment: simple sublieu-tenant though I was, the senior officers would spend their evenings with me and preferred my apartment to the café downstairs. I don't know why this should be, unless perhaps it has something to do with my ability to enter the minds and understand the ways of others. I have loved hunting and sailing as much as I have loved reading and writing. Even today, it makes no difference to me whether I speak of the commonest things or discuss the loftiest subjects. I am not much interested in wit; it is almost repugnant to me, although I am hardly a brute. No human failings shock me, except mockery and self-conceit, which I am always at great pains not to attack. I find that others are always superior to me in something, and if by chance I feel that I have an advantage over them, I am altogether embarrassed.

Certain qualities that my early upbringing had left dormant awoke in me at the Collège de Dol. My capacity for work was remarkable, and my memory was extraordinary. I made rapid progress in math-ematics, a subject to which I brought a clarity of comprehension that astounded the Abbé Leprince. At the same time, I showed a decided taste for languages. The rudiments that torment most schoolboys cost me nothing to acquire, and I awaited Latin lessons with a kind of impatience, as a form of relaxation after my equations and geo-metrical figures. In less than a year, I was ranked high in the fifth form. By some singular quirk, my Latin phrases fell so naturally into pentameters that Abbé Égault took to calling me "the Elegist," a name that took hold among my classmates.

As for my memory, here are two of its features. First, I learned my logarithm tables by heart: that is to say, when a number was given in a geometrical series, I could name its exponent in the corresponding arithmetical series, and vice versa, from memory.

Here is an illustration of the second. After evening prayers, which were recited together in the school chapel, the principal gave a sermon. One of the boys, picked at random, would be required to summarize it. We came into the chapel exhausted from playing and dying to sleep; we hurled ourselves into the pews, trying to hide in some dark corner to avoid being seen and consequently interrogated. There was above all a confessional booth that we fought over as the surest hiding place. One evening, I had the good luck of winning this refuge, and I considered myself safe from the principal. Unfortunately, he detected my strategy and decided to make an example of me. And so, slowly and deliberately, he read the second part of his sermon. Everyone fell asleep. I know not what led me to stay awake in the confessional, but the principal, who could see only the soles of my feet, believed that I was dozing like the others, and suddenly he called my name. He asked me what it was he had been reading.

The second part of the sermon had involved an enumeration of the various ways in which one can offend God. Now, not only did I relate the substance of the thing, but I recalled the divisions of the argument in their original order and repeated almost word for word several pages of mystical prose, all of which was unintelligible to a child. A murmur of applause ran through the chapel, and the principal called me up to give me a little pat on the cheek and allowed me, as a reward, to stay in bed the next day until the midday meal. I modestly shrugged off the admiration of my classmates, and I profited fully from the grace accorded me. This memory for language, which has not entirely stayed with me, has given way to another, more singular kind of memory, of which I may soon have occasion to speak.

One thing humiliates me, however. Memory is often a quality associated with stupidity. It usually belongs to slow-witted souls whom it renders still slower by the baggage it loads on them. And yet, without memory, what would we be? We would forget our friendships, our loves, our pleasures, our affairs; the genius would not be able to collect his thoughts, and the most affectionate heart would lose its tenderness, if they did not remember. Our existence would be reduced to the successive moments of an endlessly flowing present, and there would be no more past. What a misery is man! Our life is so vain that it is no more than a reflection of our memory.

2.

HOLIDAYS AT COMBOURG—PROVINCIAL CHÂTEAU
LIFE—FEUDAL WAYS—INHABITANTS OF COMBOURG

Dieppe, October 1812

I WENT to spend my holidays at Combourg. Château life in the vicinity of Paris can give no idea of château life in a remote province.

The estate of Combourg was no more than a few acres of heath, several mills, and two forests, Bourgouët and Tanoërn, in a region where timber is almost worthless. But Combourg was rich in feudal rights of various kinds. Some of these rights determined certain rents for concessions or regulated customs that had been established under the old political order; others seemed to have been merely amusements from the start.

My father had revived a few of these latter rights in order to prevent their positive prescription. When the whole family was gathered together, we took part in these Gothic entertainments. The three principal ones were the Saut des Poissonniers,[2] the Quintaine, and a fair called the Angevine. Peasants in clogs and breeches, men of a France that no longer exists, would watch the games of a France that had already ceased to be. There was a prize for the victor and a forfeit to be paid by the vanquished.

The Quintaine preserved the tradition of tournaments. No doubt it bore some relation to the ancient military duties of the fiefs. It is very well described by Du Cange (*voce Quintana*).[3] Forfeits had to be paid in old copper coinage, up to the value of two *moutons d'or à la couronne* of *25 sols parisis* each.

The fair called the Angevine was held in the meadow by the pond every September 4, my birthday. Vassals were required to take up arms and come to the castle to raise the banner of the lord. From there, they went off to the fair to keep order and enforce the collection of a toll due to the Counts of Combourg for every head of cattle: a sort of royalty. During these times, my father kept an open house. For three days, everyone danced: the masters, in the great hall, to the scraping of a fiddle; the vassals, in the Green Court, to the twanging of a bagpipe. Everyone sang, shouted huzzah, and fired arquebuses, and these noises mingled with the lowing of the cattle at the fair. The crowd drifted through the gardens and the woods, and, at least this one time of year, Combourg saw something that resembled joy.

Thus, in my lifetime, I have had the somewhat singular distinction to have been present at the contests of the Quintaine and at the proclamation of the Rights of Man; to have seen both the bourgeois militia of a Breton village and the National Guard of France, the banner of the Seigneurs de Combourg and the flag of the Revolution. It is as if I were the last surviving witness of the feudal ways.

The visitors that we received at the castle were the inhabitants of the town and the aristocrats of the township: these honest people were my first friends. Our vanity sets too much importance on the role that we play in the world. The Parisian bourgeois laughs at the small-town bourgeois; the nobleman at Court mocks the provincial noble; the well-known man disdains the unknown man, forgetting that time will do equal justice to their various pretensions, and that they will all look equally ridiculous or trivial in the eyes of generations to come.

The preeminent inhabitant of Combourg was one M. Potelet, a former sea captain in the East India Company, who used to retell long stories about his days in Pondicherry. As he recounted these tales, his elbows propped on the table, my father always looked as though he wanted to hurl a plate of food at his face. After Potelet came the tobacco bonder, M. Launay de La Billardière, the father of a family of twelve children, like Jacob, although in his case nine girls and three boys, of whom the youngest, David, was my playmate.* The

* I would meet my friend David again: I shall soon say when and how. (Geneva, 1832)

good man took it into his head to become a nobleman in 1789: he had really taken his time! In his household, there was a surplus of happiness and an abundance of debt. These men, together with the seneschal Gébert, the fiscal attorney Petit, the tax collector Le Corvaisier, and the chaplain Abbé Charmel, comprised the high society of Combourg. I did not meet more distinguished people when I visited Athens.

Messrs. Du Petit-Bois, de Château-d'Assie, de Tinteniac, and one or two other gentlemen came on Sundays to hear Mass in the parish and afterward dined with the lord of the manor. We were particularly close with the Trémaudan family: a husband, his extremely pretty wife, her sister, and several children. This family inhabited a farm where the only sign of their nobility was a dovecote and where they remain to this day. Wiser and happier than I, the Trémaudans have never lost sight of the towers of that castle I left more than thirty years ago; they continue to live as they lived when I went to eat brown bread at their table; they have never abandoned that refuge which I shall never see again. Perhaps they are speaking of me at this very moment, as I write this page: I reproach myself for dragging their name out of its protective obscurity. They doubted for a long time that the man about whom they heard so much was the *petit chevalier* that they used to know. The rector or curé of Combourg, Abbé Sévin, to whose sermons I used to listen, showed a similar incredulity. He could not be persuaded that a scamp who had been the friend of peasants became the defender of the Christian religion. At last, he came to believe, and now he quotes me in his sermons, whereas once he bounced me on his knees. These worthy people, whose image of me is not clouded with any strange ideas, who see me as I was in my boyhood and youth—would they recognize me today, after all the travesties of time? I'm afraid I would have to tell them my name before they clasped me in their arms.

I bring misfortune to my friends. A gamekeeper at Combourg named Raulx, who grew fond of me, was killed by a poacher. This murder made an extraordinary impression on me. What a strange mystery is human sacrifice! Why must it be that the greatest crime and the greatest glory lie in shedding man's blood? In my mind's eye, I used to picture Raulx, clutching his entrails in his hands, limping toward the cottage where he died; I plotted to avenge him, and would even have liked to fight the murderer myself. In this respect, I am singularly made: at the moment of the offense I hardly feel it, but it engraves itself in my memory, and the remembrance of it, instead of waning, waxes with time. It stays in my heart for months or years, and then wakes with fresh force in the least expected circumstances, when my wound becomes keener than on the first day. But if I never forgive my enemies, I never do them any harm either. I am rancorous but not at all vindictive. If I have the power to revenge myself, I lose the desire: I could only be dangerous in misfortune. Those who have thought to make me yield by oppressing me have been deceived. Adversity is to me what the earth was to Antaeus: I gather strength at my mother's breast. If happiness ever took me in its arms, I would suffocate.

3.

FURTHER HOLIDAYS AT COMBOURG—THE CONTI REGIMENT—CAMP AT SAINT-MALO—AN ABBEY —THE THEATER—MY TWO ELDEST SISTERS MARRY—RETURN TO SCHOOL—A REVOLUTION IN MY THOUGHTS

Dieppe, October 1812

I RETURNED to Dol, to my great regret. The following year, there were plans to attack the island of Jersey. A camp was established near Saint-Malo, and troops were stationed in Combourg. Out of courtesy, M. de Chateaubriand put up the colonels of the Touraine and Conti regiments: one was the Duc de Saint-Simon and the other the Marquis de Causans.* Every day, a dozen officers were invited to share my father's table. The chatter of these strangers upset me, and their strolls disturbed the peace of my woods. It was through seeing the lieutenant colonel of the Conti Regiment, the Marquis de Wignacourt, galloping beneath the trees, that the idea of travel first crossed my mind.

As I listened to our guests talk of Paris and the Court, I grew despondent. I tried to divine what society was and discovered only something blurred and distant; I was soon bewildered. From the tranquil realms of innocence, I cast my eyes on the world and felt a sort of vertigo, as if I were looking down at the earth from one of those towers that vanish in the sky.

One thing delighted me, however, and that was the parade. Every day, the guard, led by a drummer and a band, would march at the foot of the staircase in the Green Court. When M. de Causans offered to take me to see the camp on the coast, my father gave his consent.

I was driven to Saint-Malo by M. de la Morandais, a gentleman

---

*I experienced a palpable pleasure when, during the Restoration, I reencountered this gallant man, distinguished by his loyalty and Christian virtues. (Geneva, 1831)

of good family whom poverty had reduced to being the steward of the Combourg estate. He wore a gray woolen coat with a thin silver band around the collar, and a gray felt cap with earflaps and a single peak in front. He saddled me behind him on the crupper of his isabella mare, and I held on to the belt of his hunting knife, which he fastened outside his coat: I was ecstatic. When Claude de Bullion and Chairman Lamoignon's father were taken to the country as children, "they were carried in baskets, the two of them on either side of the same donkey, and, because Lamoignon was lighter than his comrade, a loaf of bread was put in with him as a counter-weight" (*Mémoires du président de Lamoignon*).

M. de La Morandais took backroads all the way:

> *Moult volontiers, de grand'manière,*
> *Alloit en bois et en rivière;*
> *Car nulles gens ne vont en bois*
> *Moult volontiers comme François.*[4]

We stopped for dinner at a Benedictine abbey, whose monks, for want of the requisite number, had recently been sent to join the chief residence of the order. The only man left there was the bursar, who had been charged with overseeing the sale of the abbey's furniture and the exploitation of its trees. He provided us with an excellent Friday dinner in what had formerly been the Prior's library: we ate a quantity of new-laid eggs with huge carp and pike. Through the arcade of a cloister, I could see a few tall sycamores along a pond. An ax struck at the foot of one of these trees; its top trembled in the air, and down it fell, as if to provide us with midday entertainment. Carpenters from Saint-Malo sawed off its green branches, as one trims a youthful head of hair, and squared away its toppled trunk. My heart bled at the sight of the ruptured forest and the disinhabited monastery. The widespread sacking of religious houses since then has always put me in mind of that desecrated place, which for me was a portent of things to come.

When I arrived in Saint-Malo, I found the Marquis de Causans and wandered through the streets of the camp under his guidance. The tents, the weapons stacks, and the horses tethered to their pickets formed a memorable scene, set against the backdrop of the sea and the ships, the high stone walls, and the distant steeples of town. It was in this camp, passing by me, in hussar's garb, going full gallop on a Barbary steed, that I saw one of those men in whom a whole world came to an end: the Duc de Lauzun. The Prince de Carignan, who was also there in that camp, would later marry M. de Boisgarin's daughter, a little crippled girl, but charming. This marriage caused a tremendous stir and led to a legal case in which M. Lacretelle the Elder is even now embroiled. But what connection do these things have with my life? "I have noticed, among some of my closest friends, that the more their memory provides them with the thing entire, the more they push their narrative so far back and load it with such pointless details that, if the tale is good, they smother its goodness, and if it isn't good, you are left cursing either the felicity of their memory or the infelicity of their judgment. I have seen some very amusing stories become very boring in the mouth of a certain gentleman."[5] I am afraid of being this gentleman.

My brother was also in Saint-Malo when M. de la Morandais deposited me there. One evening he said to me, "I'm going to take you to the theater. Go get your hat."

I lost my head: I went straight down to the cellar looking for my hat, which was up in the attic. A troupe of traveling players had just arrived in town. I had seen puppet shows and supposed that one saw far lovelier marionettes in the theater than in the street.

I arrive, with my heart pounding, at a wooden building in a deserted street of town. I proceed through dark corridors, not without a certain sense of dread. A small door is opened, and there I am with my brother in a box half filled with people.

The curtain was raised and the performance began. The play was Diderot's *Le Père de famille*. I saw two men walking around the stage and talking while everyone watched, and I took them for the puppetmasters, chatting outside Madame Gigogne's hut while they waited for the audience to file in. I was only surprised at how loudly they were speaking of their affairs and how quietly everyone else was listening to them. My astonishment redoubled when I saw other characters arrive on stage, throwing up their arms and weeping, whereupon everyone around me also started weeping, as if there were some sort of contagion. The curtain fell without my having understood any of this. My brother went down to the lobby for intermission. Left alone in the box, among strangers whose very presence was a torment to my timidity, I wished that I were back in the obscurity of my school. Such was my first impression of the art of Sophocles and Molière.

The third year of my sojourn at Dol was marked by the weddings of my two eldest sisters: Marianne married the Comte de Marigny, and Benigne the Comte de Québriac. They went with their husbands to Fougères: the first intimation of the dispersal of my family, whose members were soon to be separated forever. My sisters received the nuptial blessing on the same day, at the same moment, at the same altar, in the chapel at Combourg. They were weeping; my mother was weeping; I was stunned by such sorrow. I understand it well today. I never attend a baptism or a wedding without a bitter smile or a pang of the heart. After the unhappiness of being born, I know of none greater than that of giving life to a man.

This same year saw a revolution in my person as well as in my family. Chance brought two very different books into my hands: an unexpurgated Horace and a compendium of *Evil Confessions*. The mental upheaval that these two books caused me is incredible. A strange new world came into being around me. On one side, I began to suspect that there were secrets incomprehensible to a boy my age, an existence different from mine, pleasures beyond my childish games, charms of an unknown nature in a sex that I knew only through my mother and my sisters; on the other, ghosts dragging chains and vomiting fire promised eternal punishments for a single hidden sin. I lost sleep over it; at night, I believed I could see black and white hands passing in turn across my curtains. I came to think that the white hands were cursed by religion, and this idea stoked my fear of the infernal shades. I searched hell and heaven in vain for an explanation of this double mystery. Stricken all at once in mind and body, I was still struggling with my innocence against the storms of premature passion and the terrors of superstition.

From then on I felt sparks flying from that fire which is the transmission of life. I construed the fourth book of the *Aeneid* and read *Télémaque*. Suddenly I discovered in Dido and Eucharis two beauties who ravished me; I became attuned to the harmony of those marvelous verses and that classical prose. One day I translated on sight Lucretius's *Aeneadum genetrix, hominum divumque voluptas,* "Mother of Aeneas's sons, voluptuous delight of men and gods,"[6] with such ardor that M. Égault tore the poem from my hands and set me to studying Greek roots. I palmed a copy of Tibullus, and when I reached *Quam juvat immites ventos audire cubantem,* "What joy to hear the wild winds as I lie here,"[7] the sensual pleasure and melancholy of these verses seemed to reveal to me my true nature. The volumes of Massillon that contained the sermons on Sinful Women and the Prodigal Son never left my side. I was allowed to leaf through any book I wanted, for no one suspected what I found in them. I would steal small candle-ends from the chapel and stay up all night reading seductive descriptions of the troubles of the soul. I would go to sleep babbling incoherent phrases in which I tried to put the sweetness, the meter, and the grace of the writer who had best conveyed the euphony of Racine's verse into prose.

If I have since depicted, with some veracity, the workings of the human heart commingled with Christian synderesis,[8] I am convinced that I owe my successes to chance, which introduced me to those two inimical dominions at one and the same time. The havoc that a wicked book unleashed in my imagination was met with the corrective terrors that another book inspired, and these terrors were in turn allayed by the sweet thoughts stirred in me at seeing certain pictures unveiled.

4.

ADVENTURE OF THE MAGPIE—THIRD HOLIDAY IN COMBOURG—THE CHARLATAN—RETURN TO SCHOOL

Dieppe, End of October 1812

WHAT THEY say of troubles, that they never come alone, might also be said of the passions. They arrive together, like the Muses or the Furies. Together with the weakness that had begun to agonize me, my sense of honor was born. Honor is an exaltation of the soul that keeps the heart incorruptible in a world of corruption—a kind of restorative principle set beside the principle of depletion, like the inexhaustible spring of wonders that love asks of youth set beside the sacrifices that love imposes.

When the weather was fine, boarders were permitted to spend Thursdays and Sundays away from school. Often, we were taken to Mont-Dol, on the summit of which there were some Gallo-Roman ruins. Looking down from the heights of this isolated hillock, the eye soared over the sea and the marshes where will-o'-the-wisps flew by night, casting those magic lights that nowadays burn in our lamps. Other days, the object of our strolls was the meadowland surrounding a seminary of Eudists, named after Eudes, the brother of the historian Mézerai, who had founded their congregation.

One day in the month of May, Abbé Égault, who was prefect that week, had led us to this seminary. We were at liberty to play almost anywhere, but he expressly forbade us from climbing the trees. Then, having set us loose on a grassy path, he went off to recite his breviary.

A few tall elms bordered the path. At the very top of the tallest one, a magpie's nest seemed to glow. We looked up in admiration, all pointing to the mother bird sitting on her eggs and all seized by a keen desire to possess that superb prey. But who would dare take the risk? The prohibition was so strict, the prefect so near, the tree so tall. All hopes rested on me: I climbed like a cat. I hesitated, but soon enough visions of glory prevailed. I shed my coat, put my arms around the elm, and started my ascent. The trunk had no branches until two-thirds of the way up, where it formed a fork, one of whose tines bore the nest.

My fellow boarders gathered beneath the tree and cheered my efforts, keeping one eye on me and one eye on the path by which the prefect might come at any moment, stamping with joy in expectation of the egg, and dying of fear in expectation of punishment. I reached the nest; the magpie flew away; I plundered the eggs, put them in my shirt, and began to climb down. Unfortunately, I let myself slip between the twin trunks and was stuck straddling the fork. The tree had been so neatly pruned that I couldn't find the foothold I would have needed to lift myself up and grab hold of the main trunk again. So I remained, hanging in the air, fifty feet above the ground.

Suddenly there was a shout—"There he is! The prefect!"—and I found myself abandoned by my companions forthwith, as is the custom. One boy, named Le Gobbien, attempted to help me, but he was soon forced to give up this generous enterprise. There was but one way for me to escape my annoying predicament, and that was to dangle by my hands from one of the two branches of the fork while trying to grip the trunk with my feet somewhere below the bifurcation. I executed this maneuver at the risk of my life. Amid these tribulations, I did not let go of my treasure, although I would have been better off throwing it away, as I have since thrown away so many others. Sliding down the trunk, I skinned my hands, scraped my knees and my chest, and crushed the eggs. It was this that gave me away. The prefect had not even seen me up the tree, and I hid my blood from him easily enough; but there was no way to hide the bright yellow stuff smeared all over my clothes.

"Let's go, Monsieur," he said to me. "You shall have a flogging."

If this man had told me that he would commute his sentence to a death sentence, I would have felt a thrill of joy. The idea of shame had not yet entered into my savage education, and, at any age, there was no torture that I would not have preferred to the horror of having to blush before another living creature. Indignation rose in my throat. I replied to Abbé Égault, in the tone of a man, not a child, that neither he nor anyone else would ever lift his hand against me. This response riled him. He called me a rebel and promised to make an example of me.

"We shall see," I said, and I set to playing ball with a sangfroid that perplexed him.

We returned to the school. The prefect made me go to his room and ordered me to submit to my punishment. My exalted feelings gave way to a flood of tears. I reminded Abbé Égault that he had taught me Latin, that I was his pupil, his disciple, his child, that he could not wish to dishonor his own student and make the sight of my friends unbearable to me, that he could lock me up in prison and feed me only bread and water, deprive me of my pleasures and load me with *pensums*, and that I would be grateful to him for his clemency and love him all the more. I fell at his knees. I clasped my hands and begged him to spare me in the name of Jesus Christ, but he remained deaf to my pleas. Then I rose to my feet, flushed with rage, and kicked his legs so violently that he let out a cry. He hurried to close the door of his room, double-locked it, and turned back to face me. I entrenched myself behind his bed. He lunged at me across the mattress with a ferule in his hand. I twisted myself up in his bed linens and, rousing myself to battle, shrieked:

"Macte animo, generose puer!"[9]

This show of schoolboy erudition made my enemy laugh despite himself. He spoke of armistice, and we concluded a treaty: I agreed to yield to the principal's judgment. The principal, without pardoning me altogether, decided that I should be excused from the punishment which had so repulsed me. When this excellent priest pronounced my acquittal, I kissed the sleeve of his robe with such a heartfelt outpouring of gratitude that the man could not help but give me his blessing. Thus ended the first battle in which I defended my honor, the idol of my life, for which I have so often sacrificed tranquility, pleasure, and fortune.

The fall holidays, during which I turned twelve, were sad days. Abbé Leprince accompanied me to Combourg, and I did not go out at all except in the company of my tutor. Together we went for long and aimless strolls. He was dying of consumption; he was melancholy and silent: I was hardly more cheerful. We would walk for hours at a time, one behind the other, without speaking a word. One day, we lost our way in the woods, and M. Leprince turned to me and said, "Which way should we go?"

I replied without hesitation, "The sun is setting. Around now the light glints off the high tower. We should walk in that direction."

M. Leprince recounted this incident to my father that evening. There was already something of the future traveler in my swift decision. Many a time, seeing the sun set in the forests of America, I recalled the woods of Combourg. My memories echo one another.

Abbé Leprince suggested that I be given a horse, but according to my father's ideas the only thing a naval officer needed to know how to handle was a ship. I was thus reduced to riding one of the two fat coach horses or a big piebald, and this only behind my father's back. My piebald was not, like Turenne's piebald, one of those war horses trained to aid their masters which the Romans called "*desultorios equos*"[10]: he was a lunatic Pegasus unmanageable at a trot who bit at my legs whenever I set him to jumping a ditch. I have never much cared for horses, although I have lived the life of a Tartar, and, despite my early training, I still ride with more elegance than balance.

A case of Tertian fever, the germ of which I had brought home with me from Dol, relieved me of M. Leprince. A quacksalver was passing through the village at the time. My father, who had no faith in doctors and great faith in charlatans, sent for this man, who declared that he could cure me in twenty-four hours. The next day he returned wearing a green coat trimmed with gold braid, a large powdered wig, huge ruffles of filthy muslin around his neck, false diamonds on his fingers, threadbare satin breeches, bluish-white stockings, and shoes with enormous buckles.

He threw open my bed-curtains, felt my pulse, made me stick out my tongue, jabbered a few words in an Italian accent—something about how I needed purging—and gave me a small piece of caramel to eat. My father approved of all this, for he maintained that every illness rose from indigestion. He believed that all maladies could be cured by purging your man to the blood.

Half an hour after swallowing the caramel, I was seized by a terrific fit of vomiting. As soon as M. de Chateaubriand was told of this, he wanted to throw the poor Italian devil out the tower window. The medicine man, obviously frightened, removed his coat and rolled up his shirtsleeves, making the most grotesque gesticulations imaginable. With each gesture, his wig turned in a new direction, and he replicated my cries with his own, saying, "*Che*? Monsou Lavandier?" This M. Lavandier was the village chemist, who had been called in to help. In the throes of my suffering, I did not know whether I would die from taking the charlatan's drugs or from roaring with laughter at his absurdity.

The effects of this violent dose of emetic were halted, and I was soon on my feet again. All our life is spent wandering around our grave; all our illnesses are so many gusts of wind that bring us nearer or farther from port. The first dead man I saw was a clergyman in Saint-Malo. He lay lifeless on the bed, his face distorted by the last convulsions. Death is beautiful, she is our friend; only we do not realize it because she comes to us masked, and the mask she wears horrifies us.

I was sent back to school at the end of autumn.

5.

INVASION OF FRANCE—GAMES—THE ABBÉ DE CHATEAUBRIAND

Dieppe, Vallée-aux-Loups, December 1813

FROM DIEPPE, where the police injunction had forced me to take refuge, I have been permitted to return to the Vallée-aux-Loups, where I am now picking up the thread of my narrative again. The earth trembles under the footsteps of foreign soldiers who are at this very moment invading my native land. I write this, like the last Romans, amid the tumult of Barbarian invasion. By day, I scribble pages as agitated as the events of the moment;* by night, when the rumble of distant gunfire fades from my woods, I return in silence to those years that sleep in the grave, to the peace of my earliest memories. How narrow and short is one man's past beside the vast present of the nations and the immensity of their future!

Mathematics, Greek, and Latin occupied the whole of my winter at school. What time was not dedicated to study was given over to those childhood games that are the same in all places. The little Englishman, the little German, the little Italian, the little Spaniard, the little Iroquois, the little Bedouin—all of them roll hoops and throw the ball. Children are brothers of one great family and lose their common features only when they lose their innocence. It's the same the world over. The passions, modified by climates, governments, and customs, form the different nations; humankind ceases to speak and

De Bonaparte et des Bourbons (Geneva, 1831)

understand the same language: it is society that is the true Tower of Babel.

One morning, I was engrossed in a game of prisoner's base in the schoolyard when I was told that I was wanted. I followed the servant to the main gate. I found a large, red-faced man with a brusque and impatient way about him, a ferocious tone of voice, carrying a stick in his hand and wearing a badly curled black wig, a torn cassock that he had tucked into his pockets, dusty shoes, and stockings with gaping holes at the heels.

"You," he said. "Little wretch. Are you not the Chevalier de Chateaubriand de Combourg?"

"Yes, Monsieur," I replied, stunned by the way he spoke to me.

"And I," he said, almost foaming at the mouth, "I am the last of the oldest branch of your family. I am the Abbé de Chateaubriand de la Guérande. Take a good look at me now."

The proud priest put his hand in the fob pocket of his old plush breeches, pulled out a moldy six-franc coin wrapped in greasy paper, flung the thing at my nose, and continued his journey afoot, muttering his matins with a furious air. I have since learned that the Prince de Condé once offered this country cleric the post of tutor to the Duc de Bourbon. The bumptious priest replied that the prince, as the owner of the Chateaubriand barony, ought to know that the heirs to this barony might *have* tutors, but that they would *be* tutors to no man. Such hauteur was the chief failing of my family. In my father it was odious; my brother took it to ridiculous lengths, and it has passed down to some degree to his eldest son. I am not quite sure, despite my Republican leanings, whether I have entirely shaken it off myself, much as I have tried to conceal it.

6.

FIRST COMMUNION—I LEAVE THE COLLÈGE DE DOL

THE TIME of my first communion was drawing near, the moment when it was customary for a family to decide a child's future station. This religious ceremony among young Christians took the place of the taking of the *toga virilis* practiced among the Romans. Madame de Chateaubriand came from Combourg to attend the first communion of a son who, after being united with God, would be separated from his mother.

My piety in those days appeared sincere. I edified the whole school, my eyes were ardent, and my fasts were so frequent as to make even my teachers uneasy. They feared the excess of my devotion and sought to temper my fervor with their enlightened faith.

I had for my confessor the superior of the Eudist seminary, a man of fifty with a very austere look about him. Every time I took my seat in the confessional booth, he would question me anxiously. Surprised at the slightness of my sins, he did not know how to reconcile my agitation with the small importance of the secrets I confided to him. The closer Easter came, the more pressing the priest's questions became.

"Aren't you keeping something from me?" he would ask.

"No, Father."

"Have you not committed such and such a sin?" he would say.

And it was always "No, Father."

He would dismiss me doubtfully, sighing and trying to peer into the depths of my soul, while I, on my side, would leave his presence as pale and disfigured as a criminal.

76

I was to receive absolution on Holy Wednesday. I spent the night from Tuesday into Wednesday praying, and also reading, with a feeling of terror, the book of *Evil Confessions*. On Wednesday, at three in the afternoon, we set off for the seminary in the company of our parents. All the vain commotion that has since surrounded my name would not have given Madame de Chateaubriand an ounce of the pride she experienced, as a Christian and as a mother, when she saw her son prepared to participate in the great mystery of religion.

On entering the church, I prostrated myself before the altar and lay there as if annihilated. When I stood to go to the sacristy, where the superior was waiting, my knees trembled beneath me. I threw myself at the priest's feet, and only in the most strangled voice was I able to pronounce my Confiteor.

"Well," asked the man of God, "have you forgotten anything?"

I held my tongue. The priest's questions began again, and again the fatal "no, Father" escaped my lips. He fell into meditation and asked for the counsel of He who had conferred on the Apostles the power of binding and loosing souls. Then, making an effort, he prepared to grant me absolution.

If lightning had struck me from on high, it would have caused me less fear.

I cried out, "I have not told it all!"

And this formidable judge, this delegate of the sovereign Arbiter, whose stern face inspired such fear in me, became the tenderest of shepherds. He embraced me and burst into tears. "Come now, dear boy," he said, "have courage!"

I had never known such a moment in my life. If the weight of a mountain had been lifted from me, I could not have been more relieved: I sobbed with happiness. I would venture to say that it was on this day that I became an honest man. I felt that I could never survive the pain of remorse. How much more painful it must be for a criminal, if I could suffer so much over my childish flaws? But how divine it is that religion can take hold of what is good in us! What moral precepts can ever take the place of these Christian institutions?

After this first confession, the rest cost me nothing. The childish things that I had concealed, which would have made the world smile, were weighed on the scales of religion. The superior was very embarrassed. He would have liked to delay my communion, but I was about to leave the Collège de Dol, and very soon after I would join the navy. He wisely perceived, in the character of my juvenile sins, insignificant as they were, the nature of my proclivities. He was the first man to discern the secret of what I might one day become. He divined my future passions and did not conceal the good he thought he saw in me, but he also predicted some of the evils. "After all," he said, "you have little time for penance. But you have been cleansed of your sins by your courageous, if tardy, confession." Then, raising his hand, he pronounced the formula of absolution. And now, this second time, his disquieting arm descended on my head like the rosy dew of heaven. I bowed my head to receive his blessing, and I partook of the joy of the angels. I ran to press myself to my mother's bosom: she was waiting for me at the foot of the altar. I no longer looked the same to my teachers and my schoolmates. I walked with a light step, my head held high, my face radiant, in all the triumph of repentance.

The next day, Maundy Thursday, I was admitted to that sublime and moving ceremony which I tried to depict in *The Genius of Christianity*. I might have felt my habitual humiliations there, too: my bouquet and my clothes were not as fine as those of my companions. But that day everything was from God and for God. I know exactly what true faith is: the Real Presence of the Victim in the Blessed Sacrament was as manifest to me that day as my mother's presence at my side. When the Host was laid on my tongue, I felt as though everything were afire inside me. I trembled with respect for it, and the only material thing that intruded on my brain was the fear of profaning the sacramental bread:

> *Le pain que je vous propose*
> *Sert aux anges d'aliment,*
> *Dieu lui-même le compose*
> *De la fleur de son froment.*
> (Racine)[11]

I understood then the courage of the martyrs. At that moment, I could have borne witness to Christ on the rack or in the face of a lion.

I love to recall these ecstasies. They made their mark on my soul only a few moments before I underwent the tribulations of the wider world. Compare these ardors with the transports I will soon depict; see the same heart experience in the space of three or four years all that is sweet and worthy in the ways of innocence and religion, and all that is seductive and funereal in the ways of passion; choose between these two joys, and you may see on which side you should search for happiness and, above all, peace.

Three weeks after my first communion, I left the Collège de Dol. I still retain a pleasant memory of the place. Our childhood leaves something of itself in the places it has embellished, as a flower lends its fragrance to the objects it has touched. To this day, I find myself thinking back on the disbandment of my first schoolmates and my first teachers: Abbé Leprince, who was appointed to a benefice near Rouen, did not live much longer; Abbé Égault found a rectorship in the diocese of Rennes; and I myself saw the good principal, Abbé Portier, die in the first days of the Revolution. He was a bookish man, gentle and simple-hearted. I will always honor and cherish the memory of that obscure Rollin.[12]

7.

COMBOURG—COLLÈGE DE RENNES—I SEE GESRIL AGAIN—MOREAU, LIMOËLAN—MARRIAGE OF MY THIRD SISTER

Vallée-aux-Loups, end of December 1813

IN COMBOURG, I found a mission to nourish my piety. I followed its exercises, and, on the steps of the castle, kneeling beside the peasant boys and girls, I received the sacrament of Confirmation from the Bishop of Saint-Malo's own hands. After this ceremony, we erected a stone crucifix. It still stands below the tower where my father died. For thirty years, it has seen no one moving in the windows of that tower. It is no longer saluted by the children of the castle. Every spring it waits for them in vain, but it sees only the return of the swallows, the companions of my youth, more loyal to their nest than man to his home. I might have been happy if my life had been spent at the foot of that mission cross—if only my hair had gone white beneath its mossy beams!

It was not long before I departed for Rennes, where I was to continue my studies and finish my instruction in mathematics, which would prepare me for the Naval Guard examination in Brest.

At the Collège de Rennes, a sort of Breton Juilly, there were three distinguished teachers: Abbé de Chateaugiron in the humanities, Abbé Germé in rhetoric, and Abbé Marchand in physics. The population at Rennes was large, made up of both boarders and day students, and the classes were very difficult. In living memory, Geoffroy and Ginguené had graduated from the school—men who would have done honor to Saint-Barbe or Plessis. The Chevalier de Parny also studied at Rennes. I inherited his bed in the room that was assigned to me.

Rennes seemed a Babylon to me, and the school a world. The multitude of teachers and students, the extent of the buildings, gardens, and courtyards, at first appeared boundless, although soon enough I was accustomed to it. On the principal's birthday, we were given time off. We sang superb couplets at the top of our lungs:

> *Ô Terpsichore, ô Polymnie,*
> *Venez, venez remplir nos voeux;*
> *La raison même vous convie!*[13]

I gained the same ascendancy over my new schoolmates that I had previously exercised over my comrades at Dol. It cost me a few punches. We Breton baboons are surly types. On half days, in the garden of the Benedictine abbey which we called "the Thabor," we exchanged written challenges. We fastened mathematical compasses to the ends of sticks or battled hand to hand, more or less treacherously or courteously, according to the seriousness of the opponent's challenge. There were judges appointed to decide who should throw the gage and what weapons the warriors could employ. And the fighting did not cease until one of the two parties declared himself vanquished. Here, I found my old friend Gesril, presiding over these engagements as he had in Saint-Malo. He volunteered to be my second in a spat I had with Saint-Riveul, the young gentleman who became the first victim of the Revolution. When I fell beneath my adversary, I refused to admit defeat and paid dearly for my arrogance. I said, like Jean Desmarest on his way to the scaffold, "I cry for mercy to no one but God."

I met two men at this school who have since become famous for quite different reasons: Moreau, the general, and Limoëlan, the inventor of the infernal machine, who is today a priest in America.[14] Only one portrait of my Lucile exists, and this miserable miniature was executed by the very same Limoëlan, who turned portrait painter during the Revolutionary distress. Moreau was a day student, Limoëlan a boarder. It is rare to find at the same time, in the same province, in the same provincial city, under the roof of the same educational establishment, two destinies as singular as theirs.

Here I cannot help recounting a trick that my comrade Limoëlan once played on one of the prefects.

The prefect would usually make his rounds in the hallways after lights out, checking to see that all was well. For this purpose, he would look through the peepholes of every door. Limoëlan, Gesril, Saint-Riveul, and I slept in the same room:

More mischievous creatures, you have never met.[15]

On several previous occasions we had stopped up the peephole with paper to no avail. The prefect had simply poked the paper through and caught us jumping on our beds and breaking chairs. Then, one evening, without telling us of his plan, Limoëlan persuaded us all to get in bed and put out the light. A quarter of an hour later, we heard the prefect sneaking down the hall on tiptoe. As we were, reasonably enough, suspect in his eyes, he paused at our door, listened, went to look, and seeing no light at all. . . .

"Who has done this?" he shouted, bursting into our room.

Limoëlan choked with laughter and Gesril, in a nasal voice, asked in his half-naive, half-mocking way, "What's wrong, Monsieur Prefect?" As for Saint-Riveul and me, we laughed just as hard as Limoëlan and hid ourselves beneath the covers.

They could get nothing out of us: we were heroic. We were all four imprisoned in the *caves*. Saint-Riveul dug out the earth beneath the door that opened on the farmyard: he stuck his head up through the molehill he had made and a pig ran toward him, making as if to eat his brains. Gesril broke into the school's cellars and set a barrel of wine flowing. Limoëlan demolished a wall. For my part, like a second Perrin Dandin, I climbed to the basement window and stirred up the rabble in the street with my harangues. The terrible author of the infernal machine, playing this schoolboy prank on a school prefect, calls to mind the story of the young Cromwell flicking ink in the face of his fellow regicide, who was waiting to sign Charles I's death warrant after him.

Although the education at the Collège de Rennes was very religious, my fervor was already subsiding. The large number of teachers and students multiplied the opportunities for distraction. I made progress in the study of languages and became strong in mathematics, for which I have always had a decided knack: I would have made a fine naval officer or engineer. All in all, I was born with a natural aptitude for almost everything. Attuned to amusing things as well as serious ones, I began with poetry before coming to prose; every one of the arts enraptured me, and I have loved music and architecture with a passion. Although quick to become bored by everything, I am always patient with the smallest details: I am endowed with the fortitude to face every impediment and, even when I grow weary of my object, my persistence is always greater than my boredom. I have never abandoned any project worth the trouble of completing. There are many things in my life that I have pursued for fifteen or twenty years with as much ardor on the last day as the first.

My supple intelligence has extended itself to secondary matters also. I was deft at chess, skilled at billiards, hunting, and fencing, and I was a passable draughtsman. I would have sung well, too, if my voice had been trained. All this, combined with my unusual education and my experience as a soldier and a traveler, explains why I have never been a pedant, nor ever displayed the dull conceit, awkwardness, and slovenliness of the literary men of the last century, nor the arrogant self-assurance, the vain and envious braggadocio, of the new authors.

I left the Collège de Rennes after two years. Gesril preceded me by eighteen months and went to join the Navy. My third sister, Julie, was married sometime in the course of these years. She wedded the Comte de Farcy, a captain in the Condé regiment, and later settled with her husband in Fougères, where my two oldest sisters were already living. Julie's wedding, too, took place in the chapel at Combourg. It was there that I saw the Comtesse de Tronjoli who later distinguished herself by her courage on the scaffold: a cousin and close friend of the Marquis de La Rouërie, she would be implicated in his conspiracy. Until that day, I had not seen beauty outside of my own family, and I was flustered to discover it in a stranger's face. Each stage of my life has opened a new vista to my eyes. I was then beginning to hear the distant, seductive voice of the passions calling to me, and I rushed to meet those sirens, drawn by their unfamiliar harmonies. It turned out that, like the high priest of Eleusis, I had a different incense for each deity. But could the hymns I sang while the incense burned be called "balms,"[16] as were the verses of the hierophant?

8.

I AM SENT TO BREST TO TAKE THE NAVAL EXAM
—THE PORT OF BREST—I MEET GESRIL AGAIN—
LA PÉROUSE—I RETURN TO COMBOURG

La Vallée-aux-Loups, January 1814

AFTER Julie's wedding, I set off for Brest. On leaving the large Collège de Rennes, I did not feel anything like the regret I experienced on leaving the small Collège de Dol. Perhaps I no longer had that innocence which casts a spell over everything; my youth was no longer enveloped in its flower: time was beginning to disclose it. My mentor in my new position was one of my maternal uncles, the Comte Ravenel de Boisteilleul, who was commander of a squadron: one of his sons, a highly distinguished artillery officer in Bonaparte's army, would later marry the only daughter of my sister the Comtesse de Farcy.

On arriving in Brest, I did not find my cadet's commission waiting; I know not what accident had delayed it. I thus remained what was called an "aspirant," and as such I was exempted from the usual course of studies. My uncle found me a room on the rue de Siam, in a cadets' boarding house, and introduced me to the naval commander, the Comte Hector.

Abandoned to myself for the first time in my life, instead of fraternizing with my future comrades, I withdrew into my instinctual solitude. Other than my teachers in fencing, drawing, and mathematics, I spoke to no one.

That same sea, which I was to encounter again on so many shores, washed the tip of the Armorican peninsula at Brest. Beyond this protuberant cape, there was nothing but boundless ocean and unknown worlds. My imagination went wild in those spaces. Often, sitting on some topmast that lay along the Quai de Recouvrance, I observed the ruck and moil of the crowd. Shipbuilders, sailors, soldiers, customs workers, and convicts passed and repassed before me. Travelers embarked and disembarked, captains conned their crafts, carpenters planed blocks of wood, ropemakers spun their cables, and cabin boys lit fires under huge coppers, which gave off thick plumes of smoke and a healthy stink of tar. Loads were being carried, recarried, and rolled from the ships to the warehouses and back from the warehouses to the ships: there were bales of merchandise, sacks of victuals, and artillery trains. Over here, they were pushing carts into the water; over there, they were hoisting tackle while cranes lowered stones and dredging machines dug silt from the harbor. The forts repeated signals, and sloops came and went, even as other vessels were fitted out or tied up at the docks.

My mind seethed with vague ideas about society, its blessings and its faults. I cannot say what sadness seized me, but I would leave the mast on which I'd been sitting and start up the bank of the Penfeld River, which flows there into the harbor, until I reached the bend where the harbor disappears from sight. Here, seeing nothing before me but a peaty dale, but still hearing the confused murmur of the sea and the voices of men, I would lie down on the bank of the narrow river. Sometimes watching the surface of the water, sometimes following the flight of a jackdaw with my eyes, basking in the silence around me, or listening to the pounding of the caulker's hammer, I would fall into the profoundest reveries. In the midst of these reveries, if the wind brought me the sound of a cannon from a ship setting sail in the harbor, I would tremble and feel tears welling up in my eyes.

One day, I had directed my wanderings toward the far end of the port, beside the open sea. It was a hot day, and I had stretched out on the beach and fallen asleep, when, all of a sudden, I was woken by a tremendous noise. I opened my eyes, like Augustus waking to see the triremes in the anchorage of Sicily after the victory over Sextus Pompey.[17] The reports of the guns followed one after another, and the roadstead was strewn with ships: the great French squadron was returning after the signing of a peace treaty. The ships maneuvered under sail, swathed themselves in smoke, hoisted their colors, presented their sterns, bows, and broadsides, stopped short by dropping anchor in mid course, or scudded onward over the waves. Nothing has ever given me a loftier idea of the human spirit. At that moment, mankind seemed to borrow something from He who said to the sea, "You shall go no further." *Non procedes amplius.*[18]

All Brest rushed down to the harbor. Sloops broke off from the fleet and sailed alongside the breakwater. The officers who crowded on deck, their faces bronzed by the sun, had that foreign look that one brings back from another hemisphere and an indescribable air of gaiety, pride, and audacity, as befitted men who had just restored the honor of the national flag. This naval corps, so worthy and so illustrious, these companions of Suffern, La Motte-Picquet, Couëdic, and D'Estaing, had escaped the enemy's fire; but they were soon to fall beneath the fire of Frenchmen.

I was down at the harbor watching the brave troops march past when one of the officers broke off from his comrades and jumped up around my shoulders. It was Gesril. He seemed taller, but weak and weary from a sword wound that he had taken in the chest. He would leave Brest that same evening to go visit his family, and I would see him only once more, not long before his heroic death. I will soon relate the particulars. For now, let me say only that Gesril's appearance and sudden departure led me to make a resolution that changed the course of my life. It was written that this young man should have absolute power over my destiny.

One can see how my character was taking shape, the turn of my ideas, and the earliest symptoms of my genius, for I can speak of it as an illness, whatever this genius of mine may be, rare or common, worthy or unworthy of the name I give it for lack of a better word to express what I mean. If I had been more like other men, I would have been happier. He who could have killed my so-called talent, without robbing me of my mind, would have been my truest friend.

When the Comte de Boisteilleul took me to meet M. Hector, I listened as the sailors, young and old, told stories about their campaigns and the countries they had visited. One had recently come back from India, another from North America. This one had set sail on a voyage around the world, and that one was soon to return to the Mediterranean, where he would visit the shores of Greece. In the crowd, my uncle pointed out La Pérouse, a second Captain Cook, whose death is a secret kept by the tempests. I heard it all and saw it all without saying a word, but I could not sleep that night. I stayed up indulging myself in imaginary sea battles and explorations of uncharted lands.

Be this as it may, having seen Gesril about to return to his parents, I decided that nothing should prevent me from going home to mine. No doubt I would have enjoyed naval service if my independent spirit had not rendered me unfit for service of any kind. I have in me a deep inability to obey. Voyages tempted me, but I felt I would enjoy them better alone, following my own whims. Finally, showing the first sign of my inconstancy, without having informed my uncle Ravenel, without writing to my parents, without asking permission of anyone, and without waiting for my cadet's commission, I set off one morning for Combourg, where I dropped in as though from the sky.

I am still astonished today, given the terror my father inspired in me, that I would have dared take such a step. But what is equally astonishing is the manner in which he received me. I had expected transports of violent rage, but instead I was made gently welcome. My father was content to shake his head at me, as if to say, "Here's a fine caper!" My mother, grumbling, embraced me with all her heart, and my Lucile, with a ravishment of joy.

BOOK THREE

I.

A WALK—THE APPARITION OF COMBOURG

Montboissier, July 1817

BETWEEN the last date of these *Memoirs*, written in the Vallée-aux-Loups, January 1814, and today, in Montboissier, July 1817, three years and six months have passed. Did you hear the Empire fall? No. For nothing has troubled the sleep of these acres. And yet the Empire is obliterated. The vast ruin has crumbled in my lifetime like so much Roman rubble spilled in the current of an unknown stream. But events mean little to he who does not count on them. A few brief years from eternity's hands will do justice to all this noise with endless silence.

The previous book was written under the dying tyranny of Bonaparte and the last lightning flashes of his glory. I begin the current chapter under the reign of Louis XVIII. But I have seen kings up close before, and my political illusions have vanished as thoroughly as those lovelier chimeras whose story I am continuing to tell. So let us speak instead of what made me pick up the pen again. The human heart is anything's toy, and no one can anticipate what frivolous circumstance may cause it pleasure or sorrow. "No cause is needed to disturb our soul," Montaigne observed. "A reverie without cause or subject may dominate and disturb it."[1]

I am now in Montboissier, on the border of the Beauce and the Perche. The château here belongs to Madame la Comtesse de Colbert-Montboissier. It was sold and destroyed during the Revolution. All that remains of it today are two small buildings, separated from the main house by an iron gate, which were once inhabited by the gardener.

The park, now in the English style, bears some traces of its former French symmetry. Straight alleys and copses boxed within hedgerows give it a serious look. It has the beauty of a ruin.

Yesterday evening I was walking alone. The sky was like an autumn sky, and a cold wind blew in gusts. At a break in the thicket, I stopped to watch the sun sinking in the clouds over the tower of Alluye, where Gabrielle, who lived in that tower, watched the sun set as I did, two hundred years ago. And what has become of Henri and Gabrielle? The same thing that will have become of me by the time these *Memoirs* are published.

I was roused from my reflections by the warbling of a thrush perched on the highest branch of a birch. This magic sound brought my father's lands back before my eyes in an instant. I forgot the disasters I had only recently witnessed and, abruptly transported into the past, I saw again those fields where I so often heard the thrushes whistling. When I listened then I was sad, as I am today; but that first sadness was born of a vague desire for happiness: a privilege of the inexperienced. The sadness that I experience presently comes of the knowledge of things weighed and judged. The bird's song in the woods of Combourg spoke to me of a bliss that I was sure I would attain; the same song in the park here in Montboissier reminds me of the days I have lost in pursuit of that old, elusive bliss. There is nothing more for me to learn. I walked faster than other men and have already made the tour of my life. The hours fly past and drag me onward, and I am not at all certain that I can finish these *Memoirs* in time. In how many places have I already begun to write them, and in what place shall I bring them to an end? How many more times shall I walk along the edge of the woods? Let me profit from the few moments that remain to me; let me hasten to describe my youth while I can still recall it. A sailor, leaving his enchanted island forever, writes his journal in sight of the land that slowly slips away. It is a land that will soon be lost.

2.

COLLÈGE DE DINAN—BROUSSAIS—I RETURN TO MY
PARENTS' HOUSE

AT THE end of the previous book, I spoke of my return to Combourg and how I was welcomed there by my father, my mother, and my sister Lucile. The reader will perhaps remember that my other three sisters were married by then and living on their new families' estates near Fougères. My brother, whose ambitions had now expanded their reach, was more often in Paris than in Rennes. He first bought a post as Lord of Requests, which he then sold in order to take up a military career. He signed on with the Royal Cavalry regiment, and in the diplomatic corps, with the Comte de la Luzerne, he traveled to London, where he met André Chénier. He was on the point of obtaining the Vienna embassy when our troubles broke out. He applied for the Constantinople embassy, but he had a formidable contender in Mirabeau, to whom the post had been promised as a prize for joining the Court's party. My brother had thus only recently left Combourg when I came to live there.

Holed up in his manor, my father now never left it, not even for the meetings of the Estates of Brittany. My mother went to Saint-Malo for six weeks every year, at Eastertime, and she waited for this moment as for deliverance. She detested Combourg. A month before the trip, she and my father would begin discussing it, as if it were a hazardous enterprise. Preparations were made; horses were rested. On the eve of her departure, my parents would go to bed at seven at night in order to wake up at two in the morning. My mother, to her great satisfaction, would be on the road by three, and would spend the whole day traveling a distance of twelve leagues.

Lucile had been received as a canoness in the Chapter of L'Argentière and was now awaiting her transfer to the Chapter of Remiremont. In the meantime, she remained entombed in the country.

As for myself, after my escapade in Brest, I declared it my firm wish to embrace the ecclesiastical state. The truth is that I was only trying to buy time, for I had no idea what I wanted to do. I was sent to the Collège de Dinan to finish my education in the humanities. I knew Latin better than my instructors, but I began to learn Hebrew.

Dinan, graced with old trees and fortified with old towers, is built in a picturesque spot, on a high hill at the foot of which the Rance flows back toward the sea. The mineral waters of Dinan are well known. This town, bursting with history, is the birthplace of Duclos and boasts, among other antiquities, the heart of Du Guesclin: heroic dust, stolen during the Revolution, when it was almost ground down by a glazier to make stained glass. Who knows: perhaps it was destined for panels depicting the country's victories over its enemies?

M. Broussais, my countryman, studied with me at Dinan. The students there were taken to bathe every Thursday, like clerics under Pope Adrian I, and every Sunday, like prisoners under Emperor Honorius. One day, I thought I was going to drown; another, Broussais was bitten by some ingrate leeches, unaware of his future enthusiasm for them. Since Dinan lay an equal distance from Combourg and Plancouët, I took turns going to see my uncle de Bedée at Monchoix and my family at Combourg. M. de Chateaubriand, who found it more economical to keep me at home, and my mother, who hoped that I would follow my religious vocation but had some scruples about pressing me to do so, no longer insisted that I reside at school, and little by little I found myself becoming a fixture in my father's house.

I would take pleasure in recalling my parents' way of life even if it were nothing to me but a fond memory; but I will reproduce the picture all the more gladly because it will seem as though it were traced from an engraving in a medieval manuscript. Between the present time and the time that I am about to depict, centuries have elapsed.

3.

LIFE IN COMBOURG—DAYS AND EVENINGS
Montboissier, July 1817; Revised in December 1846

AT THE time of my return from Brest, four masters (my father, my mother, my sister, and I) inhabited the Château de Combourg. A cook, a chambermaid, two footmen, and a coachman comprised the entire domestic staff. A hunting dog and two old mares were confined in a corner of the stable. These twelve living beings easily vanished in a castle where a hundred knights, their ladies, their squires, and their pages, together with King Dagobert's warhorses and his pack of hounds, could almost have gone unnoticed.

In the whole course of the year, not a single stranger showed his face in the castle save for a pair of noblemen, the Marquis de Montlouet and the Comte de Goyon-Beaufort, who sought hospitality on their way to plead at Parliament. They came in winter, on horseback, pistols on their saddlebows and hunting knives at their sides, accompanied by a footman, also on horseback, who rode with a big livery portmanteau behind him.

My father, always a very formal man, greeted them bareheaded out on the steps amid the wind and the rain. Once inside, these country gentlemen endlessly recounted their war days in Hanover, the affairs of their families, and the history of their lawsuits. At night, they were shown up to the north tower, to Queen Christina's Chamber, a guest room furnished with a bed seven feet square, supported by four gold-leaf Cupids, and surrounded by a double set of curtains made of green gauze and crimson silk. The next morning, when I went down to the great hall and looked through the windows at the country flooded and covered over with frost, I saw only two or three travelers on the lonely lane by the pond. These were our guests, riding toward Rennes.

These strangers did not know much about the things of life; yet our view was extended a few leagues beyond the horizon of our woods by their visits. As soon as they had left, we were reduced, on weekdays, to our small family circle, and on Sundays to the company of the village bourgeoisie and the local gentry.

On Sundays when the weather was fine, my mother, Lucile, and I crossed the Little Mall and walked along a country road to the parish church. When it rained, we took the abominable rue de Combourg. We did not, like the Abbé de Marolles, travel in a light chariot drawn by four white horses captured from the Turks in Hungary.[2] My father, for his part, went down to the parish only once a year, to perform his Easter duties. The rest of the time, he heard Mass in the chapel of his own castle. Sitting in the lord's pew, he received incense and prayers across from the black marble tomb of Renée de Rohan, next to the altar. What an emblem of the honors of man!—a few plumes of smoke before a coffin.

These Sunday entertainments were over with the day. They were not even the usual fare. During the worst season, months would go by without a single human creature knocking at the door to our fortress. If the gloom was great on the moors around Combourg, it was still greater inside the castle. One experienced the same sensation, strolling beneath its vaults, as in the Carthusian monastery of Grenoble. When I visited that place in 1805, I had to roam across a mute wilderness that was perpetually growing around me. I thought it would end at the monastery, but within the very walls of the cloister the monks showed me the charterhouse gardens, which were even more forsaken than the woods. At last, in the center of the monument, I found an old graveyard swathed in folds of solitude: a sanctuary where endless silence, the presiding spirit of the place, extended its empire over the mountains and the forests for miles around.

The mournful calm of the Château de Combourg was intensified by my father's taciturn, unsociable temperament. Instead of drawing his family and his servants in around him, he had scattered them to every corner of the castle. His bedroom was in the small eastern tower, and his study was in the small western tower. The furniture of this study consisted of three black leather chairs and a table strewn with deeds and scrolls. A genealogical tree of the Chateaubriand family hung over the mantel, and in the embrasure of a window he had displayed all sorts of armaments, from a small pistol to a blunderbuss. My mother's apartment was above the great hall, between the two small towers: it was parqueted and decorated with faceted Venetian mirrors. My sister lived in a smaller room adjoining my mother's. The chambermaid slept a great distance away, in the main building between the two large towers. As for me, I made my nest in a sort of isolated cell in a turret, at the top of the staircase that led from the interior courtyard to the various wings of the castle. At the bottom of this staircase, my father's footman and another manservant lay down to sleep in the vaulted cellar. The cook had his garrison in the fat western tower.

My father arose every morning at four o'clock, in winter and summer alike. He went into the interior courtyard and called for his footman to wake. He was brought a small cup of coffee at five o'clock, and then worked in his study till noon. My mother and my sister each breakfasted in her own room at eight o'clock. I had no fixed time for either rising or for breakfasting: I was reputed to be studying until noon, but most of the time I did nothing.

At half past eleven, the bell rang for dinner, which was served at midday. The great hall served us as both dining room and sitting room: we dined in one corner on the east side, and, after the meal was over, we went and sat in the opposite corner on the west side, in front of an enormous fireplace. This hall was wainscoted, painted a whitish gray, and decorated with old portraits dating from the reign of François I to that of Louis XIV. Among these portraits, one could recognize the faces of Condé and Turenne. A painting, depicting Hector slain by Achilles beneath the walls of Troy, hung above the fireplace.

When dinner was finished, we sat together until two o'clock. Then, if it were summer, my father amused himself by fishing, or visiting his kitchen garden, or taking a walk no longer than a capon's flight. If it were autumn or winter, he went hunting. My mother meanwhile withdrew to the chapel, where she spent several hours in prayer. This chapel was a dim oratorium, prettified by good pictures by some very great painters, such as one would hardly expect to find in a feudal castle in the depths of Brittany. I have in my possession today a *Holy Family* by Albani, painted on copper, taken from this chapel: it is all that remains to me of Combourg.

My father gone and my mother at her prayers, Lucile shut herself up in her room, and I either trudged back up to my cell or went to wander in the fields.

At eight o'clock, the bell rang for supper. After supper, on fine days, we sat out on the steps. My father, armed with his gun, shot at the owls that flew from the battlements at twilight. My mother, Lucile, and I gazed at the sky, the woods, the last rays of sun, and the first stars. At ten o'clock, we would climb the stairs and go to bed.

Autumn and winter evenings were of a different nature. When supper was over and the four diners had moved from the table to the fireside, my mother sank with a sigh into an old daybed upholstered in imitation Siam; she was brought a pedestal table and a candle. I huddled by the fireside with Lucile, while the servants cleared the table and retired for the night. It was then that my father began a stroll that did not cease until he went to bed. He was dressed in a thick white woolen gown, or rather a sort of cloak, which I have never seen on anybody but him, and he covered his half-bald head with a tall white cap that stood straight up. When, in the course of this stroll, he moved away from the hearth, the vast hall was so dimly lit, by a single candle, that he was no longer visible. Only his footsteps could still be heard in the darkness. Then, slowly, he would return toward the light, emerging little by little from the shadows, like a specter, with his white gown, his white cap, and his long pale face. Lucile and I exchanged a few whispered words while he was at the far end of the hall, but we fell silent as soon as he came near. He asked, as he passed us, "What are you two chattering about?" Terror-stricken, we made no reply. Our father continued on his walk. For the rest of the evening, nothing could be heard but the measured sound of his footsteps, my mother's sighs, and the murmuration of the wind.[3]

When ten hours sounded on the castle clock, my father stopped. The same spring that had raised the hammer of the clockworks seemed to have suspended his steps. He pulled out his watch, wound it, took a large silver candlestick topped with a tall candle, went for a moment into the small western tower, then returned, torch in hand, and made his way toward his bedroom in the small eastern tower. Lucile and I would place ourselves in his path. We kissed him and wished him goodnight. He bent down to offer us his dry, hollow cheek without a word, and proceeded on his way, disappearing into the depths of the tower, whose doors we heard closing behind him.

And the spell was broken. My mother, my sister, and I, transformed into statues by my father's presence, began to recover the functions of life. The first result of our disenchantment was an overflow of words. If silence had oppressed us, it now paid us back in full.

Once this torrent of words had run its course, I called for the chambermaid and escorted my mother and sister to their rooms. Before I left them, they made me look under the beds, up the chimneys, behind the doors, and in the neighboring staircases, passageways, and corridors. All the old traditions of the castle, the tales of robbers and ghosts, came to trouble their thoughts. The servants were convinced that a certain peg-legged Comte de Combourg, who had been dead for three centuries, appeared from time to time, and that one was especially likely to encounter him on the staircase in the turret. His wooden leg also sometimes walked alone, with a black cat by its side.

4.
MY KEEP

Montboissier, August 1817

THESE tales always occupied my mother and sister at bedtime. They climbed under the covers scared to death; I retired to the top of my turret; the cook returned to his tower; and the servants went down to their subterranean abode.

The window of my keep opened onto the interior courtyard. During the day, I had a view of the crenellations on the curtain-wall opposite, where hart's-tongue fern and a wild plum tree grew. A few martins, which dove shrieking into the holes in the walls all summer long, were my sole companions. At night, I could see only a thin patch of sky and a few stars. When the moon shone and sank in the west, I was apprised of it by the rays that fell through the diamond-shaped windowpanes on my bed. Owls, flying from one tower to the other, passed back and forth between the moon and me, and cast the mobile shadows of their wings on my curtains. Relegated to the most deserted part of the castle, at the opening of the galleries, I did not miss a murmur in the dark. Sometimes, the wind would seem to scamper lightly; sometimes, it would let out groans. All of a sudden my door would be violently shaken, the underground rooms of the castle would start howling; then the noises would die away, only to start up again. At four in the morning, the master's voice calling his footman at the entrance to the ancient vaults echoed like the voice of the night's last phantom. For me, this voice took the place of the sweet music with which Montaigne's father used to wake his son.[4]

The Comte de Chateaubriand's stubborn insistence on making a child go to bed alone at the top of a tower may have had some draw-backs, but it turned out to my advantage. My father's violent way of treating me left me with a man's courage, and without robbing me of that imaginative sensitivity of which they now try to deprive the young. Instead of attempting to persuade me that ghosts did not exist, my mother and father forced me to confront them. When my father said to me, with an ironic smile, "Would Monsieur le Cheva-lier be *afraid*?" he could have made me sleep with a corpse. When my good mother said to me, "My child, nothing happens except by God's permission: you have nothing to fear from evil spirits so long as you are a good Christian," I was more reassured than by all the arguments of philosophy. My victory was so complete that the night winds which came to my disinhabited turret were soon the playthings of my inven-tion and the wings of my dreams. My enflamed imagination spread to everything around it, but nowhere did it find enough to keep it fed: had it been able, it would have devoured heaven and earth. This is the moral state that I must now describe. Delving again into the days of my youth, I am going to try to grapple with my past self, to show myself such as I was, such as I perhaps regret I no longer am, despite the torments I endured.

5.

THE PASSAGE FROM CHILDHOOD TO MANHOOD

I HAD HARDLY returned to Combourg from Brest when a revolution took place in my existence: the child disappeared and the man showed himself with all his fleeting joys and his lasting sorrows.

At first everything became a passion for me, in anticipation of the passions themselves. When, after a silent dinner during which I had not dared speak or eat, I succeeded in escaping the castle, my sense of happiness was incredible. I could not descend the stairs all at once: I would have tumbled head over heels. I was obliged to sit down on one of the steps for a while, to let my agitation subside. But the moment I reached the Green Court and the woods, I began running, jumping, bounding, skipping, gamboling, until I collapsed, drained of strength, panting for breath, intoxicated by folly and freedom.

My father took me with him when he went on the hunt. A taste for the chase took hold of me, and I pursued it to the point of madness. I can still see the field where I killed my first hare. It often happened that in autumn I stood for four or five hours up to my waist in water, waiting for wild ducks at the edge of the pond. To this day, I lose all composure when a dog stops and points. In my first ardor for the hunt, however, there was a novel element of independence: jumping ditches, tramping through fields, marshes, and moors, finding myself with a rifle in a wild place, strong and solitary: this, I felt, was my natural state of being. On my excursions, I wandered so far that I could walk no farther, and the gamekeepers were obliged to carry me home on a pallet of woven branches.

Yet soon the pleasures of the hunt were no longer enough for me, and I became troubled by a longing for happiness that I could neither control nor understand. My mind and my heart came to be like two empty temples without altars or sacrifices, and no one could say what deity would be worshipped there. I grew up beside my sister Lucile; our friendship formed the whole of our life.

6.

LUCILE

LUCILE was tall and remarkably beautiful, but solemn. Her pale face was framed by long black tresses, and she often gazed fixedly at the sky or cast around her with eyes full of sadness or fire. Her gait, her voice, her smile, and even her physiognomy had something dreamy and long suffering about them.

Lucile and I were useless to each other. When we talked about the world, it was the world that we carried within ourselves and that did not resemble the real world. She looked to me as her protector, and I looked to her as my friend. She was subject to black moods that I found very difficult to dispel. At seventeen, she mourned the passing of her youth and wanted nothing so much as to entomb herself in a nunnery. Everything was worrisome to her, everything an anguish or an injury. An expression she sought, or a chimera that she herself had created, could torment her for months on end. I often used to see her lying down with one arm flung above her head, lost in a reverie, motionless and unconscious; her life, having retreated toward her heart, ceased to make any outward appearance: even her breast no longer rose and fell. In her posture, her melancholy, her Venusian beauty, she resembled an ancient funerary spirit. I would try to console her at such times, but a moment later I would be plunged into inexplicable despair.

Lucile preferred to spend her evenings alone, reading some pious sermon or other. Her favorite chapel was the junction of two country roads, marked by a stone cross and a poplar tree whose long stem pointed to the heavens like a pencil. My devout mother, quite delighted by all this, said that her daughter reminded her of a Christian woman of the Early Church, praying at one of those stations called "Laures."[5]

The concentration of my sister's soul gave rise to extraordinary mental phenomena. Asleep, she had prophetic dreams; awake, she seemed able to read the future. On one of the landings of the staircase in the high tower, there was a clock that chimed the hours in the silence. Lucile, in her insomnia, would go and sit on a step across from this clock. She would watch its face by the light of a lamp placed on the floor. When the two hands met at midnight, generating in their ominous conjunction the hour of chaos and crime, Lucile would hear noises which gave her visions of faraway deaths. Many years later, finding herself in Paris a few days before the Tenth of August, and staying with my other sisters in the neighborhood of the Carmelite Convent, she cast her eyes on a mirror and cried out, saying, "I have just seen Death coming in."[6] On the moors of Caledonia, Lucile would have been one of Walter Scott's mystic women, gifted with second sight; on the moors of Armorica, she was merely a recluse favored with beauty, genius, and misfortune.

7.
FIRST BREATH OF THE MUSE

THE LIFE that we led in Combourg, my sister and I, heightened the enthusiasms natural to our age and character. Our principal distraction consisted of walking side by side on the Grand Mall, on a carpet of primroses in spring, on a bed of dry leaves in autumn, and in winter on a sheet of snow embroidered with the tracks of birds, squirrels, and weasels. Young as the primroses, forlorn as the dry leaves, pure as the newfallen snow, we were always in harmony with our recreations.

It was during one of these walks that Lucile, hearing me speak rapturously of solitude, said to me, "You ought to put these things down in words." This remark revealed the Muse to me: a divine breath passed through my frame. I began stammering verses as though poetry were my native tongue. Day and night, I sang of my pleasures, which is to say of my woods and my valleys. I composed a heap of little idylls and sketches of the natural world.*

I wrote in verse a long time before I wrote in prose: M. Fontanes used to claim that I had been equipped with both instruments.

But this talent that a friend foresaw, has it ever really come to me? How many things have I waited for in vain! In the *Agamemnon* of Aeschylus, a slave is posted as sentry on the roof of the palace of Argos; his eyes scan the horizon in search of the signal fire that will announce the fleet's return; he sings, to solace himself in the tedium,

---

*See my *Complete Works* (Paris, 1837)

but the hours go by, the stars go down, and the torch never shines. When, after many years, the signal's belated light appears over the waters, the slave is bent beneath the weight of time. Nothing remains to him except to reap misfortune, and the chorus tells him that "an old man is but a shadow wandering in the light of day," ὄναρ ἡμερόφαντον ἀλαίνει.[7]

8.

A MANUSCRIPT OF LUCILE'S

IN THE first enchantments of inspiration, I invited Lucile to imitate me. We spent our days in constant dialogue, telling each other what we had done and what we had intended to do. We undertook works in common. Guided by our instincts, we translated the saddest and loveliest passages of Job and Lucretius: the *Taedet animam meam vitae meae*, "my soul is weary of my life," the *Homo natus de muliere*, "man that is born of woman," the *Tum porro puer, ut saevis projectus ab undis navita*, "then the newborn, like a sailor thrown upon the waves," and so on.[8] Lucile's thoughts were indistinguishable from feelings, and they emerged with difficulty from her soul; but once she had succeeded in expressing them, there was nothing more sublime. She has left behind some thirty manuscript pages, and it is impossible to read them without being deeply moved. The elegance, the sweetness, the dreaminess, the impassioned sensibility of these pages combine the spirit of the Greeks and the spirit of the Germans.

DAWN

What sweet radiance comes to illuminate the East! Is it young Aurora who half opens her lovely eyes still heavy with languorous sleep? Nimble Goddess, go! Leave your nuptial bed and assume your purple robe; let a smooth sash enwrap you in its bow; let no sandals confine your delicate feet; let no ornaments profane your lovely hands which open the doors toward day. But you have already risen on the shadowy hill. Your golden hair falls in moist tresses upon your rosy neck. From your mouth you breathe a pure and perfumed air. Tender Goddess, all Nature smiles at your presence; you alone shed tears and give birth to flowers.

TO THE MOON

Chaste Goddess, so pure that not even the rosy blush of modesty mingles with your clear and tender light, I dare to take you into my confidence. I have no more reason than you to blush at my heart's desires. But sometimes the memory of the blind and biased judgments of man encircles my brow with clouds, like those that flock around your own. Like you, the errors and miseries of this world inspire my dreams. But happier than I, fair citizen of the heavens, you always preserve your serenity; the tempests and storms that stir up this globe of ours glide over your peaceful disc. O Goddess, still friendly to my sadness, pour your cold quietude into my heart.

INNOCENCE

Daughter of heaven, amiable Innocence, if I dared to draw a feeble portrait of a few of your features, I should say that you occupy the place of virtue in childhood, of wisdom in the springtime of life, of beauty in old age, and of happiness in misfortune; I should say that, a stranger to our errors, you shed none but pure tears, and that your smile comes wholly from heaven. Lovely Innocence! but how danger surrounds you; desire addresses all its appeals to you: and do you tremble, modest Innocence? Do you seek to surrender to the dangers that menace you? No, I see you there asleep, your head leaning on the altar.

*

Once in a while, my brother accorded the hermits of Combourg a few brief moments of his time. He had taken to bringing with him a young councilor from the High Court of Brittany, M. de Malfilâtre, a cousin of the unfortunate poet of that name. I think that Lucile, unknown to herself, harbored a secret passion for my brother's friend, and that this stifled passion was at the bottom of my sister's melancholy. She had, moreover, Rousseau's mania, though without his pride: she believed that everyone was conspiring against her. She moved to Paris in 1789, accompanied by my sister Julie, whose loss she mourned with a tenderness tinged with sublimity. All who knew her admired her, from M. de Malesherbes to Chamfort. Thrown into the Revolutionary crypts in Rennes, she was almost reincarcerated in the Château de Combourg, which became a dungeon during the Terror. When she was released from prison, she married M. de Caud, who widowed her within a year. It was not until I returned from my exile in England that I saw the friend of my childhood again. I shall soon say how she disappeared, when it pleased God to afflict me.

9.
LAST LINES WRITTEN IN THE VALLÉE-AUX-LOUPS—
REVELATION OF THE MYSTERY OF MY LIFE

Vallée-aux-Loups, November 1817

BACK FROM Montboissier, here are the last lines I shall write in my hermitage. I have to abandon it all, even the handsome saplings in their close-set rows, which were already beginning to hide and crown their father. I will no longer see the magnolia that promised its flower to the grave of my Floridian girl, the Jerusalem pine, the Lebanese cedar dedicated to the memory of Saint Jerome, the laurel from Grenada, the plane tree from Greece, the Armorican oak at the foot of which I depicted Bianca, sang of Cymodocée, invented Velléda. These trees were born and grew up together with my dreams: they were their Hamadryads. Now they are about to pass under another's sway. Will their new master love them as I have loved them? He will let them rot, maybe he will cut them down: I can keep nothing on this earth. In saying goodbye to the woods of Aulnay, I shall recall the goodbye I said to the woods of Combourg. All my days are goodbyes.

The taste for poetry that Lucile had inspired in me was like oil thrown on a fire. My feelings gathered a new measure of force, and vain ideas of fame passed through my mind. For the moment I believed in my *talent*, but soon, recovering a proper distrust of myself, I began to doubt that talent, as I doubt it still. I regarded my work as a wicked temptation, and I felt vexed with Lucile for having engendered such an unhappy inclination in me. I stopped writing, and I took to mourning my future glory as one might mourn for a glory that has passed.

Returned to my former idleness, I felt all the more sharply what my youth was missing. I was a mystery to myself. I could not so much as look at a woman without being troubled; I would blush if she spoke a word to me. My timidity, which was already excessive with everyone, was so great in the presence of a woman that I would have preferred any torment whatsoever to being left alone with her; yet no sooner did she leave the room than I wished she would return. The descriptions written by Virgil, Tibullus, and Massillon loomed in my memory; but the image of my mother and sister, covering everything with its purity, thickened the veils that nature was contriving to lift. My life as an affectionate brother and son obscured the possibility of any less disinterested affection. If the loveliest slave of a seraglio had been handed over to me, I swear I would not have known what to ask of her. Chance enlightened me.

A neighbor of ours in Combourg had come to spend a few days at the castle with his wife, who was very pretty. I don't remember what occurred in the village, but everyone ran to one of the windows of the great hall to see. I got there first, with the beautiful stranger close behind me. I wanted to yield my place to her and turned toward her. Inadvertently she blocked my path, and I felt myself pressed between her and the window. I no longer knew what was happening around me.

At that moment, I suspected that to love and be loved in a manner as yet unknown to me must be the supreme happiness. If I had done what other men do, I would soon have learned the pains and pleasures of passion, the seed of which I carried within me. But everything in my life took an unusual turn. The ardor of my thoughts, my timidity, and my solitude, instead of spurring me to action, threw me back upon myself. For lack of a real object of affection, I was prompted by the power of my vague desires to evoke a phantom that would never leave me. I do not know if the history of the human heart offers another example of this kind.

10.

A PHANTOM LOVE

I COMPOSED myself a woman from all the women I had ever seen. She had the figure, the hair, and the smile of the guest who had pressed me against her breast; I gave her the eyes of one young girl from the village and the pink cheeks of another. The portraits of great ladies from the time of François I, Henri IV, and Louis XIV that decorated the hall provided me with some other features, and I stole a few graces from the pictures of Virgins in church.

This invisible enchantress followed me everywhere. I conversed with her as though she were a real being, and she changed according to my folly: Aphrodite without her veil, Diana clothed in azure and rosy dew, Thalia with her laughing mask, Hebe with her cup of youth. Often she became a fairy who placed everything in nature under my control. I went on retouching my canvas constantly: I took one charm from my beauty and replaced it with another. I also changed her clothes. I borrowed from every country, every century, every art, and every religion. Then, when I had created a masterpiece, I dissolved my lines and colors, and my unique woman was transformed into a multitude of women, in whom I idolized separately the charms that I had worshipped together.

Pygmalion was less in love with his statue. My only trouble was how to please mine. Finding in myself none of those qualities that one needs to be loved, I lavished on my imaginary self all that I lacked. In my mind, I rode a horse like Castor or Pollux and played the lyre like Apollo; Mars wielded his arms with less strength and skill: a hero

out of history or romance—how many fictive adventures I heaped
upon those fictions! The shades of Morven's daughters, the sultanas
of Baghdad and Granada, the ladies of ancient manors; baths, perfumes, dances, and Asiatic delights: I conjured them all with my
magic wand.

Here comes a queen, bedecked in diamonds and flowers (she was
always my sylph). She seeks me out at midnight through a grove of
orange trees, in the galleries of a palace washed by the sea, on the
balmy shore of Naples or Messina, under a sky of love permeated by
the light of Endymion's star. She walks toward me like a living statue
by Praxiteles, down a path between frozen statues, faded pictures,
and frescoes silently blanched by the rays of the moon. The faint
sound of her footsteps on the marble mosaics mingles with the still
fainter sound of the breakers. Royal jealousy surrounds us. I fall to
the knees of the sovereign ruler of Enna's fields. She looses the silken
waves of her hair from beneath her diadem, and these waves brush
against my brow. And when she leans her sixteen-year-old head down
toward my face, her hands press against my chest with a shudder of
respect and desire.

On emerging from these dreams and finding myself again a poor
dark little Breton, without fame, or beauty, or talents, a young man
who would draw nobody's gaze, who would go unnoticed, whom no
woman could ever love, despair took hold of me. I no longer had the
courage to lift my eyes to the dazzling image I had created to walk
beside me.

11.

TWO YEARS OF DELIRIUM—OCCUPATIONS AND CHIMERAS

THIS DELIRIUM lasted two whole years, during which my spiritual faculties reached the highest pitch of exaltation. I used to speak little, and now I did not speak at all; I used to study, and now I tossed my books aside. My taste for solitude redoubled. I had all the symptoms of a violent passion: my eyes were sunken, I was skinny as a rail, I couldn't sleep; I was distracted, sad, ardent, sullen. My days passed in a wild, weird, insane fashion, which was nevertheless full of delights.

To the north of the castle there was a moor littered with Druidic stones. I would go and sit on one of these stones at sunset. The gilded treetops, the splendor of the land, the evening star twinkling through the rosy-colored clouds: all these things carried me back to my dreams. I would have liked to enjoy these sights with the ideal object of my desires. In my mind, I walked in step with the day star: I gave him my beautiful girl to escort, so that he might present her in all her radiance and receive homage from the universe. It was only when an evening wind stirred the networks that the insects stretched between the grass blades, and a moor lark landed on a rock, that I was recalled to reality. I plodded back along the path to the castle, crestfallen and heavy-hearted.

On stormy summer days, I would climb to the top of the big western tower. The thunder rolling beneath the attics of the castle, the torrents of rain pounding on the pyramidal roofs of the towers, and the lightning that furrowed the clouds and bounced off the copper weathercocks with its electric flames incited my enthusiasm. Like

Ismen on the ramparts of Jerusalem, I called on the thunder, hoping it might bring me Armida.[9]

And if the weather was clear? I would cross the Grand Mall until I reached the fields on the far side, which were divided by planted rows of willows. I had constructed a seat, like a nest, in one of these willows. Up there, alone between heaven and earth, I spent many hours with the warblers. My nymph was by my side. I associated her image with the beauty of those spring nights filled with the fresh dew, the nightingale's sighs, and the murmuring breezes.

Other times, I followed a long abandoned path or a small river bordered by its riverine plants. I listened to the noises that issue from unfrequented places; I pressed my ear to the trunk of every tree: I believed I could hear the moonlight singing in the wood. I would have liked to tell someone of these pleasures, but the words died on my lips. I cannot begin to count how many times I rediscovered my goddess in the timbre of a voice, the quivering of a harp, the velvet or liquid tones of a horn or a harmonium. It would take too long to recall the many gorgeous voyages that I made with my love flower: how we visited the famous ruins hand in hand—Venice, Rome, Athens, Jerusalem, Memphis, Carthage—or how we leapt across the seas, how we asked for happiness from the palms of Tahiti and the balmy groves of Ambon and Timor, how we went to wake the dawn at the zenith of the Himalayas, how we traveled down the *sacred rivers* whose waters coursed toward distant pagodas with their golden domes ablaze, or how we slept on the shore of the Ganges, while the avadavat, perched on the mast of our bamboo gondola, sang his Indian barcarole.

Heaven and earth were nothing to me anymore. I especially forgot the former. But if I no longer addressed my prayers to it, still it heard the voice of my secret misery. For I was suffering, and suffering is prayer.

12.

MY AUTUMN JOYS

THE SADDER the season, the more in tune with my nature. Snowy weather, by making travel more difficult, isolated the inhabitants of the countryside. One felt better inside human shelter.

A moral character clings to autumn scenes. Those leaves that fall like our years, those blossoms that fade like our hours, those clouds that flee like our illusions, the light that grows weak like our wits, the sun that cools like our passions, the waves that freeze over like our lives: these things have some secret rapport with our destinies.

I looked forward to the return of the stormy season with unspeakable pleasure. I loved to observe the passage of swans and woodpigeons, and to watch the crows congregating on the meadow near the pond at nightfall, when they went to perch on the tallest oaks of the Grand Mall. When the evening raised its bluish mist over the clearings of the forests, when the plaintive music of the winds wailed in the withered mosses, I would come into full possession of my natural sympathies. If I met with a farmer at the end of some fallow field, I would stop to look at this man whose seedtime was spent in the shadow of the same wheat among which he would soon be reaped, a man who, turning the earth of his own grave with the blade of his plow, mingled his hot sweat with the icy rains of autumn: the furrow he cut was the only monument destined to survive him. But what did my elegant sprite have to do with this? Through her magic, she transported me to the banks of the Nile and showed me the Egyptian pyramids bedded in sand, subject to the same laws that would one day hide the Armorican furrow beneath the heather. I congratulated myself on having placed the fables of my happiness far beyond the circle of human realities.

In the evenings, I used to take a boat across the pond, rowing alone between the cattails and the large floating leaves of the water lilies. There, gathering their strength to fly from our lands again, the swallows flocked. I did not neglect a single note of their chirruping: Tavernier as a child was less attentive to a traveler's tale.[10] The birds frolicked over the water at sunset, pursuing insects, shooting together up into the air, as if to test their wings, then swooping down again to the surface of the lake, and coming to rest on the reeds that scarcely bent beneath their weight, and they filled the air with their clamorous song.

13.
INCANTATION

NIGHT fell. The reeds, like distaffs and daggers, rattled in their fields. The feathered caravan of moorhens, ducks, kingfishers, and snipe cooed and quieted. The pond lapped against its shores. Autumn's great voices were whispering from the marsh and the woods. I ran my boat aground and returned to the castle. Ten hours sounded on the clock. The second I entered my room, I threw open my windows, fixed my gaze upon the sky, and began to recite an incantation. I levitated to the clouds with my fair magician. Wrapped in her hair and veils, I went wherever the storms willed me, stirring the treetops, shaking the mountain peaks, whirling over the seas. I plunged through space and descended from the throne of God to the gates of the Abyss. Worlds were delivered unto the strength of my passions. Amid this chaos of elements, I drunkenly wed my thoughts of danger with my thoughts of pleasure. The breath of the boreal wind brought me voluptuous sighs. The murmur of the rain invited me to lay my head on a woman's bosom. The words I spoke to this woman would have given old age back its senses and warmed the marble of a tomb. All-ignorant and all-knowing, simultaneously virgin and lover, innocent Eve and fallen Eve, my enchantress nourished my madness with a mixture of mystery and passion. I placed her on an altar and worshipped her. The pride of being loved by her increased my love twice over. When she walked, I prostrated myself so that I could be trampled beneath her feet and kiss her footsteps. I was troubled by her smile; I trembled at the sound of her voice; I shuddered with longing if I touched what she had touched. The air exhaled from her moist mouth penetrated the marrow of my bones and flowed in my veins instead of blood. A single glance from her sent me flying to the ends of the earth. What desert would not have been enough for me, as long as she was there? At her side, the lion's den would have been transformed into a palace, and thousands of centuries would have been too short to exhaust the fires by which I felt myself enflamed.

In this frenzy, there was an element of moral idolatry: by another caprice of my imagination, this Phryne who clasped me in her arms was also Glory and, above all, Honor. Virtue performing its noblest deeds or Genius giving birth to its rarest thought could hardly give an idea of this imaginary happiness. I discovered in my marvelous creation all the blandishments of the senses and all the delectations of the soul. Overwhelmed, as though submerged by these double delights, I no longer knew which was my true existence. I was a man and not a man. I became a cloud, a wind, a noise; I was pure spirit, an aerial being that chanted songs of rapture: I stripped myself of my own nature in order to merge with the daughter of my desires, to transform myself into her, to touch her beauty the more intimately, to be at the same time passion received and passion given, the love and the object of love.

And then suddenly, struck by my folly, I would throw myself on my bed; I would wallow in my desolation; I would water my sheets with burning tears that no one witnessed and that flowed miserably, for a nonexistent being.

14.
TEMPTATION

SOON, unable to stay a minute longer in my tower, I would go downstairs in the dark, open the door to the staircase as furtively as a murderer, and go wandering in the woods.

After walking a while wherever chance led me, waving my arms and embracing the winds, which escaped my grasp as surely as the shadow I pursued, I would lean against the trunk of a beech. I would gaze at the crows that my presence had sent flying from one tree to another, and at the moon gliding through the bare treetops of the forest. I would have liked to inhabit this dead world that mirrored the pallor of the grave. I felt neither the chill nor the moisture of the night air, and not even the glacial breath of dawn could have dragged me from the depths of my thoughts, if only the village bell had not begun to toll.

In most of the villages of Brittany, it is traditionally at daybreak that the bell for the dead is tolled. This peal, of three long repeated notes, makes for a somewhat droning, melancholy, bucolic air. Nothing was better suited to my sick and wounded soul than to be summoned back to the tribulations of existence by the bell that announced its end. I would picture the shepherd dead in his insignificant hut; I would see him being laid to rest in a cemetery no less obscure. What had he come to do on earth? What was I myself doing in this world? Since I should have to go in the end, would it not be better to set off in the freshness of morning, and arrive early, than to make the voyage under the burdensome heat of the day? A flush of desire rose in my face, and the idea of ceasing to be took hold of my heart like a sudden joy. In my time of youthful error, I often hoped that I would not outlive happiness: there was a degree of felicity in my first success that made me wish for annihilation.

More and more fettered to my phantom, and unable to enjoy what did not exist, I was like one of those mutilated men who dream of unattainable ecstasies and construct fantastic pleasures to equal the tortures of hell. Beyond this, I had a presentiment of my miserable future. Ingenious at inventing sufferings, I had positioned myself between two poles of despair. Sometimes, I considered myself to be no more than a cipher, incapable of rising above the vulgar herd; sometimes, I seemed to sense in myself qualities that would never be appreciated. A secret instinct warned me that, as I made my way in the world, I would find nothing of what I sought.

Everything nourished my bitterness and disgust. Lucile was unhappy; my mother did not console me; my father only made me conscious of the agonies of my life. His peevishness had increased with age; the years had stiffened his soul as well as his body. He spied on me incessantly in order to scold me. When I came back from my wild excursions and saw him sitting on the staircase, I would as soon have died as have to enter the castle. But to flee would only mean delaying my punishment. Obliged to appear at dinner, I would sit exiled on the edge of my chair, my cheeks wet with rain and my hair tangled. Beneath my father's gaze, I would hold myself motionless and feel the sweat beading on my brow. The last glimmer of reason fled from me.

I now come to a moment when I need some strength to confess my weakness. The man who attempts to take his own life shows not so much the vigor of his soul as the failure of his character.

I had a hunting rifle with a damaged trigger that often went off uncocked. I loaded this gun with three bullets and went to an unfrequented corner of the Grand Mall. I cocked the rifle, put the muzzle in my mouth, and struck the butt-end against the ground. I repeated this action several times, but the gun did not go off. When a gamekeeper appeared, I suspended my resolution. A fatalist, lacking willpower and knowledge, I reasoned that my hour had not come, and I delayed the execution of my plan. If I had killed myself, everything that I was would be buried with me. No one would know what had led me to my death. I would have gone to swell the crowd of nameless unfortunates, and no one could have followed the trail of my sorrows as one follows a wounded man by the trail of his blood.

Those who might be troubled by these descriptions and tempted to imitate these follies, those who wish to attach themselves to my memory by sympathizing with my delusions, must remember that they are hearing only the voice of a dead man. Reader, whom I shall never meet, know that nothing is left. All that remains of me is in the hands of the living God who has judged me.

15.

ILLNESS—I FEAR AND REFUSE TO ENTER THE SEMINARY—PLAN FOR A PASSAGE TO INDIA

AN ILLNESS, the fruit of this unruly life, put an end to the torments which brought me the first inspirations of the Muse and the first attacks of the passions. Those passions that overrode my soul, those still vague passions, were like tempests at sea that rush in from every point of the compass: an inexperienced pilot, I did not know how to rig the sails in such uncertain winds. My chest became swollen and fever gripped me. A message was sent to Bazouches, a little town about five or six miles distant from Combourg, calling on an excellent doctor named Cheftel, whose son later played a role in the Marquis de La Rouërie affair.* He examined me attentively, ordered the appropriate remedies, and declared it absolutely necessary that I be torn away from my current mode of life.

I was in perilous health for six weeks. One morning, my mother came to sit at the edge of my bed and said to me: "It's time for you to decide. Your brother can obtain a benefice for you. But before you enter the seminary, you must consider it carefully, for though I would like it if you embraced the ecclesiastical state, I would rather see you become a man of the world than a scandalous priest."

After what he has read in the previous pages, the reader can judge for himself whether my pious mother's proposal came at a timely

---

*The longer I live, the more people from these *Memoirs* I encounter again. The widow of Doctor Cheftel's son came to implore me to be taken into the Marie-Thérèse Infirmary: he is one more witness to my veracity. (Paris, 1834)

moment. In the major events of my life, I have always known at once what to avoid: my sense of honor prompts me. If I were a priest? I would seem ridiculous to myself. A bishop? The majesty of my office would overawe me and I would respectfully recoil from the altar. If I had become a bishop, would I have made some effort to acquire virtues or would I have been content to conceal my vices? I believe I would have been too weak for the first course and too frank for the second. Those who call me hypocritical and ambitious know little about me. I shall never succeed in this world precisely because I am lacking in one passion, ambition, and one vice, hypocrisy. Ambition might at most appear in me as wounded self-love. At times I might wish I were a minister or a king so that I could laugh at my enemies, but after twenty-four hours I would throw my portfolio or my crown out the window.

I thus told my mother that I did not feel a strong enough vocation for the ecclesiastical state. I was changing my plans for the second time. I had not wanted to be a sailor, and now I no longer wanted to be a priest. All that remained was a military career, which appealed to me. But how to endure the loss of my independence and the constraint of European discipline? I hit on a harebrained scheme: I declared that I would go to Canada, where I would clear forests, or to India, where I would try to serve in the army of one of that country's princes.

By one of those contrasts to be found in every man, my father, who was otherwise so pragmatic, was not greatly shocked by my adventurous plans. He grumbled a bit to my mother about my beating around the bush, but he decided to help me on my way to India. I was sent to Saint-Malo, where a ship was being outfitted for Pondicherry.

16.

A MOMENT IN MY NATIVE TOWN—RECOLLECTION OF LA VILLENEUVE AND THE TRIBULATIONS OF MY CHILDHOOD—I AM CALLED BACK TO COMBOURG —LAST CONVERSATION WITH MY FATHER—I ENTER THE SERVICE—GOODBYE TO COMBOURG

TWO MONTHS rolled by: I found myself alone on my native island. La Villeneuve had only recently died there. Going to mourn beside the poor empty bed where she had passed away, I saw the little wicker cart in which I had first learned to stand upright on this sad globe, and I pictured my old nurse, confined to her bed, turning her weakened gaze on this wheeled basket. This first memento of my existence set beside the last memento of the existence of my second mother made me see that the good Villeneuve must have prayed for the happiness of her foster child even on her deathbed. The thought of her fondness for me, so constant, so disinterested, so pure, broke my heart with tenderness, regrets, and gratitude.

Otherwise, nothing of my past remained in Saint-Malo. In the harbor I looked in vain for the ships in whose rigging I had played: they had departed or been dismantled. In the village, the building where I was born had been transformed into an inn. I was hardly out of my cradle, and already a whole world had vanished; I had become a stranger in my childhood haunts, and everyone I met asked me who I was for no reason except that my head had risen a few inches above the ground toward which, in a year or two, it will bow again. How quickly and how often we change our lives and our illusions! Some friends leave us, and others take their place; our relationships alter: there is always a time when we possessed nothing of what we now possess, a time when we have nothing of what we used to have. Man has not one and the same life; he has several lives laid end to end, and that is the cause of his misery.

Friendless now, I explored the strand that had once seen me building sandcastles: *campos ubi Troja fuit*.[11] I walked along a beach forsaken by the sea. The sands, abandoned by the tides, seemed to me an emblem of those desolated spaces that illusions leave around us when they fade. My fellow countryman Abelard once gazed at the waves as I did, eight hundred years ago, remembering Héloïse. Like me, he watched the ships departing (*ad horizontis undas*), and his ears, like mine, were lulled by the droning surf.[12] I waded through the breakers and gave myself over to those lethal fantasies that I had brought with me from the woods of Combourg. Only Cape Lavarde put an end to my wanderings. Seated on the point of this headland, lost in the bitterest thoughts, I recalled that these same rocks had served as my hiding place on festival days. Here, I had swallowed my tears while my friends grew drunk with joy. I did not feel any more loved nor any happier than I did then. Soon I would leave my native land and fritter away my days in foreign climes. These reflections grieved me half to death, and I was tempted to let myself fall into the breakers.

A letter summoned me back to Combourg. I arrived and sat down to supper with my family. My father said not a word; my mother sighed. Lucile seemed dismayed. At ten o'clock we went to bed. I questioned my sister, but she knew nothing. The next morning at eight o'clock a servant came to fetch me. I went downstairs. My father was waiting for me in his study.

"Monsieur le Chevalier," he said to me, "you must renounce your follies. Your brother has obtained a sublieutenant's commission for you in the Navarre Regiment. You shall go to Rennes and from there to Cambrai. Here are a hundred louis d'or. Do not squander them. I am old and sick. I am not long for this world. Conduct yourself as a good man should, and never dishonor your name."

He kissed me, and I felt that rough, stern face pressed tenderly against mine: it was to be my last paternal embrace.

At that moment, the Comte de Combourg, a man who had always been so formidable in my eyes, appeared to me simply as a father most worthy of my affection. I grabbed his gaunt hand and wept. He was already suffering then from the paralysis that would lead him to the grave. His left arm had a convulsive tremor, which he was obliged to keep still with his right hand. It was holding his arm in this way, and after presenting me with his old sword, that, without giving me time to recover myself, he led me to the cabriolet waiting for me in the Green Court. He made me board it in his presence. The postilion drove off even as I bade farewell to my mother and my sister, who were dissolving in tears on the steps.

We drove up the lane by the pond. I looked at the reeds where my swallows perched, the millstream, and the meadow. I cast my gaze back toward the castle. And then, like Adam after his sin, I went forth into an unknown country: *and the world was all before him*.[13]

Since that day, I have seen Combourg three times. After my father's death, the family met there in mourning, to divide our inheritance and say our goodbyes. Another time I accompanied my mother to Combourg, when she was busy furnishing the castle for my brother, who was to bring my sister-in-law to live in Brittany. My brother never arrived. Beside his young wife, at the executioner's hands, he was to receive a very different place to lay his head than the pillow my mother prepared for him. Finally, I passed through Combourg a third time, on my way to Saint-Malo, before I embarked for America. The castle was abandoned, and I had to spend the night in the steward's house. When, wandering on the Grand Mall, I looked down a dark alley of trees and saw the empty staircase and the closed windows and doors, I felt faint. I dragged myself back to the village and sent for my horses. I left in the middle of the night.

After fifteen years away, before leaving France once more and traveling to the Holy Land, I raced to Fougères to embrace what remained of my family. But I did not have the heart to make a pilgrimage to those fields where the most vivid part of my life took place. It was in the woods of Combourg that I became what I am, that I began to feel the first onslaught of that ennui which I have dragged with me through all my days, and that sadness which has been both my torment and my bliss. There, I searched for a heart in sympathy with mine; there, I saw my family join together and disband; there, my father dreamed of seeing his name reestablished and the fortune of his house renewed: yet another chimera that time and the Revolution dispelled. Of the six children that we were, only three are left. My brother, Julie, and Lucile are no more; my mother is dead of grief; my father's ashes were filched from his tomb.

If my work survives me and my name endures, maybe one day, guided by these *Memoirs*, some traveler will visit the places I have described. He may still recognize the castle, but he would look in vain for the great woods: the cradle of my dreams has vanished, like the dreams themselves. Left alone on its rock, my old keep mourns the oaks, its ancient companions, who surrounded it and shielded it from storms. Isolated as that keep, I too have seen them falling around me, the family that once eased my days and gave me shelter. Happily, my life is not built on the earth as solidly as the towers where I passed my youth, and man offers less resistance to the storms than the monuments raised by his hands.

BOOK FOUR

I.

BERLIN—POTSDAM—FREDERICK

Berlin, May 1821;
Revised in July 1846

IT IS A long way from Combourg to Berlin, and a long way from a young dreamer to an old minister. Among the pages I have written, I find these words: "In how many places have I already begun to write these *Memoirs*, and in what place shall I bring them to an end?"

Between the last date attached to these *Memoirs* and today, when I pick up the pen again, nearly four years have passed. A thousand things have intervened. Another man has appeared in me, a political man: I do not much care for him. I have defended the liberties of France, which alone can make the legitimate monarchy endure. With the *Conservateur*, I have put M. de Villèle in power. I have seen the Duc de Berry die, and I have honored his memory.[1] With the aim of reconciling all parties, I have left France; I have accepted an ambassadorship in Berlin.

Yesterday I was in Potsdam, an ornate barrack now devoid of soldiers: I made a study of the false Julian in his false Athens.[2] I was shown, at Sans-Souci, the table where a great German monarch put the Encyclopedists' maxims into French versets; Voltaire's room, decorated with carved wooden monkeys and parrots; the mill which he who laid waste to whole provinces played at respecting; and the tombs of the horse César and the greyhounds Diane, Amourette, Biche, Superbe, and Pax. The impious king took pleasure in profaning even the sanctity of tombs by raising mausoleums for his dogs; he marked out a place for his sepulcher near theirs, less out of contempt for humanity than out of an ostentatious belief in nothingness.

I was taken to the New Palace, which is already falling down. In the old castle of Potsdam, the tobacco stains, the torn and soiled armchairs, indeed every trace of the renegade prince's uncleanliness, is preserved. These rooms immortalize the filthiness of a cynic, the impudence of an atheist, the tyranny of a despot, and the glory of a soldier.

Only one thing held my attention: the hands of a clock stopped at the minute that Frederick expired. I was deceived by the stillness of the image. The hours never suspend their flight; it is not man who stops time, but time that stops man. In the end it matters little what part we have played in life. The brilliance or obscurity of our doctrines, our wealth or poverty, our joy or pain: these things have no effect on the measure of our days. Whether the hand moves around a golden face or a wooden one, whether the dial fills the bezel of a ring or the rose window of a cathedral, the length of the hour is still the same.

Down in the crypt of the Protestant church, immediately beneath the pulpit of the defrocked schismatic, I saw the tomb of the sophist to the crown.[3] The tomb is made of bronze; if one taps it, it rings aloud. But the gendarme who sleeps forever in this bronze bed would not be torn from sleep even by the rumor of his reputation. He will not wake until the trumpet sounds to summon him to his final battlefield, where he shall come face to face with the Lord of Hosts.

I had such a need to alter my impressions that I found relief in visiting the Marble Palace. The king who ordered its construction had once addressed a few honorable words to me, when, as a humble officer, I passed through his army. At least this king shared the ordinary weaknesses of men: vulgar like them, he took refuge in his pleasures. These two skeletons, do they trouble themselves about the differences that once existed between them, when one was Frederick the Great and the other was Frederick William II? Today, Sans-Souci and the Marble Palace are both ruins without masters.

Taken all together, though the enormity of events in our time has dwarfed the events of the past, and though Rosbach, Lissa, Liegnitz, Torgau, etc., etc., were merely skirmishes compared with the battles of Marengo, Austerlitz, Jena, and Moscow, Frederick suffers less than others by comparison with the giant chained on Saint-Helena. The King of Prussia and Voltaire are two of the most bizarrely grouped figures who ever lived: the latter destroyed a society with the same philosophy that helped the former to found a kingdom.

The evenings are long in Berlin. I live in a house that belongs to Madame la Duchesse de Dino. At nightfall, my secretaries abandon me. When there aren't festivities at Court celebrating the marriage of the Grand Duke and the Grand Duchess Nicholas,* I stay at home. Shut up in my room, alone with a very gloomy-looking stove, I hear nothing but the shouts of the sentinels at the Brandenburg Gate and, outside in the snow, the footsteps of the watchman who whistles the hours. What should I do with my time? Read? I have scarcely any books. What if I were to continue my *Memoirs*?

You last saw me on the road from Combourg to Rennes. I alighted in this latter town at the house of a relative. This man announced to me with great enthusiasm that a lady of his acquaintance, who was going to Paris, had a spare seat in her carriage, and that he had managed to persuade this lady to take me with her. Cursing my kinsman's courtesy, I accepted. He settled the matter and soon presented me to my traveling companion, a blithe and uninhibited fashionmonger, who burst into laughter the moment she saw me. At midnight the horses came and we departed.

There I was in a post-chaise, alone with a woman in the middle of the night. I, who had never looked at a woman without blushing—how was I to stoop from the heights of my dreams to this dreadful reality? I did not know where I was; I stuck myself in a corner of the carriage for fear of touching Madame Rose's dress. When she spoke to me, I babbled, then lost the power of speech entirely. She had to pay the postilion and see to everything else as well, for I was capable of nothing. At daybreak, she looked with renewed amazement at this simpleton with whom she must have regretted entangling herself.

*Now Emperor and Empress of Russia. (Paris, 1832)

As the look of the countryside began to change and I no longer recognized the clothing and the accent of Brittany, I fell into a deep despondency, which only increased Madame Rose's contempt for me. I took note of the feelings that I inspired in her, and this first contact with the judgments of the wider world left me with an impression that time has not completely effaced. I was born savage, but not ashamed; I had the modesty of my years, but not the embarrassment. When I surmised that I was made ridiculous by my good side, my savagery turned into an insurmountable timidity. I would not say another word. I felt that I had something to conceal, and that this something was a virtue: I resolved to sink within myself so that I might wear my innocence in peace.

We were now approaching Paris. On the descent from Saint-Cyr, I was struck by the width of the roads and the symmetry of the fields. Soon we reached Versailles: the orangery and the marble staircases enthralled me. The success of the American war had brought back triumphs to Louis XIV's palace; the Queen reigned there in all the splendor of her youth and beauty; the throne, so near its downfall, never seemed to have been more solid. And I, an obscure traveler, I was destined to outlive all this pomp: I would remain to see the woods of Trianon as deserted as the woods that I had just abandoned.

At last, we entered Paris. I saw a mocking expression on every face: like Molière's Gentleman of Périgord, I believed that everyone was looking at me only to jeer at me. Madame Rose told the postilion to take me to the Hôtel de l'Europe in the rue du Mail and wasted no time disburdening herself of her imbecile. I had hardly stepped down from the carriage before she said to the porter, "Give this gentleman a room."

She nodded at me.

"Your servant," she said, making a brief curtsy.

I never saw Madame Rose again in my life.

2.

MY BROTHER—MY COUSIN MOREAU—MY SISTER THE COMTESSE DE FARCY

Berlin, March 1821

A WOMAN climbed before me up a dark, steep staircase, holding a labeled key in her hand; a Savoyard followed behind me, carrying my little trunk. On the third floor, the woman unlocked the door to a room; the Savoyard balanced the trunk across the arms of a chair.

"Does Monsieur need anything else?" asked the chambermaid.

"No," I replied.

There were three sharp blasts from a whistle; the chambermaid shouted, "Coming!" and turned brusquely, closed the door, and crashed down the stairs together with the Savoyard. Finding myself shut up alone in my room, my heart was gripped by such strange qualms that I nearly took the road back to Brittany. Everything I had ever heard said of Paris flooded into my mind, and I felt embarrassed in a hundred ways. I would have liked to go to bed, but the bed was not made; I was famished, but I had no idea how to set about dining. I feared committing some impropriety. Should I call for the hotel's service? Should I go downstairs? How would I know whom to speak to? I took the liberty of sticking my head out the window: I could see nothing but a small interior courtyard as deep as a well, where people passed to and fro who would never in their lives give a thought to the prisoner on the third floor. I went and sat down again, next to the dirty alcove where I would have to sleep, reduced to contemplating the figures on the wallpaper. Then a sound of distant voices drifted toward me, swelled, approached. My door burst open and in came my brother and one of my cousins, Moreau, the son of my mother's sister, who had made a rather poor marriage. So Madame Rose had taken pity on her simpleton after all! She had sent word to my brother, whose address she had learned in Rennes, that I had arrived in Paris. My brother embraced me. My cousin stood by: a big fat man, whose clothes were always stained with snuff, Moreau ate like an ogre, talked unremittingly, and was always pacing, panting, choking, with his mouth half open and his tongue half out; he knew everyone on earth and lived out his life in gambling halls, waiting rooms, and parlors.

"Well, Chevalier," my cousin said, "here you are in Paris. I am going to take you to see Madame de Chastenay."

Who was this woman whose name I was hearing for the first time? My cousin's proposition turned me against him.

"The Chevalier is no doubt in need of a rest," my brother said. "We'll go see Madame de Farcy, and then he'll come back here for his dinner and go to bed."

A feeling of joy washed over me. In this indifferent world, the memory of my family was a balm. We went out. Cousin Moreau raised a stink about the dreadful room I had been given and admonished my host to bring me down at least one floor. Then we got into my brother's carriage and drove to the convent where Madame de Farcy was living.

Julie had already been in Paris for some time, to consult with physicians. Her charming face, elegance, and wit had soon made her the center of attention. I have already said that she was born with a true talent for poetry. She became a saint, after having been one of the most attractive women of her century. The Abbé Carron has written her life. These apostles who go everywhere in search of souls feel the same love for them that a Father of the Church attributes to the Creator: "When a soul arrives in Heaven," says this Father, with the simpleheartedness of an early Christian, and the naiveté of the Greeks, "God takes them on his knee and calls her his daughter."

Lucile has left a poignant lamentation: "For the Sister I Have Lost." Abbé Carron's admiration for Julie explains and justifies Julie's words. The holy priest's account also goes to show that I spoke truth in my preface to *The Genius of Christianity* and serves as proof of some portions of my *Memoirs*.

Innocent Julie delivered herself into the hands of repentance; she dedicated the riches won from her austerities to the redemption of her brothers; and, following the illustrious example of the African woman who was her patron saint, she became a martyr.

Abbé Carron, my countryman and the author of *The Life of the Just*, is that priest—that Francis of Paola of the exiles—whose reputation, broadcast by the afflicted, pierced even the reputation of Bonaparte. The voice of this poor banished clergyman was not stifled by the resounding ruckus of a revolution that overturned society. He seemed to have returned from foreign lands expressly to write an account of my sister's virtues: he searched among our ruins, and he discovered a victim and her forgotten grave.

When this hagiographer describes Julie's religious cruelties, one thinks of Bossuet's sermon on Mademoiselle de la Vallière's profession of faith:

> Will she dare to touch that body so tender, so cherished, so well treated? Will there be no pity for this delicate complexion? On the contrary! It is principally to this that the soul imputes its most dangerous temptations; she sets bounds for herself: closed in upon all quarters, she can no longer breathe except on the side of Heaven.

I still cannot rid myself of a certain bewilderment on discovering my name in the last lines written by Julie's venerable chronicler. Why should my weaknesses be compared with her sublime perfections? Have I adhered to all that my sister's note made me promise since I received it during my exile in London? Is a book enough for God? And has my life really been lived in accordance with *The Genius of Christianity*? What does it matter if I have traced more or less brilliant images of religion if my passions cast a shadow on my faith! I have not gone very far; I have not shouldered the hair shirt: this tunic of my viaticum would have drunk up and dried all my sweat. A weary traveler, I have sat down by the wayside; but weary or not, I must get up again and go where my sister has already gone.

Julie's glory lacks for nothing: Abbé Carron has written her life, and Lucile has mourned her death.

3.

JULIE IN SOCIETY—DINNER—POMMEREUL—MADAME DE CHASTENAY

Berlin, March 30, 1821

WHEN I visited Julie in Paris, she was in all the pomp of worldly luxury; she appeared surrounded by those flowers, bedecked with those necklaces, and veiled in those perfumed fabrics that Saint Clement forbids the early Christians. Saint Basil wants midnight for the solitary hermit to be what morning is for others, so that he may take advantage of nature's silence. Midnight was the hour when Julie used to go to gatherings where the principal attraction was her poetry, which she recited in a wonderful, mellifluous voice.

Julie was infinitely more beautiful than Lucile. She had warm, soft blue eyes and long dark hair that she wore in plaits or in large waves. Her hands and arms were models of whiteness and form, and their graceful gestures lent an added charm to her already charming figure. She was brilliant, lively, and laughed often and easily, and when she laughed she showed teeth as white as pearls. A host of portraits of women from the time of Louis XIV resembled Julie, among others those of the three Mortemarts; but she was more elegant than Madame de Montespan.

Julie welcomed me with that tenderness which belongs only to a sister. I felt myself protected in the clutch of her arms, her ribbons, her roses, and her lace. Nothing can take the place of the affection, the delicacy, and the devotion of a woman. A man may be forgotten by his brothers and his friends; he may be misjudged by his companions; but he is never forgotten or misjudged by his mother, his sister, or his wife. When Harold was killed in the battle of Hastings, no one could pick him out from the crowd of dead; they went to ask for the help of a young girl, Harold's sweetheart. She came, and the doomed prince was found by swan-necked Edith: *Editha swanes-hales, quod sonat collum cycni*.[4]

My brother brought me back to my hotel. He made arrangements for my dinner and left me. I dined alone and went sadly to bed. I spent my first night in Paris longing for the moors of Combourg and trembling at the obscurity of my future.

At eight o'clock the next morning, my fat cousin arrived. He was already on his fifth or sixth visit of the day. "*Eh bien! Chevalier,*" he said, "we'll go have breakfast, then we'll dine with Pommereul, and this evening I'll take you to meet Madame de Chastenay."

This seemed to be my fate, and I resigned myself to it. Everything transpired as my cousin had planned. After breakfast, he claimed that he was going to show me Paris and proceeded to drag me through the dirtiest streets in the neighborhood of the Palais-Royal, lecturing me on the dangers to which a young man might be exposed. We were punctual to our dinner, at a restaurant. Everything that was served there tasted bad to me. The conversation and the company showed me an unfamiliar world. Talk turned on questions of the Court, finances, the sittings of the Academy, the women and the intrigues of the moment, the latest play, and the success of actors, actresses, and authors.

Several Bretons were around that table, among others the Chevalier de Guer and Pommereul. The latter was a good conversationalist, who has since chronicled some of Bonaparte's campaigns and whom I was destined to meet again when he was in charge of the State Press.

Pommereul, under the Empire, enjoyed a sort of renown for his hatred of the nobility. When a gentleman was appointed court chamberlain, he cheerfully shouted: "Another chamberpot on the nobles' heads!" And yet Pommereul claimed, and with reason, to be a gentleman. He signed his name "Pommereux," which would make him a descendant of the Pommereux family mentioned in Madame de Sévigné's letters.

After dinner, my brother wanted to take me to the theater, but my cousin insisted that I go with him to Madame Chastenay, and I went with him, to meet my fate.

I saw a beautiful woman no longer in the first flush of youth, but who could still inspire affection. She greeted me warmly, tried to put me at ease, and asked me about my province and my regiment. I was awkward and embarrassed; I signaled to my cousin to cut the visit short. But he, without looking at me, would not stop singing my praises, affirming that I had written poetry in my mother's womb and even asking me to celebrate Madame Chastenay in rhyme. She released me from this painful situation by begging my pardon, she had to go out that evening, but would I like to come back tomorrow morning? Her voice was so sweet that I involuntarily promised to obey.

I returned the next day alone. I found her reclining in an elegantly furnished room. She told me that she was feeling a bit indisposed, and that anyhow she had the bad habit of rising late. I found myself for the first time at the bedside of a woman who was neither my mother nor my sister. She had noticed my timidity the previous night, and now she conquered it to the point that I dared express myself with a sort of abandon. I have forgotten what I said to her, but I can still see the look of astonishment on her face. She stretched out a half-naked arm to me, and the most beautiful hand in the world, and she said with a smile, "We shall tame you."

I did not even kiss that beautiful hand; I retreated at a loss. The next day I left for Cambrai. Who was this Madame de Chastenay? I know nothing about her. She passed through my life like a charming shade.

4.
CAMBRAI—THE NAVARRE REGIMENT—LA MARTINIÈRE

Berlin, March 1821

THE MAIL courier brought me to my garrison. One of my brothers-in-law, the Vicomte de Chateaubourg (he had married my sister Bénigne, the Comte de Québriac's widow), had written me letters of recommendation to the officers of my regiment. The Chevalier de Guénan, a very companionable man, invited me to a mess hall where I met several officers distinguished by their talents: Messrs. Achard, des Mahis, and La Martinière. The Marquis de Mortemart was colonel of the regiment, and the Comte d'Andrezel was the major. I was placed under the private tutelage of the latter. I would meet them both again, by and by. The one became my colleague in the Chamber of Peers, and the other applied to me for certain services that I was happy to render him. There is a sad pleasure in reencountering people whom we have known during a different period of our lives, and in considering the changes that have taken place in their existence as well as ours. Like stones left behind us, they trace the paths we have followed through the desert of the past.

I joined the regiment in civilian garb, but within twenty-four hours I had assumed the clothes of a soldier. It seemed to me I had always worn them. My uniform was blue and white, like the old coat of my vows: I marched under the same colors as a young man as when a child. I was not subjected to any of the trials that the sublieutenants usually made newcomers undergo. I don't know why no one dared pull those puerile military pranks on me, but I had not been in the regiment fifteen days before my fellow men treated me as an "old hand." I picked up the operation and theory of firearms with ease, and I rose through the ranks of corporal and sergeant with the commendations of my instructors. My room became a meeting place for old captains and young lieutenants alike: the former told me stories of their campaigns, and the latter confided their love affairs.

One of these young lieutenants, La Martinière, used to come fetch me to go walk with him past the door of a beautiful Cambrésienne whom he worshipped: we happened by five or six times a day. La Martinière was a very ugly man with a face furrowed by smallpox; he spoke to me of his passion while drinking big glasses of red currant syrup, for which I sometimes paid.

Everything would have been wonderful if it weren't for my extravagant love of clothes. The army then affected the stiffness of the Prussian uniform: small hat, short curls cropped close to the head, tight pigtail, coat buttoned to the collar. This very much displeased me. I would submit to these fetters in the morning, but in the evening, when I hoped never to be seen by my superior officers, I would crown myself with a larger hat, unbutton my coat, cross my lapels, and have the barber let down my hair and loosen my pigtail. In this informal state of dress, I went courting, on La Martinière's behalf, under the window of his cruel Walloon.

Then one evening I found myself face to face with M. d'Andrezel. "What's this, Monsieur?" the terrifying major said to me. "Consider yourself under arrest for the next three days."

I was a bit humiliated, but I recognized the truth of the proverb that it is an ill wind that blows nobody good, for I was at last delivered from my comrade's love affairs.

Beside Fénelon's tomb, I reread *Télémaque*, but I was not in the proper mood for the philanthropic tale of the cow and the bishop.[5]

I am amused to recall the beginning of my career. Years later, passing through Cambrai with the King, after the Hundred Days, I looked for the house where I once lived and the café I used to frequent, but I could not find them. Everything had disappeared, both men and monuments.

5.

MY FATHER'S DEATH

THE SAME year I was serving my military apprenticeship in Cambrai, I heard the news of Frederick II's death: today, I am ambassador to that great king's nephew and write this section of my *Memoirs* in Berlin. This news, important to the public, was followed by another piece of news, sorrowful to me: Lucile wrote to tell me that my father had been carried off by an apoplectic attack two days after the Angevine fair, one of the joys of my childhood.

Among the authentic documents that serve to guide me, I find the death certificates of my parents. As these documents record, in a particular manner, the "death of the century," I hereby consign them to the pages of history.

First, a certificate from the register of deaths in the Parish of Combourg, year 1786:

> The body of the high and puissant Messire René de Chateaubriand, Chevalier, Comte de Combourg, Lord of Gaugres, Plessis-l'Épine, Boulet, Malestroit en Dol, and other places, husband to the high and puissant Lady Apolline-Jeanne-Suzanne de Bédée de la Bouërtadais, Comtesse de Combourg, at the age of about sixty-nine, died in his castle in Combourg, on September 6, around eight in the evening, and was buried on September 8 in the family vault, on the grounds of our church in Combourg, in the presence of the gentlemen and officers of the jurisdiction as well as other notable burghers whose names

are subscribed. Witnessed by le Comte du Petitbois, de Molouët, de Chateaudassy, Delaunay, Morault, Noury de Mauny, advocate; Hermer, procurator; Petit, advocate and fiscal procurator; Robiou, Portal, Le Douarin, de Trevelec, rector and dean of Dingé; Sévin, Rector.

I observe that, in the "collated copy" delivered in 1812 by M. Lodin, who was then mayor of Combourg, the nineteen words expressive of titles ("high and puissant Messire," etc.) are struck through.

Second, a certificate from the register of deaths in the town of Saint-Servan, first arrondissement of the *département* of Ille-et-Vilaine, year VI of the Republic, folio 35:

On the twelfth Prairial, year six of the French Republic, there appeared before me one Jacques Bourdasse, municipal officer of the Commune of St. Servan, chosen an officer of the public the 4th of last Floréal, Jean Baslé, gardener, and Joseph Boulin, day-laborer, who have declared in my presence that Apolline-Jeanne-Suzanne de Bédée, widow of René-Auguste de Chateaubriand, died at the house of citizen Gouyon, in La Ballue, in that Commune, this day, at one o'clock, p.m. After this declaration, whose truth I have ascertained, I have drawn up the present document, which Jean Basléalone has signed along with me, Joseph Boudin, having declared his inability to do so when summoned.

Made at the public office, the day and year stated above. Signed Jean Baslé and Bourdasse.

In the first certificate, the old society subsists. M. de Chateaubriand is a "high and puissant lord," etc., etc., and the witnesses are the "gentlemen" and "burghers of note." I note the signature of the Marquis de Monlouet, who stopped over one winter day at the Château de Combourg, as well as the signature of the curé Sévin, who was so difficult to persuade that I was the author of *The Genius of Christianity*. Both men were loyal friends to my father until his final hour. But my father did not lay long in his winding sheet: he was tossed out of it when the old France was tossed on the garbage pile.

In my mother's death certificate, the earth turns on different poles. There is a new world, a new era. Even the computation of years and the names of the months have changed. Madame de Chateaubriand is only a poor woman who passed away in the house of "citizen" Gouyon. The only witnesses to my mother's death are a gardener and an illiterate farmhand: no relatives, no friends, no funeral pomp. The only bystander is the Revolution.

6.

REGRETS—WOULD MY FATHER HAVE APPRECIATED ME?

Berlin, March 1821

I WEPT for M. de Chateaubriand. His death showed me more clearly what he was worth. I remembered neither his strictures nor his failings. I could still see him taking his evening stroll in the great hall at Combourg, and I was moved by the thought of those familial scenes. If my father's affection for me was curbed by the severity of his character, deep down it was nonetheless real. The fierce Marshal de Montluc, whose nose was mutilated by terrible wounds, and who was reduced to hiding the horror of his glory beneath a shroud, this man of carnage reproached himself for the harsh treatment of a son whom he had lost.

"This poor boy," he writes, "having never seen me except with a scowling and scornful countenance, lived in the belief that I neither knew how to love him nor how to esteem his merits. To what purpose did I curb the singular affection that I bore him in my soul? Was it not he who ought to have had all the pleasure and all the obligation of that affection? I have constrained myself and scourged myself in order to keep this vain mask in place, and I have thereby lost the pleasure of his conversation and his will, likewise, which could not have been other than ill-borne toward me, as I had never treated him in anything but a harsh and tyrannical fashion."[6]

My "will was not at all ill-borne" toward my father, and I do not doubt, despite his own "tyrannical fashion," that he loved me tenderly. He would, I am sure, have mourned my loss had Providence called me away before him. But if he had remained on earth beside me, what would he have thought of all the clamor that has come of my life? A literary reputation would have wounded his gentlemanly pride; he would have seen nothing in his son's aptitudes but degeneration. Even my embassy in Berlin, won by the pen, not the sword, would have given him but middling satisfaction. His Breton blood made him a political reactionary, a great opponent of taxation and a violent enemy of the Court. He read the *Gazette de Leyde*, the *Journal de Francfort*, the *Mercure de France*, and the *Histoire Philosophique des Deux Indes*, whose declamations particularly charmed him; he called the author, Abbé Raynal, a "mastermind." In diplomatic matters he was anti-Mussulman: he declared that forty thousand "Russian wretches" would crush the Janissaries and conquer Constantinople. Turk-hater though he was, my father had an equally heartfelt loathing of the "Russian wretches," due to his encounters at Danzig.

I share M. de Chateaubriand's feeling about reputations, literary or otherwise, but for reasons different from his. I am not aware of any kind of fame in history that would tempt me. Should I have to stoop, in order to pick up at my feet, and to my advantage, the greatest glory in the world, I would not give myself the inconvenience. If I had molded my own clay, perhaps I would have made myself a woman, out of passion for them, or, if I had made myself a man, I would have bestowed myself with beauty first of all; then, as a safeguard against boredom, that tenacious enemy of mine, it might have suited me to be a superior artist, but unknown, putting my talent to use only for the good of my solitude. In this life, weighed by its light poundage, measured by its short distance, and with all the loaded dice thrown away, there are only two true things: intelligent religion and youthful love, which is to say the future and the present. The rest is not worth the trouble.

With my father's death, the first act of my life came to a close. The paternal hearth was empty, and I pitied it, as though it were capable of feeling its abandonment and its solitude. Henceforth I would be masterless and enjoy my own fortune; but such liberty frightened me. What was I going to do with it? To whom should I give it? I distrusted my strength, and I recoiled from myself.

7.

RETURN TO BRITTANY—A SOJOURN IN MY ELDEST
SISTER'S HOUSE—MY BROTHER CALLS ME TO PARIS

Berlin, March 1821

I OBTAINED a furlough. M. d'Andrezel, appointed Lieutenant Colonel of the Picardy regiment, was leaving Cambrai: I acted as his courier. We passed through Paris, where I didn't want to stop for even a quarter of an hour. I saw the moors of my Brittany again with more joy than a Neapolitan, banished to our lands, would the shores of Portici or the fields of Sorrento. My family gathered at Combourg and divided the inheritance. This done, we disbanded like birds flying from the paternal nest. My brother had come from Paris and went straight back; my mother left to settle in Saint-Malo; Lucile went with Julie; and I spent a length of time with Mesdames de Marigny, de Chateaubourg, and de Farcy. Marigny, my eldest sister's château, three leagues from the town of Fougères, was agreeably situated between two ponds in a landscape of woods, rocks, and meadows. I stayed there for a few tranquil months, until a letter from Paris came to trouble my repose.

Though on the verge of joining the military and marrying Mademoiselle de Rosambo, my brother had not yet rid himself of the long robe. For this reason, he was not allowed to ride in the King's carriages. His hasty ambition gave him the idea of procuring the honors of the Court for me, the better to pave the way for his own advancement. Our proofs of nobility had already been drawn up for Lucile, when she was admitted to the Chapter of L'Argentière, and everything was in order: Marshal de Duras would act as my patron. My brother said that I was on the high road to fortune, that already I had the honorific and gentlemanly rank of cavalry captain, and that it would therefore be easy for me to join the Order of Malta, by means of which I would enjoy large benefices.

This letter struck me like a lightning bolt. The prospect of returning to Paris and being presented at Court—when I found myself almost sick every time I was introduced to three or four strangers in a parlor! How was I to understand my brother's ambitions, when all I wanted was to live forgotten?

My first impulse was to reply to my brother that, being the eldest, it was his duty to uphold the family name; that, as for me, an obscure little Breton, I would not be resigning from the service, for there was a chance of war; that, though the King had need of a soldier in his army, he had no need of a poor gentleman in his Court.

I hastened to read this romantic rejoinder to Madame de Marigny, who shrieked aloud and called for Madame de Farcy, who mocked me. Lucile would have liked to take my side, but she did not dare do battle with her sisters. They snatched the letter from my hands, and, always weak in matters where I am concerned, I wrote to tell my brother that I would go.

Indeed I went; I went to be presented at the First Court of Europe, to make the most brilliant debut in life, and all the while I had the look of a man being dragged to the galley, or a man about to be sentenced to death.

8.

MY HERMIT'S LIFE IN PARIS

Berlin, March 1821

I ENTERED Paris by the same road that I had followed the first time, and I alighted at the same hotel in the rue du Mail: I knew none other. I was lodged across the hall from my first room, but this second one was slightly larger and the windows gave onto the street.

My brother, perhaps because he was embarrassed of my manners, or perhaps because he took pity on my shyness, did not take me into society or introduce me to anyone. He was living on the rue des Fossés-Montmartre, and I used to go there every day to dine with him at three o'clock. We then said our farewells and did not see each other again until the following day. My fat cousin Moreau was no longer in Paris. I walked past Madame de Chastenay's house three or four times without asking the porter what had become of her.

It was early autumn. Every day I would get up at six o'clock, go to the riding school, and have breakfast. I had a happy rage for Greek in those days, and I would translate the *Odyssey* and the *Cryopaedia* until two o'clock, interspersing my labors with historical research. At two o'clock I would dress and go to my brother's apartment. He would ask me what I had been doing, what I had seen, and I would answer: "Nothing." He would shrug his shoulders and turn his back to me.

One afternoon, we heard a noise in the street. My brother ran to the window and called to me, but I had no desire to leave the armchair where I sprawled at the other end of the room. My poor brother predicted that I would die unknown, useless to myself and my family.

At four o'clock, I went back to my hotel and took my seat behind the windowpanes. Two young girls of fifteen or sixteen came at that hour to sketch at the window of a hotel directly across the street. They had noticed my punctuality, as I had noticed theirs. From time to time, they would raise their heads and glance at their neighbor; I owed them infinite gratitude for this sign of attention: they were my only company in Paris.

When night came down, I went to some show or another. The wilderness of the crowd pleased me, though it still cost me a little effort to buy my ticket at the door and mingle with other men. I rectified the ideas that I had formed of the theater in Saint-Malo. I saw Madame de Saint-Huberti as Armida, and I felt that there had been something missing from the sorceress I had created. Whenever I was not imprisoning myself in the Opéra or the Français, I wandered from street to street or along the quais until ten or eleven in the evening. To this day, I cannot look at the line of streetlamps from the Place Louis XV to the Barrière des Bons-Hommes without recalling the agonies I suffered when I followed that route on the way to my presentation at Versailles.

Back in my room, I spent a part of the night gazing into my fire. It told me nothing. I did not possess, like the Persians, an imagination lavish enough to envision the flames as anemones or the embers as pomegranates. I listened to the carriages coming, going, and crossing paths, and their distant rumbling seemed to imitate the murmur of the breakers on the beaches of my Brittany, or the wind in my woods at Combourg. These noises of the world, which recalled the noises of solitude, reawakened my regrets. I conjured up my old despondency, or my imagination invented stories about the people that the carriages were conveying through the streets; I pictured radiant salons and balls, love affairs and conquests. Soon enough, though, I fell back on myself, and saw myself as I was: forsaken in a hotel room, looking at the world through my window and hearing its echoes in my hearth.

Rousseau believes that he owes it to his sincerity, and to the edification of mankind, to confess the suspect sensual pleasures of his life. He even supposes that he is being seriously interrogated and asked to account for his sins with the *donne pericolanti* of Venice. If it were true that I had prostituted myself to the courtesans of Paris, I would not consider myself obliged to enlighten posterity; but I was too timid on the one hand, and too idealistic on the other, to let myself be seduced by the *filles de joie*. When I shouldered my way through packs of these unhappy women, who grabbed at the arms of passersby to pull them up to their quarters like Saint-Cloud cabmen trying to make travelers climb into their carriages, I was overcome by disgust and horror. The pleasures of such adventure would only have appealed to me in times past.

In the fourteenth, fifteenth, sixteenth, and seventeenth centuries, our imperfect civilization, our superstitious beliefs, and our strange and half-barbarous customs lent romance to all things. Characters were strong; imagination was powerful; existence was mysterious and hidden. By night, around the high walls of the cemeteries and the convents, under the deserted ramparts of the city, along the chains and ditches of the marketplaces, on the outskirts of the closed quarters, in the narrow streets without streetlamps, where thieves and murderers lay in ambush, where meetings took place by torchlight or in impenetrable darkness, it was at the risk of your head that you kept a rendezvous with some Héloïse. To give himself over to such chaos, a man would have to be truly in love; to violate the prevailing moral code, he would have to make great sacrifices. Not only would it be a question of facing unforeseen dangers, and braving the killing blade of the law, but also of having to conquer within himself the power of fixed habits, the authority of his family, the tyranny of domestic conventions, the opposition of his conscience, and the terrors and duties of a Christian. All these obstacles would double the energy of one's passions.

In 1788, I was not about to follow a starving wretch who would have dragged me into her hovel under the surveillance of the police, but it is possible that, in 1606, I would have pursued an adventure of the kind so beautifully recounted by Marshal Bassompierre.

"About five or six months ago," the marshal writes, "every time I crossed the Petit-Pont (for in those days the Pont-Neuf was not yet built), a beautiful woman, a seamstress at Les Deux-Anges would make me a deep curtsy and follow me with her eyes as long as she could; and as I had taken note of this gesture, I began to look at her and treat her with new attention.

"It happened that one day I was returning from Fontainebleau to Paris over the Petit-Pont, and as soon as she saw me coming she stood in the doorway of her shop and said as I passed: 'I am your servant, Monsieur.' I bowed to her, and, turning back to look at her from time to time, I saw that she followed me with her eyes as long as she could."

Bassompierre arranged a rendezvous. "I found," he says, "a very beautiful woman, aged twenty, her hair done up for the night, dressed in nothing but a very thin chemise and a little skirt made of emerald ratteen, with slippers on her feet and a shawl wrapped around her. She was very pleasing to me. I asked if I could not see her again. 'If you wish to see me again,' she replied, 'it will have to be in the rue Bourg-l'Abbé, near Les Halles, next to the rue aux Ours, the third door on the rue Saint-Martin side. I shall wait for you there from ten until midnight, and later still. I shall leave the door open. In the entryway there is a little passage that you must hurry through, for my aunt's door opens onto it, and there you will find a stairwell that will take you up to the second floor.'

"I went at ten o'clock and found the door she had described, and I saw a big bright light, not only on the second floor, but on the third and the first floor as well. The door, however, was shut. I knocked to announce my arrival, but I heard a man's voice, which asked me who I was. I turned around and walked to the rue aux Ours, and then, circling back again, and finding the door open, I went up to the second floor. I found that the light came from the straw of a bed that was being burned there, and I saw two naked bodies laid out on a table in this same room. I staggered backward quite astonished. Then, on my way out, I encountered a group of crows (*buriers of the dead*) who asked me what I was after; and I, so as to have done with them, took my sword in hand and went past them, returning to my lodgings, not a little disturbed by this unexpected sight."

I went, in my turn, on a quest for the address given two hundred and forty years earlier by Bassompierre. I crossed the Petit-Pont, passed Les Halles, and followed the rue Saint-Denis until the rue aux Ours appeared on my right; the first street on the left, joining the rue aux Ours, is the rue Bourg-l'Abbé. The street sign, blackened by time and smoke, gave me high hopes. The storyteller's information was so accurate that, on the rue Saint-Martin side, I soon found the "third door on the left." There, sadly, the two and a half centuries that I had at first thought remained in the street disappeared. The façade of the house is modern, and no light shone from the first, nor the second, nor the third floor. From the windows of the attic, beneath the roof, there was a garland of nasturtiums and sweet peas; on the ground floor, a hairdresser's shop displayed a multitude of braided hair behind its glass.

Quite disappointed, I entered this Museum of Éponines. Ever since the Roman conquest, the Gauls have been selling their blond tresses to less well-adorned heads. My countrywomen in Brittany still have themselves shorn on certain feast days: they trade their natural headdress for an Indian kerchief. Addressing myself to a wigmaker busy dragging his iron comb through a wig, I said, "Monsieur, by any chance have you purchased the hair of a young seamstress who used to live at the Deux-Anges, near the Petit-Pont?" He stared at me flabbergasted, unable to say yes or no; I excused myself, muttering a thousand apologies, through a labyrinth of toupees.

Now I wandered from door to door. I found no twenty-year-old seamstress making "deep curtsies" to me; no frank, disinterested, passionate young woman, "her hair done up for the night, dressed in nothing but a very thin chemise and a little skirt made of emerald ratteen, with slippers on her feet and a shawl wrapped around her"; only a grumpy old crone ready to rejoin her teeth in the grave who tried to beat me with her crutch: perhaps she was the aunt of the rendezvous.

What a wonderful story, this story of Bassompierre's! It allows us to understand one of the reasons why he was so resolutely beloved. In his day, the French were still separated into two distinct classes, one dominant and the other half-servile. The seamstress held Bassompierre in her arms like a demigod descended into the heart of a slave: he gave her the illusion of glory, and French women, above all other women, are prone to be intoxicated by this illusion.

But who will reveal to us the obscure agents of the catastrophe? Was it the fetching grisette of the Deux-Anges whose body lay on the table beside the other body? And who was this second person? Was it the husband, or the man whose voice Bassompierre had heard? Was it the plague (for there was plague at that time in Paris) or jealousy that rushed down the rue Bourg-l'Abbé ahead of love? The imagination runs wild with such a subject. Combine a poet's inventions with music-hall songs, the gravediggers rushing onto the scene, the "crows" and Bassompierre's sword—a superb melodrama would come of the adventure.

You will no doubt admire the chastity and restraint of my youth in Paris. In this capital where I was free to surrender myself to all my whims, as in the Abbey of Thélème, where everyone did whatever he desired, I did not abuse my independence in the least.[7] The only congress I had was with a two-hundred-and-sixteen-year-old courtesan who had formerly been smitten with a French marshal, Henry IV's rival for the affections of Mademoiselle de Montmorency and the lover of Mademoiselle d'Entragues, whose sister the Marquise de Verneuil spoke so unfavorably of Henry IV. Louis XVI, whom I was about to meet, would never have suspected my secret connections with his family.

9.
PRESENTATION AT VERSAILLES—HUNTING WITH THE KING

Berlin, March 1821

THE FATAL day came, and I had to set off for Versailles more dead than alive. My brother accompanied me there on the eve of my presentation and brought me to the house of the Marshal de Duras, a gallant man, whose wit was so unremarkable that it made his fine manners seem somewhat bourgeois. This good man inspired me nonetheless with a horrible fear.

The next morning, I went to the palace alone. He has seen nothing who has not seen the pomp of Versailles, even after the dismissal of the King's old entourage: the spirit of Louis XIV was still there.

Things went well so long as I only had to pass through the guardrooms. Military pageantry has always pleased me and has never overawed me. But when I entered the Oeuil-de-Boeuf and found myself among the courtiers, my difficulties began. They peered at me; I heard them asking who I was. One must remember the former prestige of royalty to understand the importance of a presentation in those days. A mysterious sense of destiny attached itself to the debutant; he was spared the self-protective expressions of contempt, mixed with extreme politesse, which defined the inimitable manners of the grandees. Who knew whether this debutant would not became a favorite of the King? He was respected for the future servitude with which he might be honored. Today, we rush to the palace with even more enthusiasm than in former times and, what is strange, without illusions: a courtier reduced to living on truths is bound to die of hunger.

When the King's levee was announced, the people who were not to be presented withdrew. I felt a touch of vanity: I was not proud of remaining, but I would have been humiliated to leave. The door to the King's bedroom opened, and I saw the King, in accordance with custom, finishing his toilette, which is to say taking his hat from the first gentleman-in-waiting. The King approached on his way to Mass. I bowed, and the Marshal de Duras introduced me: "Sire, the Chevalier de Chateaubriand."

The King looked at me, returned my bow, hesitated, and for a moment seemed as if he wanted to stop and say a word to me. I would have replied with a calm countenance: my timidity had vanished. Speaking to the general of an army or a head of state has always seemed quite simple to me, though I cannot explain why that has been my experience. The King, more embarrassed than I, found nothing to say to me and passed on. The vanity of human destinies! This sovereign, whom I was seeing for the first time, this profoundly powerful monarch was Louis XVI six years from the scaffold. And this new courtier whom he had scarcely looked in the eye, charged with sorting bones from bones, many years after being presented upon proof of nobility to the grandeurs of this descendant of Saint Louis, would one day be presented, upon proof of loyalty, to his dust.[8] A twofold mark of respect for the twofold royalty of the scepter and the pen! Louis XVI might have answered his judges as Christ answered the Jews: "Many good works I have shown you: for which of these works do you stone me?"

We hurried to the gallery to see the Queen as she came back from the chapel. She appeared, surrounded by a copious and radiant retinue. She made us a stately curtsy; she seemed enchanted by life. One day, those lovely hands, then carrying the scepter of a long line of kings with such grace, were destined, before being bound by the executioner, to mend the rags of a widow, a prisoner in the Conciergerie!

My brother had obtained a sacrifice from me, but it was not in his power to make me pursue my privileges any further. He begged me in vain to stay in Versailles to attend the Queen's card game in the evening. "You will be presented to the Queen," he told me, "and the

King will speak to you." He could not have given me a better reason to flee. I hastened to hide my glory in a furnished room, happy to have escaped the Court, but seeing before me the terrible day of the carriages, February 19, 1787.

The Duc de Coigny had sent a message informing me that I was to hunt with the King in the Forest of Saint-Germain. I set out early in the morning to meet my punishment in full debutant attire: a gray coat, red waistcoat and trousers, lace-topped riding boots, a hunting knife at my side, and a little gold-laced French hat on my head. There were then four debutants at the Palace of Versailles: myself, the two Messieurs de Saint-Marsault, and the Comte d'Hautefeuille.* The Duc de Coigny, whose name was so fatal to the Queen, gave us our instructions.[9] He warned us not to cross the scent, as the King became angry if anyone came between him and his game. The place of the meet was to be Laval, in the Forest of Saint-Germain, an estate leased by the Crown from the Marshal de Beauvau. The horses of the first hunt, in which the debutants took part, were to be provided, as tradition dictated, by the Royal Stables.†

The drummers beat the march: a voice gave the order to present arms. They cried: *The King*! And the King came out and climbed into his coach: we rode in carriages behind him. It was a long way from this hunting expedition with the King of France to my hunting excursions on the moors of Brittany, and an even longer way to my hunting expeditions with the savages of North America. But my life has been full of such contrasts.

We reached the rallying point, where a number of saddle horses, held in hand beneath the trees, were betraying signs of impatience.

---

*I have met M. le Comte d'Hautefeuille again. He is in the midst of translating a few selected poems by Lord Byron; and Madame la Comtesse d'Hautefeuille is the very talented author of the *Exiled Soul*, etc. etc.

†In the *Gazette de France* of Tuesday, February twenty-seventh, 1787, one may read: "Le Comte Charles d'Hautefeuille, le Baron de Saint-Marsault, le Baron de Saint-Marsault-Chatelaillon, and le Chevalier de Chateaubriand who had previously had the honor of being presented to the King, have received, on February nineteenth, the honor of riding in His Majesty's carriages, and of following the hunt."

The carriages drawn up in the forest with their guards standing by; the groups of men and women; the packs of hounds barely contained by the huntsmen; the dogs barking, the horses neighing, and the sound of the horns: all this made for a lively scene. The hunts of our kings brought to mind both the old and the new customs of the monarchy: the primitive pastimes of Clodion, Chilpéric, and Dagobert, and the elegant amusements of François I, Henri IV, and Louis XIV.

I was too full of my reading not to see Comtesses de Chateaubriand, Duchesses d'Étampes, Gabrielles d'Éstrées, La Vallières, and Montespans everywhere. My imagination took this hunt historically, and I felt myself at ease. Besides, I was in a forest: I was at home.

Stepping down from the carriage, I presented my ticket to the huntsmen. I was destined for a mare named "l'Heureuse," a light-footed beast, but hard-mouthed, skittish, and capricious: a fair enough image of my fate, which never ceases setting back its ears. The King mounted and rode off; the hunting party followed him by a different route. I was left in the dust to do battle with l'Heureuse, who was unwilling to let her new master straddle her. Finally, I somehow managed to launch myself on her back. The hunt was already far off.

I mastered l'Heureuse well enough at first. Forced to shorten her stride, she arched her neck, chewed the bit till it was white with foam, and bounded along sideways; but when she came near the action, there was no holding her. She thrust forth her head, jerked my hands past her withers, and galloped hard into a knot of hunters, sweeping aside everything in her path and stopping only when she collided with the horse of a woman who nearly tumbled to the ground, to the roaring laughter of some and the frightened shouts of others. I have tried in vain today to recall the name of this woman, who accepted my apologies graciously. Word quickly spread of the debutant's "adventure."

But I had not come to the end of my trials. About half an hour after my first blunder, I was riding across a wide clearing in a deserted part of the woods; there was a pavilion at the end of the clearing, and I began to think of the palaces scattered everywhere around the royal forests, recalling the longhaired kings and their mysterious pleasures, when suddenly a shot rang out. L'Heureuse veered abruptly, charged headfirst into a thicket, and carried me to the very spot where a stag had just been brought down. The King appeared.

I remembered then, but too late, the Duc de Coigny's injunctions. The damned Heureuse had violated them all. I leapt to the ground, pushed back my mare with one hand, and held my hat low in the other. The King looked at me and saw only a debutant who had arrived at the kill before him. He felt he had to speak, but instead of losing his temper he laughed and said, in a good-humored voice, "He did not hold out long!" These were the only words that I ever had from Louis XVI. People swarmed in from every side, amazed to find me "chatting" with the King. The debutant Chateaubriand stirred up some rumors with his two adventures, but, as it has always been since, he did not know how to profit from either good fortune or bad.

The King brought down three more stags. Since debutants were only permitted to run after the first animal, I went back to Le Val with my companions to wait for the other hunters to return.

When the King arrived at Le Val, he was in good spirits and talked cheerfully about the mishaps of the hunt. We then took the road back to Versailles. Another disappointment for my brother: instead of going to get dressed for the King's unbooting ceremony, a moment of triumph and favor, I threw myself into the depths of my carriage and returned to Paris, elated to be free of all honors and humiliations. I told my brother that I was determined to return to Brittany.

Content to have made his name known, and hoping one day to bring to term, by means of his own presentation, that which had been aborted in mine, he did not oppose the departure of his freakish younger brother.*

Such was my first glimpse of the City and the Court. Society seemed to me even more odious than I had imagined it; but if it

* The *Mémorial historique de la Noblesse* published an unedited document, annotated in the King's hand, pulled from the Royal Archives, *section historique*, register M 813 and box M 814. This document contains the "Entrances." My name and my brother's name appear in it: further proof that my memory has served me well regarding these dates. (Paris, 1840)

frightened me, it did not discourage me. I felt, in a confused way, that I was superior to what I had seen. I came away with an unconquerable disgust for the Court, and this disgust, or rather this contempt, which I have never been able to conceal, will prevent me from succeeding, or it will bring about my downfall at the high point of my career.

But if I judged the world without knowing it, the world, in its turn, knew nothing of me. No one present at my debut guessed what I was worth, and when I went back to Paris no one there guessed any better. Since my sad fame has spread, many people have said to me, "How we should have noticed you, if we had met you in your youth!" This friendly pretension is nothing but an illusion produced by an already established reputation. Men are all alike on the outside. In vain does Rousseau tell us that he had two small, very charming eyes. It makes us no less certain, in light of his portraits, that he looked like a schoolmaster or a grouchy cobbler.

To have done with the Court, I should say that, after returning to Brittany and then going back to Paris to live with my sisters Lucile and Julie, I plunged more deeply than ever into my solitary habits. One may ask what became of the story of my presentation. In truth, it went no further.

"Then you never hunted with the King again?"

"No more than I did with the Emperor of China."

"And you never returned to Versailles?"

"I went as far as Sèvres a couple of times, but my heart failed me, and I turned back to Paris."

"And you made nothing of your position?"

"Nothing."

"So what did you do?"

"I got bored."

"Then you felt no ambition?"

"I did indeed. By dint of much worry and intrigue, I achieved the glory of publishing an idyll in the *Almanach des Muses*. Its appearance nearly killed me with hope and fear. I would have given all the King's carriages to have written the ballad 'Ô ma tendre musette!' or 'De mon berger volage.'"

Good for anything where others are concerned, good for nothing when it comes to myself: there you have me.

10.

JOURNEY TO BRITTANY—GARRISON IN DIEPPE— RETURN TO PARIS WITH LUCILE AND JULIE

Paris, June 1821

EVERYTHING that you have read so far in this fourth book was written in Berlin. I have since returned to Paris for the Duc de Bordeaux's baptism, and I have resigned my embassy out of political loyalty to M. de Villèle, who has left the ministry. Now that I've surrendered myself to leisure, let me write. As these *Memoirs* fill up with my bygone years, they put me more and more in mind of the lower bulb of an hourglass which shows me just how much dust has dropped out of my life: when all the sand has sifted down, I would not flip my glass timepiece over again, even if God granted me the power to do so.

The new solitude into which I entered in Brittany after my presentation was not like the solitude at Combourg: it was neither so absolute, nor so grave, nor, to tell the truth, so obligatory. It was permissible for me to leave it, and so it lost its value. An ancient Lady engraved on a shield and an old Baron emblazoned on a panel, keeping watch over the last of their daughters and the last of their sons in a feudal house, offered up what the English call "characters": there was nothing provincial or constricting about this life, because it was not the life led by the rest of the world.

Where my sisters lived, the whole province seemed to come together in the fields. Neighbors danced at neighbors' houses and put on plays in which I was sometimes an inept actor. In wintertime, one had to endure the small town society of Fougères: the balls, the assemblies, and the dinners where I could not, as in Paris, be forgotten.

Then again, I had not seen the Army and the Court without undergoing a change of ideas. Despite my natural tastes, something in me was rebelling against obscurity and imploring me to emerge from the shadows; Julie held provincial life in horror; the instincts of genius and beauty were pushing Lucile toward a wider stage. I therefore began to feel uneasy about my existence in Brittany. Something told me that this existence was not my destiny.

Yet I loved the country, and the country near Marigny was delightful.* My regiment had changed its quarters: the first battalion was garrisoned in Le Havre, the second in Dieppe. I rejoined the latter and discovered that my presentation had made a celebrity of me. I began to develop a taste for my profession. I worked hard at my drills, and I was put in charge of recruits, whom I marched up and down the pebbles by the sea. That sea has formed the background of almost every scene of my life.

La Martinière did not concern himself in Dieppe with his namesake, Lamartinière, nor with the Father Simon, who wrote against Bossuet, Port-Royal, and the Benedictines, nor with the anatomist Pecquet, whom Madame de Sévigné called "*le petit* Pecquet"; but La Martinière was in love in Dieppe, as he had been in Cambrai. He wilted at the feet of a formidable Norman whose headdress and coiffure were near half a fathom high. She was not a young woman. By a singular coincidence, she was named Cauchie, a granddaughter of that Anne Cauchie of Dieppe who, in 1645, was one hundred and fifty years old.[10]

It was in 1647 that Anne of Austria, looking at the sea, as I did, through the windows of her room, passed the time by watching the fire-ships burn for her amusement. She let the people who had been loyal to Henri IV keep watch over the young Louis XIV, and she showered these people with infinite benedictions, "in spite of their vile Norman tongue."[11]

---

*Marigny has changed significantly since the days when my sister lived there. It was sold and today belongs to the Pommereuls, who have had the house rebuilt and completely renovated.

Some of the feudal royalties that I had seen paid in Combourg still prevailed in Dieppe: to a householder named Vauquelin there were due three pigs' heads, each with an orange between its teeth, and three sous of the oldest known coinage.

I went back to spend a six-month leave in Fougères. The place was now presided over by a noble old maid named Mademoiselle de La Belinaye, the aunt of that Comtesse de Tronjoli whom I have already mentioned. An agreeably ugly young woman, the sister of an officer in the Condé Regiment, attracted my attention. I would not have had the temerity to raise my eyes to beauty; it was only in the presence of a woman's imperfections that I dared risk a respectful homage.

Madame de Farcy, still suffering, had finally resolved to decamp from Brittany. She decided that Lucile should go with her, and Lucile, in her turn, conquered my repugnance. Together we took the road to Paris, in a sweet partnership of the three youngest birds of the nest.

My brother was married by then, and residing with his father-in-law, the President de Rosambo, in the rue de Bondy. We decided to settle in the same neighborhood. Through the good offices of M. Delisle de Sales, who lived in the Saint-Lazare pavilions, we secured an apartment in these same pavilions, at the top of the Faubourg Saint-Denis.

11.

DELISLE DE SALES—FLINS—LIFE OF A MAN OF LETTERS

Paris, June 1821

MADAME de Farcy was already acquainted, I know not how, with Delisle de Sales, who had once been confined in the Vincennes for some philosophical nonsense or other. In those days, men became famous if they scribbled a few lines of prose or published a quatrain in the *Almanach des Muses*. This elderly man, very kind, very cordially mediocre, was content to relax his mind and let the years roll by him. He had amassed a fine library of his own works, which he lent out to strangers and which no one in Paris ever read. Every year, in the spring, he would replenish his ideas in Germany. Fat and unwashed, he carried with him everywhere a roll of dirty paper that could be seen protruding from his pocket: he used to stop on street corners and consign his passing thoughts to this filthy scroll. On the pedestal of his marble bust, he had with his own two hands traced the following inscription, borrowed from a bust of Buffon: GOD, MAN, NATURE, HE HAS EXPLAINED THEM ALL. Delisle de Sales had explained them all! Such pomposities are quite amusing, but also quite disheartening. Who can flatter himself and claim that he has real talent? Might it not be that, so long as we live, we are under the sway of an illusion similar to that of Delisle de Sales? I would wager that some author who is reading this sentence believes himself a writer of genius and is in fact nothing but a cretin.

If I have lingered overlong on my account of this good man of the Saint-Lazare pavilions, it is only because he was the first literary person I ever met. He introduced me into the company of others.

The presence of my sisters made my sojourn in Paris less intolerable, and my taste for letters still further weakened my disgust for the place. Delisle de Sales seemed to me a titan. At his apartment, I met Carbon Flins des Oliviers, who fell in love with Madame de Farcy. She mocked him for it, but he took the thing well, for he prided himself on being good company. Flins introduced me to Fontanes, his friend, who would soon become a friend of mine.

The son of a Warden of Waters and Forests in Reims, Flins had a negligible education; even so, he was a man of wit and sometimes of talent. It would be impossible to see anything fatter than him. He was a short, bloated man with large protruding eyes, bristly hair, dirty teeth, and yet, in spite of all this, a not ignoble bearing. His style of life, which resembled that of almost all Parisian men of letters at the time, merits some description.

Flins occupied an apartment on the rue Mazarine, not far from La Harpe's apartment on the rue Guénégaud. Two Savoyards, disguised as lackeys by means of livery cloaks, waited on him hand and foot. In the evenings they accompanied him everywhere, and in the mornings they opened the door to all his visitors. Flins went regularly to the Théâtre-Français, which was then in the Odéon and especially known for its comedies. Brizard was coming to the end of his career; Talma was just starting out. Larive, Saint-Phal, Fleury, Molé, Dazincourt, Dugazon, Grandmesnil, Mesdames Contat, Saint-Val, Desgarcins, and Olivier were all at the height of their powers, and waiting in the wings was Mademoiselle Mars, the daughter of Monvel, about to make her debut at the Théâtre Montansier. Actresses looked after their authors then, and were frequently the occasion of their fortune.

Flins, who received only a small allowance from his family, lived on credit. When Parliament was not in session, he would pawn his Savoyards' livery cloaks, his two watches, his rings, and his linen, pay with the loan what he had to pay, and set off for Reims, where he would stay three months before returning to Paris, redeeming what he had pawned at Mont-de-Piété with the money his father had given him, and resuming the rounds of his life, always cheerful and well received.

12.

MEN OF LETTERS—PORTRAITS

Paris, June 1821

IN THE course of the two years that passed between my settling in Paris and the opening of the Estates-General, my social circle widened. I knew the Chevalier du Parny's elegies by heart, as I know them still, and I wrote him, asking permission to meet a poet whose works delighted me. He sent me a courteous reply: I went to call on him in the rue de Cléry.

I found a still-youngish man, very proper, very tall and thin, with a face marked by smallpox. He returned my visit, and I introduced him to my sisters. He did not much care for society and was soon driven from it by his politics: he was then of the old party. I have never known a writer more similar to his works. A poet and a creole, he lacked for nothing but the Indian sky, a spring, a palm tree, and a wife. He recoiled from fame and tried to glide through life unnoticed. He sacrificed everything to his idleness and was never betrayed in his obscurity except by his pleasures, which played in passing on his lyre:

> *Que notre vie heureuse et fortunée*
> *Coule en secret, sous l'aile des amours,*
> *Comme un ruisseau qui, murmurant à peine,*
> *Et dans son lit resserrant tous ses flots,*
> *Cherche avec soin l'ombre des arbrisseaux,*
> *Et n'ose pas se montrer dans la plaine.* [12]

It was his inability to tear himself away from his indolence that turned the Chevalier de Parny from a frenzied aristocrat into a miserable revolutionary, attacking a persecuted religion and its priests on the scaffold, buying his peace at any price, and lending to the Muse that sang of Éléonore the language of those places where Camille Desmoulins went to haggle for his whores.

The author of the *Histoire de la littérature italienne*, who stole into the Revolution in Chamfort's wake, came to meet us through that *cousinage* which exists among all Bretons: Ginguené lived in society on the reputation of a stylish enough piece of verse, *La Confession de Zulmé*, which earned him a pitiful place in M. de Necker's offices; hence his piece on entering the Contrôle-Général. I don't know who claimed that Ginguené hadn't written *La Confession de Zulmé*, the title that won him his glory, but he was in fact responsible for it.

This poet from Rennes knew music well and composed ballads. His origins were humble, but the more he attached himself to well-known men, the more arrogant he became. Around the time that the Estates-General convened, Chamfort tasked him with scribbling some articles for the newspapers and some speeches for the clubs. Suddenly he was superior. At the first Federation he said, "What a lovely affair! But we could light the place better if we burned four aristocrats, one at each corner of the altar." There was nothing original in his wish. Long before him, Louis Dorléans, the Leaguer, had written in his *Banquet du Comte d'Arête*, "We ought to stack the Protestant ministers like faggots on the Midsummer's Night bonfire and drown Henri IV like a cat in a barrel."

Ginguené had advance knowledge of the Revolutionary murders. Madame Ginguené warned my sisters and my wife about the massacre that was to take place at the Carmelite convent and gave them refuge. My sisters were then living in the cul-de-sac Férou, close to the place where so many throats were cut.

After the Terror, Ginguené became what might as well have been the Minister of Public Education of France. It was then that he sang "l'Arbre de la liberté" at the Cadran-Bleu, to the tune of "Je l'ai planté, je l'ai vu naître."[13] He was judged philosophically smug enough to serve as an envoy to one of those kings that were dethroned. He wrote from Turin to M. de Talleyrand that he had "conquered a prejudice" because he had caused his wife to be received at Court *en pet-en-l'air*.[14] Tumbling from mediocrity into importance, from importance into foolishness, and from foolishness into ridiculousness, he ended his days as a distinguished literary critic and, what's better still, an independent writer in the *Décade Philosophique*. Nature had carried him back to the place from which society had dragged him to no good purpose. His knowledge is secondhand, his prose heavy, his poetry correct and sometimes pleasant.

The poet Lebrun was Ginguené's friend. Ginguené protected him as a man of talent, who knows the world, protects the simplicity of a man of genius; Lebrun, in his turn, shed his luster on the eminence of Ginguené. Nothing was more comical than the roles played by these two friends, rendering each other, by amiable commerce, every service that can be rendered by two men superior in different spheres.

Lebrun was quite simply a pretender to the Empyrean. His vigor was as cold as his ecstasies were frozen. His Parnassus, an upper room on the rue Montmartre, was furnished exclusively with books piled pell-mell on the floor, a burlap bed with two dirty towels for curtains hanging from a rusty iron rod, and a broken water jug propped against a broken-down chair. It was not so much that Lebrun was poor, but that he was miserly and devoted to loose women.

At M. de Vaudreuil's classical dinner, Lebrun played the character of Pindar. Among his lyric poems, one finds energetic and elegant stanzas, as in the ode to the ship *Le Vengeur* and in the ode to *Les Environs de Paris*. But his elegies emerged from his head, rarely from his soul; he possessed a studied rather than a natural originality, and he created nothing except by force of artifice. He wore himself out perverting the sense of words and conjoining them in monstrous combinations. His real talent was for satire, and his epistle on *la bonne et la mauvaise plaisanterie* has enjoyed well-deserved praise. A few of his epigrams are comparable to those of J.-B. Rousseau; in this regard,

La Harpe in particular inspired him. And one more justice must be done to him: he remained independent under Bonaparte and has left some wrathful verses lambasting the oppressor of our freedoms.

But, without question, the most bilious man of letters I knew in Paris at that time was Chamfort. Infected by the same malady that made the Jacobins, he could not forgive mankind for the accident of his birth. He betrayed the confidence of the houses into which he was admitted. He mistook his own cynical language for an accurate description of the manners of the Court. No one can deny that he had wit and talent, but wit and talent of the kind that does not reach posterity. When he saw that he would come to nothing under the Revolution, he turned against himself those same hands that he had once raised against society. The red cap appeared to his pride as no more than another sort of crown and sans-culottism as another sort of nobility, of which the Marats and the Robespierres were high and puissant lords. Furious to find inequalities of rank persisting in this world of sorrow and tears, condemned to be no more than a *vilain* in the feudality of the executioners, he tried to kill himself to escape from the magnificos of crime. He failed. Death laughs at those who summon it and confuse it with nothingness.

I did not know the Abbé Delille until 1798, in London, and I never saw Rulhière, who lives through Madame d'Egmont and who makes her live, nor Palissot, nor Beaumarchais, nor Marmontel. The same goes for Chénier, whom I never met, who has attacked me (I never replied), and whose seat at the Institute would cause one of the crises of my life.[15]

When I reread most of the eighteenth-century writers today, I am puzzled by both the ruckus they raised and by my former admiration of them. Whether our language has progressed or retrogressed, whether we have marched toward civilization or beat a retreat toward barbarism, I know that I find something exhausted, passé, pallid, lifeless, and cold in these authors who were the delight of my youth. Even in the greatest writers of the Voltairean age, I find a poverty of feeling, thought, and style.

Who is to blame for my mistake? I am afraid that I have been the most at fault. I was a born innovator, and it may be that I have communicated to the new generations the same malady with which I was infected. Horrified, I have often yelled at the young, "Don't forget your French!" They reply as the Limousin did to Pantagruel, "From alme, inclyte and celebrate academy, which is vocitated Lutetia."[16]

The mania for Hellenizing and Latinizing our language is not really new, as we can discern: Rabelais cures it, it reappears in Ronsard, Boileau attacks it. In our days, it has been resuscitated by science. Our revolutionaries, great Greeks by nature, have obliged our shopkeepers and our peasants to learn hectares, hectoliters, kilometers, millimeters, and decagrams. Politics have "Ronsardized" everything.

I might have said something here about M. La Harpe, whom I still know and to whom I will return; I might also have added a portrait of Fontanes to my gallery; but, although my connection with that excellent man began in 1789, it was only in England that we formed a friendship which has always been intensified by bad fortune and has never been diminished by good. I shall tell you more about this later, and with the full effusions of my heart. In doing so, I will have nothing to describe except talents that no longer console the earth. My friend's death came unexpectedly, at the very moment when my memories were leading me to retrace the beginning of his life. Our existence is so fleeting that if we do not record the events of the morning in the evening, the work overburdens us and we no longer have the time to bring it up to date. This doesn't prevent us from wasting our years and scattering to the winds those hours that for man are the seeds of eternity.

13.

THE ROSAMBO FAMILY—M. DE MALESHERBES: HIS PREDILECTION FOR LUCILE—APPEARANCE AND TRANSFORMATION OF MY SYLPHIDE

Paris, June 1821

IF MY INCLINATIONS and those of my sisters had launched me into Parisian literary society, our position forced us to frequent another circle. The family of my brother's wife was naturally at the center of this circle.

President Le Pelletier de Rosambo, who later died with such courage, was, when I arrived in Paris, a model of frivolity. In those days, everything was deranged in minds and in morals: it was a symptom of the revolution to come. Magistrates were ashamed to wear their robes and mocked the solemnity of their fathers. The Lamoignons, Molés, Séguiers, and d'Aguessaus wanted to fight, not deliberate. The presidents' wives, ceasing to be venerable mothers, left their dark mansions in search of radiant adventures. The priest in his pulpit steered clear of the name of Jesus Christ and spoke only of the "Christian Legislator." Ministers fell one after another. Power was slipping through everyone's fingers. The height of fashion was to be American in town, English at Court, and Prussian in the army: to be anything, in other words, except French. What people did and said was no more than a succession of inconsistencies. They pretended to care about priests, but they wanted nothing to do with religion. No one could be an officer if he wasn't a gentleman, but it was good form to rail against the nobility. Equality was introduced into the parlors, and flogging was introduced into the camps.

M. de Malesherbes had three daughters: Mesdames de Rosambo,

d'Aulnay, and de Montboissier. He was most affectionate toward Madame de Rosambo because her opinions most resembled his. Chairman de Rosambo also had three daughters: Mesdames de Chateaubriand, d'Aulnay, and de Tocqueville, and a son, whose brilliant mind is crowned with Christian perfection. M. de Malesherbes took pleasure in the company of his children, grandchildren, and great-grandchildren. Many a time, in the early days of the Revolution, I saw him come into Madame de Rosambo's house heated from politics, throw off his wig, lie down on the carpet in my sister-in-law's room, and start yelling and romping with the rowdy children. He would have been a man of rather vulgar manners had he not possessed a certain brusqueness that saved him from seeming common. At the first phrase that came from his lips, one sensed that he was both a man of old family and a superb magistrate. His natural virtues were a bit tainted by affectation, however, as a result of the philosophy that he had mingled with them. He was full of knowledge, probity, and courage; but he was hot-headed and passionate to the point that one day, in speaking to me of Condorcet, he said, "That man was my friend once, but today I would have no scruples about killing him like a dog." The tides of the Revolution swept over him, and his death brought him glory. The great man's merits would have remained forever hidden had bad luck not revealed them to the world. A Venetian noble once lost his life, retrieving his title deeds from a crumbling palace.

M. de Malesherbes's frankness freed me from all constraint. He found me not uneducated, and this was our first point of connection: we discussed botany and geography, two of his favorite subjects of conversation. It was in the course of talking with him that I conceived the idea of traveling to North America in search of the ocean first seen by Hearne and later by Mackenzie.* We understood each other's politics as well. The fundamentally generous sentiments of our first troubles appealed to my independent character, and the natural

*In recent years navigated by Captain Franklin and Captain Parry. (Geneva, 1831)

antipathy I felt for the Court only strengthened these leanings: I sided with M. de Malesherbes and Madame de Rosambo and against my brother, whom we nicknamed "the rabid Chateaubriand." The Revolution would have caught me up in its flow if it had not started with crimes. When I saw the first head carried at the end of a pike, I recoiled. In my eyes, murder will never be an object of admiration or an argument for freedom; I know of nothing more servile, more despicable, more cowardly, more narrow-minded than a terrorist. Right here in France, have I not met this whole race of Brutus hired out by Caesar and his police? The levelers, regenerators, and cutthroats were transformed into footmen, spies, sycophants, and, still less naturally, into dukes, counts, and barons! How medieval!

Finally, what made me so fond of the distinguished old man was his predilection for my sister. In spite of the Comtesse Lucile's shyness, he and I succeeded, with the help of a splash of champagne, in making her play a part in a little show put on for M. de Malesherbes's birthday. Lucile was so moving in this role that the good and great man's head was turned. He insisted even more strongly than my brother that she should be transferred from the Chapter of L'Argentière to Remiremont, where the rigorous and difficult proof of Sixteen Quarterings was required. Philosopher though he was, M. de Malesherbes held the principles of birth in high regard.

This picture of men and the world at the time I first appeared in society must be understood to occupy the space of about two years, from the closing of the first Assembly of Notables on May 25, 1787, to the opening of the Estates-General on May 5, 1789. During these two years, my sisters and I did not always stay in Paris or even in the vicinity of Paris. In the next book, I shall regress and take my readers back to Brittany.

All the while I was still half mad with my illusions. I missed my woods, but now past epochs, rather than distant places, had opened my eyes to another kind of solitude. In the old Paris, in the neighborhoods of Saint-Germain des-Prés, in the cloisters of monasteries, in the vaults of Saint-Denis, in Sainte-Chapelle and Notre-Dame, in all the narrow streets of the city, and at Héloïse's dark door, I saw my enchantress again. But, under the Gothic arches and among the tombs, there was something deathlike about her. She seemed pale and looked at me with sad eyes; she was no more than the shade or *manes*[17] of the dream I had loved.

BOOK FIVE

I.

FIRST POLITICAL STIRRINGS IN BRITTANY—A BRIEF
LOOK AT THE HISTORY OF THE MONARCHY

Paris, September 1821;
Revised in December 1846

MY POLITICAL education began during several different visits to
Brittany in 1787 and 1788. The Estates of the province furnished a
model of the Estates-General: the provincial troubles that broke out
in the Estates of Brittany and Dauphiné were harbingers of the national troubles to come.

The transformations that had been developing for two centuries
were coming to term. France had gone from a feudal monarchy to a
monarchy of the Estates-General, from a monarchy of the Estates-
General to a parliamentary monarchy, from a parliamentary monarchy
to an absolute monarchy, now tending, through the struggle between
the magistracy and the royal power, toward representative monarchy.

The Maupeou Parliament, the establishment of provincial assemblies in which individuals could vote, the first and second Assemblies
of Notables, the Plenary Court, the formation of large bailiwicks,
the civil reintegration of Protestants, the partial abolition of torture
and forced labor, and the equal division of taxation: all these things
were successive proofs of the revolution in progress. But then we could
not see these facts together: each event seemed to be an isolated accident. In all historical periods, there is a presiding spirit. Seeing only
one point, it is impossible for us to perceive the rays converging from
all the other points on a common center; we cannot trace back the
hidden agent that gives life and movement to the whole, as water or
fire gives life to machines. That is why, at the start of revolutions, so

many think it should suffice to break merely one wheel or another to keep the torrent from rushing forth or the steam from exploding.

The eighteenth century, a century of intellectual rather than material action, would not have succeeded in changing the laws so rapidly had it not stumbled on a suitable vehicle: the parliaments, and most notably the parliament of Paris, became the instruments of a philosophical system. Every opinion dies powerless or mad if it lacks an assembly to lend it strength and willpower, to give it hands and a tongue. It is and will always be through bodies, legal or illegal, that revolutions arise and continue to arise.

The parliaments had their own reasons for vengeance. Absolute monarchy had robbed them of the authority that they had usurped from the Estates-General. Enforced registrations, beds of justice, and sentences of exile increased the magistrates' popularity and drove them to plead for liberties in which they did not sincerely believe. They called for the restoration of the Estates-General, but they didn't dare admit that they wanted political and legislative power for themselves. In this way, they hastened the resurrection of a body whose inheritance they had reaped, a body that, on returning to life, would instantly reduce them to their own special function: the administration of justice. Men, whether they are moved by wisdom or passion, are almost always mistaken about what is in their own interest: Louis XVI restored the parliaments that forced him to summon the Estates-General; the Estates-General, transformed into the National Assembly and the Convention, destroyed both the throne and the parliaments, and condemned to death both the judges and the monarch from whom justice emanated. Louis XVI and the parliaments acted as they did because they were, without knowing it, instruments of a social revolution.

The idea of the Estates-General was already on everyone's mind, only no one could see where it would lead. It was, for the masses, a question of how to make up a deficit that today the lowliest banker would be sure to eliminate. Such a violent remedy, applied to such a trivial evil, proved that we were being carried into uncharted political waters. In 1786, the only year for which financial accounts are well established, receipts added up to 412,924,000 livres and expenditures were 593,542,000 livres. Thus the deficit was 180,618,000 livres, reduced to 140 million by 40,618,000 livres in savings. According to this budget, the King's household is reckoned to have cost the immense sum of 37,200,000 livres: debts owed by the Princes, the acquisition of castles, and the depredations of the Court were the cause of this excess.

Everyone wanted the Estates-General to take the form they had in 1614. Historians always cite their form at that time as if, after 1614, nobody ever heard tell of the Estates-General or called on them to assemble. Yet, in 1651, the orders of the Nobility and the Clergy, at a meeting in Paris, did call on them to assemble: there is a fat bundle of acts passed and speeches delivered in the archives. The all-powerful Paris Parliament, far from seconding the wishes of the Nobility and the Clergy, dissolved their assemblies as illegal, which they were.

And while I am on the subject, I want to take note of another serious fact, which has escaped those who have meddled and are still meddling with writing the history of France without understanding it. Men speak of the "three orders" as the essential constituents of the so-called Estates-*General*. Well, in fact, it often happened that bailiwicks only nominated representatives from one or two of the orders. In 1614, the bailiwick of Amboise nominated no representative of the clergy or the Third Estate; Le Puy, La Rochelle, Le Lauraguais, Calais, La Haute-Marche, and Châtellerault sent no representative of the clergy; Montdidier and Roy sent no representative of the Nobility. Nevertheless, the Estates of 1614 were called the Estates-*General*. The old chronicles therefore express themselves more correctly when they speak of our national assemblies as including the "three Estates," or the "notable bourgeoisie," or the "barons and the bishops," as the case may be, and when they attribute to all of these assemblies, so composed, the same legislative power. In other provinces, the Third Estate, though having the right to be represented, appointed no delegates, for unremarked but quite natural reasons. The Third Estate had acquired total control of the magistracy and driven out all military men. It reigned there with absolute authority, except in a few noble parliaments, as judge, advocate, prosecutor, clerk, etc. It made both the criminal and the civil laws, and, by dint of its parliamentary usurpation, it took hold of great political power. The fortune, honor, and lives of citizens depended on the Third Estate. Everyone abided by its decrees, and every head fell beneath the broadsword of its justice. When it thus enjoyed such limitless power, what need was there for it to go looking for a paltry fraction of that power in assemblies where it could only appear on its knees?

The people, metamorphosed into monks, took refuge in cloisters and governed society by the power of religious opinion; the people, metamorphosed into tax collectors and bankers, took refuge in finance and governed society by the power of money; the people, metamorphosed into magistrates, took refuge in tribunals and governed society by the power of the law. The great kingdom of France, aristocratic in its parties and its provinces, was democratic as a whole: it acted under the direction of its king, with whom it maintained a marvelous understanding and almost always marched in step. It is this that explains the kingdom's long existence. There is a whole new history of France to be written about this, or, rather, the history of France remains unwritten.

All the great questions mentioned above were under continual debate in 1786, 1787, and 1788. The minds of my fellow Bretons found in their natural vivacity, in the privileges of the province, the clergy, and the nobility, in the clashes between the Parliament and the Estates, plenty of inflammatory material. M. de Calonne, the intendant of Brittany for a brief moment, further intensified divisions by favoring the cause of the Third Estate. M. de Montmorin and M. de Thiard were not strong enough leaders to gain power for the Court party. The Nobility formed a coalition with the Parliament, which was also noble: now it resisted M. Necker, M. de Calonne, and the Archbishop of Sens; now it repressed the popular movement, which its own early resistance had favored. It assembled, deliberated, and protested. And the communes and municipalities assembled, deliberated, and protested in opposition. The particular business of "hearth money," mixed up with general business, had only increased animosities. In order to understand this, one must first understand how the Duchy of Brittany was constituted.

2.

THE ESTATES OF BRITTANY—THE MEETING OF THE ESTATES

Paris, September 1821

THE ESTATES of Brittany were more or less varied in their constitution, as were all the other Estates of feudal Europe which they resembled. The kings of France had come into the full rights of the
dukes of Brittany. The marriage contract of the Duchesse Anne,
drawn up in the year 1491, not only gave Brittany as part of her dowry
to the crown of Charles VIII and Louis XII, it also stipulated a
transaction which was meant to end a disagreement dating back to
the days of Charles de Blois and the Comte de Montfort. The duchy
of Brittany maintained that the line of succession passed down through
daughters; the kingdom of France held that it passed solely through
sons and that, when the male line came to an end, Brittany, like a
giant fiefdom, should be returned to the crown. Charles VIII and
Anne, followed by Anne and Louis XII, mutually yielded their rights
and claims. Then Anne and Louis XII's daughter, Claude, who married François I, bequeathed the Duchy of Brittany to her husband.
François I, upon the petition of the Estates assembled at Vannes,
issued a public edict at Nantes, in 1532, which united the Duchy of
Brittany with the Crown of France while still guaranteeing this duchy
its liberties and privileges.

In those early days, the Estates of Brittany convened once each
year, but in 1630 their meetings became biannual. The governor would
announce the opening of the Estates. The three orders would assemble, according to their stations, in a church or in the halls of a
monastery, and each order would deliberate separately. There were

thus three private assemblies, raging with their three private storms, which turned into a collective hurricane when the Clergy, the Nobility, and the Third Estate convened. The Court then exuded discord, and on this cramped battlefield, as in a larger arena, talent, vanity, and ambition were in play.

In the dedication to his *French-Breton Dictionary*, Father Grégoire de Rostrenen, the Capuchin, speaks to our Lordships of the Estates of Brittany as follows:

> If it were unsuitable for a Roman orator to praise the dignified and august assembly of the Roman Senate, should it be suitable for me to venture an ode to your own august assembly, which so worthily recalls to us the idea of all that was honorable and majestic in Rome, both ancient and new?

Rostrenen goes on to prove that Celtic is one of the primitive languages that Gomer, Japhet's eldest son, brought to Europe, and that Bas-Bretons, despite their stature, are descended from giants. It's only too bad that the Breton children of Gomer, separated from France for such a long time, have let so many of their old title-deeds decay. Their charters, on which they did not place nearly enough importance as points of connection with the history of the world, too often lack the authenticity in which decipherers of certificates, on their side, put far too much value.

The season of the Estates of Brittany was a season of galas and balls. A person dined with M. the Commandant; he dined with M. the President of the Nobility; he dined with M. the President of the Clergy; he dined with M. the Treasurer of the Estates; he dined with M. the Intendant of the Province; he dined with M. the President of the Parliament: he dined everywhere, and drank everywhere too! Du Guesclin farmers and Duguay-Trouin sailors sat at long refectory tables with old-fashioned guardman's swords or short cutlasses at their sides. Seen all together, the gentlemen attending the Estates resembled a Polish Diet, but Poland on foot, not on horseback; a Diet of Scythians, not Sarmatians.

Unfortunately, everyone enjoyed himself too much; the balls never ended: Bretons are famous for their dances and their dancing tunes. Madame de Sévigné compared our political revels among the moorlands to the festivities of fairies and witches that used to take place on the heaths.

"I must tell you a bit of news about our Estates," she writes, "as your penalty for being Breton. M. de Chaulnes arrived on Sunday evening with all the noise that Vitré could muster. On Monday morning he wrote me a letter and sent it by one of his gentlemen. I answered by going to dine with him. Food is served at two tables in the same room; there are fourteen covers at each table; Monsieur presides at one and Madame at the other. There is far too much to eat, and whole platters of roast meat are carried away untouched; and the pyramids of fruit are so tall that doorways must be made higher. Our forefathers never anticipated mechanics such as these, since they had no notion that a door should be any taller than themselves.... After dinner, Messieurs de Lomaria and Coëtlogon danced some marvelous *passepieds* and minuets with two Breton ladies, to a tune which our own courtiers cannot even approach: they do Gypsy and Lower Breton steps with charming delicacy and precision.... Night and day there is gaming, good food and freedom, which attracts everybody. I had never seen the Estates; it is a very pretty thing. I cannot imagine any provincial assembly with so grand an air as this one. This province is full of nobility. Not one of them is away at the war or at Court except your brother, who may come back here one day like the rest.... A multitude of presents, pensions, road repairs and town restorations, fifteen or twenty huge tables, continual gaming, eternal balls, plays three times a week, lots of showing off, and there you have the Estates. Oh, and I am forgetting the four hundred pipes of wine drunk there."[1]

Bretons find it difficult to forgive Madame de Sévigné her mockery. I am less severe, but I do not like it when she says: "You speak very pleasantly of our miseries; we are no longer so roué: *one* in eight days is entirely given up to the business of justice. It is true that a hanging now seems to me quite refreshing." This is taking the cheerful language of the Court too far: Barère would speak of the guillotine with the same nonchalance. In 1793, the drownings at Nantes were referred to as "Republican marriages." Popular despotism reproduced the jaunty style of royal despotism.

The Parisian fops who traveled to the Estates with the King's men used to joke that we country squires lined our pockets with tin plate, so as to take home a few pieces of the Commandant's fricasseed chicken to our wives. These jokes cost the jokesters dearly. Not long ago, a Comte de Sabran was left dead in the square in return for one such flippant remark. This descendant of troubadours and Provençal kings, tall as a Swiss, was killed by a little hare-hunter from Morbihan no larger than a Laplander. This Ker yielded nothing to his adversary in genealogy.[2] If Saint Elzéar de Sabran was a close relative of Saint Louis, this noble Ker's great-uncle, Saint Corentin, was the Bishop of Quimper under King Gallon II, three hundred years before Christ.[3]

3.

THE KING'S REVENUE IN BRITTANY—PRIVATE
REVENUE OF THE PROVINCE—HEARTH MONEY—
MY FIRST POLITICAL GATHERING—SCENE

THE KING'S revenue in Brittany consisted of freely given sums that varied according to needs, income from the royal domains adding up to three or four hundred thousand francs, and the stamp tax, etc., etc.

Brittany had revenues of its own to meet its expenditures. The great duty, and the small duty laid on liquor and the transportation of liquor furnished two million a year. Finally, there were the sums raised by "hearth money." No one suspects the importance of hearth money to our history; but in fact it was to the French Revolution what the stamp tax was to the American.

Hearth money, or *fouage* (*census pro singulis focis exactus*), was a feudal censure, or a sort of tallage, levied on each commoner's fire. By gradually increasing *fouage*, the province covered its debts. In wartime, expenditures rose by more than seven million from one session to the next: a sum that exceeded the revenue. A plan was proposed to create capital from the funds collected by the tax and to consolidate this capital in a stock that would be to the benefit of the taxpayers. The injustice (although a *legal* injustice according to custom) lay in taxing only the property of commoners. The communes never stopped complaining; the Nobility, clinging less to their money than to their privileges, refused to entertain any arrangement that would make their property taxable. Such was the state of affairs in December 1788, when the bloody Estates of Brittany convened.

Minds were then agitated by various causes: the Assembly of Notables, territorial taxation, the coffee trade, the imminent meeting of the Estates-General and the affair of the necklace, the Plenary Court and the *Marriage of Figaro*, the large bailiwicks and Cagliostro and Mesmer, and a thousand other serious or trivial things that were the topic of controversy in every family.

The Breton nobility, on its own authority, had assembled in Rennes to protest the establishment of the Plenary Court. I went to this assembly. It was the first political gathering that I ever experienced. I was aghast and amused at the shouting I heard. Some climbed on tables and chairs; others gesticulated or talked over each other. The Marquis de Trémargat, a peg-leg, spoke out in stentorian voice: "Let us go to the Commandant, M. de Thiard, and say to him: 'The Breton nobility is at your door; we ask to speak with you. The King himself would not refuse!'"

At this eloquent eruption, cheers shook the rafters.

He raised his voice again: "The King himself would not refuse!"

The shouts and stamping redoubled.

We went to see M. le Comte de Thiard, a courtier, an erotic poet, a gentle and frivolous-minded man mortally tired of our agitation. He regarded us as so many screech owls, wild boars, and beasts of the jungle. He longed to be somewhere far from our Armorica, and had no desire whatsoever to refuse us entry to his house. Our spokesman told him what he wanted, after which we went back and drew up the following declaration: "We declare dishonorable all those who would accept any post either in the new administration of justice or in the administration of the Estates, which will not be sanctioned by the constitutional laws of Brittany." Twelve gentlemen were chosen to deliver this document to the King. On arriving in Paris, they were locked up in the Bastille, from which they soon emerged as heroes; they were greeted with laurels on their return. We wore coats trimmed in ermine with big mother-of-pearl buttons, and sewn around these buttons was a Latin motto: DEATH BEFORE DISHONOR. We triumphed over the Court, over which everyone would triumph, and we fell with it into the same abyss.

4.

MY MOTHER RETIRES TO SAINT-MALO

Paris, October 1821

IT WAS at this time that my brother, still pursuing his plans, took it upon himself to have me admitted to the Order of Malta. This meant that I would have to join the clergy, a favor that could be granted me by M. Courtois de Pressigny, the Bishop of Saint-Malo. I therefore went back to my native town, where my excellent mother had retired. She no longer had her children around her. She passed her days in church and her evenings in knitting. Her absent-mindedness was incredible: I saw her one morning in the street carrying one of her slippers under her arm instead of her prayer book. From time to time, a few old friends would come to visit her in her retreat and talk about the good old days. When she and I were alone, she would make up lovely stories in verse, which she improvised. In one of these stories the devil carried off a chimney (a heretic had been trapped inside it) and the poet cried out:

> All along the avenue
> The devil went so fast
> That he was lost to view
> Before an hour had passed.

"It seems to me," I said, "that the devil does not walk so fast after all."

But Madame de Chateaubriand proved to me that I didn't know what I was talking about: she was charming, my mother.

She knew by heart a long ballad about the True Story of a Wild Duck in the Town of Montfort-la-Cane-lez-Saint-Malo. A certain lord had imprisoned a young girl, a great beauty, in the Château de Montfort, and was planning to ravish her. At that moment, through a window, she saw the Church of Saint-Nicolas. She prayed to the saint with her eyes full of tears and was miraculously transported outside the castle walls. But she fell into the hands of some of the villain's servants, who wanted to use her as they supposed their master had already done. The poor girl was distraught. She looked around her in every direction for help but saw nothing except a few wild ducks on a pond. Renewing her prayers to Saint Nicolas, she besought him to make these animals witnesses to her innocence, so that, if she lost her life and could not discharge the vows she had made to the saint, the birds would fulfill these vows in their own fashion, in her name and on her behalf.

The girl died within the year: and behold, on the Feast of the Translation of the Bones of Saint Nicolas, on the ninth of May, a wild duck with her little ducklings came to the Church of Saint-Nicolas. The duck entered the church, flew before the image of the Blessed Liberator, and celebrated him by batting her wings; then she returned to the pond, having left one of her young ones behind as an offering. Some time later, the duckling went home too, though no one had seen it go. For two hundred years and more, the duck, and always the same duck, has come back with her brood, always on the same day, to the Church of Saint-Nicolas, in Montfort. This story was written down and printed in 1652. The author remarks, rightly enough, that "a wretched little duck is not a very considerable thing in the eyes of God, yet still she renders homage to God's greatness: Saint Francis's cicada was of even less account, yet his trilling charmed the heart of a seraph." But Madame de Chateaubriand followed a false tradition. In her version of the ballad, the girl imprisoned at Montfort was a princess who had herself been changed into a duck, in order to escape her captor's violence. I can recall but one verse of my mother's song:

The beautiful maid was made a duck,
Was made a duck, was made a duck,
And through the lattice off she flew till
She came to a pond full of lentils.

5.

TONSURE—THE LANDS AROUND SAINT-MALO

Paris, October 1821

AS MADAME de Chateaubriand was a true saint, she obtained the Bishop of Saint-Malo's promise to give me tonsure. The good man had some scruples about it. Bestowing the ecclesiastical mark on a military man seemed to him a profanation approaching simony. M. Courtois de Pressigny, today the Archbishop of Besançon and a peer of France, is a good and worthy man. He was young then. The Queen was his protector, and he was on the high road to fortune, which he later reached by a better route: persecution.

I knelt at the feet of this priest—dressed in my uniform, sword at my side—and he cut two or three locks of hair from the crown of my head. This was called tonsure, and I was given formal letters to prove it. With these letters, two hundred thousand livres a year would devolve to me, once my proofs of nobility had been accepted in Malta: an abuse, without question, of the ecclesiastical order, but a useful thing in the old political order. Wasn't it better for this sort of military benefice to be attached to the sword of a soldier than to the cloak of an abbot, who would have eaten up his fat revenues on the sidewalks of Paris?

The tonsure, conferred on me for reasons already mentioned, has caused some ill-informed biographers to say that I was once a man of the Church.

This happened in 1788. I had horses then, and I used to go riding in the country or galloping alongside the waves, my moaning friends of old: I would get down from my horse and frolic with them. All the baying family of Scylla jumped at my knees and nuzzled me: *Nunc vada latrantis Scyllae.*[4] I have gone far to admire natural scenes, but I should have been content with those offered me by my native lands.

Nothing is more charming than the landscape around Saint-Malo. The banks of the Rance, from the mouth of the river down to Dinan, are enough to warrant any traveler's attention: a continuous mixture of rock and verdure, beaches and forests, brooks and hamlets, ancient manors of feudal Brittany and modern houses of commercial Brittany. These latter houses were built at a time when the merchants of Saint-Malo were so rich that on spree days they used to fricassee pennies and throw them out the window to the crowd. They are extremely luxurious. Bonabant, the château of the Messieurs de Lasaudre, is built partly of marble imported from Genoa and has a magnificence that we scarcely imagine even in Paris. La Brillantais, Le Beau, Montmarin, La Balue, and Le Combier are, or were, adorned with orangeries, gushing fountains, and statues. Sometimes, the gardens slope down to the shore behind arcades formed by a portico of linden trees, through a colonnade of pine trees, to the end of a lawn. Over the tulip beds, the sea displays its ships, its calms, and its tempests.

Every peasant, sailor, and farmer owns a little white cottage with a garden. Among the potted herbs, the gooseberries, the roses, the irises, and the marigolds, you will find a shoot of Cayenne tea, a head of Virginia tobacco, or a Chinese flower: some souvenir of another shore and another sun, which forms the itinerary and the map of the gardener. The tenant farmers on the coast are of good Norman stock. The women are tall, slim, nimble; they wear gray woolen bodices, short petticoats made of calimanco and striped silk, and white stockings stitched with colorful clocks. Their foreheads are shaded by tall dimity or chambray headdresses whose flaps can either be turned up like a cap or worn loose like a veil. A silver chain hangs in knotted loops at their left side. Every morning, in spring, these daughters of the North step down from their boats as if they were invading the region once again. They carry baskets of fruit and scallop shells filled with curds to sell at market. When they steady with one hand the black jugs of milk or flowers balanced on their heads, and the white strings of their bonnets set off their blue eyes, their pink faces, and their blond hair beaded with dew, not even the Valkyries of the *Edda*, of whom the youngest is the *Future*, or the Canephori of Athens could have looked so graceful.[5] Does this picture still bear some resemblance to reality? These women, no doubt, are no more. Nothing remains of them but my memories.

6.

THE REVENANT—ILLNESS

Paris, October 1821

I LEFT my mother and went to see my elder sisters near Fougères. I stayed for a month with Madame de Châteaubourg. Her two country houses, Lascardais and Le Plessis, close to Saint-Aubin-du-Cormier, famous for its tower and its battle, were situated in a country of rocks, moors, and woodlands. For her steward, my sister had a man named M. Livoret, formerly a Jesuit, who had stumbled into a strange adventure.

When M. Livoret was appointed the steward of Lascardais, the elder Comte de Châteaubourg had only recently died. M. Livoret, who had never met him, was installed as the caretaker of the castle. The first night he slept there alone, he saw a pale old man in a dressing gown and a nightcap come into his bedroom holding a short candle. The apparition went to stand beside the hearth, placed his candlestick on the mantel, rekindled the fire, and then sat down in an armchair: M. Livoret trembled all over. After two hours of silence, the old man stood up, took his candlestick, and left the room, closing the door behind him.

The next day the steward recounted his adventure to the farmers, who, after listening to his description of the *lemur*, said they were sure it was their former master. But it did not end there. For if M. Livoret glanced behind him in the forest, he would see the phantom; if he had to climb over a stile in the fields, the shade would be straddling the wall beside him. One day, the poor persecuted wretch worked up the courage to say to the ghost, "Monsieur de Châteaubourg, please leave me alone."

To which the ghost replied, "No."

M. Livoret, a cold and matter-of-fact man with no great powers of imagination, would retell this story to anyone who wanted to hear it, always in the same tone of voice and with the same conviction.

Not long after, I traveled to Normandy with a brave officer who had suffered an attack of brain fever. We were given lodgings in a farmhouse. An old tapestry lent to us by the owner of the place separated my bed from the bed of the sick man. Behind this tapestry, the patient was bled and, to ease his suffering, plunged repeatedly into icy baths. He shivered under this torture. His nails turned blue, his face purple and haggard. He gritted his teeth. His head was shaven, and the long beard that grew down from his pointed chin was the only thing that covered his bare, wet, emaciated chest. Whenever the sick man started to weep, he opened an umbrella, thinking it would shelter him from his tears. If this strategy had proved effective, a statue should have been erected in his honor.

My only happy moments were those when I went for walks in the churchyard of this hilltop hamlet. My companions were the dead, a few birds, and the setting sun. As I walked, I would daydream about Paris society, my childhood, my sylph, and the woods of Combourg: so near in space, so distant in time. After a while, I would go back to my poor sick man. It was the blind leading the blind.

Alas! A blow to the head, a fall, an affliction of the brain could rob even Homer, Newton, or Bossuet of his genius. Then these exalted men, instead of exciting our profound pity, our bitter and eternal regret, would become the objects of our smiles! Many people I have known and loved have seen their reason disturbed in my presence, as if I carried the germ of the contagion within me. I can understand the cruel gaiety of Cervantes's masterpiece only through a melancholy meditation: considering the whole of human existence, weighing good and evil, one might be tempted to wish for any accident that brings forgetfulness, as a means of escaping from oneself. A happy drunk is a fortunate creature. Religion aside, happiness comes of being ignorant of yourself and arriving in the grave without having felt the sting of life.

I brought back my compatriot completely cured.

7.

THE ESTATES OF BRITTANY IN 1789—INSURRECTION —SAINT-RIVEUL, MY FORMER SCHOOLMATE, IS KILLED

Paris, October 1821

MADAME Lucile and Madame de Farcy, who had returned with me to Brittany, now wished to go back to Paris; but I was detained by troubles in the province. The Estates were convened on the last day of December 1788. The commune of Rennes, and after it all the other communes of Brittany, had passed a decree forbidding their deputies to involve themselves in any other business until the matter of hearth money had been settled.

The Comte de Boisgelin, who was to preside over the Order of the Nobility, rushed to Rennes. Gentlemen were summoned by private letters, even those who were, like me, still too young to have a vote in the deliberations. Seeing that we could be attacked, it was a matter of arms as well as votes: we went to our posts.

Several meetings were held at M. de Boisgelin's house before the Estates opened. Here, all the scenes of confusion at which I had been present repeated themselves. My uncle, the Comte de Bedée, called "Bedée the Artichoke" on account of his fatness and to distinguish him from another Bedée, tall and skinny, called "Bedée the Asparagus," broke several chairs by climbing on them to hold forth. The Marquis de Trémargat, the peg-legged naval officer, made plenty of enemies for his order. One day, everyone was discussing the establishment of a military school where the sons of poor aristocrats could be educated, when a member of the Third Estate cried out, "And what about our sons? What of them?"

"Your sons have the workhouse," Trémargat replied.

These words fell among the crowd and promptly took root.

I noticed during these meetings a tendency of my character that I have since rediscovered in all matters of politics and war: the more hot-tempered my friends and colleagues, the cooler-headed I became. I could see a tribunal or a cannon set on fire with indifference. I have never cheered either for speeches or bullets.

The result of our deliberations was that the Nobility would deal first of all with general business and would not occupy themselves with the matter of hearth money until all other matters had been resolved—a resolution directly opposed to that of the Third Estate. The nobles had no great confidence in the clergy, who had often abandoned them in the past, especially when they were presided over by the Bishop of Rennes, a fawning, plodding personage who spoke with a slight lisp, not without elegance, and who always made the best of his opportunities at Court. A newspaper, *La Sentinelle du Peuple*, printed up in Rennes by a scribbler lately arrived from Paris, helped foment hatred.

The Estates were convened in the Jacobin Convent on the Place du Palais. We entered the main hall in the mood I have just described, and no sooner were we in session than the people besieged us. The twenty-fifth, twenty-sixth, twenty-seventh, and twenty-eighth of January 1789 were unhappy days. The Comte de Thiard had only a few troops. An ineffective and indecisive leader, he maneuvered without accomplishing anything at all. The law school in Rennes, led by Moreau, had sent for the young men of Nantes. They arrived four hundred strong, and the Commandant, no matter how he pleaded, could not prevent them from invading the city. Meetings of various kinds, held on the Champ-Montmorin and in cafés, ended in violent brawls.

Tired of being blockaded in our chamber, we made a resolution to sally forth, swords in hand. It made for a very fine sight. At a signal from our president, we all drew our swords at once, to the cry of *Vive la Bretagne!* and, like a garrison deprived of resources, we executed a furious sortie, trying to pass through the heart of our besiegers. The people received us with howls, stones, iron poles, and pistols. We forced a gap in the surging crowd, but they closed in on us again. Several gentlemen were wounded, dragged, lacerated, and covered with bruises and contusions. Only with great difficulty did we manage to disengage ourselves and thread our ways back to our separate lodgings.

Duels followed, between gentlemen and the law students and their friends from Nantes. One of these duels took place publicly on the Place Royale. The honors rested with the old naval officer Keralieu, who fought with such incredible vigor that he won the applause of his young adversaries.

Another mob had formed. The Comte de Montboucher caught sight of a student named Ulliac in the crowd and called out to him, "Monsieur, this concerns the two of us!" A circle was formed around them. Montboucher made the sword jump from Ulliac's hand and then returned it. They embraced, and the crowd dispersed.

At least the Breton nobles did not yield without honor. They refused to send deputies to the Estates-General because the Estates had not been assembled according to the fundamental laws of the province's constitution. Later, they would go in great numbers to join the Army of Princes, to be decimated with Condé or Charette in the Vendée Wars. Would it have made any difference to the majority of the National Assembly, if they had taken part? It is unlikely. In these great social transformations, individual resistance, however honorable for those who resist, is powerless against the facts. Even so, it's difficult to say what might have come of a man of Mirabeau's genius, but of opposite opinions, had he been found in the ranks of the Breton nobility.

The young Boishue and Saint-Riveul, my former schoolmate, had died before these conflicts began, on their way to the Chamber of Nobles: Boishue was defended in vain by his father, who served as his second.

Reader, I ask you to pause. Consider the first drops of blood that the Revolution spilled. It was ordained that they should come from the veins of my childhood companion. Suppose I had fallen instead of Saint-Riveul: they would have said of me, changing only the name, exactly what they said of the victim with whom the great immolation began. "A gentleman, named Chateaubriand, was killed on his way to the Estates." These few words would have taken the place of my long story. Would Saint-Riveul then have played my part on earth? Was he destined for the noise of fame or for silence?

Pass on now, reader; wade the river of blood that separates forever the old world, which you are leaving, from the new world at whose beginning you shall die.

8.

THE YEAR 1789—JOURNEY FROM BRITTANY TO
PARIS—TURBULENCE ALONG THE WAY—HOW PARIS
LOOKED—DISMISSAL OF M. NECKER—VERSAILLES—
THE HIGH SPIRITS OF THE ROYAL FAMILY—GENERAL
INSURRECTION—THE TAKING OF THE BASTILLE

Paris, November 1821

THE YEAR 1789, so famous in our history and in the history of the
human race, found me still on the moors of my Brittany. I could not
leave the province until late in the year and did not get to Paris until
after the pillaging of the Maison Réveillon, the opening of the Estates-
General, the transformation of the Third Estate into the National
Assembly, the Tennis Court Oath, the Royal Speech of June 23, and
the incorporation of the Clergy and the Nobility into the Third
Estate.

There was great turbulence on the way to Paris. In the villages,
peasants were stopping carriages, demanding to see passports, and
interrogating travelers. The closer we came to the capital, the more
disorderly things became. Passing through Versailles, I saw troops
quartered in the orangery, artillery trains parked in the courtyards,
makeshift chambers for the National Assembly erected on the Place
du Palais, and deputies coming and going amid a swarm of sightseers,
palace servants, and soldiers.

In Paris, the streets were glutted with crowds standing at bakery
doors; passersby stopped to talk on street corners; merchants left their
shops and stood on their doorsteps to hear and tell the latest news;
agitators massed together at the Palais-Royal: Camille Desmoulins
was just beginning to stand out from the throng.

I had hardly alighted, with Madame de Farcy and Madame Lucile,
at a hotel in the rue de Richelieu, when a riot broke out. The people
rushed to the Abbaye to liberate a few French Guards who had been

206 · MEMOIRS FROM BEYOND THE GRAVE

arrested on the order of their officers, and the noncommissioned officers of an artillery regiment quartered at the Invalides went with them. Military defection had begun.

The Court, sometimes yielding, sometimes trying to resist, a tangle of stiff-necked bravado and craven fear, let itself be harangued by Mirabeau, who asked that the troops be removed, but would not make any effort to remove them: it accepted the affront and did not destroy the cause. A rumor spread through Paris that an army was going to come up through the Montmartre sewers, and that dragoons were going to force the barricades. Somebody suggested that they tear up the paving stones from the streets, carry them up to the fifth floor, and hurl them at the tyrant's henchmen; everyone went to work. In the midst of this babble, M. Necker received an order to resign. The new ministry was to consist of Messrs. de Breteuil, de la Galaisière, Marshal de Broglie, de la Vaugoyon, de Laporte, and Foulon, who would be replacing Messrs. de Montmorin, de la Luzerne, de Saint-Priest, and de Nivernais.

A Breton poet, newly arrived in Paris, had asked me to take him to Versailles. There are people who visit fountains and gardens while empires are being overthrown. Scribblers especially have this capacity for isolating themselves in the world of their obsessions, even during the most historic events: for them, their sentence or their stanza takes the place of everything.

I took my Pindar to Mass in the gallery of Versailles. The Oeil-de-Boeuf was radiant: M. Necker's dismissal had lifted everyone's spirits, and they were feeling sure of victory. Perhaps Sanson and Simon, mingling in the crowd, were spectators of the royal family's good cheer.

The Queen passed by with her two children. Their blond heads seemed to be awaiting their crowns. The eleven-year-old Madame le Duchesse d'Angoulême, in particular, attracted all eyes with her virginal dignity. Beautiful by dint of her noble blood and her girlish innocence, she seemed to say, like Corneille's orange flower in the *Guirlande de Julie*:

I have all the splendor of my birth.

The little Dauphin walked under his sister's guidance, and M. Du Touchet followed close behind his pupil. He noticed me and obligingly pointed me out to the Queen. Casting her eyes on me with a smile, she made me the same charming curtsy as she had on the day of my presentation. I will never forget those eyes, which were so soon to be extinguished. When Marie-Antoinette smiled, the shape of her mouth was so clear that the memory of this smile (horrible thought!) allowed me to recognize the jaw of this daughter of kings when the unfortunate woman's head was discovered in the exhumations of 1815.

The counter-blow to the blow struck in Versailles resounded in Paris. On my return, I ran headlong into a multitude of people who carried busts of M. Necker and the Duc d'Orléans draped in mourning sheets. They shouted, "Long Live Necker! Long Live the Duc d'Orléans!" and among these shouts a bolder and more unexpected cry could be heard: "Long Live Louis XVII!" Long live a child whose very name would have been forgotten in his family's funeral epitaph if I hadn't recalled it to the Chamber of Peers! If only Louis XVI had abdicated, Louis XVII would have been placed on the throne, the Duc d'Orléans would have been declared regent, and what would have happened then?

In the Place Louis XV, the Prince de Lambesc, at the head of the Royal German Guards, drove the people back into the Tuileries garden and wounded an old man. Suddenly the signal bell sounded. Munitions shops were looted and thirty thousand muskets were taken from the Invalides. The people provided themselves with pikes, staves, pitchforks, sabers, and pistols; they pillaged Saint-Lazare and burned the barricades. The voters of Paris took over the government of the capital, and, in one night, sixty thousand citizens were organized, armed, and equipped as National Guards.

As for July 14, the taking of the Bastille: I was present as a spectator at this attack on a few invalids and a timorous governor. If they had kept the gates shut, the people never could have stormed the fortress. I saw two or three cannonballs fired, not by the invalids, but by French Guardsmen who had already climbed the towers. De Launay, the governor, was dragged from his hiding place, suffered a thousand outrages, and was bludgeoned to death on the steps of the Hôtel de Ville. Flesselles, the provost of merchants, had his brains blown out by a pistol. This was the spectacle that the heartless bigots found so beautiful. Between these murders, the people gave themselves over to orgies, as during the troubles in Rome under Otho and Vitellius. The so-called "conquerors of the Bastille"—those happy drunks declared victorious in every cabaret—were paraded through the streets in hackney cabs, escorted by prostitutes and sans-culottes, who were then just beginning their reign. Bystanders, out of a respect born of fear, doffed their hats to these heroes, some of whom died of fatigue in the course of their triumph. Keys to the Bastille quickly multiplied and were sent to all the simpletons of importance in every corner of the world. I am always missing my chance at fortune! If only I, a spectator, had signed my name in the registry of conquerors, I would have a pension today.

The experts rushed to conduct an autopsy of the Bastille. Makeshift cafés were set up under tents, and people congregated there as if it were the Saint-Germain fair or Longchamp. A long line of carriages threaded past or stopped at the foot of the towers whose stones were now being thrown to the ground in a maelstrom of dust. Elegantly appareled women and fashionable young men stood on the various levels of the Gothic rubble and mingled with half-naked laborers who were busy demolishing the walls to the cheers of the crowd. At this rendezvous one saw the most famous orators, the best-known men of letters, the most celebrated painters, the most renowned actors and actresses, the most acclaimed dancers, the most illustrious foreigners, the grandees of the Court, and the ambassadors of Europe. Old France had gone there to end, new France to begin.

No event, no matter how wretched or odious in itself, should be treated lightly when its circumstances are serious and it brings about a new epoch. What should have been seen in the taking of the Bastille (and what no one saw at the time) was not the violent act of emancipating the people, but the emancipation itself, which resulted from that act.

Everyone admired what he should have condemned, the accident, and no one looked to the future to see what was in store for the people, the changes in manners, ideas, and political power—a renovation of the human race in which the taking of the Bastille was only the prelude to an era, a sort of bloodstained jubilee. Brutish anger made ruins, and beneath this anger was a hidden intelligence that laid among these ruins the foundations of a new edifice.

But the nation, deceived by the grandeur of material facts, was not deceived by the grandeur of moral facts. In the nation's eyes, the Bastille was the trophy of its servitude; it seemed erected at the entryway to Paris, across from the sixteen pillars of Montfaucon, as a gallows on which liberties were hanged.* By razing this fortress of the State, the people thought to break the military yoke and thereby tacitly agreed to take the place of the army that they were disbanding. And we know what marvels were born when the people became soldiers.

*Fifty-two years later, fifteen Bastilles have been erected to oppress that same liberty in the name of which they razed the first one. (Paris, 1841)

9.

EFFECT OF THE TAKING OF THE BASTILLE ON THE COURT—THE HEADS OF FOULON AND BERTIER

Paris, November 1821

WOKEN by the fall of the Bastille as by a noise foreboding the fall of the crown, Versailles had gone from vauntery to despondency. The King rushes to the National Assembly, gives a speech from the President's own chair, announces that the troops have been ordered to withdraw, and returns to his palace with everybody's blessings. What useless pageantry! No party ever believes in converting their opponent: neither liberty capitulating nor power abasing itself ever obtains mercy from its enemies.

Eighty deputies came from Versailles to declare peace in the capital. Illuminations followed. M. de Lafayette was named commander of the National Guard and M. Bailly the Mayor of Paris: I never knew this poor but respectable scholar except through his misfortunes. Revolutions find men for all their phases: some follow these revolutions to the end, while others start them but do not see them to the finish.

Everyone was scattering. Courtiers left for Bâle, Lausanne, Luxembourg, and Brussels. Madame de Polignac in flight met M. Necker returning. The Comte d'Artois, his sons, and the three Condés emigrated, dragging behind them the high clergy and a portion of the nobility. Officers, threatened by their insurgent soldiers, yielded to a torrent that would soon set them adrift. Louis XVI alone stayed to face the nation with his two children and a few women: the Queen, the King's aunts Mesdames Adélaide and Victoire, and Madame Élisabeth. *Monsieur*, who remained until the flight to Varennes, was of no great help to his brother.[6] Though he had helped decide the Revolution's fate by supporting, in the Assembly of Notables, the right to individual votes, the Revolution would nonetheless defy him. *Monsieur* had little liking for the King, did not understand the Queen, and was disliked by them in turn.

Louis XVI came to the Hôtel de Ville on the seventeenth. A hundred thousand men armed like the monks of the League received him. He was harangued by Messrs. Bailly, Moreau de Saint-Méry, and Lally-Tolendal, who wept: the latter is still prone to tears. The King was moved in his turn. He put an enormous tricolor ribbon in his hat and declared, there and then, that he was "an honest man, Father of the French, and King of a free people," even as these people prepared, by virtue of their freedom, to cut off the head of this honest man, their Father and their King.

A few days after this reconciliation, I was at the window of my hotel with my sisters and a few other Bretons. We heard shouting: "Bolt the doors! Bolt the doors!"

A group of ragged men appeared at one end of the street; from their midst rose two flagpoles, which we couldn't see very well at that distance. Only when they came closer could we make out the two disheveled and disfigured heads that Marat's predecessors carried on the points of their pikes. These were the heads of Messrs. Foulon and Bertier.[7] Everyone else drew back from the windows: I alone remained. The murderers stopped below me and thrust their pikes up toward me, singing, rollicking, and leaping to shove the pale effigies in my face. An eye in one of those heads, gouged from its socket, hung over the dead man's darkened countenance; the pike came through the open mouth so that the teeth chomped down on metal.

"Brigands!" I shouted. "Is this what you take liberty to be?"

If I had had a gun, I would have shot at those derelicts as at a pack of wolves. They howled and pounded harder against the front door, hoping to force it and add my head to those of their victims. My sisters fainted, and the cowards in the hotel heaped reproaches on me. But the murderers were being pursued; they had no time to invade the building and so moved on. These heads, and others that I would encounter soon after, changed my political leanings. I was horrified by these cannibal feasts, and the idea of leaving France for some distant country began to take root in my mind.

10.

Paris, November 1821

RECALLED to office on July 25, inaugurated, and welcomed with celebrations thrown in his honor, M. Necker, third successor of Turgot, following Calonne and Taboureau, was soon eclipsed by events and fell out of popular favor. It is one of the singularities of the times that so grave a character as M. Necker should have been raised to the post of minister by the savoir-faire of a man as mediocre and insubstantial as the Marquis de Pezay. The *Compte-rendu*, which in France replaced the system of taxation with a system of loans, stirred up ideas. Women started discussing incomes and expenditures; for the first time, one saw, or thought one saw, something in the calculating machine. Its calculations, painted in sunny colors *à la Thomas*, had established Necker's reputation as the Director-General of Finance. A skillful treasurer, but an inexpedient economist; a noble writer, but bombastic; an honest man, but without any great virtue, the banker was like one of those ancient characters who recite the prologue, explaining the play to the public, and then vanish as soon as the curtain rises. M. Necker was Madame de Staël's father. His vanity would hardly have permitted him to think that his true claim to the memory of posterity would be through his daughter's glory.

The monarchy was demolished just as surely as the Bastille when the National Assembly met on the evening of August 4. Those who, out of hatred for the past, rail against the nobility today seem to forget that it was a member of this nobility, the Vicomte de Noailles,

who, with the support of the Duc d'Aiguillon and Mathieu de Montmorency, tore down the edifice that had prompted the Revolutionary
measures. On a motion made by a feudal deputy, all feudal rights—
the rights of the hunt, dovecotes, and warrens; the privileges of the
orders, towns, and provinces; tithes and champerty; personal servitude;
manorial jurisdiction; the purchase of offices—were abolished. The
greatest blows against the old constitution of the State were struck
by gentlemen. Patricians started the Revolution, and plebeians finished
it. As the old France once owed the French nobility its glory, so the
new France owes it its liberty, if there is any such thing as liberty in
France.

The troops camped around Paris had been sent away, and by one
of those contradictory counsels that vexed the King, the Flanders
Regiment was summoned to Versailles. The bodyguards held a banquet for the office of this regiment; heads grew hot; the Queen appeared in the middle of the banquet with the Dauphin; toasts were
drunk to the royal family's health; the King came in his turn, and
the military band struck up the stirring and well-loved tune "Ô
Richard, ô mon roi!" No sooner did the news of this banquet reach
Paris than the opposite opinion took hold; people shouted that Louis
refused to sanction the Declaration of the Rights of Man and was
planning to flee to Metz with the Comte d'Estaing. It was Marat
who propagated this rumor. He was already writing the *Ami du
peuple*.

Then came October 5. I was not there to witness the events of that
day. The story of what happened reached the capital early the next
morning. We were told, at the same time, to expect a visit from the
King. Timid as I was in parlors, I was bold in public places: I used to
feel I was made either for solitude or for the forum. I rushed to the
Champs-Élysées. First came the cannon, with harpies, molls, and
streetwalkers straddling their barrels, making the coarsest remarks
and the lewdest gestures. Next, in the middle of this horde of every
age and sex, the King's bodyguards marched past on foot, having
exchanged their hats, swords, and baldrics for those of the National
Guard. Behind them, every one of their horses carried two or three

filthy-drunk fishwives like bedraggled bacchantes. Next came the delegation of the National Assembly, followed by the King's carriages, which moved in the dusty shade of a forest of pikes and bayonets. Tattered ragpickers and butchers, with their aprons bloody to the thigh, bare knives at their belts, and their shirtsleeves rolled, clung to the carriage doors. Some other black-hearted satyrs had climbed onto its roof; still others hung from the lackeys' footboard or lolled on the box. They fired muskets and pistols; they shouted: "Here comes the baker, the baker's wife, and the little baker's boy!" Instead of an oriflamme, before this son of Saint Louis, Swiss halberds held high the heads of two bodyguards, curled and powdered by a wigmaker from Sèvres.

At the Hôtel de Ville, the astronomer Bailly announced to Louis XVI that the "humane, respectful, and loyal" people had conquered their King, and the King, for his part, "greatly touched and greatly pleased," announced that he had come to Paris "of his own free will": shameful falsities, born of the violence and the fear that did dishonor to every party and every man alive. Louis XVI was not a liar. He was weak, but weakness is not falsity, even when it takes its place and serves its functions. The respect that this martyred King's virtues and misfortunes should inspire in us renders all human judgment almost sacrilegious.

II.
CONSTITUENT ASSEMBLY

THE DEPUTIES left Versailles and held their first meeting on October 19, in one of the halls of the Archbishop's palace. On November 9, they moved to the Riding House, near the Tuileries. The rest of the year 1789 saw the decrees that despoiled the clergy, destroyed the old magistracy, and created the currency of *assignats*; the resolution of the Commune of Paris that formed the first Committee of Inquiry; and the mandate that instructed the judges to prosecute the Marquis de Favras.[8]

The Constituent Assembly, despite everything that can be said against it, remains the most illustrious popular assembly that has ever appeared among the nations, as much for the grandeur of its transactions as for the magnitude of its results. There was no political question so profound that the Assembly did not discuss and properly resolve it. What it could have achieved, if it had held itself to the notebooks of the Estates-General and not tried to go beyond! All that human experience and human intelligence has ever conceived, discovered, and elaborated over the last three centuries can be found in these notebooks. The many different abuses of the old regime are indicated in them, along with proposed remedies for their cure. Every kind of freedom is demanded, even the freedom of the press; every improvement necessary for industry, factories, commerce, roads, the army, taxation, finance, schools, public education, etc. We have crossed over abysses of crime and heaps of corpses to no profit. The Republic and the Empire have achieved nothing. The Empire only regulated the brute strength of arms that the Republic set in motion and has bequeathed us centralization, a vigorous type of administration which I look on as an evil, but which was perhaps the only system that could replace the local administrations once these had been destroyed and ignorant anarchy led men around by the nose. All in all, we haven't advanced one step since the Constituent Assembly: its labors were like those of Hippocrates, that great physician of antiquity, who established and extended the boundaries of science at one and the same time. Let us speak of a few members of this Assembly, beginning with Mirabeau, who epitomizes and towers over them all.

12.

MIRABEAU

Paris, November 1821

MIXED up in world events by the chaos and coincidences of his life, in contact with fugitives of justice, rapists, and adventurers, Mirabeau, the tribune of the aristocracy, the deputy of democracy, had something of Gracchus and Don Juan, of Catiline and Guzmán d'Alfarache, of Cardinal de Richelieu and Cardinal de Retz, of the Regency rake and the Revolutionary savage; he had, moreover, something of "Mirabeau," an exiled Florentine family that carried with them a memory of those fortified palaces and great factions celebrated by Dante: a naturalized French family in which the Republican spirit of the Italian Middle Ages and the feudal spirit of our Middle Ages were to be united in a succession of extraordinary men.

Mirabeau's ugliness, laid over the foundation of the beauty particular to his race, gave him a powerful figure, as though he had stepped out of the *Last Judgment* by Michelangelo, Arrighetti's countryman. The furrows plowed by smallpox in the orator's face looked more like scars left by fire. Nature seemed to have molded his head either for imperium or for the gallows, chiseled his arms to annul a nation or abduct a woman. When he shook his mane and looked at the people, he stopped them cold; when he lifted his paw and showed his claws, the plebes ran wildly away. In the middle of one horribly disorderly session, I saw him at the rostrum, dark, ugly, and motionless. He called to mind Milton's Chaos, impassive and formless, standing at the center of his own confusion.[9]

Mirabeau took after his father and uncle, who, like Saint-Simon, could write immortal prose offhand. Speeches were often written for Mirabeau, but he borrowed only what his spirit could amalgamate with its own substance. If he adopted them in their entirety, he delivered them badly; one could hear that they were not his by the stray words which he added to them, and which revealed the man. He pooled his energy from his vices, but these vices weren't born of a frigid temperament but of deep, burning, tempestuous passions. Cynicism of manners, by annihilating the moral sense, brings society back to a kind of barbarism, but these social barbarians, prone to destruction like the Goths, have no power to create like the Goths. The barbarians of old were enormous children of virgin nature; the new ones are the monstrous abortions of nature depraved.

Two times I met Mirabeau at a banquet: once at the house of Voltaire's niece, the Marquise de Villette, and once more at the Palais-Royal, with some deputies of the opposition to whom Chapelier had introduced me. Chapelier would go to the scaffold in the same tumbrel as my brother and M. de Malesherbes.

Mirabeau talked a great deal, especially about himself. This son of lions was himself a lion with a chimera's head; this man so practical when it came to facts was all romance, poetry, and enthusiasm when it came to language and imagination. One could see in him the lover of Sophie, exalted in his feelings and capable of sacrifice. "I found her," he wrote, "this adorable woman . . . I knew what her soul was—that soul formed by Nature's hand in a moment of magnificence."

Mirabeau enchanted me with his stories of love and his dreams of escape, which he interspersed with dry discussions. He interested me in another way also: like me, he had been treated severely by his father, who, like mine, had stood by the inflexible tradition of absolute paternal authority.

The great talker expounded on foreign politics and said almost nothing of domestic affairs, although these were what occupied him. But he did let slip a few words of sovereign contempt for those men who proclaim themselves superior by reason of the indifference that they affect toward disasters and crimes. Mirabeau was by nature generous, given to friendship, and quick to pardon offenses. Despite his immorality, he could not warp his conscience, and he was corrupt only within himself. His firm and upright mind never made an intellectual sublimity of murder. He had no admiration for slaughterhouses and garbage heaps.

Mirabeau was not, however, lacking in pride. He boasted about himself outrageously. Although he had become a cloth merchant in order to be elected a member of the Third Estate (the Order of the Nobility having had the honorable madness to reject him), he was enamored of his birth: "a haggard-looking bird whose nest was up between four turrets," his father said of him. He would not forget that he had appeared at Court, ridden in coaches, and hunted with the King. He demanded to be addressed by the title of Comte and, sticking to his guns, clothed his servants in livery even when everyone else had ceased doing so. Whenever possible, and often when it seemed almost impossible, he brought up his "ancestor," Admiral Coligny. Once the *Moniteur* referred to him as Riquet and he said angrily to the journalist, "Do you realize that with your 'Riquet,' you have disoriented all of Europe for three days?" He often repeated this impudent and well-known pleasantry: "In any other family, my brother the Vicomte would be a wit and a vagabond; in my family, he is a fool and a good man." Biographers attribute this bon mot to the Vicomte himself, as though he were humbly comparing himself to other members of his family.

Deep down, Mirabeau was a Royalist. He once spoke these fine words: "I wanted to cure the French of superstition about the monarchy and replace it with worship for the monarchy." In a letter, destined for the eyes of Louis XVI, he wrote, "I would not like to have labored only to make way for a vast destruction." This is, however, exactly what happened to him. Heaven, to punish us for talents badly employed, makes us repent of our success.

Mirabeau moved public opinion by two levers. With one hand, he pivoted his fulcrum among the masses, of whom he had fashioned himself the defender while loathing them; with the other, though a traitor to his order, he maintained its sympathy through caste affinities and common interests. This wouldn't have been possible for a plebeian, if one had managed to become a champion of the privileged classes: such a man would have been abandoned by his party without winning over the aristocracy, who are by nature ungrateful and un-winnable if one isn't born within their ranks. The aristocracy cannot, besides, simply improvise a noble, since nobility is the daughter of time.

Mirabeau founded a school. By freeing themselves from moral shackles, men dreamed that they were transforming into statesmen. But these imitations produced only perverse dwarfs: one who prides himself on being a corrupt thief and is no more than a debauched scoundrel; another who thinks himself vicious and is merely vile; still another who brags of his criminality but who is merely infamous.

Too soon for him and too late for it, Mirabeau sold himself to the Court, and the Court bought him. He staked his reputation on a pension and an embassy: Cromwell, in his day, was once on the brink of bartering his future for a title and the Order of the Garter. Yet, in spite of his arrogance, Mirabeau didn't value himself highly enough. Now that the abundance of cash and positions has raised the price of a conscience, there is not an errand-boy who doesn't fetch hundreds of thousands of francs and the highest honors that the State can bestow. Only the grave relieved Mirabeau of his promises and rescued him from perils that he probably could not have overcome. His life would have showed his weakness for good; his death has left him in possession of his capacity for evil.

On leaving our dinner, there was some talk of Mirabeau's enemies. I found myself beside him without having uttered a word. He looked me in the face with eyes full of arrogance, depravity, and genius, and, putting his hand on my shoulder, he said to me, "They will never forgive me my superiority!" I still feel the impression of that hand, as if Satan had touched me with his fiery claw.

When Mirabeau fixed his gaze on a young mute, did he have an inkling of my futuritions? Did he consider that one day he would figure in my memories? I was destined to become the historian of great personages: they have filed away before me, without my having to hang on their coattails and be dragged with them into posterity.

Mirabeau has already undergone the metamorphosis that has its way with everyone whose memory will survive. Carried from the Panthéon to the gutter, and from the gutter back to the Panthéon, he has been raised to the pinnacle of those times that today form his pedestal. The real Mirabeau is no longer anywhere to be found; only the idealized Mirabeau, the Mirabeau of the artists, who has become a symbol or a myth of the epoch he represents. In this way he becomes more false and more true. Among so many reputations, so many actors, so many events, so many ruins, only three men remain—each of them attached to one of the great Revolutionary epochs: Mirabeau for aristocracy, Robespierre for democracy, Bonaparte for despotism. The monarchy has nothing: France has paid dearly for those three reputations that Virtue can never acknowledge.

13.

MEETINGS OF THE NATIONAL ASSEMBLY—
ROBESPIERRE

Paris, December 1821

THE SESSIONS of the National Assembly offered a spectacle of interest that the meetings of our Chambers are far from approaching. One had to get up very early to find a seat in the crowded gallery. The deputies arrived eating, talking, and gesticulating; they formed groups in different parts of the room, according to their opinions. The minutes were read aloud, and then a prearranged subject was discussed or an extraordinary motion was set forth. It was never a matter of some insipid article of law. The order of the day rarely lacked a scheme of destruction. Deputies spoke pro or contra, and everyone, for better or worse, improvised their speeches. These debates grew tempestuous. The galleries joined in the discussion, applauded and cheered, hissed and booed at the speakers. The president rang his bell, while the deputies shouted at each other from bench to bench. Mirabeau the Younger seized his opponent by the collar; Mirabeau the Elder cried out, "Silence! The thirty votes!"

One day, I was sitting behind the Royalist opposition. In front of me was a gentleman from Dauphiné, a swarthy little man, who jumped on his chair in a fury and called to his friends, "Let us fall upon those beggars, sword in hand!"

He pointed toward the majority. The ladies of the market, who sat knitting in the galleries, heard him, rose from their seats, and shouted all together, with stockings in their hands and foaming mouths, "Hang them from the lampposts!"

The Vicomte de Mirabeau, Lautrec, and a few other young nobles wanted to take the galleries by storm.

Soon this fracas was drowned out by another: petitioners armed with pikes appeared at the bar.

"The people are dying of hunger," they said. "It's time to take action against the aristocrats and rise *to the level of the situation*."

The chairman assured these citizens of his respect. "We have our eyes on the traitors," he replied, "and the Assembly will see that justice is done."

At this, another uproar broke out: the deputies of the Right shouted that we were on the road to anarchy; the deputies of the Left replied that the people were free to express their will, that they had every right to complain of men who collaborated with despotism, seated in the very midst of the nation's representatives. That was how they described their colleagues to the sovereign people, who waited outside beneath the streetlamps.

The evening sessions were even more scandalous than the morning sessions: men spoke better and more boldly by candlelight. The Riding House was then as good as a theater, where one of the greatest dramas in the world was being played out. The leading characters still belonged to the old order of things; their terrible understudies, hidden behind them, hardly said a word. At the end of one violent debate, I saw a common-looking deputy mount the rostrum. His face was gray and inexpressive, and his hair was neatly combed. He was very properly dressed, like the steward of a good house or a village notary careful of his appearance. He read a long and boring report to which no one listened. I asked his name: it was Robespierre. The well-heeled were just getting ready to leave their parlors, and already the sabots were kicking at the door.[10]

14.
SOCIETY—PARIS

Paris, December 1821

WHEN, before the Revolution, I read the history of public disturbances among the different nations, I could not conceive of how
people had lived in such times. I was astonished that Montaigne could
write so cheerfully in a castle that he could not so much as stroll
around without running the risk of being abducted by bands of
Leaguers or Protestants.

The Revolution made me understand how possible it is to live
under such conditions. Moments of crisis redouble the life of man.
In a society that is dissolving and recomposing itself, the struggle of
two spirits, the clash of past and future, the intermingling of old ways
and new, makes for a transitory concoction that leaves no time for
boredom. Passions and characters set at liberty are displayed with an
energy unimaginable in a well-regulated city. The breaches of the law,
the freedom from duties, customs, and good manners, even the dangers intensify the appeal of this disorder. The human race on holiday
strolls down the street, rid of its masters and restored for a moment
to its natural state; it feels no need of a civic bridle until it shoulders
the yoke of the new tyrants, which license breeds.

I can think of no better way to describe the society of 1789 and 1790
than to compare it to architecture from the days of Louis XII and
François I, when the Greek orders began to be combined with the
Gothic style, or, rather, by likening it to the collection of ruins and
tombs of all the centuries, piled up pell-mell after the Terror in the
cloisters of the Petits-Augustins: except the ruins of which I speak were

alive and constantly changing. In every corner of Paris, there were literary gatherings, political meetings, and theater shows; future celebrities wandered in the crowd unknown, like souls on the banks of the Lethe before they bask in the light. I saw Marshal Gouvion-Saint-Cyr play a part in Beaumarchais's *La Mère Coupable* at the Théâtre du Marais. People went from the Club des Feuillants to the Club des Jacobins, from balls and gambling houses to the crowds at the Palais-Royal, from the gallery of the National Assembly to the gallery of the open air. Popular delegations, cavalry pickets, and infantry patrols marched every which way in the streets. Beside a man in French dress, with powdered hair, a sword at his side, a hat under his arm, leather shoes, and silk stockings, walked a man with unpowdered hair cropped close to his skull, dressed in an English frock coat and an American cravat. In the theaters, actors announced the latest news, and the pit burst into patriotic song. Topical plays drew the crowds: a priest would appear on stage, and the people would shout, *Calotin! Calotin!* and the priest would reply: *Messieurs, Vive la Nation!*[11] Everybody hastened to hear Mandini and his wife, Viganoni, sing with Rovedino at the Opéra-Buffa, only minutes after hearing "Ça ira" howled in the street; they went to admire Madame Dugazon, Madame Saint-Aubin, Carline, little Olivier, Mademoiselle Contat, Molé, Fleury, and the young sensation Talma, fresh from seeing Favras hanged.

The promenades on the boulevard du Temple and the boulevard des Italiens, nicknamed "the Coblentz," and all the paths in the Tuileries garden were inundated with fashionable women. Grétry's three young daughters shone there, as white and pink as their dresses: all three of them would soon be dead. "She fell asleep forever," Grétry said of the eldest, "sitting on my lap, as beautiful as she was in life." A multitude of carriages plowed the muddy crossroads where the sans-culottes splashed, and the beautiful Madame de Buffon could be seen sitting alone in a phaeton belonging to the Duc d'Orléans, parked outside the door of some club.

Everything elegant and tasteful in aristocratic society gathered at the Hôtel de La Rochefoucauld, at the soirées of Mesdames de Poix, d'Hénin, de Simiane, and de Vaudreuil, or in those few salons of the high magistracy that still remained open. In the houses of M. Necker, M. le Comte de Montmorin, and the various other ministers, gathered (together with Madame de Staël, the Duchesse d'Aiguillon, Mesdames de Beaumont and de Sérilly) all the icons of the new France and all the liberties of the new manners. A cobbler in the garb of the National Guard knelt down to measure your foot; a monk, who dragged a black or white robe along the ground on Friday, on Sunday wore a round hat and a layman's coat; a clean-shaven Capuchin read the newspaper in a tavern; and in a circle of frivolous women sat a grave-looking nun, an aunt or sister turned out of her convent. Crowds now visited these monasteries open to the world as travelers in Granada walk through the abandoned halls of the Alhambra, or as they linger, in Tivoli, beneath the columns of the Temple of the Sybil.

For the rest, there were many duels and love affairs, prison liaisons and mysterious trysts among the ruins, under a tranquil sky, in the peace and the poetry of nature; many far-flung, silent, solitary walks punctuated by undying oaths and unutterable affections, to the dull tumult of a fleeing world, to the distant noise of a crumbling society, which threatened to fall and crush every chance for happiness placed at the foot of events. When a person was lost from sight for twenty-four hours, no one was sure of seeing him again. Some went the Revolutionary route; others contemplated civil war; others left for Ohio, sending ahead plans for châteaux to be built among the savages; others went to join the Princes: all of them blithely, often without a sou in their pockets, the Royalists alleging that one of these mornings an act of parliament would bring everything to an end, and the patriots, just as heedless in their hopes, declaring a reign of peace, happiness, and liberty. They sang:

> La sainte chandelle d'Arras,
> Le flambeau de la Provence,
> S'ils ne nous éclairent pas,
> Mettent le feu dans la France;
> On ne peut pas les toucher,
> Mais on espère les moucher.[12]

228 · MEMOIRS FROM BEYOND THE GRAVE

And this was how they thought of Robespierre and Mirabeau! "It is as little within the power of any earthly faculty to keep the French from talking," says L'Estoile, "as it is to bury the sun in the earth or drown it in a well."[13]

The Tuileries Palace, transformed into a great jailhouse filled with prisoners, towered over these festivals of destruction. Even the condemned enjoyed themselves while awaiting the cart, the shears, and the red shirt that had been hung up to dry. From the windows they could gaze out at the dazzling illuminations of the Queen's circle.[14]

Pamphlets and newspapers proliferated by the thousands. Satires, poems, and songs from the *Actes des Apôtres* responded to the *Ami du peuple* or the *Modérateur*, put out by the Royalist club and edited by Fontanes. In the political section of the *Mercure de France*, Mallet-Dupan wrote in opposition to La Harpe and Chamfort, who contributed to the literary section of that same paper. Champcenetz, the Marquis de Bonnay, Rivarol, Boniface Mirabeau the Younger (a Holbein of the sword who, in the Rhineland, raised a legion called the Hussars of Death), and Honoré Mirabeau the Elder—all these men amused themselves drawing caricatures over dinner and composing a *Little Almanack of Great Men*. After dinner, Honoré would go and declare martial law or seize the clergy's property. He would spend the night with Madame Le Jay after having announced that he would not leave the National Assembly except under the prodding of bayonets. "Equality" conferred with the devil in the Montrouge quarries and then went back to the Jardin de Monceau to preside over orgies organized by Laclos.[15] The future regicide had not at all degenerated from his forefathers: twice prostituted, Debauchery drained and delivered him into the hands of Ambition. Lauzun, already wrinkled and withered, dined in his little house at the Barrière du Maine with dancers from the Opéra who sat carelessly intertwined with Messrs. de Noailles, de Dillon, de Choiseul, de Narbonne, de Talleyrand, and some other elegant men of the day, of whom two or three mummies still remain.

Most of the courtiers famous for their immorality at the end of Louis XV's reign and during the reign of Louis XVI had enrolled under the tricolor flag: almost all of them had fought in the American war and bedaubed their ribbons with Republican colors. The Revolution made use of them so long as it was only of middling stature, and they even became the first generals of its armies. The Duc de Lauzun, the romantic lover of Princess Czartoryska, a woman-chaser of the high-roads, a Lovelace who had *had* this one and *had* that one, according to the chaste and noble jargon of the Court, this Duc de Lauzun became the Duc de Biron, who commanded the forces of the Convention in the Vendée Wars. —What a pity! The Baron de Besenval, the mendacious and cynical revelator of corruption in high society, a fly buzzing around the puerilities of the old dying monarchy, this tedious Baron, compromised by the business of the Bastille, was saved by M. Necker and Mirabeau only because he was Swiss. —What miserable stuff! Why had such men become involved in such events? As the Revolution grew, it disdainfully abandoned these frivolous apostates of the throne. It had needed their vices and now it needed their heads. No blood was above contempt; not even the blood of Madame du Barry.[16]

15.

WHAT I DID AMID THIS TURMOIL—MY SOLITARY
DAYS—MADEMOISELLE MONET—I MAKE PLANS TO
JOURNEY TO AMERICA—BONAPARTE AND I—THE
MARQUIS DE LA ROUËRIE—I EMBARK AT SAINT-MALO
—LAST THOUGHTS ON LEAVING MY NATIVE LAND

Paris, December 1821

THE YEAR 1790 brought to completion the measures outlined in
1789. Church property, put at first into the hands of the nation, was
confiscated, the civil constitution of the clergy decreed, and nobility
abolished.

I was not present at the Federation of July 1790: a rather serious
illness kept me in bed. But I was amused beforehand to see the
wheelbarrows on the Champ-de-Mars. Madame de Staël has described
this scene marvelously. I will always regret not having seen M. de
Talleyrand saying the Mass with Abbé Louis, as I regret not having
seen him, saber at his side, granting an audience to the ambassador
of the Grand Turk.

Mirabeau's popularity plummeted in 1790: his connections with
the Court were obvious. M. Necker resigned his office and retired
from public life without anyone attempting to dissuade him. The
King's aunts left for Rome with a passport issued by the National
Assembly. The Duc d'Orléans returned from England and declared
himself the King's most humble and obedient servant. Societies of
Friends of the Constitution multiplied upon the earth and attached
themselves to the mother society, from which they took inspiration
and orders.

It turned out that my character was favorably inclined toward
public life. What happened in the streets attracted me because, in
the crowd, I kept my solitude and did not have to face my timidity.
Salons, too, participating in the general agitation, seemed a little less

foreign to my turn of mind, and I had despite myself made a few new acquaintances.

Among these was the Marquise de Villette. Her husband, whose reputation had been slandered, wrote with *Monsieur*, the King's brother, in the *Journal de Paris*. Madame de Villette, still a charming woman, lost a sixteen-year-old daughter, even more charming than her mother, and for whom the Chevalier de Parny wrote a few verses worthy of the *Anthologie*:

> *Au ciel elle a rendu sa vie,*
> *Et doucement s'est endormie,*
> *Sans murmurer contre ses lois;*
> *Ainsi le sourire s'efface,*
> *Ainsi meurt sans laisser de trace*
> *Le chant d'un oiseau dans les bois.*[17]

My regiment, garrisoned at Rouen, maintained its discipline until fairly late. It had a brush with the people over the execution of the actor Bordier, who suffered the last sentence issued by parliamentary power: hanged one day, he would have been a hero the next, if only he had lived another twenty-four hours. But finally insurrection took hold among the soldiers of the Navarre. The Marquis de Mortemart emigrated, and the officers followed suit. I myself had neither adopted nor rejected the new ideas. As little disposed to attack them as to serve them, I wanted neither to emigrate nor to continue my military career, and I resigned my commission.

Cut loose from all ties, I had, on one hand, rather animated quarrels with my brother and the President de Rosambo; on the other, no less bitter discussions with Ginguené, La Harpe, and Chamfort. Ever since my youth, my political impartiality has pleased no one. What's more, I attached importance to the questions at issue only when they concerned universal ideas of liberty and human dignity; personal politics bored me. My real life lay on higher ground.

The streets of Paris, clogged with people day and night, no longer permitted me my aimless strolls of old. In search of desert places, I found shelter in the theater: I tucked myself away in the back of the box and let my thoughts wander to the verse of Racine, the music of Sacchini, or the dances of the Opéra. I must have been intrepid enough to see *Barbe-Bleu* and the *Sabot Perdu* twenty nights running at the Italiens, boring myself in an effort to drive boredom away, perched like an owl in a hole in the wall. All the while the monarchy collapsed, I heard neither the cracking of the ancient vaults, nor the caterwauling of vaudeville, nor the thundering voice of Mirabeau at the tribunal, nor Colin singing to Babet of the theater:

> *Qu'il pleuve, qu'il vente ou qu'il neige,*
> *Quand la nuit est longue, on l'abrège.*[18]

Sometimes, Madame Ginguené sent M. Monet, the Director of Mining, and his young daughter to disturb my savage solitude: Mademoiselle Monet would take her seat at the front of the box, and I would sit down, half glad and half grouchy, behind her. I don't know whether I liked or loved her, but I was certainly scared of her. When she had gone, I regretted her absence and rejoiced to be free of the sight of her. Yet I would sometimes go call on her, sweating at the brow, and take her for a stroll: I would give her my arm, and I believe that I may have squeezed hers a little.

One idea and one idea alone had begun to dominate me, and that was the idea of going to the United States. I needed only a practical purpose for my journey: I proposed to discover (as I have said in these *Memoirs* and in several of my works) the Northwest Passage. This plan was not out of keeping with my poetic nature. No one paid what I did any mind; I was then, like Bonaparte, a slim sublieutenant, completely unknown to the world. We emerged together, he and I, from the obscurity of the same epoch: I to seek my fame in solitude, he to seek his glory among men. Now, not having given myself to any woman, my sylph still obsessed my imagination, and I was ardent to realize my fantastic wanderings with her in the forests of the New

World. Under the influence of another nature, my love flower, my nameless phantom of the Armorican woods, would become *Atala*, in the shade of a Floridian grove.

M. de Malesherbes made me dizzy with excitement about this voyage. I went to see him every morning. With our noses pressed to the maps, we compared different drawings of the Arctic Circle; we calculated the distances between the Bering Stait and the far end of Hudson Bay; we read the various narratives of English, Dutch, French, Russian, Swedish, and Danish sailors and travelers; we traced the routes to be followed overland in order to reach the shores of the Polar Sea; we discussed the difficulties to be overcome and the precautions to be taken against the severe climate, the attacks of wild beasts, and the dwindling of provisions. The great man said to me: "If I were younger, I would go with you and spare myself the sight of all the crimes, betrayals, and insanities of Paris. But at my age a man must die wherever he happens to be. Don't forget to write me by every ship, and keep me abreast of your progress and your discoveries: I will show them to the ministers. It's only too bad you don't know a thing about botany!"

After a conversation such as this, I would leaf through Tournefort, Duhamel, Bernard de Jussieu, Grew, Jacquin, Rousseau's *Dictionary*, and the *Flores Élémentaires*; I would rush to the Jardin du Roi, and soon considered myself a second Linnaeus.

Finally, in January 1791, I made up my mind in all seriousness. The chaos was intensifying. It was enough to bear an "aristocratic" name to be exposed to persecution: the more conscientious and moderate your opinions, the more suspect and prone to attack. I therefore resolved to strike my tent: I left my brother and sisters in Paris and made my way toward Brittany.

In Fougères I met the Marquis de la Rouërie and asked him for a letter of introduction to General Washington.[19] "Colonel Armand" (the name that the marquis was given in America) had distinguished himself in the American War of Independence. He was to become famous, in France, for his part in the Royalist conspiracy that made such poignant victims in the Désilles family. Having died while organizing this conspiracy, he was exhumed, identified, and caused misfortune to his hosts and friends. A rival of Lafayette and Lauzun, a forerunner of La Rochejaquelin, the Marquis de la Rouërie was more spirited than any of those men: he had fought more battles than the first; he had seduced as many Opéra actresses as the second; and he would have become the comrade-in-arms of the third. He used to go foraging with an American major in the woods of Brittany, accompanied by a monkey that perched on his horse's rump. The law students of Rennes loved him for the boldness of his actions and the liberality of his ideas: he had been one of the twelve Breton gentlemen imprisoned in the Bastille. He was elegantly tall, well mannered, honest-looking, handsome, and bore a striking resemblance to the portraits of the young lords of the League.

I decided to embark from Saint-Malo, in order to embrace my mother. I have already said in the third book of these *Memoirs* how I passed through Combourg and what feelings oppressed me there: I stayed for two months in Saint-Malo, busy with preparations for my voyage, as I had done years earlier when I planned to go to India.

I struck a deal with a captain named Desjardins: he would take me as far as Baltimore with Abbé Nagot and several of the seminary students placed under his care. These traveling companions would have been better suited to me four years prior: I had since gone from being a Christian zealot to a freethinker, which is to say a very vacant thinker indeed. This change in my religious convictions came from the reading of philosophical books. Now I believed, in good faith, that a religious mind was partly paralyzed—that there were truths which would always escape it, no matter how superior it might be in other respects. This self-righteous arrogance led me to suppose that the religious mind suffered from a deficiency, which is exactly the deficiency suffered by the philosophical mind: a limited intelligence thinks it can see everything because it keeps its eyes open; a superior intelligence consents to close it eyes, for it perceives that everything is within. Finally, one other thing brought about the change in my thinking, and that was the bottomless despair I carried with me in the depths of my heart.

A letter from my brother has fixed the date of my departure in my memory. He wrote to my mother from Paris, informing her of Mirabeau's death. Three days after the arrival of this letter, I went to board my ship in the harbor. My luggage was already stowed. We weighed anchor: a solemn moment among sailors. The sun was setting when the coast guard left us, having led us through the channels. The sky was dark, the breeze soft, and the waves beat heavily against the reefs only a few cable-lengths from the ship.

My eyes remained fixed on Saint-Malo; I had just left my mother there in tears. I could still make out the steeples and the domes of the churches where I had prayed with Lucile; the walls, the ramparts, the forts, the towers, and the beaches where I had spent my childhood with Gesril and my other companions. I was abandoning my fractured country at the very moment she had lost a man whom no one could replace; I was going away as uncertain about what destiny had in store for my homeland as for myself. Who would be lost to France, or to me? Would I ever see France or my family again?

As night fell, we were becalmed at the mouth of the roadstead; the beacons and the fires of town were kindled: those bright shapes that had glimmered beneath my father's roof seemed simultaneously to smile at me and bid me farewell, lighting my way among the rocks, through the shadows of the night and the darkness of the waves.

I was taking nothing with me but my youth and my illusions; I was deserting a world whose dust I had trampled and whose stars I had counted for a world where the soil and the sky were unknown to me. What would have happened to me if by some chance I had reached my journey's end? Bewildered on the hyperborean shores, the years of discord that have crashed over so many generations with so much noise would have broken in silence over my head. Society would have renovated its face in my absence. Probably I would never have had the misfortune to write. My name would have remained obscure, or it would have been linked with one of those quiet, less-than-glorious reputations which are disdained by envy and left in peace. Who knows if I would ever have re-crossed the Atlantic, or if I might not have settled a place in the vast solitudes, explored and discovered at my risk and peril, like a conqueror among his conquests?

But no! I would have to return to my country, to a change of misery, and I would then be something different from what I had been. The sea, in whose lap I was born, would be the cradle of my second life. I was carried by her, on my first voyage, as if at my nurse's breast—as if in the arms of the first being who shared my pleasures and my tears.

The ebb tide, in the absence of a breeze, tugged us out to sea, and the lights on the shoreline dwindled little by little until they disappeared. Exhausted by reflections, vague regrets, and still vaguer hopes, I went down to my cabin: I lay swaying in my hammock to the noise of the waves that lapped against the ship's side. The wind rose, the unfurled sails that had hung flapping from the masts began to swell, and, when I climbed on deck the next morning, the land of France was nowhere to be seen.

Here my destinies changed. As Byron says: *Encore à la mer!* Again to sea![20]

BOOK SIX

I.

PROLOGUE

London, April to September 1822;
Revised in December 1846

THIRTY-ONE years after having set sail for America as a simple sublieutenant, I set sail for London with a passport conceived in the following terms: *Laissez passer sa seigneurie le Vicomte de Chateaubriand, pair de France, ambassadeur du Roi près Sa Majesté Britanique,* etc., etc. "Let pass his lordship the Vicomte de Chateaubriand, Peer of France, Ambassador of the King to His Majesty, the King of Britain." No description; my greatness was supposed to be enough to make my face familiar everywhere. A steamboat, chartered for me alone, carried me from Calais to Dover. When I set foot on English soil, on April 5, 1822, I was saluted by the cannon of the fort. An officer came on behalf of the commandant to offer me an honor guard. Down at the Shipwright Inn, the owner and the waiters of the place received me with deep bows and bared heads. Madame the Mayoress invited me to a soirée in the name of the loveliest ladies of the town. Monsieur Billing, an attaché of my embassy, was awaiting my arrival. A meal of enormous fish and monstrous quarters of beef restored *Monsieur l'Ambassadeur,* who had no appetite at all and who was not tired in the least. The townspeople, gathered beneath my windows, filled the air with their loud *huzzahs.* The officer returned and, despite my protest, posted sentries at my door. The next day, after distributing no small amount of my master the King's money, I was on my way to London, to the booming of cannon, in a light carriage driven at full trot by a pair of elegantly dressed jockeys. My servants followed in other carriages, and couriers dressed in my livery rode alongside the cavalcade. We passed through Canterbury, drawing the gaze of John Bull and of every horse and rider that crossed our path. At Blackheath, a common once haunted by highwaymen, I found an entirely new village. Soon after, I saw the immense skullcap of smoke that covers the city of London.

Plunging into this gulf of carbon vapor, as though into one of the maws of Tartarus, and crossing the entire town, whose streets I well remembered, I landed at the embassy in Portland Place. There the chargé d'affaires, M. le Comte Georges de Caraman, the secretaries of the embassy, M. le Vicomte de Marcellus, M. le Baron Élisée Decazes, M. de Bourqueney, and the other attachés welcomed me with dignified deferentiality. Every usher, porter, valet, and footman of the house stood assembled on the sidewalk. I was presented with the cards of English ministers and foreign ambassadors, who had already been informed of my upcoming arrival.

On May 17, in the year of grace 1793, I disembarked at Southampton on my way to this same city of London, an obscure and humble traveler coming from Jersey. No mayoress took notice of me. On May 18, William Smith, the mayor of Southampton, handed me a travel permit for London to which a copy of the Alien Bill had been attached. My description read, in English: "François de Chateaubriand, French officer in the emigrant army, five feet four inches high, thin shape, brown hair and brown side whiskers."[1] I modestly shared the least expensive carriage with a few sailors on leave. I changed horses at the most miserable inns. Poor, sick, and unknown, I entered a rich and opulent city, where Mr. Pitt reigned. I found lodgings, for six shillings a month, under the laths of a garret at the end of a little street off the Tottenham Court Road, which a cousin from Brittany had prepared for me:

> *Ah!* Monseigneur, *que votre vie,*
> *D'honneurs aujourd'hui si remplie,*
> *Diffère de ces heureux temps!*[2]

Yet another sort of obscurity has come to darken my days in London. My political position is overshadowing my literary fame, and there is not a fool in the three kingdoms who doesn't prefer the ambassador of Louis XVIII to the author of *The Genius of Christianity*. I shall see how things turn out once I'm dead, or once I've ceased to fill M. le Duc Decazes's post in the Court of George IV—a succession as bizarre as the rest of my life.

Now that I am in London as the French ambassador, one of my greatest pleasures is to abandon my carriage in the corner of a square and go wandering on foot through the backstreets I used to frequent; the cheap, working-class suburbs where sufferings refuge with similar sufferings; the unheralded shelters I haunted with my partners in distress, never knowing whether I would have enough bread to survive the morrow—I, whose table is laden with three or four courses today. In all those narrow and destitute doorways that once were open to me, I meet only unfamiliar faces. No longer do I see my compatriots wandering the streets, recognizable by their gestures, their gait, the state and cut of their clothes; no longer do I catch sight of those martyred priests, wearing their little collars, their big three-cornered hats, and their long black threadbare frocks, to whom the English used to tip their hats as they passed by. Wide streets lined with palaces have been cut, bridges built, and promenades laid: Regent's Park occupies the site, close to Portland Place, where once there were meadows covered with herds of cattle. A graveyard, which dominated the view from the window of one of my garrets, has disappeared into the confines of a factory. When I go to see Lord Liverpool, I am hard pressed to pick out the empty spot where Charles I's scaffold once stood. New buildings, closing in around the statue of Charles II, have encroached, along with forgetfulness, on memorable events.

How I mourn, amid my insipid pomp, that world of tribulations and tears, that time when my sorrow mingled with the sorrows of a whole colony of exiles! It's true then that everything changes, that the poor die the same as the prosperous. And what has become of my brothers in emigration? Some are dead, and others have suffered their

242 · MEMOIRS FROM BEYOND THE GRAVE

various fates: like me, they have seen their family and their friends disappear, and they find themselves less at home in their own country than they were in a foreign land. Was it not in that land that we had our gatherings, our amusements, our celebrations, and above all our youths? Mothers and young maidens starting their lives in adversity brought home the weekly fruit of their labors, then went out to revel in some hometown dance. Friendships were struck up in the small talk of the evenings, after the day's work, on the grass of Hampstead or Primrose Hill. In chapels, decorated with our own hands in dilapidated rooms, we prayed together on January 21 and on the day of the Queen's death, deeply moved by the funeral oration delivered by the emigrant *curé* of our village. We strolled along the Thames, gazing at the ships towering over the docks and loaded with the riches of the world, admiring the country houses of Richmond—we who were so poor, we who were deprived of our father's roofs. All these things were true happiness!

When I come home in 1822, instead of being greeted by my friend, trembling with cold, who opens the door of our garret calling me by my first name, who goes to bed on a pallet next to mine, covering himself with a thin coat and with nothing but the moonlight for a lamp, I walk by torchlight between two lines of footmen ending in five or six respectful secretaries, and arrive, riddled along the way by the words *Monseigneur, My Lord, Your Excellency, Monsieur l'Ambassadeur,* at a parlor draped in gold and silk.

—I'm begging you, young men, leave me be! Enough with these *My Lords*! What do you want me to do with you? Go and laugh in the chancery, as if I weren't here! Do you think you can make me take this masquerade seriously? Do you think I'm stupid enough to believe that my nature has changed because I've changed my clothes? The Marquess of Londonderry is coming to call, you say; the Duke of Wellington has left his card; Mr. Canning came looking for me; Lady Jersey expects me for dinner with Lord Brougham; Lady Gwydir hopes that I will join her in her box at the Opera at ten o'clock; Lady Mansfield, at midnight, at Almack's....

Have mercy on me! After all, where can I hide? Who will deliver me? Who will rescue me from these persecutions? Come back, you lovely days of indigence and solitude! Rise up and live again, my companions in exile! Let us go, old comrades of the camp-bed and the pallet, let us go out into the country, into the little garden of some forgotten tavern, and drink a bad cup of tea on a wooden bench, talking of our foolish hopes and our ungrateful homeland, mulling over our troubles, looking for ways to help each other or one of our relations even worse off than ourselves.

This is how I've felt and what I've thought these first days of my embassy in London. Only by saturating myself in the less ponderous sadness of Kensington Gardens have I been able to escape the sadness that besieges me beneath my own roof. At least these gardens haven't changed (I assured myself of this again in 1843); the trees alone have grown taller: here, in perpetual solitude, the birds build their nests in peace. It's no longer even the fashion to meet in this place, as it was in the days when Madame Récamier, the most beautiful of Frenchwomen, used to walk here followed by the crowd.[3] Now, from the edge of the deserted lawns of Kensington, I love to gaze at the running of the horses across Hyde Park and the high society carriages among which one might pick out my tilbury, standing empty, while I, become once again a poor little émigré, climb the path where the banished confessor not long ago recited his breviary.

It was in Kensington Gardens that I contemplated the *Essai historique*. It was there that, reading over the journal of my travels overseas, I drew from it the loves of *Atala*. It was there, too, after wandering in the country, under a low English sky, glowing, as though shot through with polar light, that I penciled the first sketches of the passions of *René*. By night, I stored the harvests of my daydreams in the *Essai historique* and *The Natchez*. The two manuscripts advanced side by side, though I often lacked the money to buy paper, and, for want of thread, fastened what sheets I had together with tacks pulled from the windowsill of my garret.

These places where I had my first inspirations make me feel their power; they refract the sweet light of memories over the present—and I feel myself prodded to take up the pen again. So many hours are wasted in embassies! I have as much time here as in Berlin to continue my *Memoirs*, this edifice that I'm building from dry bones and ruins. My secretaries in London want to go picnicking in the morning and dancing at night, and I am glad to let them go. The men, Peter, Valentin, and Lewis, go to the tavern; the maids, Rose, Peggy, and Maria, for a stroll on the sidewalks; and I am delighted. I have been left the key to the street door: *Monsieur l'Ambassadeur* is in charge of the house. If you knock, he shall open. Everyone is gone, and I am here alone. Let us get down to work.

It was twenty-two years ago, as I have just said, that I sketched *The Natchez* and *Atala* here in London; I am now at the precise moment in my *Memoirs* when I set sail for America: this coincidence suits me marvelously. Let us cancel out those twenty-two years, as they have in effect been canceled out of my life, and set off for the forests of the New World. The story of my embassy will be told when the time is right, if it pleases God; but as long as I remain here for a few months, I should have the leisure to proceed from Niagara Falls in New York to the Army of the Princes in Germany, and from the Army of the Princes to my refuge in England. The Ambassador of the King of France can then recount the story of the French émigré in the same place where the latter was exiled.

2.

CROSSING THE OCEAN

London, April to September 1822

THE LAST book ended just after I boarded the ship in Saint-Malo. Soon we left the Channel, and an immense swell from the west let us know that we had reached the Atlantic.

It is difficult for those who have never been to sea to imagine the feelings that a man experiences aboard a ship when he looks around him and sees nothing but the solemn face of the deep. In the dangerous life of a sailor, there is a freedom that comes of the absence of land. The passions of men are abandoned on shore, and between the world that they leave and the world that they seek, the element on which the sailors are borne is all that there is of love and country. There are no more duties to fulfill, no more visits to pay, no more newspapers, no more politics. The very language of sailors is different from ordinary language: it is a language such as the ocean and the sky, the calm and the tempest might speak. Aboard a ship, you inhabit a universe of water among creatures whose clothing, tastes, manners, and faces do not resemble those of the autochthonic tribes. They have the wildness of the sea wolf and the lightness of the bird; their brows are free of society's cares, and the wrinkles that do cross it resemble the folds of a slackened sail, formed less by age than by the North wind, like the wrinkles formed upon the waters. The salt-steeped skin of these creatures is red and chapped, like the surface of a reef battered by the waves.

Sailors have a passion for their ship. They cry ruefully when they leave it, tenderly when they see it again; they cannot stay at home with their families. After having sworn a hundred times that they will never again expose themselves to the sea, they find it impossible to live without it, like a young man who cannot tear himself from the arms of a fickle and unfaithful mistress.

On the docks of London and Plymouth, it is not unusual to find sailors who were born on ships. From their childhood until their old age, they never set foot on shore. They see the land only from the sides of their floating cradle, spectators of a world that they will never enter. In this life reduced to so small a space, under the clouds and above the abyss, all things are animate to the mariner: an anchor, a sail, a mast, or a cannon are characters worthy of affection, each of which has a story of its own.

The sail was torn on the coast of Labrador; the master sail-maker put on that patch you see there.

The anchor saved the ship when all the other anchors had dragged in the coral reefs near the Sandwich Islands.

The mast snapped during a hurricane off the Cape of Good Hope; it was originally made of a single pole, but it is much stronger now that it is made of two.

The cannon was the only one not dismounted in the Battle of the Chesapeake.

The news on board is most interesting: the log has been thrown and the ship is making ten knots.

At noon the sky is clear; a measurement is taken: we are at such-and-such a latitude.

A reckoning: it is calculated that we have gone so many leagues on our course.

The declination of the compass is so many degrees: we are traveling north.

The sand in the hourglass is falling fitfully: it is going to rain.

Some of the sailors notice storm petrels in the ship's wake: a squall is coming.

Flying fish to the south: the weather will be calm.

To the west, a clear spot forms in the clouds; it is the footprint of the wind: tomorrow, the wind will blow from that direction.

The water has changed color; we have seen driftwood and seaweed, gulls and ducks, and a little bird that came and perched on the shrouds: we must turn our course back out to sea, for we are nearing land, and it is no good to sail too close to the coast at night.

In the coop there is a favorite and, so to speak, sacred rooster who has outlived all the others. He is famous for having crowed during a battle as though he were on a farmyard among his hens. Below deck there lives a cat: coat streaked with green, tail hairless, whiskers bushy, firm on his feet, shifting his weight against the pitch and balancing against the roll.[4] He has traveled twice around the world and was saved from a shipwreck on a floating barrel. The ship's boys give the rooster biscuits steeped in wine, and Tom has the privilege of sleeping, whenever he pleases, curled up in the second mate's fur coat.

An old sailor resembles an old farmer. Their harvests are different, it's true: the sailor has led a wandering life, and the farmer has never left his fields; but they both know the stars and predict the future as they plow their furrows. To the one, the nightingale, the lark, and the robin, and to the other, the petrel, the curlew, and the halcyon are prophets. They both retire at evening-time, the one to his hut, the other to his cabin. They both lay their heads down in these frail dwellings, and yet the hurricane that batters them does not disturb their tranquil consciences.

> If the wind tempestuous is blowing,
>   Still no danger they descry;
> The guiltless heart its boon bestowing,
>   Soothes them with its Lullaby, etc., etc.[5]

The sailor knows not where death will take him by surprise, nor on what coast he will lose his life. Perhaps, when his last sigh has mingled with the wind, he shall be launched into the bosom of the tides, bound to two oars, and allowed to continue his journey, or perhaps he will be buried on a desert island that no man will ever find again, and sleep there as isolated as when he slept in his hammock on the open sea.

The vessel alone is a sight to behold. Sensitive to the slightest movement of the helm, a hippogryph or a winged stallion, she responds to the touch of the skipper as a horse to the touch of a rider. The elegance of the masts and the rigging, the nimbleness of the sailors who flit over the shrouds, the different aspects of the ship, when she heels under a contrary blast, or when she scuds before a favorable boreal wind, makes this intelligent contrivance one of the wonders of man's genius. Sometimes, the swell and its foam break and burst against the hull; sometimes, the peaceful waves divide themselves unresisting before the prow. The flags, the pennants, and the sails complete the beauty of this palace of Neptune: the lowest sails, deployed in all their grandeur, bulge like enormous cylinders, and the topsails, cinched around their middle, resemble the breasts of a Siren. Brought to life by an impetuous breath, the ship's keel, like a plowshare, loudly creases the blue fields of the sea.

On this ocean road, along which there are no trees, no villages, no towns, no towers, no spires, and no tombstones; on this highway without signposts or milestones, with no borders but the waves, no relays but the winds, no lights but the stars, the most beautiful of adventures, when you are not in search of undiscovered lands or waters, is the meeting of two ships. They catch sight of each other on the horizon through the spyglass, and begin to navigate one toward the other. The crew and the passengers rush upon deck. The structures approach, hoist their flags, take in their reefs, and heave to. When all is silence, the two captains, standing on their quarterdecks, hail one another through speaking-trumpets: "Name of ship? Out of what port? Name of captain? Where are you coming from? How many days out? Latitude and longitude? Farewell now! Farewell!"

They let go the reefs and the sails tumble down again. The sailors and the passengers of the two ships watch each other disappear without saying a word. These ones go to seek the sun of Asia; these others, the sun of Europe; no matter which way they go, the same sun shall see them die. Time carries off and separates travelers on land even more promptly than the wind carries off and separates them at sea. So we make our signals from afar: *Farewell now! Farewell!* The common port is Eternity.

And if the vessel encountered were that of Cook or La Pérouse?[6]

The boatswain of my Maloan ship was a former cargo supervisor named Pierre Villeneuve, whose very name pleased me, for it recalled my nurse. This Villeneuve had served in India under the Bailli de Suffern and in America under the Comte D'Estaing: he had taken part in a host of engagements. Leaning on the fore of the ship beside the bowsprit, as though he were a veteran seated beneath the trellis of his little garden in the ditch around the Invalides, Pierre would chew a quid of tobacco that filled his cheek like a swelling and describe for me the moment when the decks were cleared, the effect of artillery detonations below board, the damage done by cannonballs and their ricochets against the gun carriages, the guns, and the timber-work. I made him tell me about Indians, Negroes, and colonists. I asked him how these people dressed, how trees were shaped, the color of the earth and the sky, the taste of fruits, if pineapples were better than peaches, if palm trees were more beautiful than oaks. He explained it all to me by drawing comparisons with things I knew. He said that palm trees were large cabbages, that an Indian's dress was like my grandmother's dress, that a camel looked like a hunchbacked donkey, and that all the peoples of the Orient, most notably the Chinese, were thieves and cowards. Villeneuve was from Brittany, and we never failed to finish our conversations by praising the incomparable beauty of our native land.

The ship's bell inevitably interrupted our talk. It rang for the changing of the watch, for dressing, for roll call, and for meals. In the mornings, at its signal, the crew clambered on deck, stripped off the blue shirts they were wearing, and donned another blue shirt that had been left to dry in the shrouds. The cast-off shirts were immediately washed in the same tubs in which this boarding-house of seals lathered their leathery faces and their tar-black paws.

At midday and evening meals, seated in a circle around the mess, the sailors would plunge their pewter spoons one after another, rhythmically and without any cheating, into the swashing and roiling soup. Those who weren't hungry sold their share of biscuit and salted meat to their mates for a plug of tobacco or a glass of eau-de-vie. The passengers meanwhile ate in the captain's cabin. When the weather was fine, a sail was spread over the quarterdeck, and we dined in sight of the blue sea, flecked here and there by the white marks made by the skimming of the breeze.

Wrapped in my cloak, I would lie on the deck at night, contemplating the stars above my head. The swelling sails brought me down the cool breeze, which lulled me asleep beneath the celestial dome: half drowsing and driven onward by the wind, I seemed to see the sky change with my changing dreams.

The passengers aboard a ship form a society different from that of the crew. They belong to another element, and their destinies lie on land. Some are running away to find fortune, and some to find rest; that one is returning to his homeland, and this one is leaving it; others are journeying to learn the ways of foreign peoples or to study the arts and sciences. Every one has time to get to know each other on this wandering hotel that travels with the traveler; time to hear many adventures recounted, conceive antipathies, and contract friendships. When they come and go, those young women born of English blood and Indian blood, who combine the beauty of Clarissa and the delicacy of Shakuntala,[7] then chains are formed that bind and unbind the fragrant breezes of Ceylon, which are sweet like them, and like them nimble.

3 .

FRANCIS TULLOCH—CHRISTOPHER COLUMBUS—CAMÕES

London, April to September 1822

AMONG my fellow passengers was an Englishman named Francis Tulloch. He had served in the artillery; he was a painter, a musician, a mathematician, and spoke several languages. The Abbé Nagault, a Superior of the Sulpiciens, had met this Anglican officer and made him a Catholic. He was now taking his neophyte to Baltimore.

I struck up a friendship with Tulloch. As I was then a deep philosopher, I urged him to return to his family. The sights that we had before our eyes sent him into transports of admiration. We used to get up at night, when the deck was abandoned to the officer on watch and a few sailors who smoked their pipes in silence: *Tuta aequora silent.*[8] The ship rolled at the mercy of the slow and soundless waves, as sparks of fire coursed in the white foam along her sides. Thousands of stars shining in the somber azure of the celestial dome and a shoreless sea: infinity in the sky and on the waters! Never has God more impressed me with his grandeur than on those nights when I had such immensity above my head and such immensity below my feet.

Westerly winds interspersed with calms slowed our progress. On May 4, we had only got as far as the Azores. On the sixth, around eight o'clock in the morning, we came in sight of the Island of Pico, that volcano which has long towered over innavigable seas, a useless beacon by night and an invisible landmark by day.

There is something magical about seeing land rising up from the bottom of the ocean. Christopher Columbus, hemmed in by his mutinous crew and ready to return to Europe without having reached his journey's end, spied a little light shining on a beach that night had hid. The flight of birds had guided him toward America. Now the glow of a savage hearth revealed to him a new universe. Columbus must have experienced the kind of feeling that scripture ascribes to the Creator when, having drawn up the earth out of nothingness, he saw that his work was good: *vidit Deus quod esset bonum.*[9] Columbus also created a world. One of the first biographies of the Genoese navigator is that which Giustiniani, publishing his Hebrew psalter, placed in the form of a note beneath the psalm: *Caeli enarrant gloriam dei.*[10]

Vasco de Gama must have been no less amazed when, in 1498, he touched the coast of Malabar. In a moment, everything changed on the globe. Nature took on a new appearance, and the curtain, which for thousands of centuries had hidden a part of the earth, was lifted. The sailors discovered the country of the sun, the place where he rose each morning "like a bridegroom or a giant," *tanquam sponsus, ut gigas.*[11] They saw, in all her nakedness, that wise and brilliant Orient whose mysterious history was blended with the travels of Pythagoras, the conquests of Alexander, the memory of the crusades, and whose perfumes came to us from across the fields of Arabia and the sea of Greece. Europe sent her a poet to pay her tribute: Camões, the swan of Tagus, made his sweet sad voice heard over the shores of the Indies. He borrowed from them their radiance, their fame, and their misfortune. He left them only their riches.

4·

THE AZORES—THE ISLAND OF GRACIOSA

WHEN GONZALO Villo, Camões's maternal grandfather, discovered a part of the Azorean archipelago, he would have reserved, if he had foreseen the future, a concession of six feet of earth to cover his grandson's bones.

We anchored in a bad roadstead, over a rocky bottom, forty-five fathoms deep. The island of Graciosa, in sight of which we moored, displayed slightly rounded hills whose shape recalled the ellipses of an Etruscan amphora: they were draped in green grains and exhaled a pleasant, wheaty odor, peculiar to the Azorean harvest. Up and down these carpets one could see the border walls, made of volcanic stones, parti-colored black and white, and stacked one atop the other. An abbey, a monument of an old world on a new soil, stood on the summit of a low hill, and at the foot of this hill, in a pebbly cove, the red roofs of the town of Santa Cruz shimmered in the sun. The entire island, with its carved bays, promontories, inlets, and capes, was repeated in the inverted landscape of the waters. Sheer rock walls rising up from the waves formed an outer belt. In the background, the cone of the Pico volcano, planted on a cupola of clouds, pierced the aerial panorama beyond Graciosa.

It was decided that I would go ashore with Tulloch and the second mate. The longboat was lowered and rowed toward land, which was about two miles distant. We noticed some movement on the coast: a pram was coming toward us. As soon as it was within shouting distance, we could see a great number of monks aboard. They hailed us in Portuguese, Italian, English, and French, and we replied in all four languages. Alarm reigned. Our ship was the first vessel of large tonnage that had dared to anchor in the dangerous roadstead where we were now drifting with the tide. What's more, the islands were seeing the tricolor flag for the first time; they didn't know whether we came from Algiers or Tunisia: Neptune did not yet recognize this flag carried so gloriously by Cybele. When they saw that we had human faces and understood what they said, however, their joy was extreme. The monks gathered us into their boat, and we rowed cheerfully toward Santa Cruz. There we disembarked with some difficulty, due to the rather violent surf.

All the island rushed down to meet us. Four or five *alguazils*, armed with rusty pikes, took us with them. His Majesty's uniform made them treat me with deference, and I was mistaken for the leading member of this deputation. We were escorted to the Governor's House, or Hovel, where His Excellency, dressed in a wretched green coat that had once been braided with gold, granted us a solemn audience: he permitted us to restore our provisions.

Our monks then brought us to their monastery, a commodious and well-lighted building adorned with balconies. Tulloch had meanwhile found a countryman: the chief monk, who had directed all our movements, was a sailor from Jersey whose vessel had foundered off the coast of Graciosa. He was the only survivor of this shipwreck, and no fool; he was amenable to the lessons of the catechists. He learned Portuguese and a few words of Latin. His Englishness served in his favor, and they soon converted and made a monk of him. The Jerseyan sailor found it much more agreeable to be fed, clothed, and lodged at the altar than to go taking in the mizzen topsail; but still he remembered his old trade: having gone so long without speaking his own language, he was delighted to meet someone who understood it, and he laughed and swore with Tulloch like a true seaman. He accompanied us everywhere on the island.

The houses of the village were built of wood and stone, and prettified by exterior galleries that gave a clean air to these shanties, for they let in plenty of light. Almost all the peasants were vinedressers and went around half-naked, bronzed by the sun; the women were small, yellow like mulattoes, but lively and naively coquettish with their mock orange bouquets and the rosaries that they wore as crowns and necklaces.

The hillsides glowed with vine stocks whose wine tasted almost like the wine of Fayal. Water was scarce, but wherever a spring welled up there was a fig tree and a small chapel with its portico painted in fresco. The arches of the portico framed several views of the island and several stretches of sea. It was on one of those fig trees that I saw a flock of blue teals—those seabirds whose feet are not webbed. The tree was leafless, but it bore red fruits set in its branches like crystals. When it was ornamented by the cerulean birds who came there to rest their wings, the fruits seemed to turn a dazzling crimson, and it was as though the tree had suddenly burst forth with azure leaves.

It is probable that the Azores were known to the Carthaginians, and it is certain that some Phoenician coins have been unearthed on the island of Corvo. The modern navigators who first landed on the island, it is said, found an equestrian statue on which the rider's right arm was extended and pointed to the west—assuming that this statue isn't one of those invented images that sometimes decorate ancient portulans.

I imagined, in the manuscript of *The Natchez*, that Chactas, returning from Europe, touched land on the island of Corvo, and that he encountered this mysterious statue. He expresses the feelings that occupied me on Graciosa and that put me in mind of the legend: "I approached this extraordinary monument. On its base, bathed by the foam and the spray of the waves, strange characters had been engraved: the moisture and the saltpeter of the seas had corroded the surface of the ancient bronze. The Halcyon, perched atop the helmet of the colossus, cried out at intervals in a languorous voice; mollusks clung to the flanks and the bronze mane of the steed, and, when I pressed my ear to its flared nostrils, I seemed to hear a clamorous rumbling within."

The monks served us a good supper after our day of wandering. We spent the night in the monastery, drinking with our hosts. Then, the next day around noon, with our provisions loaded, we returned to our ship. The monks were entrusted with our letters to Europe. The ship we found endangered by a strong southeasterly wind. The anchor was heaved, but it was ensnared down among the rocks and lost, as expected. At last, we got under weigh. The wind continued to freshen, and soon the Azores were behind us.

5.

SAILORS' GAMES—THE ISLAND OF SAINT-PIERRE
London, April to September 1822

Fac pelagus me scire probes, quo carbasa laxo.[12]

SO SAID my countryman, Guillaume le Breton, some six hundred years ago. Restored to the sea, I began to contemplate its vast solitudes again; but across the ideal world of my daydreams, like stern monitors, loomed the realities of France and its troubles. My refuge during the day, when I wanted to escape the other passengers, was the roundtop of the main mast: I used to climb up limberly, to the applause of the sailors, and take my seat there, high above the waves.

Space stretched out before me in its double azure, as though it were a canvas ready to receive the future creations of a great painter. The color of the water was like liquid glass. In the gullies that opened between its long, steep undulations, one caught glimpses of the desert that we call the Ocean: those wobbling landscapes made clear to me what the scriptures mean when they say that the earth reels like a drunken man before the Lord.[13] At times, one would have said that space was narrow and limited, for there was no vanishing point; but if a wave happened to rear its head, the billow would curl in imitation of a distant coast, until a school of dogfish passed along the horizon and created a scale of measurement. The expanse was revealed all the more when the mist, spreading over the surface of the deep, appeared to increase its immensity.

Climbing down from the eyrie of the mast, as I had formerly climbed down from the nest I had made in my willow, reduced as always to a solitary existence, I would eat a ship's biscuit and a bit of sugar with a lemon, and then go lie down, either on deck in my cloak or below deck in my bunk: I only had to stretch out my arms to reach from my bed to my coffin.

The wind forced us to bear north, and in a matter of days we were coasting along the banks of Newfoundland. Icebergs prowled in the cold pale mist.

Men of the trident have some games handed down to them by their ancestors: when you cross the Line, you must be "baptized." The same ceremony takes place in the Tropics as on the banks of Newfoundland, and, whatever the locale, the leader of the masquerade is always "the Old Man of the Tropics." Tropical and dropsical are synonymous to sailors: the Old Man of the Tropics therefore has an enormous paunch. Even under the tropical sun, he is outfitted in all the sheepskins and fur coats that the crew can find. He sits crouching on the maintop, bellowing from time to time like a wild animal. Everyone stares up at him. Then he starts climbing down the shrouds, heavy as a bear and staggering like Silenus. When he lands on deck, he roars some more, leaps, seizes a pail, fills it with water from the sea, and pours it over the head of anyone who has never crossed the Line or reached the icy latitude. You may flee below deck, leap onto the hatches, or shinny up the masts, but Old Man Tropic is always after you. It all ends with the sailors getting a large sum of drink money. Such are the games of Amphitrite, which Homer might have celebrated as he did Proteus, if old Oceanus had only been more fully charted in Ulysses' time; but then no one had seen anything except his head, at the Pillars of Hercules: his hidden body covered the world.

We steered for the islands of Saint-Pierre and Miquelon, looking for a new port of call. When we came in sight of the former, one morning between ten and noon, we were almost on top of it. Its coast, in the shape of a dark lump, pierced the fog.

We dropped anchor before the island's capital. We could not see it, but we could hear the sound of land. The passengers hurried to disembark. The Superior of the Sulpiciens, perpetually harried by seasickness, was so weak that he had to be carried to shore. I took a room apart, where I waited for a squall to tear through the fog and show me the place I inhabited and, so to speak, the face of my hosts in this country of shadows.

The port and anchorage of Saint-Pierre lie between the eastern coast of the island and an elongated islet called the Île aux Chiens. The port, known as the Barachois, runs deep into the land and terminates in a brackish swamp. A few barren crags are clustered together in the center of the island. Some of these, detached from the others, overhang the shoreline; others have a strip of leveled and peaty lands at their base. A watchtower atop one of these crags can be seen from town.

The Governor's House stands across from the wharf. The church, the rectory, and the provisions shop stand in this same place; then come the houses belonging to the naval commissary and the harbormaster, beyond which, along the pebbles of the beach, runs the town's only street.

I dined two or three times with the governor, an extremely hospitable and courteous officer; he was cultivating a few European vegetables on a glacis: after dinner, he showed me what he referred to as his garden.

A sweet and subtle scent of heliotrope was exhaled by a small patch of beans in flower; it was brought to us not by a breeze from home but by a wild Newfoundland wind with no relation to this exiled plant and with no sympathy of shared memory or pleasure. In this fragrance not breathed by beauty, not cleansed in her breast, not scattered in her footsteps, in this fragrance of another dawn, another culture, and another world, there was all the melancholy of regret, and absence, and youth.

Up from the garden, we climbed the slope until we stood at the base of the flagpole beside the watchtower. The new French flag floated above our heads, and, like the women in Virgil, we stared at the sea *in tears*;[14] it separated us from our native land! The Governor was anxious. He belonged to the defeated party, and besides, he was bored in this safe haven, well suited to a dreamer of my type, but merely a rude sojourn for a man interested in worldly affairs, or for anyone not carried along by that passion which suffuses everything and makes the rest of the world disappear. My host inquired about the Revolution, and I asked him for news of the Northwest Passage. He was on the front lines of the wilderness, but he knew nothing of Eskimos, and the only thing he had acquired from Canada were some partridges.

One morning, I went alone to the Cap-à-l'Aigle to watch the sun rise from the direction of France. There, a brumal stream had formed a cascade that with its last leap reached the sea. I sat down on a rocky ledge with my feet dangling over the water which frothed at the bottom of the cliff. A young fisher-girl appeared on the upper declivities of the crag. Her knees were bare despite the cold, and she walked barefoot in the dew. Her black hair came down in tufts from under the Indian kerchief she had wrapped around her head, and over this kerchief she wore a hat woven from local reeds and shaped like a cradle or a keel. A bouquet of purple heather peeked from between her breasts, which were outlined by the white fabric of her blouse. From time to time, she stooped to forage the leaves of an aromatic plant known on the island as "wild tea." With one hand, she dropped these leaves into a basket that she held in the other. She caught sight of me, and came fearlessly to sit by my side, setting her basket beside her. Like me, she dangled her legs over the sea and calmly watched the rising sun.

We sat for a few minutes without speaking. At last, I was the more courageous and I said, "What are you gathering there? The season for bilberries and cranberries is over."

She lifted her large dark eyes to me, timidly but with great dignity, and said, "I was gathering tea." And she showed me her basket.

"You are taking the tea home to your father and mother?"

"My father is away fishing with Guillaumy."

"What do you do on this island all winter?"

"Oh. We weave nets. We fish the ponds through holes in the ice. On Sundays, we go to Mass and vespers and sing hymns. And then we play games in the snow and watch the boys hunt polar bears."

"Will your father be back soon?"

"Oh, no," she said. "The captain is taking the ship to Genoa with Guillaumy."

"But Guillaumy will come back?"

"Oh, yes," she said. "Next season, when the fishermen return. He will bring me home a striped silk corset, a muslin petticoat, and an ebony necklace."

"And you shall be decked out for the winds, the mountains, and the sea," I said, musing. "Would you like it if I sent you a corset, a petticoat, and a necklace?"

"Oh, no!"

She got up, grabbed her basket, and hurried down a steep path along a forest of pines. She was singing a Mission hymn in a sonorous voice:

> *Tout brûlant d'une ardeur immortelle,*
> *C'est vers Dieu que tendent mes désirs.*[15]

On her way, she sent flying some of those lovely birds called egrets, because of the tufts on their heads: at that moment she looked as though she were one of their number. When she came to the sea, she hopped into her boat, unfurled the sail, and sat down at the rudder. One might have taken her for Fortune: she sailed away from me.

Oh, yes, oh, no, Guillaumy! The image of this young sailor up on the shrouds in the howling winds transformed that awful rock of Saint-Pierre into a land of delights: *L'isole di Fortuna ora vedete.*[16]

We spent fifteen days on the island. From its desolate shores, one looks across at the still more desolate shores of Newfoundland. The inland crags extend in diverging chains, the highest of which stretches northward toward Rodriguez Bay. In the valleys, granitic rock, mixed with red and greenish mica, is padded with mats of sphagnum, lichen, and dicranum.

Small lakes are fed by tributary streams: the Vigie, the Courval, the Pain de Sucre, the Kergariou, and the Tête Galante. These puddles are called the Ponds of the Savoyard, the Cap Noir, the Ravenel, the

Colombier, and the Cap à l'Aigle. When the whirlwinds descend on these ponds, they split the shallowest waters and lay bare a few scattered stretches of underwater meadowland, which are soon hidden again beneath the newly woven veil of water.

The flora of Saint-Pierre is the same as that of Lapland and the Strait of Magellan: the variety of vegetable life diminishes toward the Pole. In Spitzbergen, there are fewer than forty species of phanerogamous plants. When they change their place, the plant races become extinct. Those that thrive on the frozen steppes of the north, in the south become the daughters of the mountains; those that thrive in the tranquil atmosphere of the thickest forests, decrease in height and vitality, and die on the stormy ocean shores. On Saint-Pierre, the marsh myrtle (*vaccinium fuliginosum*) is reduced to the state of a creeper; it is quickly buried beneath the wadding and padding of the mosses that serve as humus. Being a traveling plant myself, I have taken precautions to disappear on the seashore, where I was born.

The sloping crags of Saint-Pierre are overlain with balsam firs, medlars, dwarf palms, larches, and black firs whose buds are used to brew an antiscorbutic beer. None of these trees grows taller than a man. The ocean wind pollards them, shakes them, prostrates them like ferns, and then, gliding underneath this forest of shrubs, it raises them up again; but the wind finds no trunks, nor branches, nor vaults, nor echoes to respond to its howling, and it makes no more noise here than on a heath.

These rickety woods contrast with the tall woods of Newfoundland, on the neighboring shore, where the firs are overgrown with a silvery lichen (*alectoria trichodes*), as though polar bears, the strange creepers of these trees, had torn their fur against the branches. The swamps on this island explored by Jacques Cartier contain paths beaten by these bears that look like the rustic footpaths around a sheepfold. All night, the cries of hungry animals resound through the forest. The traveler is reassured only by the no less despondent sound of the sea, whose waves, so rough and unsociable, become his companions and friends.

The northernmost point of Newfoundland reaches the latitude

of the Cape of Charles I in Labrador. A few degrees higher, the polar region begins. If we are to believe the accounts of travelers, these landscapes have their charm. In the evening, the sun, touching down upon the earth, seems to remain motionless, but then climbs into the sky again instead of dipping below the horizon. The mounts swathed in snow, the valleys carpeted in white moss on which the reindeer browse, the seas covered with whales and strewn with icebergs, and the whole scene agleam, as though illuminated simultaneously by the fires of the setting sun and the light of dawn, makes it impossible to know whether one is present at the creation or at the end of the world. A small bird, similar to the one that sings at night in our woods, makes his plaintive warbling heard, and love leads the Eskimo to the icy rocks where his companion awaits him. These human nuptials, at the farthest ends of the earth, are not without dignity or happiness.

6.

THE COAST OF VIRGINIA—SUNSET—DANGER— I LAND IN AMERICA—BALTIMORE—FAREWELL TO MY FELLOW PASSENGERS—TULLOCH

London, April to September 1822

AFTER we had taken on fresh provisions and replaced the anchor lost at Graciosa, we left Saint-Pierre. Sailing southward, we reached the latitude of 38 degrees. Calms stopped us a short distance from the coasts of Maryland and Virginia. The foggy skies of the boreal regions had given way to the most beautiful sunlight. We could not yet see the land, but the fragrance of the pine forests came to us across the waves. Dawn and daybreak, sunrise and sunset, twilight and night were all magnificent. I could never get my fill of gazing at Venus, whose rays seemed to fall around me like the cool hair of my sylph.

One evening as I sat reading in the captain's cabin, the bell rang for prayers. I went to mingle my vows with those of my companions. The officers and passengers filled the quarterdeck; the chaplain, book in hand, stood a little ways in front of us, near the helm; the sailors crowded pell-mell everywhere on deck. We stood with our faces toward the prow, and all the sails were furled.

The orb of the sun, about to plunge into the waves, appeared through the interwoven rigging as though in the midst of boundless space. One would have said, by the swaying of the ship, that the radiant star changed its horizon with each passing second. When I came to paint this picture in its entirety in *The Genius of Christianity*, my religious feelings were in harmony with the scene; but, alas, when I was there in person, the former man was still alive in me. It was not God alone that I contemplated over the waves, in all the splendor of his works. I saw an unknown woman and the miracles of her smile, the beauties of the sky seemed to bloom at her breath, and I would have traded eternity for one of her caresses. I imagined that she was throbbing behind the veil of the universe that hid her from my eyes. Oh, if only it had been in my power to tear back the curtain and press this unreal woman to my heart—to let myself be consumed on her breast by that love which was the source of my inspirations, my despair, and my life! While I was giving myself over to these emotions (so much in keeping with my future career as a furrier), an accident occurred that nearly put an end to all my plans and dreams.

That day the heat oppressed us. The ship, in a dead calm, sails furled and overburdened by its masts, was rolling tumultuously. Sunburned and weary of the swaying of the ship, I longed to bathe, and, although we had no boats down, hurled myself from the bowsprit into the sea. Everything was wonderful at first, and several passengers followed my example. I swam and swam without looking at the ship; but when I came to turn my head, I saw that the current had already dragged her far away. The sailors, alarmed, had tossed a rope to the other swimmers. Sharks were looming in the ship's wake, and rifles were fired to scare them away. The swell was so high that it slowed my return and sapped my strength. I had a whirlpool churning beneath me, and at any moment the sharks could have made off with an arm or a leg. Aboard the ship, the boatswain was trying to lower a boat into the sea, but first the hoist had to be threaded, and this took considerable time.

By the greatest good luck, an almost impalpable breeze began to blow. The ship answered a bit to the helm and came toward me. I was just able to catch the end of a cord; but my companions in audacity were already hanging onto this cord, so that every time we were hauled up the side of the ship, I found myself at the end of the rope, where they pressed down on me with all their weight. In this way, we were fished out of the water one by one, which took a long time. Meanwhile, the rolling continued, and at every other roll we were plunged six or seven feet underwater, or suspended as many feet in the air, like so many fish on the end of a line. On my final immersion, I felt I was about to lose consciousness. One more roll, and I would have been done for. I was hoisted on deck half dead: if I had drowned, it would have been good riddance to me and to everyone else.

Two days after this accident, we came in sight of land. My heart pounded when the captain pointed it out to me—America! It was faintly delineated by the tops of a few maples emerging from the water: since then, the palms at the mouth of the Nile have indicated the shore of Egypt to me in the same manner. A pilot came aboard and steered us into the Chesapeake Bay. That same evening a boat was sent ashore to look for fresh provisions. I joined the party and soon found myself treading American soil.

I cast my eyes around me and stood motionless for a few moments. This continent, perhaps unknown through the whole duration of ancient times and a great number of modern centuries; the first, wild destiny of this continent and its second destiny, since the arrival of Christopher Columbus; the old monarchical dominion that this new world had shaken off; the old society coming to an end in young America; a republic of a hitherto unimaginable type heralding a change in the human spirit; the part that my country had played in these world-altering events; these seas and these shores that owed their independence partly to French blood and to the French flag; a great man issuing from the depths of discord and wilderness; Washington at home in a flourishing city, in the same place where William Penn had purchased his patch of forest; the United States sending back to France the Revolution that France had supported with her guns; and my own future, the virgin muse that I had come to give over to the passions of a new nature; the discoveries that I wanted to make in the wilds whose huge kingdom still lay spread behind the narrow sway of a foreign civilization: such were the things that coursed through my mind.

We made our way toward a dwelling. Forests of balsam and Virginia cedar alive with mockingbirds and cardinals declared, by their shapes and their shadows, their colors and their songs, that we were entering another climate. The house, where we arrived after half an hour's walk, was something between an English farmhouse and a Creole hut. Herds of European cattle grazed in a pasture surrounded by a slatted fence, over which striped-tailed squirrels cavorted. Blacks were sawing pieces of wood, and whites were tending to tobacco plants. A negress of thirteen or fourteen, nearly naked and singularly beautiful, opened the gate of the enclosure to us like a young Goddess of the Night. We bought corncakes, chickens, eggs, and milk, and returned to the ship with our demijohns and baskets. I gave my silk handkerchief to the little African. It was a slave who welcomed me to the land of liberty.

The anchor was raised and we headed for the roads and the port of Baltimore. As we approached, the waters narrowed; they became smooth and still, as if we were sailing up a sluggish stream bordered by avenues of trees. Baltimore came into view as though at the far end of a lake. Across from the city stood a wooded hill, at the foot of which they were beginning to build. We moored alongside a quay in the harbor; I slept on board and did not set foot on land until the next morning. Then I went to find a room at the inn with my baggage in tow, while the seminarians withdrew to the establishment that had been prepared for them, whence they would go their separate ways into America.

And what became of Francis Tulloch? The following letter was delivered to me in London, April 12, 1822:

Thirty years have gone by, my dear Vicomte, since the epoch of our voyage to Baltimore, and I suppose it is quite possible that you have forgotten even my name. But if I trust to the feelings of my heart, which have always been true and loyal to you, it cannot be so, and I flatter myself that you would not be displeased at seeing me once again. Although we live opposite one another (as you will see by my address), I am only too well aware how many things separate us. But should you show the least desire to see me, I will hasten to prove to you, as much as shall be possible, that I am and have always been your faithful and devoted friend,

Fran. Tulloch

P.S. The distinguished rank you have attained and which you have earned by so many claims is right here before my eyes, but the memory of the Chevalier de Chateaubriand is so dear to me that I cannot write to you (at least this time around) as Ambassador etc., etc. Please pardon the style for the sake of our old alliance.

Friday, April 12
Portland Place, no. 30

So, Tulloch is in London. He did not become a priest after all. He is married, and his adventures are over, like mine. This letter testifies to the truthfulness of my *Memoirs* and the fidelity of my memory. Who could have borne witness to an *alliance* and a *friendship* formed thirty years ago on the waves, if the other party hadn't reappeared? But what a mournful and retrograde perspective this letter unfolds before me! In 1822, Tulloch lives in the same city as I do, and on the same street; the door of his house almost faces mine, just as when we met, on the same ship, on the same deck, cabin facing cabin. How many other friends I will never meet again! Every night as he goes to bed, a man can count his losses; it's only his years that do not leave him, though they pass. When he looks them over and calls them by their names, they respond, "Present!" Not one shirks the call.

7.

PHILADELPHIA—GENERAL WASHINGTON

London, April to September 1822

BALTIMORE, like every other metropolis in the United States, was not then as large as it is today: it was a pretty little Catholic town, very clean and lively, where the mores and manners still bore a close resemblance to the mores and manners of Europe. I paid the captain for my passage and bought him a farewell dinner. I reserved a seat in the stagecoach that made the journey to Pennsylvania three times a week. At four o'clock in the morning I climbed in, and there I was, rolling along the highways of the New World.

The route that we followed, more marked out than made, took us across a rather flat stretch of country: almost no trees at all, scant few farms, and some scattered villages. The climate was French, and the swallows skimmed over the waters as they did over the pond at Combourg.

As we approached Philadelphia, we crossed paths with peasants on their way to market, public cabs, and private carriages. Philadelphia struck me as a fine town, with wide streets, some of which were planted with trees, and all of which intersected with one another at right angles and in a regular pattern, north and south, east and west. The Delaware River runs parallel to the street that follows the city's western bank.[17] In Europe, this river would be considered tremendous; in America, no one mentions it. Its banks are low and not very picturesque.

At the time of my journey (1791), Philadelphia did not yet extend as far as the Schuylkill River, but the ground over toward that tributary had already been divided into lots, and on these lots several houses were under construction.

Philadelphia has a monotonous look. In general, what is missing from the Protestant cities of the United States are any great works of architecture: the Reformation, young in years, sacrifices nothing to the imagination and has rarely raised those domes, those airy naves, or those twin spires with which the ancient Catholic religion has crowned Europe. Not one monument in Philadelphia, New York, or Boston pyramids above the mass of walls and roofs. The eye is saddened to behold such an even level.

First I alighted at an inn, but soon I found an apartment in a boarding house occupied by planters from Santo Domingo and French émigrés with ideas quite different from mine. A land of liberty was offering asylum to people fleeing from liberty.[18] Nothing better proves the high value of generous institutions than these partisans of absolute power voluntarily exiling themselves in a pure democracy.

A man who landed in the United States as I did, full of enthusiasm for the classical world, a settler looking everywhere for the regularity of early Roman life, was bound to be shocked at finding the luxuriousness of the carriages, the frivolity of the conversations, the inequality of wealth, the immorality of banks and gaming houses, and the noise of dancehalls and theaters. In Philadelphia, I might easily have thought myself in Liverpool or Bristol. The people there were attractive: the Quaker girls, with their gray dresses, their identical little bonnets, and their pale faces, looked lovely.

At that time in my life, I greatly admired Republics, although I did not believe them possible at the stage of world history that we had reached: I understood Liberty as the ancients did, as the daughter of a nascent society's ways; but I knew nothing of Liberty as the daughter of enlightenment and an old civilization, Liberty of the kind that the representative republic has proved to be a reality: God grant that it may be durable! No longer does one have to till his own little field, grumble about the arts and sciences, or grow long fingernails and a dirty beard to be free.

When I arrived in Philadelphia, George Washington was not there.[19] I was obliged to wait eight or so days to meet him. One morning, I saw him pass in a carriage drawn by a team of spirited horses, driven four-in-hand. Washington, according to my ideas at the time, had to be a sort of Cincinnatus; Cincinnatus in a chariot was a bit out of keeping with my notion of the Roman Republic, year 296. Could Washington the Dictator be anything other than a rustic, prodding his oxen with a goad and steadily gripping the handle of his plow? But when I did go to him with my letter of introduction, I discovered the simplicity of an old Roman.

A small house, which looked just the same as the neighboring houses, was the palace of the President of the United States. There were no guards, and not even footmen. I knocked, and a young maid opened the door. I asked her if the General was at home, and she replied that he was. I told her that I had a letter to present him. The maid asked me my name, which is difficult to pronounce in English and which she could not keep in her mind. She then said to me softly, "*Walk in, sir,*" and she went before me down one of those narrow hallways that serve as foyers in English houses. She showed me into a parlor, where she asked me to wait for the General.

I was unmoved. Great souls and great fortunes do not impress me at all: I admire the former without being overawed, and the latter inspire in me more pity than respect. No man's face will ever disturb me.

After a few minutes, the General came in: a tall man, with a cold and calm rather than a noble demeanor, he resembled his portraits. I presented him with my letter in silence. He opened it and his eyes went straight to the signature, which he read aloud, exclaiming, "Colonel Armand!" This was the name by which he knew the Marquis de La Rouërie and with which the Marquis had signed.

We sat. I explained to him as best I could the reason for my journey. He replied to me in English and French monosyllables, listening to me with a sort of amazement. I noticed this and said to him somewhat heatedly, "But it is less difficult to discover the Northwest Passage than to create a nation, as you have done!"

"*Well, well, young man!*" he cried, taking me by the hand. He invited me to dinner the next day, and we said good night.

I took care not to be late. There were only five or six of us at table. The conversation turned on the French Revolution, and the General showed us a key from the Bastille. These keys, as I have already remarked, were rather silly trinkets then widely distributed. The same exporters of locksmith-wares, three years later, might have sent the President of the United States the bolt that sealed the cell of the monarch who gave liberty to France and America alike. If Washington had seen the "conquerors of the Bastille" in the gutters of Paris, he would have had less respect for his relic. The gravity and the force of the Revolution did not spring from those blood-smeared orgies. When the Edict of Nantes was revoked in 1685, the same populace from the Faubourg Saint-Antoine demolished the Protestant church at Charenton with as much zeal as they laid waste to the cathedral of Saint-Denis in 1793.

I left my host at ten o'clock in the evening and never saw him again. He departed the next day, and I continued on my journey.

Such was my encounter with the soldier-citizen, the liberator of a world. Washington went to his grave before even the smallest bit of fame attached itself to my footsteps; I passed before him as the most anonymous entity. He was in all his glory, I in all my obscurity, and I doubt whether my name stayed more than a day in his memory. I am nevertheless happy that his gaze once fell upon me. I would feel warmed by it for the rest of my life. There is a virtue in the gaze of a great man.

8.

PARALLELS BETWEEN WASHINGTON AND BONAPARTE

BONAPARTE has only recently breathed his last. As I have just gone knocking at Washington's door, the parallels between the founder of the United States and the emperor of France come naturally to mind, especially considering, at the moment I trace these lines, Washington himself is no more. Ercilla, singing and battling his way through Chile, halted in the middle of his journey to recount the death of Dido; so I, for my part, will halt at the beginning of my travels in Pennsylvania to compare Washington and Bonaparte.[20] I might have put off the comparison until I came to the days when I first encountered Napoleon; but if I should happen to stumble into the grave before reaching the year 1814 in my chronicle, no one would know anything of what I had to say about these two mandatories of Providence. I recall Castelnau: like me, an ambassador to England; like me, he wrote a part of his life in London. On the last page of Book Seven, he says to his son, "I will treat of this subject in Book Eight." But Book Eight of Castelnau's *Memoirs* does not exist. This reminds me to take advantage of being alive.

Washington does not belong, like Bonaparte, to that race which surpasses ordinary human stature. There is nothing astonishing about him. He is not posed in a vast theater; he does not take on the most competent generals and the most powerful monarchs of the age; he does not rush from Memphis to Vienna, from Cádiz to Moscow. He defends himself with a handful of citizens on unheralded ground, within the narrow circle of the domestic hearth. He fights no battles that recall the triumphs of Arbela and Pharsalus; he overturns no thrones only to rebuild others from their ruins; he never says to the kings at his door: *He has been kept waiting too long; now Attila is bored.*[21]

Silence envelops Washington's deeds. He moved cautiously; one could say that he felt charged with the liberty of future generations and feared compromising it. It was not his own destiny that this new species of hero carried; it was the destiny of his country. He did not permit himself to enjoy what did not belong to him, and from this profound humility, what light bursts forth! Look around the forests where Washington's sword once gleamed, and what do you find? Tombstones? No: a world! Washington left the United States as a trophy on his battleground.

Bonaparte has nothing in common with this serious American. He wages war loudly in the Old World; the only thing he wants to create is his reputation; he is burdened by nothing but his own lot. He seems to know that his mission will be cut short, that the torrent that falls from such heights must rush swiftly down. He hurries to enjoy and abuse his glory as if it were his fleeting youth. Like one of Homer's gods, he reaches the end of the earth in four bounds. He appears on every shore, hastily scrawls his name in every nation's annals, and tosses crowns to his family and his soldiers. He is precipitous in his monuments, his laws, and his victories. Hunched over the world, he lays kings low with one hand, while with the other he fells the Revolutionary giant; but, as he crushes anarchy, he smothers liberty, and he ends up losing his own liberty on his last battleground.

Each one is rewarded according to his works. Washington raises a nation into independence; a magistrate at rest, he falls asleep beneath his own roof amid the laments of his countrymen and the veneration of the people. Bonaparte robs a nation of its independence; a deposed emperor, he is launched into exile, where the frightened land still does not believe that he is well enough imprisoned, even in the ocean's custody. He dies, and the news of his death, proclaimed at the door of the palace before which the conqueror has previously announced so many funerals, neither detains nor surprises the passersby: for what do the citizens have to mourn?

Washington's Republic survives; Bonaparte's Empire is destroyed. Washington and Bonaparte both issued from the womb of democracy: they were both children of Liberty; but while the first was faithful, the second betrayed her.

Washington was the representative of the needs, ideas, intelligence, and opinions of his epoch. He seconded, instead of suppressed, the movements of the public mind. He longed for only what he had to long for, the very thing to which he had been called; and this is the reason for the coherence and the longevity of his work. This man who hardly strikes us at all, because he is in his just proportion, has merged his existence with that of his country. His glory is the patrimony of civilization. His reputation has risen like one of those public sanctuaries at a flourishing and inexhaustible fount.

Bonaparte, too, might have enriched the common domain; he acted on the most intelligent, the most courageous, and the most brilliant nation on earth. How would he have been ranked today, if he had added the quality of magnanimity to whatever he possessed of heroism; if, Washington and Bonaparte at the same time, he had named Liberty the universal heiress of his glory?

But that giant could never join his destiny with that of his contemporaries. His genius belonged to the modern age, but his ambition was from the old days. He could not see that the miracles of his life were worth more than a diadem, and that anyhow this Gothic ornament suited him badly. One moment he was hurrying toward the future, and the next he was recoiling toward the past; whether he rode with or against the current of the times, his prodigious strength dragged or repulsed the waves. Men were nothing in his eyes but a means to power; no sympathy linked their happiness with his. He had promised them deliverance, and he enchained them; he isolated himself from them, and they became estranged from him. The Kings of Egypt placed their funereal pyramids not among the flowering fields but amid the barren sands: Bonaparte built the monument to his fame in their image.

BOOK SEVEN

I.

JOURNEY FROM PHILADELPHIA TO NEW YORK AND BOSTON—MACKENZIE

London, April to September 1822;
Revised in December 1846

I WAS IMPATIENT to continue my journey. It was not Americans that I had come to see but something completely different from the men that I knew, something more in accordance with the habitual order of my ideas. I yearned to throw myself into an enterprise for which I had prepared nothing but my imagination and my courage.

When I formed the idea of discovering the Northwest Passage, no one knew whether the northern part of America extended to the Pole and adjoined Greenland, or whether it terminated in some body of water that linked the Hudson Bay with the Bering Strait. In 1772, Hearne had discovered the sea at the mouth of the Copper Mine River, latitude 71 deg. 15 min. north, longitude 119 deg. 15 min. west of Greenwich.*

On the coast of the Pacific Ocean, the efforts of Captain Cook and the explorers who followed him had left some doubts. In 1787, a ship was said to have entered the inland sea of North America. According to the account of this ship's captain, all that had been taken for the uninterrupted coastline north of California was merely a chain of islands set extremely close together. The English Admiralty sent Vancouver to verify these reports, which were found to be false. Vancouver had not yet made his second voyage.

In the United States, in 1791, rumors of Mackenzie's course were just beginning to circulate: departing from Fort Chipewyan on

---

* This latitude and longitude are now considered too high by 4¼ deg. (Geneva, 1832)

Mountain Lake, June 3, 1789, he had made his way to the Arctic Ocean by the river to which he gave his name.

This discovery might have made me change my direction and head due north; but I would have had some scruples about altering the plan drawn up by me and M. de Malesherbes. I therefore decided to travel west, in order to cut across to the northwest coast above the Gulf of California: from there, following the profile of the continent, keeping always in sight of the sea, I intended to explore the Bering Strait, double around the northernmost cape of North America, come down southeastward along the shores of the Polar Sea, and return to the United States by way of Hudson Bay, Labrador, and Canada.

What means did I have to carry out this prodigious peregrination? None. Most French travelers have been solitary men, abandoned to their own resources; it is rare that a government or a company employs or assists them. Englishmen, Americans, Germans, Spaniards, and Portuguese have accomplished, with the aid and support of their nations, what certain forsaken Frenchmen have begun in vain. Mackenzie and several others after him have made conquests in the vastitude of America, to the advantage of the United States and Great Britain, such as I dreamed of making for my native land. If I had succeeded, I would have had the honor of imposing French names on unexplored regions, endowing my country with a colony on the Pacific Ocean, robbing a rival power of the rich commerce of the fur trade, and preventing that rival from opening a shorter route to the Indies by putting France herself in possession of that route. I have recorded these plans in my *Essai historique*, published in London in 1796, and these plans were drawn directly from the notebook of my travels written in 1791. These dates prove that I was ahead, both in my hopes and my works, of even the latest explorers of the Arctic ice.

I found no encouragement in Philadelphia. I had begun to sense that I would not reach my destination on this first journey and that my travels were only the prelude to a second and longer journey. I wrote something along these lines in a letter to M. de Malesherbes, and while I waited for the future to arrive, I promised to poetry whatever might be lost to silence. Indeed, even if I did not find what

I was seeking in America, the polar world, I did find a new muse there.

A stagecoach similar to the one that had brought me from Baltimore carried me from Philadelphia to New York, a gay, populous, commercial city, but far from being what it is today, and further still from what it will be in a few years: for the United States are growing faster than this manuscript. I made a pilgrimage to Boston to salute the first battleground of American liberty. I saw the fields of Lexington and searched there, as I have since searched in Sparta, for the tomb of those warriors who died "in obedience to the sacred laws of their country."[1] What a memorable example of the interrelation of all human things! A finance bill passed in the English Parliament in 1765 gives rise to a new empire on this earth in 1782, and then causes the disappearance of one of the oldest kingdoms of Europe in 1789!

2.

THE HUDSON RIVER—THE PASSENGER'S SONG—
ALBANY—MR. SWIFT—DEPARTURE FOR NIAGARA
FALLS WITH A DUTCH GUIDE—M. VIOLET

London, April to September 1822

IN NEW YORK, I boarded a packet boat bound for Albany, a city situated far up the Hudson River. The company was numerous. Toward evening on the first day, we were served a collation of fruits and milk; the women sat on benches on the upper deck, the men on the boards at their feet. Conversation was not long maintained. At the sight of a beautiful natural tableau, we fall involuntarily into silence. All of a sudden, someone cried out, "Over there is the spot where Asgill was captured!" A Quaker girl from Philadelphia was implored to sing the ballad called "Asgill."[2] We were sailing between mountains, and the passenger's voice faded over the water, then rang out when we skimmed nearer the shore. The sad fate of a young soldier, a lover, a poet, and a worthy man, honored by Washington's interest and the generous intervention of a doomed queen, lent added charm to the romantic scene. The friend whom I have lost, M. de Fontanes, let fall a few courageous words in memory of Asgill when Bonaparte was poised to ascend the throne upon which Marie Antoinette once sat. The American officers seemed touched by the Pennsylvanian girl's song. The memory of their country's past troubles made them more sensitive to the present moment's calm. With great emotion, they contemplated those places which had only recently been burdened with troops, resounding with the noise of warfare, and which now were buried in profoundest peace: those places gilded by the last fires of daylight, animated by the whistling of cardinals, the cooing of blue wood pigeons, and the song of the mockingbirds, whose inhabitants, resting their elbows on fences fringed with begonias, watched as our boat passed by below them.

On arriving in Albany, I went in search of a Mr. Swift, to whom I had been given a letter of introduction. This Mr. Swift traded furs with the Indian tribes enclaved in the territory that England had ceded to the United States: for the civilized powers, republican and monarchic alike, divide land among themselves that does not belong to them. After hearing me out, Mr. Swift raised some very reasonable objections. He told me that I could not undertake a voyage of this magnitude straightaway, alone, with no assistance or letters of recommendation addressed to the English, American, and Spanish outposts through which I would have to pass. He said that if I was lucky enough to traverse so many solitudes, I would arrive in icy regions where I would die of cold and hunger. He advised me to begin by acclimating myself, urged me to learn the languages of the Sioux, the Iroquois, and the Eskimo, and to try living among the fur-trappers and the agents of the Hudson Bay Company. With this preliminary experience under my belt, I might then, in four or five years, with the aid of the French government, proceed on my hazardous mission.

This advice, which deep down I recognized as reasonable, rubbed me the wrong way. Yet if I'd really believed in myself, I should have departed for the North Pole at once, as one sets off from Paris for Pontoise. Instead I hid my displeasure from Mr. Swift. I asked him to hire me a guide and some horses to take me to Niagara and Pittsburgh. From Pittsburgh, I would travel down the Ohio and gather useful notions for my future expeditions. I still had it in my head to follow my earlier plan.

Mr. Swift hired a Dutchman for me who spoke several Indian dialects, and I bought a pair of horses and left Albany.

The whole stretch of country between the city of Albany and Niagara Falls today is cleared and inhabited; the New York canal crosses it;[3] but at that time a large part of this country was wilderness.

When I had crossed the Mohawk and entered a forest where no tree had ever been felled, I was seized by a sort of drunken fit of independence. I went from tree to tree, to the left, to the right, saying to myself, "Here, there are no more paths, no more cities, no more monarchies, no more republics, no more presidents, no more kings, no more men!" And, to test whether I was really reestablished in my original rights, I gave myself over to acts of buffoonery that infuriated my guide, who, in his heart of hearts, must have thought me mad.

Alas! I imagined myself alone in that forest where I held my head so high, when, all of a sudden, I nearly rammed my nose against a lean-to shack. Under this lean-to, I set my flabbergasted eyes on the first savages that I ever saw in my life. There were about twenty of them, as many men as women, their half-naked bodies painted up like sorcerers, their ears slit, crow feathers on their heads, and rings pierced through their nostrils. A little Frenchman, with hair powdered and curled, wearing an apple-green coat, a drugget vest, and a muslin jabot, was scraping a pocket fiddle and making these Iroquois dance to "Madelon Friquet." M. Violet (for this was his name) was a dancing instructor among the savages. He was paid for his lessons with beaver skins and bear meat. He had been a scullion in the service of General Rochambeau during the American war. Staying on in New York after our army had departed, he resolved to instruct the Americans in the fine arts. His successes widened his purview, and soon this new Orpheus was carrying civilization all the way to the New World's savage hordes. Speaking to me of the Indians, he always said, "These savage ladies and gentlemen." He was very proud of the sprightliness of his students, and indeed I have never seen such gamboling. M. Violet, holding his little violin between his chin and his chest, tuned the fatal instrument, then cried out to the Iroquois: *À vos places!* And the whole troupe started jumping like a band of demons.

Was it not a devastating thing for a disciple of Rousseau, to be introduced to savage life by a forest ball organized for the Iroquois by a former scullion in the army of General Rochambeau? I wanted very much to laugh, but I felt cruelly humiliated.

3.

MY SAVAGE REGALIA—A HUNT—THE WOLVERINE
AND THE CANADIAN FOX—THE MUSKRAT—
FISHING-DOGS—INSECTS

London, April to September 1822

I BOUGHT a complete outfit from the Indians, including two bear-skins: one for a demi-toga and one for a bed. In addition to these, I bought a red cap ribbed in cloth, a cloak, a belt, a horn for calling dogs, and the bandolier customarily worn by trappers. My hair hung loose over my bare neck; I wore a long beard: all in all, my appearance combined something of the savage, the hunter, and the missionary. I was invited to a hunt that was to set out the next day on the trail of a wolverine. This race of animal has now been almost totally anni-hilated in Canada, like the beaver.

We cast off in boats before daybreak, paddling upriver, into the forest where the wolverine had been sighted. There were about thirty of us, as many Indians as American and Canadian trappers: a part of the troupe walked alongside the flotilla on shore, with the dogs and the women, who carried our provisions.

We never encountered the wolverine, but we did kill a few lynxes and muskrats. In the old days, the Indians went into deep mourning when they sacrificed any of these latter animals by mistake, the female muskrat being, as everyone knows, the mother of humankind. The Chinese, with their finer powers of observation, hold for a fact that the rat changes itself into a quail, and that the mole changes itself into an oriole.

Our table was soon abundantly supplied with river birds and fish. The dogs are trained to dive, and whenever they are not hunting they go fishing, hurling themselves into the rivers and fetching fish from as far down as the riverbed. The women prepared our meal over a huge fire, around which we sat, or rather lounged horizontally, faces to the ground, in an effort to shield our eyes from the cloud of smoke that floated above our heads and protected us, in spirit, from the mosquitoes.

These various carnivorous insects, viewed through a microscope, are intimidating creatures. Once, perhaps, they were those winged dragons whose skeletons are still discovered from time to time. Gradually diminishing in size, as their matter diminished in energy, these hydras, griffons, and other monsters might find themselves reduced today to the condition of insects. The antediluvian giants are the little men of the present day.

4.

ENCAMPMENT ON THE SHORE OF THE ONONDAGAS' LAKE—ARABS—A COURSE IN BOTANY—THE INDIAN AND THE COW

London, April to September 1822

M. VIOLET offered me his credentials for the Onondagas, the last remnant of one of the six Iroquois nations. I first arrived at the lake that bears the Onondagas' name. There, the Dutchman searched out a suitable spot to set up camp: a river flowed from the lake, and at a bend in this river we pitched our shelter. We hammered two stakes into the ground, six feet apart, and hung a long pole horizontally in the forks of these stakes. Strips of birch bark, one end resting on the ground, the other draped over the transversal pole, formed the slanted roof of our palace. Our saddles had to do for pillows and our cloaks for blankets. We fastened bells to our horses' necks and turned them loose in the woods near our camp. They did not wander far.

When, fifteen years later, I bivouacked in the desert sands of Saba, a few paces from the Jordan, on the banks of the Dead Sea, our horses, those swift sons of Arabia, appeared to be listening to the tales of the sheik, as if they were partaking in the stories of Antar and the horse in Job.[4]

It was no more than four hours past midday when we finished making camp, and I took up my gun and went wandering in the vicinity. There were few birds. Only a solitary couple flew before me, like those birds that I had followed in my father's woods. By the male's color, I recognized the white sparrow, the *passer nivalis* of the ornithologists. I also heard the osprey, so well characterized by its cry. The flight of this screamer had guided me through the woods to a narrow valley that lay between bare and rocky heights. Halfway up stood a lowly cabin; a rawboned cow grazed in a meager meadow below.

I like small shelters. *A chico pajarillo chico nidillo*, as the Spanish say: "For a little bird, a little nest." I sat down on the slope across from the hut, which was planted on the hillside opposite.

After a few minutes, I heard voices in the valley. Three men were driving five or six fat cows. They put them to pasture and drove the skinny cow away with a switch. Then a savage woman came out of the hut and went after the frightened animal, calling to it. The cow ran to her, stretching out its neck and lowing softly. The settlers threatened the Indian woman from a distance until she returned to her cabin. The cow followed behind her.

I stood up, walked down the slope of the hillside, crossed the valley, and climbed the far hill until I came to the hut.

I pronounced the greeting that I had been taught: "*Siegoh!* I have come." But the Indian woman, instead of responding to my greeting with the usual reply, "You have come," said nothing. I stroked the cow. The Indian woman's gloomy yellow face softened ever so slightly, and I was moved by the mysterious relations of the unfortunate. There is a sweetness in grieving over wrongs over which no one else will grieve.

My hostess looked at me for a long time with lingering doubt before she came toward me and placed her hand on the brow of her companion in misery and solitude.

Encouraged by this mark of confidence, I said, in English, for I had exhausted my Indian, "She is very thin!"

The Indian replied in halting English, "She eats very little."

"They chased her away very roughly," I said.

And the woman replied, "We're used to it, both of us."

"Is this meadow then not yours?" I asked.

"This meadow was my husband's," she said. "He is dead. I have no children, and the paleskins drive their cattle through my fields."

I had nothing to offer this child of God. We took our leave of each other. My hostess had said many things to me that I did not understand at all. They were no doubt wishes for my prosperity. If they were not heard in heaven, it was not the fault of the one who prayed but of the infirmity of the one for whom those prayers were offered. Not all souls have an equal aptitude for happiness, just as not all lands bear an equal harvest.

I returned to my *ajoupa*, where a collation of potatoes and corn awaited me. The evening was breathtaking. The lake, as smooth as an unsilvered looking-glass, had not a single wrinkle. The murmuring river lapped against our peninsula, and the calycanthuses perfumed the air with the scent of apples. Again and again, the whippoorwill sang its song. We heard it, now nearer, now farther, as the bird changed the location of its love calls. No one called for me. Weep, poor William! *Weep, poor Will!*

5.

AN IROQUOIS—THE SACHEM OF THE ONONDAGAS— VELLY AND THE FRANKS—HOSPITALITY CEREMONY —ANCIENT GREEKS

London, April to September 1822

THE NEXT day I went to pay a visit to the sachem of the Onondagas. I reached his village at about ten in the morning. No sooner had I arrived than I was surrounded by a group of young savages who addressed me in their own language, mixed with English phrases and a few French words. They were noisy and jovial, like the Turks I met years later, in Koroni, when I first set foot on the soil of Greece. These Indian tribes, enclaved in clearings made by the whites, have horses and herds; their huts are stocked with utensils bought in Québec, Montréal, and Detroit, or from the markets of the United States.

The explorers of the North American interior found, among the various savage nations, every form of government known to civilized man. The Iroquois belonged to a race that seemed destined to conquer the other Indian races, if outsiders had not come to drain his blood and quash his spirit. These intrepid men were not awed by firearms when they were first used against them. They stood tall while bullets whistled and cannon boomed, as though they had heard these things all their lives: they appeared to pay them no more mind than they would a thunderstorm. As soon as he could get his hands on a rifle, the Iroquois put it to better use than any European. He did not, however, abandon the tomahawk, or the scalping knife, or the bow and arrow; instead, he added to them the carbine, the pistol, the dagger, and the hatchet, as if he could never have enough weaponry to equal his valor. Doubly armed with the murderous instruments of Europe and America, his head adorned with feathers, his ears slit, his face striped with ceremonial paint, his arms tattooed and dyed with blood, this New World champion became as daunting to see as he was to fight on the shores that he defended, foot by foot, against the invaders.

The sachem of the Onondagas was an old Iroquois in the strictest sense of the word: he preserved, in his person, the ancient traditions of the wilderness.

English accounts never fail to call the Indian sachem "the old gentleman." Now, the old gentleman is completely naked. He has a feather or a fishbone going through his nose, and sometimes he covers his head, which is as smooth and round as a cheese, with a lacy three-cornered hat, as a sign of European honor. Has Velly not inscribed history with the same truth? The Frankish chieftain Khilpéric rubbed his hair with rancid butter, *infudens acido comam butyro*, painted his cheeks with woad, and wore a colorful coat or tunic made from the skins of wild beasts; he is depicted by Velly as a prince, magnificent to the point of ostentation in his furniture and his retinue, voluptuous to the point of debauchery, and hardly believing in God, whose ministers he scorned and mocked.

The sachem of the Onondagas received me well and offered me a seat on his braided mat. He spoke English and understood French; my guide knew Iroquois: conversation was easy. Among other things, the old man told me that, although his nation had always been at war with mine, he had always respected it. He complained of the Americans, whom he found unjust and greedy. He regretted that in the distribution of Indian lands his tribe had not gone to increase the lot of the English.

The women served us a meal. Hospitality is the last virtue left to the savages in the midst of European civilization; from them, one knows well what hospitality must have been in ancient days, when the hearth was as sacred as the altar.

Whenever a tribe was driven from its woods, or whenever a man came asking for hospitality, the stranger began what was called the Dance of the Supplicant: a child put his hand to the threshold of the hut and said, "Here is the stranger!" And the chief replied, "Child, lead this man in!" Then the stranger, entering under the child's protection, would go and sit on the ashes of the hearth. And the women would recite the Song of Consolation: "The stranger has found a mother and a wife; the sun will rise and set for him, as it did of old."

These customs seem borrowed from the Greeks: Themistocles, in the house of Admetus, kisses the *penates* and the youngest son of his host (in Megra, years later, I may have trod on the poor woman's hearthstone, under which Phocion's cinerary urn lay concealed);[5] and Ulysses, in the palace of Alcinous, implores Arete: "Noble Arete, daughter of Rhexenor, having suffered cruel misfortunes, I throw myself at your feet...."[6] Once he has finished saying these words, the hero goes off to sit on the ashes of the hearth.

I took my leave of the old sachem. He had been present at the taking of Québec. Among all the disgraceful events of the reign of Louis XV, this episode of the Canadian War consoles us, as though it were a page of our ancient history recovered from the Tower of London: Montcalm, charged with defending Canada, unaided, and fighting against forces frequently replenished and four times as numerous, battles on successfully for two years. He defeats Lord Loudon and General Abercrombie. Finally, Fortune abandons him. Wounded beneath the walls of Québec, he collapses, and two days later he breathes his last. His grenadiers bury him in a crater opened by a bomb, a grave worthy of the honor of our arms. His noble enemy, Wolfe, dies a few feet away from him; he pays for Montcalm's life with his own, and has the glory of dying on a few French flags.

6.

JOURNEY FROM THE ONONDAGAS' LAKE TO THE GENESEE RIVER—BEES—CLEARINGS—HOSPITALITY—BED—A CHARMED RATTLESNAKE

London, April to September 1822

MY GUIDE and I mounted our horses again. Our route, which now became more and more grueling, was marked only by a line of felled trees. The trunks of these trees served as bridges over streams and fascines over bogs. The American population was then moving toward the Genesee land grants, which sold for a higher or lower price depending on the quality of the soil and the trees, and on the course and abundance of the waters.

It has been observed that settlers are often preceded in the woods by honeybees: the vanguard of farmers, they are the symbol of the industry and civilization they announce. Strangers to America, having arrived in the wake of Columbus's sails, these peaceable conquerors have robbed the New World's flowers only of those treasures that the natives did not know how to use, and they have made use of these treasures only to enrich the soil from which they harvested them.

The clearings on both sides of the path that we traveled offered a curious mixture of nature and civilization. In the depths of a forest that had never heard anything but the screams of savages and the bellowing of wild beasts, we came across a plowed field; from this same vantage point, we might also see an Indian wigwam and a planter's dwelling. Some of these dwellings, already finished, recalled tidy Dutch farmhouses; others were not yet half completed and had no roof but the sky.

I was welcomed into these houses, the work of a morning, where I often found a family with all sorts of European accoutrements, mahogany furniture, a piano, carpets, and mirrors a stone's throw from an Iroquois hut. At night, when the servants had come back from the woods and the fields with their hatchets and their hoes, the windows were thrown open. My host's daughters, their pretty blond hair in ringlets, would sing the duet from Paisello's *Pandolfetto* or one of Cimarosa's cantabiles in sight of the wilderness and sometimes to the murmur of a waterfall.

On the best sites, market towns had been built. The spires of new churches soared from the depths of an ancient forest. As English customs follow the English wherever they go, after crossing miles and miles of country where there was no trace of habitation, I would see the wooden sign of an inn swinging from the branch of a tree. Trappers, planters, and Indians converged at these caravansaries. The first time I stayed at one, I swore it would be the last.

Entering one of these hostelries, I stood dumbfounded by the sight of an immense bed built in a circle around a post. Each traveler took his place on this bed with his feet against the center-post and his head at the circumference of the circle, so that the sleepers were arranged symmetrically, like the spokes of a wheel or the sticks of a fan. After some hesitation, having established that nobody was there, I inserted myself into this contraption. I was just beginning to doze when I felt something sliding against me: it was the leg of my big Dutchman. Never in my life have I experienced a greater horror. I leapt out of this hospitable basket, heartily cursing the customs of our good old forefathers, and went to sleep in my cloak beneath the moonlight, out where the traveler's bedfellow was nothing less than agreeable, fresh, and pure.

On the bank of the Genesee, we found a ferry. A troupe of settlers and Indians crossed the river with us. We camped in meadows slathered with butterflies and flowers. In our various costumes, our different groups around the fire, our horses tethered or grazing nearby, we had the look of a caravan. It was there that I encountered the rattlesnake that let itself be charmed by the sound of a flute. The Greeks would have transformed my Canadian into Orpheus, his flute into a lyre, and the snake into Cerberus, or perhaps Eurydice.

7.

AN INDIAN FAMILY—NIGHT IN THE FOREST—THE FAMILY DEPARTS—INDIANS OF NIAGARA—CAPTAIN GORDON—JERUSALEM

London, April to September 1822

WE RODE on toward Niagara. We were no more than eight or nine leagues distant when we glimpsed, in a grove of oaks, the fire of some savages who had stopped on the bank of a stream where we had thought to bivouac. We benefited from their encampment: after grooming our horses, and getting ready for the night, we slunk alongside the horde; legs crossed tailorwise, we sat with the Indians around the woodpile and roasted our corncobs on their fire.

The family consisted of two women, two suckling infants, and three warriors. Conversation was general, which is to say peppered by a few words on my part and by a great many gestures all around. Then each went to asleep in the place where he sat. When I saw that I was the only one who remained awake, I went to sit by myself on a root that trailed along the bank of the stream.

The moon rose above the treetops, and a balmy breeze, which that Queen of Night brought with her from the Orient, seemed to precede her in the forest, as though it were her own cool breath. The solitary beam climbed higher and higher in the sky, now following her course, now fording groups of clouds like the summits of a mountain chain crowned with snow. Everything would have been silence and stillness but for the fall of a few leaves, the passage of a sudden wind, the whoop of an owl; in the distance, you could hear the muted roar of Niagara prolonged, in the calm night, from wilderness to wilderness, slowly fading through the lonely forests. It was in these nights that an unfamiliar muse appeared to me. I gathered some of her accents, and I marked them down in my book, by starlight, as a common musician might transcribe the notes dictated to him by some great master of harmonies.

The next day the Indian men armed themselves, and the women gathered up their baggage. I distributed a bit of gunpowder and vermilion among our hosts, and we parted by touching foreheads and chests. The warriors shouted the order to march and walked in front; the women took to the path behind them carrying the children, who, slung in furs on their mothers' shoulders, turned their heads to look at us. I followed them with my eyes until the entire troupe had vanished among the trees of the forest.

The savages of Niagara Falls in the English dominion were charged with policing that side of the border. This bizarre police force, armed with bows and arrows, refused to let us pass. I was obliged to send the Dutchman to Fort Niagara for a permit to enter British territory. This weighed heavy on my heart, for I remembered that France had once controlled Lower as well as Upper Canada. My guide returned with the permit, which I still possess: it is signed by "Captain Gordon." Is it not peculiar that I found the same English name on the door of my cell in Jerusalem? "Thirteen pilgrims had written their names on the door and the walls of the room: the first was Charles Lombard, who had traveled to Jerusalem in 1669; the last was John Gordon, and the date of his visit was 1804" (*Itinerary, from Paris to Jerusalem*).

8.

NIAGARA FALLS—RATTLESNAKE—I FALL BY THE EDGE OF THE ABYSS

London, April to September 1822

I STAYED two days in the Indian village, where I wrote another letter to M. de Malesherbes. The Indian women busied themselves with various tasks, while their infants slept suspended in large wicker nets hung from the arms of a purple beech. The grass was covered with dew, the wind carried with it the scent of the woods, and the native cotton plants, spilling over with white capsules, looked like white rose bushes. The breeze rocked the children's aerial cradles almost imperceptibly. From time to time, the mothers glanced over their shoulders to see whether their children were still asleep, or whether they had been woken by the birds. From this Indian village to the Falls, it was about three or four leagues. It would take as many hours for my guide and me to reach them. Six miles away, a column of mist already showed me the place where the waters tumbled low. My heart pounded with a joy mixed with terror as I entered those woods that hid from view one of the greatest spectacles nature has offered mankind.

We dismounted. Leading our horses by the bridle, we traveled across glades and thickets to the bank of the Niagara River, seven or eight hundred paces above the Falls. I was walking relentlessly forward when my guide seized me by the arm; he stopped me at the very edge of the water, which flowed past at the speed of an arrow. It did not foam at all but glided in a single mass over the rocky slope. Its silence before the Falls contrasted wildly with the roar of the Falls themselves.

Scripture often compares a people to great waters; here, it was a dying people, who, deprived of their voice by long struggle, were now hurling themselves into the abyss of eternity.

The guide still held onto me, for I felt myself drawn, so to speak, by the river: I had an involuntary desire to throw myself in. I cast my eyes first upstream, to the riverbanks, then downstream, to the island that divided the waters and where these waters suddenly ceased to be, as if they had been cleft in the sky.

After a quarter of an hour of perplexity and inexpressible admiration, I made my way to the Falls. One can consult the *Essai historique* and *Atala* for the two descriptions I have made of them. Today, highways lead to the cataract. There are inns on both the American and the English banks, and mills and factories below the chasm.

I could not convey the thoughts that stirred in me at the sight of such a sublime disorder. In the desert of my early life, I had to invent people to decorate the wastes around me; I drew on my own substance to make beings that I did not find elsewhere, and I carried these beings within me. Thus I placed the recollections of Atala and René on the banks of Niagara to express their sadness. For what is a cascade that falls eternally before the insensible face of the earth and the sky, if human nature is not there with its motives and its misery? How joyless to be submerged in that solitude of waters and mountains and then not know whom to tell about this great spectacle! To have the waves, the rocks, the woods, and the mountain streams to oneself alone! Give the soul a companion, and the smiling verdure of the hills, and the cool breath of the mist, will enrapture it. The day's journey, the sweet repose at its end, the rocking of the waves, the soft slumber on the moss—these things will draw the deepest tenderness from the human heart. I have seated Velléda on the shores of Armorica, Cymodocée under the porticos of Athens, and Blanca in the halls of the Alhambra. Alexander created cities wherever he roamed: I have left dreams wherever I have dragged my weary days.

I have seen the cascades of the Alps with their chamoises and those of the Pyrenees with their izards; I have not gone far enough up the Nile to see its cataracts, which are no more than rapids; and I will not speak of the azure zones of Terni and Tivoli, those elegant lines of ruins fit for the poet's song:

Et praeceps Anio ac Tiburni lucus.[7]

Niagara eclipses them all. I contemplated this waterfall that was revealed to the Old World, not by lowly little travelers like myself, but by missionaries who, searching for God in these solitudes, threw themselves on their knees at the sight of nature's marvels, and were martyred while they sang their hymns of praise. Our priests hailed the beautiful sites of America and consecrated them with their blood; our soldiers clapped their hands at the ruins of Thebes and presented arms in Andalusia: the whole genius of France lies in the double militia of our camps and our altars.

I was holding my horse's bridle twisted around my arm, when a rattlesnake rustled in the undergrowth. My startled horse reared and recoiled toward the Falls. I could not seem to untangle my arm from the reins. The horse, growing more and more frightened, dragged me after him. Already his forefeet were off the ground; poised over the brink of the abyss, he kept himself from falling only by the strength of his loins. It was all over for me, when suddenly the animal, astonished by this new danger, pirouetted back to dry ground. If I had left this life in the Canadian woods, would my soul have brought to the supreme tribunal any sacrifices, or any good works, or any virtues, like those of Father Jogues and Father Lallemand? Or would I have died with nothing to show but empty days and miserable illusions?

This was not the only risk I ran at Niagara. To get to the lower basin of the Falls, the savages used a ladder of vines, which was at that time broken. Desirous to see the height of the cataract from below, and despite my guide's protestations, I ventured down the side of an almost perpendicular rock. Ignoring the roar of the water that frothed below me, I kept my head and succeeded in getting about forty feet from the bottom. At that point, the bare and vertical stone offered nothing more for me to grip. So I remained, hanging by one hand from the last available root, and feeling my fingers gradually giving way beneath the weight of my body: there are few men who have counted two minutes of their lives as I counted those. At last my exhausted hand let go, and I fell. By an incredible stroke of good fortune, I found myself on a ledge of rock, upon which I should have been broken a thousand times, and I did not even feel great pain. I was half a foot from the abyss, but somehow I had not rolled into it. When the cold and the damp began to work upon me, however, I discerned that I had not gotten away so cheaply after all: I had broken my left arm above the elbow. The guide, who was looking down at me from above and to whom I was making signals of distress, ran off to find the savages. They hoisted me up on a rope along an otter path and carried me to their village. It was only a simple fracture. Two splints, a bandage, and a sling sufficed for my cure.

9.

TWELVE DAYS IN A HUT—THE CHANGING MANNERS OF THE INDIANS—BIRTH AND DEATH—MONTAIGNE —SONG OF THE ADDER—A LITTLE INDIAN GIRL, THE ORIGINAL OF MILA

London, April to September 1822

FOR TWELVE days, I remained under the care of my doctors, the Indians of Niagara. There, I saw other tribes who were coming from Detroit or from the country southeast of Lake Erie. I inquired about their customs, and in exchange for little gifts I received reenactments of their old customs, for these customs had already ceased to exist. Yet, at the start of the War of American Independence, the savages were still eating their prisoners, or at least the ones who were killed: an English captain, dipping a ladle into an Indian stewpot, once drew out a hand.

The Indian traditions surrounding birth and death are the least forgotten, for they do not pass lightly, like the life that intervenes; they are not things of fashion that come and go. The oldest name of the family is still conferred on the newborn, as a sign of honor: the name of his grandmother, for example, for names are always taken from the maternal line. From then on, the child occupies the place of the woman whose name he has taken, and he is addressed as the ancestor that this name brings back to life: thus an uncle may address his nephew by the title of "grandmother." This custom, laughable as it may seem, is nonetheless touching. It resurrects the dead; it reproduces the weakness of old age in the weakness of infancy; it connects the two extremities of life, and the beginning and the end of the family; it conveys a kind of immortality to one's ancestors and supposes that they are present among their descendants.

As regards the dead, it is easy to find motives for the savage's attachment to holy relics. Civilized nations, to preserve their country's memories, have the mnemonics of writing and the arts; they have cities, palaces, towers, columns, and obelisks; they have the scarring of the plow on formerly cultivated fields; their names are carved in bronze and marble, and their actions are inscribed in books. Not so for the peoples of the wilderness: their names are not written on the trees; their hut, built in a matter of hours, may disappear in a matter of moments; their labor hardly grazes the earth and cannot even raise a furrow. Their traditional songs fade with the last memory that retains them and vanish with the last voice that repeats them. The tribes of the New World thus have only one monument: their graves. Take the bones of their fathers from these savages and you take their history, their laws, and even their gods; you rob these men, and their future generations, of the proof that they ever existed or that they were ever annihilated.

I wanted very much to hear my hosts sing. A little Indian of fourteen named Mila, who was very pretty (Indian women are only pretty at that age), sang a charming song. Was it not the very verse quoted by Montaigne? "Adder, stay; stay, adder, that my sister may, by the pattern of thy many-colored coat, fashion and work a rich ribbon, which I shall give to the one I love; so may thy beauty and thy ornament be forever preferred above all other serpents."

The author of the *Essais* met a few Iroquois in Rouen who, according to him, were very reasonable characters. "But what's the use?" he added. "They don't wear breeches."[8]

If I ever publish the *stromates* or follies of my youth, and speak as freely as Saint Clement of Alexandria, you shall surely encounter Mila there.

10.

OLD CANADA—THE INDIAN POPULATION—
DEGRADATION OF THE OLD INDIAN WAYS—TRUE
CIVILIZATION PROMOTED BY RELIGION, FALSE
CIVILIZATION INTRODUCED THROUGH TRADE—
TRAPPERS—FACTORIES—HUNTING—THE MÉTIS,
OR BURNTWOODS—WARS BETWEEN TRADING
COMPANIES—DEATH OF THE INDIAN LANGUAGES

London, April to September 1822

THE CANADIANS are no longer such as they were described by Cartier, Champlain, Lahontan, Lescarbot, Laffiteau, Charlevoix, and the *Lettres Édifiantes*. The sixteenth century and the beginning of the seventeenth were still a time of great imagination and naive customs; the wonder of the former reflected a virgin nature and the candor of the latter mimicked the simplicity of the savage. Champlain, at the end of his first voyage to Canada, in 1603, recounts that "close to the Bay des Chaleurs, to the south, is an island where a dreadful monster dwells that the savages call Gougou." Thus Canada had its giant, the same as the Cape of Good Hope. Homer is the true father of all such inventions: there are always Cyclopes, Charybdis and Scylla, ogres and gougous.

The savage population of North America, not including the Mexicans or the Eskimos, numbers less than four hundred thousand souls today, and that includes both sides of the Rocky Mountains. Some travelers even put the number as low as one hundred and fifty thousand. The degradation of Indian customs has gone hand in hand with the depopulation of the tribes. Religious traditions have become confused; the instruction spread by Jesuits in Canada has mixed foreign ideas with the native ideas of the indigenes: one sees, in their rudimentary fables, disfigured Christian beliefs. Many savages wear crosses as though they were ornaments, and the Protestant merchants sell them what the Catholic missionaries give away. I will say, to the honor of our country and the glory of our religion, that the Indians are strongly attached to us, that they have never stopped regretting our absence, and that the black robe (the missionary's cassock) is still an object of veneration in the American forests. The savage continues to love us beneath the trees where we were his first guests, on the land where we have left our footprints, and where we have entrusted him with our graves.

When the Indian was naked or dressed in skins, there was something great and noble about him; in our day, European rags attest to his wretchedness without covering his nakedness: he has become a beggar at the counting-house door and no longer a savage in his forest.

Lately, a group of half-bred people have formed, born of settlers and Indian women. These people, sometimes called "Burntwoods" because of the color of their skin, act as brokers between the two authors of their double origin. They speak the language of their fathers and their mothers, and they have the vices of both races too. These bastards of civilized nature and savage nature sell themselves by turns to the Americans and the English, promising to give them a monopoly on furs. They keep up the rivalries between the English Hudson's Bay Company and the North West Fur Company, and the American Columbian-American Fur Company, Missouri's Fur Company, and others. They go hunting in the pay of individual traders and with other huntsmen in the pay of the companies.

Everyone remembers the great War of American Independence, but we forget about the blood that has flowed for the petty interests of a handful of merchants. In 1811, the Hudson's Bay Company sold a tract of land on the banks of the Red River to Lord Selkirk, which was settled in 1812. The North West or Canada company took exception to this. The two companies, allied with different Indian tribes and backed by "Burntwoods," came to blows. This domestic conflict, the details of which are horrible, took place in the icy wilds of the Hudson Bay. Lord Selkirk's colony was destroyed in the month of June 1815, exactly the same moment as the Battle of Waterloo. In these two theaters, so different in their brilliance and obscurity, the sorrows of the human race were the same.

It is no use looking in America today for those artistically constructed political constitutions about which Charlevoix once wrote: the Huron monarchy and the Iroquois republic are no more. Something of this destruction has been accomplished and goes on being accomplished in Europe before our very eyes. A Prussian poet, at a banquet given by the Teutonic Order, around the year 1400, recited the heroic deeds of his country's ancient warriors: no one understood him, and in payment they gave him one hundred empty nuts. Today, Bas Breton, Basque, and Gaelic are dying from cottage to cottage, as the goatherds and the farmers pass away. A fisherman told a traveler, "I hardly know four or five people who speak Breton, and they are all old folks like me, somewhere between sixty and eighty. The young no longer know a word of it."

In the English county of Cornwall, the language of the indigenes became extinct around the year 1676. The clans of the Orinoco no longer exist: nothing remains of their dialect but a dozen words uttered in the treetops by parakeets set free, as Agrippina's thrush once warbled a few Greek words on the balustrades of a Roman palace.[9] Such will be the fate of our modern jargons, sooner or later: they too will become Greek and Latin rubble. Some crow, flown from the cage where the last French priest kept it, will perch atop a ruined steeple and cry to the strange peoples who have taken our place, "Accept these last efforts of a voice that you once knew well: now you shall put all such talking to an end."[10]

Aspire to be like Bossuet then. In the end, perhaps your masterpiece will outlive your language and your memory in the minds of men, and survive in the memory of a bird!

II.

FORMER FRENCH POSSESSIONS IN AMERICA— REGRETS—MANIA FOR THE PAST—A NOTE FROM FRANCIS CONYNGHAM

Thinking of Canada and Louisiana, looking over the old maps of the former French colonies in America, I must ask myself how my country's government could have let go of these colonies, which would today be an inexhaustible source of prosperity.

From Acadia and Canada down to Louisiana, from the mouth of the St. Lawrence to the mouth of the Mississippi, the territory of Nouvelle-France once bordered all the first thirteen United States: the eleven others, together with the District of Columbia, the territories of Michigan, the Northwest, Missouri, Oregon, and Arkansas, belonged to us, or would belong to us, as they now belong to the United States by the cession of the English and the Spanish, our successors in Canada and Louisiana. The country between the Atlantic to the northeast, the Polar Sea to the north, the Pacific and the Russian possessions to the northwest, and the Gulf of Mexico to the south, which is to say more than two-thirds of North America, would now be governed by the laws of France.

I'm afraid that the Restoration will ruin itself by maintaining ideas contrary to the ones I am about to express here. The mania of holding onto the past, a mania that I never cease combatting, would mean nothing if it toppled only me and deposed only me from the Prince's favor; but it may well topple the throne itself. Political stasis is impossible. We must advance with the march of human intelligence. By all means, let us respect the majesty of time; let us reverently contemplate the bygone centuries, made holy by the memory and the relics of our fathers; but let us not try to return to them, for they no longer have to do with our reality, and if we tried to take hold of them, they would slip away. Around the year 1450, the Chapter of Notre-Dame d'Aix-la-Chapelle ordered the tomb of Charlemagne opened. They found the emperor sitting in a gold chair, holding in his skeleton hands a Book of the Gospels written in gold letters. Before him lay his scepter and his gold shield. At his side he had his sword, Joyeuse, sheathed in a gold scabbard. He was still clad in the Emperor's robes, and on his head, held upright by the strength of a gold chain, a winding sheet topped with a gold crown covered what had been his face. They reached out to touch the phantom, and it crumbled to dust.

Once we possessed vast lands overseas: they offered asylum to the surplus of our population, a market for our commerce, and nourishment for our navy. We are now excluded from the new universe, where the human race is starting over again. The English, Portuguese, and Spanish languages serve in Africa, in Asia, in Polynesia, on all the islands of the South Sea, and on the continent of the two Americas to express the thoughts of several million men, while we, disinherited from the conquests made by our courage and our genius, rarely hear the language of Colbert and Louis XIV spoken even in the market towns of Louisiana or Canada, which are now under foreign control. The French language lingers there only as evidence of our fortune and the errors of our politics.

And what kind of man is the king whose dominion now takes the place of the King of France in the Canadian forests? The kind who wrote me this note yesterday:

> Royal Lodge, Windsor, June 4, 1822
>
> M. le Vicomte,
>
> I have orders from the King to invite Your Excellency to come dine and sleep here Thursday the 6th *inst.*
>
> Your very humble and very obedient servant,
>
> Francis Conyngham

It is my destiny to be tormented by princes. But I have interrupted myself: I have recrossed the Atlantic and reset the arm I broke at Niagara; I have traded my bearskin for a gold-stitched coat; I have left an Iroquois wigwam for the Royal Lodge of His Majesty, Monarch of the Three United Kingdoms and Controller of the Indies; I have left behind my slit-eared hosts and the beaded little savage girl. I only wish Lady Conyngham had Mila's charm, and was of that age which still belongs to the earliest springtime—to those days that lead up to the month of May and that our Gallic poets used to call "*l'Avrillée*."[11]

Revised July 26, 1846

BOOK EIGHT

I.

ORIGINAL MANUSCRIPT FROM AMERICA—LAKES OF CANADA—A FLEET OF INDIAN CANOES—NATURE'S RUINS—VALLEY OF TOMBS—HISTORY OF THE RIVERS

London, April to September 1822;
Revised in December 1846

THE LITTLE beaded girl's tribe departed. My guide, the Dutchman, refused to go with me beyond the Falls. I paid him and joined a party of traders who were leaving to go down the Ohio. But before I went, I cast a glance at the lakes of Canada. Nothing is so sad as the face of these lakes. The plains of the Ocean and the Mediterranean open paths to the nations, and their shores are or were inhabited by many powerful civilized peoples; the Canadian lakes offer nothing but bare waves that lap against denuded lands: solitudes dividing other solitudes. Uninhabited coastlines look out on shipless seas, and you step down from desolate waves onto desolate sands.

Lake Erie is more than one hundred leagues in circumference. The riverine nations were exterminated by the Iroquois two centuries ago. A chilling thing it is, to see the Indians venturing out in bark canoes on this lake famous for its tempests, where in the old days a myriad of serpents swarmed. These Indians suspend their manitous from the sterns of their boats and launch themselves into whirlwinds among the churning waves. The lakewater, level with the apertures of the canoes, seems ready to swallow them at any moment. The hunting dogs, paws resting on the sides, howl while their masters, in total silence, strike the waters rhythmically with their paddles. The canoes advance in a line. At the prow of the first stands a chief who chants the diphthong *oah*; *o* on a long, dull note, *ah* in a short, sharp tone. In the last canoe is another chief, also standing, and maneuvering an oar that serves as rudder. The other warriors crouch on their heels at the bottom of the boats. Through the fog and the winds, one sees only the feathers that decorate the Indians' heads, the outstretched necks of the baying dogs, and the shoulders of the two sachems, the pilot and the augur: one might call them the gods of these lakes.

The Canadian rivers have no history in the Old World: theirs is different from the destiny of the Ganges, the Euphrates, the Nile, the Danube, and the Rhine. What changes have those rivers not seen on their banks? How much sweat and blood have conquerors shed in order to traverse those waters that a goatherd can step over at their source!

2.

COURSE OF THE OHIO

London, April to September 1822

LEAVING behind the lakes of Canada, we came to Pittsburgh and the confluence of the Kentucky and the Ohio. Here, the landscape displays an extraordinary splendor. Yet this magnificent country is called Kentucky, after the name of its river, which means "river of blood." It owes this name to its beauty. For over two centuries, the nations on the Cherokee side and those on the Iroquois side have been fighting over its hunting grounds.

Will the European generations on its banks prove more virtuous and free than the annihilated American generations of old? Will slaves not plow the earth beneath the lashing of their masters in these wastelands of man's primordial independence? Will prisons and gallows not take the place of the open hut and the tall tulip tree where the bird built its nest? Will the richness of the soil not engender new wars? Will Kentucky ever cease to be a *land of blood* and let the monuments of art make the banks of the Ohio still more beautiful than the monuments of nature?

Beyond the Wabash, the great Cypress, the Cumberland, the Cherokee or Tennessee, and the Yellow Banks, the traveler arrives at a strip of land frequently flooded by high waters. Here, at 36 deg. 51 min. latitude, the Ohio and the Mississippi converge. The two rivers resist each other, and this equal resistance slackens their course. Side by side, but without mingling, they slumber together for a few miles, like two great peoples of separate origins, which come to form a single race; like two famous rivals, sharing the same resting place after a battle; like husband and wife, but of enemy blood, who at first have no desire to mix their destinies in the marriage bed.

And I, too, like the powerful urns of the rivers, have divided the short course of my life between one side of the mountain and the other. Whimsical in my errors but never consciously wicked, I have preferred poor valleys to rich plains, and stopped for flowers rather than palaces. By now, I was so enraptured by my travels that I gave almost no thought to the Pole. A company of traders, lately arrived from the land of the Creeks, in the Floridas, allowed me to go with them.

We made our way toward the country then known under the general name of the Floridas, which today encompasses the states of Alabama, Georgia, South Carolina, and Tennessee. We were following very close to the trails which now link the high road from Natchez to Nashville by way of Jackson and Florence, and which returns to Virginia by way of Knoxville and Salem: country which, at that time, was little frequented, and where Bartram had already explored the lakes and the sites. Planters from Georgia and the Florida Maritimes traveled all the way to the diverse tribes of the Creeks to buy horses and half-wild beasts, which multiplied to infinity on the dry savannahs interrupted only by those wellsprings beside which I had Atala and Chactas take their rest. Some of them extended their journeys even as far as the Ohio.

We were pushed onward by a fresh wind. The Ohio, swollen by a hundred streams, was sometimes lost in the lakes that spread before us, sometimes in the thick of the forests. Islands rose up in the middle of the lakes. We set sail for one of the largest, where we landed at eight in the morning.

I crossed a meadow sown with yellow-flowered ragwort, pink-plumed hollyhocks, and purple-tufted obelarias.

An Indian ruin struck my sight. The contrast between this ruin and the youthfulness of nature, this monument of man in a desert landscape, gave me a chill. What people once lived on this island? What was their name? Their tribe? How long had they endured? Were they alive when the continent on which they were concealed was unknown to the other three quarters of the globe? The silence of these people was perhaps contemporary with the noise of certain great nations since fallen, in turn, into silence.*

From the sandy anfractuosities of the ruins, or tumuli, there grew a species of poppy with red flowers that weighed down the tops of their pale green stalks. The stem and the flower have a scent that stays on your fingers long after you have touched the plant. An emblem of the memory of a life spent in solitude, this fragrance that outlives its flower.

I observed the water lilies, which began to hide their white buds in the water at the close of day, and the *arbor tristis*, which uncloses its flowers only at the dawn of night: the wife goes to bed when the courtesan rises.

The pyramidal oenothera, which grows up to seven or eight feet tall and has notched oblong leaves of a greenish black, follows other customs toward other ends. Its yellow flower starts to unfold toward evening, in the time it takes Venus to sink below the horizon; it continues to open beneath the starlight; dawn finds it in all its splendor; but halfway through morning it begins to fade; by noon, it withers and dies. It lives no more than a few hours, but it spends these hours beneath a tranquil sky, between the breaths of Venus and Aurora. What does it matter then, the briefness of life?

I came to a stream garlanded with dionea over which a thousand dragonflies buzzed. There were also hummingbirds and butterflies that, in their bright regalia, vied in splendor with the variegations of the flowers. Yet in the midst of these wanderings and these studies, I was often struck by their futility. What! Could the Revolution, which drove me into the woods and weighed upon my every moment, not inspire me to do something more serious? While my country was wracked and overturned, could I not find something to occupy me besides descriptions, and plants, and butterflies, and flowers? Human individuality reminds us of the smallness of the greatest events. For

*The ruins of Mitla and Palenque in Mexico now prove that the New World rivals the Old World in its antiquity. (Paris, 1834)

how many men are indifferent to these events, and how many others have not even heard of them? The total population of the globe is estimated to be between eleven and twelve hundred million. One of these people dies every *second*. Thus, in every *minute* of our existence, even as we enjoy ourselves and smile, sixty people perish; sixty families weep and mourn. Life is an interminable plague. The chain of mourning and funerals that encircles us is never broken; it is always growing: we ourselves form one of its links. And still we magnify the importance of catastrophes that seven-eighths of the world will never so much as mention! Let us pant after a vain reputation that will never fly more than a few leagues from our grave! Let us dive into an ocean of bliss where every minute sixty coffins float by, incessantly renewed!

> *Nam nox nulla diem, neque noctem aurora secuta est,*
> *Quae non audierit mixtos vagitibus aegris*
> *Ploratus, mortis comites et funeris atri.*

"No day has ever followed night, nor night ever followed dawn, that has not heard the sound of weeping mingled with mournful wailings, attendants of death and dark funerals."[1]

3.

FOUNTAIN OF YOUTH—MUSKOGEES AND SEMINOLES
—OUR CAMP

London, April to September 1822

THE SAVAGES of Florida tell of an island in the middle of a lake inhabited by the most beautiful women on earth. Many times the Muskogees have tried to conquer it; but this Eden flees before their canoes: a natural emblem of those chimeras that retreat before our desires.

This land also contained a Fountain of Youth. But who would want to live his life over again?

These fables very nearly took on a kind of reality in my eyes. At a moment when we least expected it, we saw a flotilla of canoes come out of a bay, some by oar, and others by sail. They landed on our island. All in all, there were two Creek families, one Seminole and the other Muskogee, among whom there were a few Cherokees and "Burntwoods." I was struck by the elegance of these savages, who did not at all resemble the savages of Canada.

Seminole and Muskogee men are quite tall, but, by an extraordinary contrast, their mothers, wives, and daughters are the smallest race of women known in America.

The Indian women who landed near us, of mixed Cherokee and Castilian blood, were tall of stature. Two of them resembled creoles from Santo Domingo or Mauritius, but they were yellow and delicate like the women of the Ganges. These two Floridians, paternal cousins, served me as models: the one for Atala and the other for Céluta. They surpassed the portraits that I made of them only in that variable and fugitive truth of nature, that physiognomy of race and climate which I could not render. There was something indefinable in their oval faces; their shadowy complexions that one seemed to see through a light, orange mist; their soft black hair; their long eyes half concealed beneath satin lids that opened ever so slowly; in short, in the double seductions of the Indian and the Spaniard.

The meeting with our hosts slowed our gait a bit: our trading agents began asking about horses, and it was decided that we should go set up camp in sight of the studs.

The plain around our camp was covered with bulls, cows, horses, bison, buffalo, cranes, turkeys, and pelicans: these birds mottled the green background of the savannah with streaks of white, black, and pink. .

A multitude of passions stirred our traders and our huntsmen to action: not passions of rank, education, or prejudice, but natural passions, full and absolute, making straight for their object, with no witnesses but a fallen tree in the depths of an unknown forest, an unmapped valley, or a nameless river. Relations between the Spaniards and the Creek women formed the background of most adventures, and the "Burntwoods" play a principal role in all of these romances. One story was legendary: that of an eau-de-vie merchant seduced and ruined by a "painted woman" (a courtesan). Men used to sing this story, put into Seminole verse under the title of *Tabamica*, as they made their way through the forests.* Kidnapped in their turn by the settlers, the Indian women soon die forsaken in Pensacola: their misfortunes went to swell the *Romanceros*, and to be set alongside the sad songs of Ximena.[2]

---

*I have given the words in my *Travels in America*. (Geneva, 1832)

4.

THE TWO FLORIDIANS—RUINS ON THE OHIO

THE EARTH is a charming mother; we issue from her womb; in our infancy, she holds us to her breasts swollen with milk and honey; in our youth and maturity, she lavishes us with her cool waters, her harvests, and her fruits; everywhere, she offers us shade, a bath, a table, and a bed; at our death, she opens her entrails to us once again, and throws a blanket of grass and flowers over our grave, silently transforming us into her own substance, only to reproduce us in some new and graceful form. That is what I said to myself when I woke and blinked my eyes at the sky, the canopy of my bed.

The hunters had set out to do the day's work, and I was left behind with the women and children. I did not stray from my two sylvan goddesses: the one was proud, the other melancholy. I understood not a word of what either of them said to me, but I went to fetch water for their cups, twigs for their fire, and mosses for their bed. They wore the short petticoat and wide slashed sleeves of the Spanish woman, the bodice and the cloak of the Indian. Their bare legs were laced in latticed birch bark. They threaded garlands of flowers and rushes through their hair and strung chains and glass necklaces around their necks. They wore crimson berries as earrings and possessed a pretty talking parrot, bird of Armida, that they set on their shoulder like an emerald, or hooded and carried on their hand, as the grandes dames of the tenth century carried their hawks. To firm their breasts and arms, they rubbed themselves with apoya or supplejack. In Bengal, the bayadères chew betel; in the Levant, the almes suck the mastic of Chios; the Floridians crushed, between their bluish-white teeth, the blades of *liquidambar* and the roots of *libanis*, which mingled the fragrances of angelica, cedrat, and vanilla: they lived in an atmosphere of scents that they themselves exuded, as orange trees and flowers live in the pure exhalations of their leaves and calyxes. I amused myself by placing small trinkets in their hair, and, sweetly scared, they submitted. Being magicians, they believed I was casting a spell over them. One of them, the proud one, often prayed; she seemed to be half Christian. The other sang songs in a velvety voice, ending every phrase with an unsettling cry. Sometimes they spoke sharply to one another, and I thought I could detect the accents of jealousy; but then the sad one wept, and silence returned.

Weak as I was, I sought examples of weakness to embolden myself. Hadn't Camões, in the Indies, fallen in love with a black Barbary slave? Couldn't I, in America, offer homage to two young jonquil sultanas? Camões, after all, had addressed a few *endechas*, or stanzas, to his *barbara escrava*:

> Aquella captiva,
> Que me tem captivo,
> Porque nella vivo,
> Já naõ quer que viva.
> Eu nunqua vi rosa
> Em soaves mólhos,
> Que para meus olhos
> Fosse mais formosa.
> . . . .
> Pretidaõ de amor,
> Taõ doce a figura,
> Que a neve lhe jura
> Que trocára a côr.
> Léda mansidaõ,
> Que o siso acompanha:
> Bem parece estranha,
> Mas Barbara naõ.

"This captive who holds me captive, because I live in her, does not spare my life. Never has a rose, not even in the sweetest bouquet, been more charming to my eyes. . . . Oh, seductress: her face is so sweet the snow wants to change its color for her; her gaiety walks hand in hand with restraint. She is a foreigner, but a barbarian, no."

A fishing party was arranged. The sun had almost set. In the foreground, there were sassafras, tulip trees, catalpas, and oaks whose boughs held long skeins of white moss. Beyond this foreground rose the most charming of trees, the papaya, which might have been taken for a column of chased silver topped with a Corinthian urn. The background was dominated by balsams, magnolias, and *liquidambars*.

The sun sank behind this curtain. A ray glided across the dome of a thicket, sparkling like a carbuncle set in the dark foliage, and the light, fractured by the trees and branches, projected crescent columns and shifting arabesques on the grass. Below were lilac bushes, azaleas, and bindweed in gigantic bunches; above were clouds like promontories or ancient towers, others floating past like pink smoke or carded silk. Transformations followed one after another; furnaces heaped with glowing embers turned into a flowing river of lava: everything was dazzling, radiant, gilded, opulent, and saturated with light.

After the Morean insurrection in 1770, Greek families sought refuge in Florida, where they could still believe themselves in their old Ionian climate, which seems to have softened, like men's passions: at Smyrna in the evening, nature sleeps like a courtesan worn out by love.

To our right were the ruins of one of those enormous fortifications found along the Ohio; to our left was what had formerly been an Indian camp. The island where we sat, reflected in the water and reproduced by a mirage, flung its doubled image before us. To the east, the moon was resting on the distant hills; to the west, the vault of the sky had melted into a sea of diamonds and sapphires in which the half-drowned sun seemed to be dissolving. All the animals of creation kept watch, and the earth, in an act of adoration, appeared to scatter her incense in the sky. The ambergris she exhaled would soon fall back to her as dew, as prayers return upon the heads of the one who prays.

Abandoned by my companions, I rested alone at the edge of a clump of trees: their shadows, glazed with light, formed the penumbra in which I sat. Fireflies shone among the dark shrubs and were eclipsed as they passed through the irradiations of the moon. I heard the ebb and flow of the lake, the leap of the goldfish, and the rare cry of the wild duck. My gaze fixed upon the rippled surface of the water, and I slipped little by little into that drowsiness familiar to all men who travel the roads of this world. No distinct memory remains with me. I felt myself living and vegetating with nature in a sort of pantheistic stupor. I leaned my back against the trunk of a magnolia and went to sleep. My slumber floated on a vague sea of hope.

When I emerged from this Lethe, I found myself between two women. The odalisques had returned. They had not wanted to wake me and had sat down in silence by my side. Either feigning sleep or truly dozing, their heads had fallen on my shoulders.

A breeze traveled through the grove and showered us with a rain of magnolia petals. Then the younger of the Seminoles began to sing. Let he who is unsure of himself keep far from such temptations! One never knows what passion steals into man's heart with a song. To this voice, a rough and jealous voice replied: a "Burntwood" was calling to the two cousins, who shuddered and stood. Dawn was beginning to break.

I have since reexperienced this scene, though without Aspasia, on the shores of Greece. Climbing to the columns of the Parthenon at dawn, I have seen Mount Cythera, Mount Hymetus, the Acropolis of Corinth, the tombs, and the ruins bathed in a dewy golden light, transparent, scintillant, reflected by the seas, and diffused like a perfume by the zephyrs of Salamis and Delos.

We brought our wordless journey to a close on shore. At midday, the traders struck camp to go inspect the horses that the Creeks wanted to sell and that they wanted to buy. All the women and children were assembled, according to custom, to witness these solemn transactions. Stallions of every age and every color, foals and mares together with bulls, cows, and heifers, began to sprint and gallop around us. In this confusion, I was separated from the Creeks. A thick group of horses and men massed at the edge of the woods. Suddenly, I caught sight of my two Floridians in the distance. Vigorous hands were pushing them up onto the cruppers of two Barbary mares ridden bareback by a "Burntwood" and a Seminole. O Cid! If only I'd had your swift Babieca to chase after them! The mares gallop away, and the immense squadron follows after them. Now the horses kick, rear, bound, and neigh among the clashing horns of bulls and buffalo, their hoofs smacking midair, their bloody tails and manes flying. A maelstrom of terrible insects envelops the globe of this wild cavalry. My Floridians disappeared like Ceres' daughter, spirited away by the god of the underworld.

So it is that everything proves abortive in my story, and nothing is left to me but pictures of what has passed so swiftly by: I shall go down to the Elysian Fields with more shades than any man has ever brought with him. The fault lies in my character. I do not know how to profit from any kind of fortune, and I am uninterested in what may be interesting to others. Outside of religion, I have no beliefs. Were I a shepherd or a king, what would I do with my scepter or my crook? I would tire of glory and genius, work and leisure, prosperity and misfortune alike. Everything wearies me: I haul my boredom through my days like a chain, and everywhere I go I yawn away my life.

5.

THE YOUNG MUSKOGEE LADIES—THE KING IS ARRESTED IN VARENNES—I INTERRUPT MY TRAVELS TO RETURN TO EUROPE

RONSARD paints us a picture of Mary Stuart, about to depart for Scotland after François II's death:

> *De tel habit vous estiez accoustrée,*
> *Partant hélas! de la belle contrée*
> *(Dont aviez eu le sceptre dans la main)*
> *Lorsque pensive et baignant vostre sein*
> *Du beau crystal de vos larmes roulées,*
> *Triste, marchiez par les longue allées*
> *Du grand jardin de ce royal chasteau*
> *Qui prend son nom de la source d'une eau.*[3]

Did I resemble the widowed Mary Stuart strolling in Fontainebleau as I strolled on the savannah, after being widowed by my Floridians? What is certain, in any case, is that my mind, if not my person, was enveloped by "a long veil, fine and flowing," as Ronsard, that old poet of the new school, goes on to say.

The devil having carried off the Muskogee ladies, I learned from the guide that a "Burntwood," who was in love with one of the two women, had been jealous of me and that he had conspired with a Seminole, who was the other woman's brother, to deprive me of "Atala" and "Céluta." The guides bluntly called them "painted women," which wounded my vanity. I felt still more humiliated when I learned that the "Burntwood," my favored rival, was a measly mosquito, ugly and dark, and with all the other characteristics of those insects that, according to the definitions of the Great Lama's entomologists, are creatures who wear their flesh on the inside and their bones on the outside. The solitudes looked empty to me after my misadventure. I turned a cold shoulder to my sylph when she generously rushed to console her faithless lover, like Julie when she forgave Saint-Preux his Parisian Floridians.[4] I hastened to leave the wilderness, where I have since revived the drowsy companions of my night. I do not know if I have given them back the life that they gave me; but at least I made a virgin of one and a chaste wife of the other, by way of expiation.

We crossed over the Blue Mountains again and returned to the European clearings near Chillicothi. I was no wiser about the principal object of my journey to America; but I was escorted by a world of poetry:

> Like a young bee working in the dew,
> My muse returned with honey, too.

Along the bank of a stream, I caught sight of an American house with a farm on one wing and a mill on the other. I went in, seeking food and shelter, and I was well received.

My hostess led me up a ladder into a room over the mill wheel. My little window, festooned with ivy and cobaea flowering with iris bells, overlooked the stream that flowed, narrow and solitary, between two thick borders of willow, elm, sassafras, tamarind, and Carolina poplar. The mossy mill wheel turned in their shade, letting fall long ribbons of water. Perch and trout leapt in the swirling foam, wagtails flew from one bank to the other, and a kind of kingfisher hovered above the current on bright blue wings.

I thought how happy I would have been here with the *melancholy* Muskogee girl, supposing she were faithful; how I would sit at her feet lost in dreams with my head against her knees, listening to the noise of the falling water, the revolutions of the wheel, the rolling of the millstone, the sifting and bolting of the flour, the even beat of the mill-clapper, breathing in the fresh scent of the water and the efflorescence of the pearl barley.

Night fell. I climbed down to the farmhouse parlor. It was lit only by the corn straw and the bean shells blazing in the fireplace. The miller's rifles, laid horizontally in the gun-rack, glinted in the firelight glow. I sat down on a stool at the corner of the wide hearth beside a squirrel, who amused himself by jumping back and forth between the neck of an enormous dog and the shelf of a spinning wheel. A little cat took possession of my knee to watch this game. The miller's wife hung a large cooking pot over the fire, and the flames embraced its black base like a crown of radiant gold. While the potatoes for my supper boiled under my supervision, I passed the time reading, by the light of the fire, an English newspaper that had fallen to the floor at my feet. I saw, printed in large letters, these words: FLIGHT OF THE KING. It was the story of Louis XVI's attempted escape and the doomed monarch's arrest in Varennes. The paper also recounted the progress of the emigration and the gathering of military officers under the flag of the French princes.

My mind instantly underwent a complete conversion. Rinaldo saw his weakness in the Mirror of Honor in Armida's gardens.[5] I am no hero out of Tasso, but the same mirror showed me my image in the depths of an American orchard. The clash of arms and the tumult of the world resounded in my ears beneath the thatched roof of a mill, hidden in the darkness of a foreign wood: I said to myself, "Return to France," and I abruptly put an end to my travels.

Thus, what seemed to me a duty overthrew my original plans, and brought about the first of those vicissitudes with which my career has been scored. The Bourbons needed a Breton cadet to return from overseas and offer them his obscure devotion no more than they would need his services later, when he emerged from his obscurity. If I had lit my pipe with the newspaper that changed my life, and gone on with my travels, no one would have noticed my absence; my life then was as anonymous and slight as the smoke from my calumet. A simple dispute between myself and my conscience cast me onto the world's stage. I might have done whatever I wished, seeing that I was the sole witness to the struggle; but of all witnesses, this is the one before whom I am most ashamed to blush.

Why do the solitudes of Erie and Ontario present themselves to my mind today with a charm that my memory does not find even in the brilliant spectacle of the Bosphorus? It is because, at the time of my travels in the United States, I was full of illusions. The troubles in France began at the same moment that I began my journey, and nothing was decided, neither in myself nor in my country. Those days are sweet to me, because they recall the innocent feelings inspired by my family and the pleasures of youth.

Fifteen years later, after my voyage to the Levant, I found the Republic, swollen with rubble and tears, disploding like a deluge into despotism. I no longer soothed myself with chimeras; my memories, which had begun to take their material from society and passions, had lost their innocence. Disappointed in my pilgrimages to the West and to the East, I had failed to discover the passage to the Pole, I had failed to win glory on the banks of Niagara, where I had gone to seek it, and I had left it undisturbed on the ruins of Athens.

Setting out to be an explorer in America, returning to be a soldier in Europe, I saw neither of these careers through to the end. An evil spirit tore the baton and the sword from me, and put a pen in my hand. Another fifteen years have passed since I contemplated the night sky above Sparta, remembering the many countries that had already witnessed me sleeping in peace or with trouble in mind: among the woods of Germany, on the moors of England, in the fields of Italy, on the open ocean, in the Canadian forests, I had already looked up at the same stars that I saw shining above the homeland of Helen and Menelaus. But why bother complaining to the stars, those motionless witnesses to my vagabond destinies? One day their gaze shall no longer weary itself pursuing me. For the moment, indifferent to my fate, I will not ask these astral bodies to shield it with a gentler influence, or to restore me whatever it is that a traveler leaves of himself in the places he visits.

If I were to see the United States again, I would no longer recognize it. Where I left forests, I would find cultivated fields; where I cleared a path through a thicket, I would ride on a highway. In Natchez, where Céluta's hut once stood, there is now a town of five thousand inhabitants. Chactas might today be a representative to Congress. Not long ago I received a pamphlet printed by the Cherokees, which was addressed to me, on behalf of the tribe, as "a defender of the freedom of the press."

In the land of the Muskogees, the Seminoles, and the Chickasaws, there is a city called Athens, another called Marathon, as well as a Carthage, a Memphis, a Sparta, and a Florence. There is a District of Columbia and a county of Marengo. The glory of every nation leaves a name in the same wilderness where I met Father Aubry and the obscure Atala. Kentucky has its Versailles, and a territory called Bourbon has Paris for its capital.

All the exiles, all the oppressed who have found sanctuary in America, have carried the memory of their homelands with them:

> ... *Falsi Simoentis ad undam*
> *Libabat cineri Andromache.*[6]

The United States offer in their bosom, under the protection of liberty, an emblem and a memory of the most celebrated places of antiquity and modern Europe. Hadrian, in his garden in the Roman countryside, had the monuments of his empire reproduced.

Thirty-three highways leave Washington today, as in former times the roads of Rome radiated from the Capital. These highways describe, in their ramifications, the circumference of the United States, tracing a circuit of 25,747 miles. On most of these roads, post offices have been built. One hires a stagecoach bound for the Ohio or Niagara as in my day one hired a guide or an Indian interpreter. Modes of transportation have doubled. Lakes and rivers are everywhere, linked together by canals. One can travel beside terrestrial paths in rowboats or sailboats, barges or steamers. Fuel is inexhaustible, for immense forests cover coal mines that rise to the earth's surface.

The population of the United States has increased decade by decade, between the years 1790 and 1820, at the rate of thirty-five individuals per one hundred. One may assume then that by 1830 there will be twelve million eight hundred and seventy-five thousand souls. If these numbers continue to double every twenty-five years, there will be twenty-five million in 1855, and, twenty-five years later, in 1880, there will be more than fifty million.

This human sap makes every part of the wilderness flower. The lakes of Canada, once devoid of sails, today resemble dockyards: frigates, corvettes, cutters, and barques cross paths with Indian pirogues and canoes, like the big ships and galleys mingling with the pinks, rowboats, and caiques in the waters of Constantinople.

The Mississippi, the Missouri, and the Ohio no longer flow in solitude: three-masters ascend them, and more than two hundred steamboats invigorate their shores.

This immense inland navigation, which by itself would ensure the prosperity of the United States, has never stopped them from making more distant expeditions. Their ships sail on every sea, engage in every kind of enterprise, and transport the starred flag from the land of the setting sun to the land of the dawn that has never known anything but servitude.

To complete this staggering picture, one must imagine the cities of New York, Philadelphia, Boston, Baltimore, Charleston, Savannah, and New Orleans lighted up at night, filled with horses and carriages, adorned with cafés, museums, libraries, dance halls, and theaters, offering all the pleasures of luxury.

At the same time, it is no use looking in the United States for that which sets man apart from other created beings—that which is the certificate of his immortality and the ornament of his days: literature is unknown in the new republic, although a great many establishments may have called for it. The American has replaced intellectual activity with practical activity. But do not impute his mediocrity in the arts to the American's inferiority, for he has not yet turned his attention to their making. Cast by various causes on a desert soil, he has so far cared only for agriculture and commerce. Before being able to think, one must survive; before planting trees, one must fell them in order to plow. The earliest colonists, their minds steeped in religious dissension, brought, it is true, a passion for argument even into the bosom of the forests; but first they had to conquer the wilderness with hatchets on their shoulders. When they rested from their labors, their only pulpit was the elm tree that they themselves had squared. The Americans have not passed through the successive ages of other nations. They have left behind their childhood and youth in Europe, and the naive prattling of the cradle is unknown to them; they have enjoyed the comforts of the hearth only through regret for a homeland that they have never seen: they mourn its eternal absence and its rumored charms.

There is no such thing on the new continent as classical literature, romantic literature, or Indian literature: Americans have no model for the classical, no Middle Ages for the romantic, and, as for the Indian, Americans despise the savages and regard the forest with horror, as though it were a prison to which they had once been condemned.

For these reasons, literature as a thing apart, literature properly defined, does not exist in America. There is applied literature that serves various social causes, and there is a literature of workers, merchants, sailors, and farmers. Americans have hardly succeeded in anything except engineering and science, and that is because the sciences have their material side: Franklin and Fulton have harnessed lightning and steam to the benefit of mankind. It fell to America to supply the world with discoveries that will make it impossible for any continent to evade the navigator's search.

Poetry and imagination, the share of a very small number of idlers, are regarded in the United States as puerilities of childhood and old age. But then, Americans have not had a childhood; they have not yet experienced old age.

From this it follows that the men engaged in serious studies have necessarily taken part in the affairs of their country, in order to become acquainted with them, and that these same men necessarily found themselves taking part in their Revolution. But one sad thing must be noted: the rapid degeneration of talent, from the first men to involve themselves in the American troubles down to the men of recent times. Yet these men have something in common nevertheless. The old Presidents of the American Republic had characters defined by their piety, simplicity, honor, and calm: qualities of which one finds no trace in the bloody fracas of our Republic or our Empire. The solitude by which Americans were surrounded acted upon their nature, and they achieved their liberty in silence.

General Washington's farewell address to the people of the United States might have been spoken by one of the gravest characters of antiquity:

"How far in the discharge of my official duties," says the General, "I have been guided by the principles which have been delineated, the public records and other evidences of my conduct must witness to you and to the world. To myself, the assurance of my own conscience is, that I have at least believed myself to be guided by them. Though, in reviewing the incidents of my administration, I am unconscious of intentional error, I am nevertheless too sensible of my defects not to think it probable that I may have committed many errors. Whatever they may be, I fervently beseech the Almighty to avert or mitigate the evils to which they may tend. I shall also carry with me the hope that my country will never cease to view them with indulgence; and that, after forty-five years of my life dedicated to its service, with an upright zeal, the faults of incompetent abilities will be consigned to oblivion, as myself must soon be to the mansions of rest."

Jefferson, in his house at Monticello, after the death of one of his two children, writes:

"The loss which I have experienced is great indeed. Others may lose of their abundance, but I, of my want, have lost even the half of all I had. My evening prospects now hang on the slender thread of a single life. Perhaps I may be destined to see even this last cord of parental affection broken!"

Philosophy, which is so rarely touching, is here touching in the highest degree. And this is not the idle sorrow of a man who has played no part in life: Jefferson died July 4, 1826, at the age of eighty-four, in the fifty-fourth year of his country's independence. His remains lie covered by a stone engraved with a simple epitaph: THOMAS JEFFERSON, *author of the Declaration of Independence*.

Pericles and Demosthenes once delivered a eulogy for those young Greeks that fell defending a people that disappeared soon after them; so Brackenridge, in 1817, celebrated the death of those young Americans whose blood gave birth to a people.

There exists a national gallery of portraits of distinguished Americans, in four octavo volumes, and, what is even more remarkable, a biographical compendium that records the lives of more than one hundred Indian chiefs. Logan, Chief of the Cayuga, delivered these words to Lord Dunmore: "Colonel Cresap, the last spring, in cold blood and unprovoked, murdered all the relations of Logan, not even sparing my women and children. There runs not a drop of my blood in the veins of any living creature. This called on me for revenge. I have sought it. I have killed many. I have fully glutted my vengeance. For I rejoice at the beams of peace; but do not harbor a thought that mine is the joy of fear. Logan never felt fear. He will not turn on his heel to save his life. Who is there to mourn for Logan? No one!"

Without loving nature, Americans have applied themselves to the study of natural history. Townsend set out from Philadelphia to walk across the regions separating the Atlantic from the Pacific, jotting down numerous observations in his journal. Thomas Say, an explorer of the Floridas and the Rocky Mountains, has published a work on American entomology. Alexander Wilson, who started as a weaver before he became an author, has painted some rather accomplished pictures.

As regards literature properly defined, although there is not much of it, a few novelists and poets bear mention. A Quaker's son, Charles Brockden Brown, is the author of *Wieland*, which has been the source and model for many novels of the new school. Unlike his countrymen, "I prefer," Brown says, "roaming in the forests to threshing corn." Wieland, his novel's hero, is a Puritan whom Heaven has ordered to kill his wife. "I have brought thee hither," he says to her, "to fulfill a divine command. I am appointed thy destroyer, and destroy thee I must." Brown's narrative continues:

> Saying this I seized her wrists. She shrieked aloud, and endeavored to free herself from my grasp...
>
> "Wieland.... Am I not thy wife? And wouldst thou kill me? Thou wilt not; and yet... Spare me—spare—help, help—"
>
> Till her breath was stopped she shrieked for help—for mercy.

Wieland strangles his wife and experiences unspeakable delights beside her expired corpse. The horror of our modern inventions is here far surpassed. Brown's imagination was formed by reading *Caleb Williams*, and in *Wieland* he imitates a scene from *Othello*.

At the present time, the American novelists James Fenimore Cooper and Washington Irving are forced to take refuge in Europe, where they find materials and readers. In America, the language of the great writers of England has been "creolized," "provincialized," "barbarized," without having gained any energy from the new country's virgin nature. It has even been found necessary to compile catalogues of American expressions.

As for American poets, their language is pleasant enough; but they rise only a little above the level of mediocrity. Bryant's "The Evening Wind," Longfellow's "Sunrise on the Hills," Sigourney's "Native Scenery," and a few other poems are worth our attention. Fitz-Greene Halleck has sung of the dying Botsaris, and George Hill has wandered among the ruins of Greece. "O Athens!" he writes, "you, the lonely queen dethroned! O Parthenon, king of temples, you have seen your fellow monuments abandoned to time's deprivations, despoiled of their priests and their gods."[7]

It pleases me, I who have traveled to the shores of Hellas and Atlantis, to hear the independent voice of a land unknown to antiquity mourning the lost liberty of the Old World.

6.

DANGERS FOR THE UNITED STATES

BUT WILL America preserve its form of government? Will the States not sunder? Has a representative from Virginia not already argued for the ancient theory of liberty which accepted slavery, and which was the result of paganism, against a representative from Massachusetts who defended the cause of modern liberty without slavery, which Christianity has wrought? Aren't the Northern and the Southern states opposed in their opinions and interests? Wouldn't the Western States, so far from the Atlantic, prefer their own regime? One wonders whether the federal bond is strong enough to preserve the union and compel each state to stand ranked around it. On the other hand, if the power of the presidency were increased, would despotism not be close behind, bringing with it all the obligations and privileges of a dictator?

The isolation of the United States has given them birth and space to grow. It is doubtful whether such a state could have lived, let alone thrived, in Europe. The Swiss Federation subsists among us, it's true. But why? Because it is small, poor, and walled in by mountains, a nursery for royal soldiers and a destination for travelers.

Separated from the Old World, the population of the United States still inhabits a sort of wilderness: its solitude has made it free, but already the conditions of its existence are being altered.

The presence of democracies in Mexico, Columbia, Peru, Chile, and Buenos Aires, constantly troubled as these democracies are, is a danger. When the United States had nothing near them except the colonies of a transatlantic kingdom, serious warfare was unlikely. But today, isn't a rivalry to be feared? If there were a rush to arms on all sides, if the military spirit seized the children of Washington, a great captain might emerge to take the throne. Glory loves a crown.

I said that the Northern, Southern, and Western states are divided in their interests, which is common knowledge. But if these states broke from the union, would they be reduced to bearing arms? If so, what enmities will ferment and spread through the body politic! If the dissident states were to claim their independence, every kind of discord would erupt across the emancipated states! These overseas republics, come undone, would form debilitated units of no weight on the social scale or be successively subjugated by some single state among them. (I pass over the serious subject of alliances and foreign intervention.) Kentucky—peopled by a bolder, more rustic, more militant race—would seem destined to be the conquering State. In this State that would devour the others, the power of one would soon rise above the ruins of the power of all.

I have spoken of the danger of war, but I must also recall the dangers of prolonged peace. Since their emancipation, the United States have enjoyed, apart from a few short months, a period of the most profound tranquility: while hundreds of battles shook Europe to its roots, they went on securely cultivating their fields. The consequence has been an increase of population and wealth, with all the inconveniences that follow from a superabundance of people and money.

If hostilities descend on an unwarlike people, would they be able to resist? How could they bring themselves to renounce their indolent ways, their comforts, and the gentler habits of life? China and India, asleep in their muslins, have been constantly subject to foreign domination. What best suits the complexion of a free society is a state of peace tempered by war or a state of war tempered by peace. The Americans have already worn the olive-crown for too long a time: the tree that provides it is not native their shores.

The mercantile spirit is beginning to take hold of them; self-interest is becoming a national vice. Already the gambling spirit of the banks of the different States has hindered them, and bankruptcies are threatening the common weal. So long as liberty produces gold, an industrial republic performs wonders; but when the gold is spent or exhausted, the republic loses this love of liberty that is founded not on moral sentiment but originates in a thirst for profit and a passion for industry.

What's more, it is difficult to create a *homeland* from States which have no community rooted in religion or material interests, which have arisen from different sources at different times, and which survive on different soils and under different suns. What connection is there between a Frenchman from Louisiana, a Spaniard from the Floridas, a German from New York, and an Englishman from New England, Virginia, the Carolinas, or Georgia—all of whom are reputed to be Americans? One is a frivolous duelist; one a proud and lazy Catholic; one a Lutheran farmer who owns no slaves; one a Puritan merchant. How many centuries will it take to render these elements homogeneous!

A chrysogeneous aristocracy, with a passionate love of distinctions and titles, is ready to emerge. It is supposed that there is one common level in the United States, but this is completely untrue. There are groups in American society that disdain one another and remain wholly exclusive; there are parlors where the host's haughtiness surpasses that of a German Prince with his Sixteen Quarterings. These plebeian nobles aspire to be a caste despite the progress of enlightenment that has made them equal and free. Some of them are forever talking about their ancestors, proud barons, apparently bastards, and companions of William the Bastard; on their walls, they display the emblazoned chivalry of the Old World decorated with New World serpents, lizards, and parakeets. A cadet from Gascony, landing with no more than a cloak and an umbrella on these republican shores, as long as he remembers to refer to himself by the title of "marquis," is guaranteed to be well received on every steamboat.

The enormous imbalance of wealth is a more serious threat to the spirit of equality than any other. A few Americans possess one or two million in income. The Yankees of high society no longer live like

Benjamin Franklin: the true "gentleman," disgusted by his new country, goes to Europe looking for the old. He can be found in every hotel, making a "tour" of Italy, and vying with the English in extravagance and spleen. These vagrants from Carolina and Virginia buy up ruined abbeys in France and plant English gardens with American trees in Melun. Naples may send New York her singers and performers, Paris her fashions and dancers, London her grooms and boxers; but these exotic delights don't give the Union any great pleasure. In America, men amuse themselves by leaping into Niagara Falls to the cheering of fifty thousand planters: half-savages who laugh only at the sight of pain and death.

And what is still more extraordinary is that, even as the imbalance of wealth increases and an aristocracy is beginning to form, the great egalitarian impetus of the culture at large obliges the owners of factories and lands to hide their luxuries and lie about their wealth for fear of being bludgeoned by their neighbors. No one pays the executive powers any mind; local authorities, only recently elected, are removed from office and replaced by others. This does not disturb the social order. In fact, practical democracy is observed at the same time that people laugh at the laws decreed by this same democracy, in theory. Family feeling scarcely exists: as soon as a child is in a condition to work, he must fly on his own two wings like a fledgling bird. From these generations, emancipated into premature orphanhood, and from the emigrants constantly arriving from Europe, come bands of nomads who clear the lands, dig canals, and exercise their industry everywhere, but without ever attaching themselves to the soil; they begin building houses in the wilderness where the transient proprietor will not stay for more than a few brief days.

A cold hard egotism rules the towns. Piastres and dollars, banknotes and silver, the rise and fall of stocks: this is all anyone discusses. A man might believe he was at the Bourse or the counting-house of a large boutique. The newspapers, of huge dimensions, are rife with business articles and crass gossip. Could the Americans be suffering, without knowing it, from the law of a climate where vegetable nature seems to have thrived at the expense of sentient beings? This law has been dismissed by distinguished minds, but perhaps its implications are not entirely swept away by its refutation. One might wonder whether the American has not become too quickly accustomed to philosophical liberty, as the Russian has become accustomed to civilized despotism.

In sum, the United States give the impression of being a colony, not a mother country: they have no past, and their mores are not a result of their laws. The citizens of the New World took their place among the nations at a moment when political ideas were in the ascendant, and this explains how they transformed themselves with such unusual rapidity. Anything resembling a permanent society appears to be impracticable among them. On one hand, this is due to the extreme ennui of its individual citizens; on the other, to the impossibility of remaining in place and the need for motion that dominates their lives: for man is never truly settled when the household gods are wanderers. Placed upon the ocean roads, at the forefront of progressive opinions as new as his country, the American seems to have inherited from Columbus the mission to discover new worlds rather than create them.

7.

RETURN TO EUROPE—SHIPWRECK

London, April to September 1822

HAVING returned from the wilderness to Philadelphia, as I have already said, and having hastily written on the road "what I have just related," like the old man in La Fontaine, I did not find the remittances waiting for me as I had expected.[8] This was the first of those pecuniary embarrassments in which I would be submerged for the rest of my life. Fortune and I took a dislike to each other at first sight. According to Herodotus, certain Indian ants gather heaps of gold; according to Athenaeus, the sun gave Hercules a vessel of gold to land on the island of Erytheia, the home of the Hesperides: although I am an ant, I do not have the honor of belonging to the mighty Indian family, and although I have been a sailor, I have never crossed the waters in anything but a vessel made of pine.[9] Such was the ship that carried me from America back to Europe. The captain gave me passage on credit. On December 10, 1791, I embarked in the company of several of my countrymen, who, for manifold reasons, were like me returning to France. The ship's destination was Le Havre.

A gust of wind took us at the mouth of the Delaware and propelled us across the Atlantic in a mere seventeen days. Often we scudded under bare masts and bore off only with great effort. The sun did not show its face once. The ship, steered by dead reckoning, was swept along before the surge. I crossed the ocean under shadows; never had it seemed to me so sad. But I myself was sadder still: I was returning dismayed by the first step I had taken into life. "Palaces are not built on the sea," says the Persian poet Farid ud-Din.[10] I felt an indescribable heaviness of heart, such as one feels at the approach of a great misfortune. I let my eyes wander over the waves, and asked them about my destiny, or I wrote, more disturbed by their motion than by their menace.

Far from calming, the tempest grew in fury the nearer we came to Europe; but it blew steadily, and the uniformity of its rage produced a sort of furious stillness in the livid sky and on the leaden sea. The captain, unable to sound the depths, became uneasy; he climbed the shrouds and looked through his spyglass at every point of the horizon. A lookout was stationed on the bowsprit, another on the maintop. The waves turned choppy; the sea changed color: these were signs of approaching land, but of *what* land? Breton sailors have a proverb: "Who sees Belle-Isle, sees his isle; who sees Groie, sees his joy; who sees Ouessant's shore, is not long for this world."

I had spent two nights pacing on the upper deck, while the waves hissed in the darkness, and the wind whistled in the rigging, and the sea leapt back and forth over the boards. All around us was a riot of waves. On the third night, weary from these jolts and jostlings, I went below early. The weather was horrible. My hammock swung and shuddered with each blow from the sea which, breaking on the ship, shook it from stem to stern. Soon, I heard loads of cordage falling on one part of the deck after another, and I experienced the reeling sensation one feels when a ship starts to tack. The hatchway to the ladder between boards was thrown open. A terrified voice called out—*captain, captain!* This voice, amid the darkness and the roaring tempest, was an ominous thing. I prick up my ears, and I seem to hear the sailors talking about the lie of the coast. I hurl myself down from my wobbly hammock, and at that moment a wave bursts into the forecastle, floods the captain's cabin, overturning tables, beds, chests, and guns in a roiling mess. I climb to the deck half-drowned.

When I put my head out the hatchway, I was dumbfounded by a sublime spectacle. The ship had attempted to put about, but, failing the attempt, she had been embayed by the wind. Under the light of a sickle moon that emerged from the clouds only to be submerged in them again, I squinted through the thick yellow fog and spied, on either side of the ship, a coast bristling with rocks. The sea was blistered with waves like mountains that rolled all over the bay in which we found ourselves engulfed. Sometimes, these mountains sparkled with spume and spray; sometimes, they appeared oily and vitreous at the surface, marbled with black, coppery, or greenish stains, according to the color of the bottom over which they churned. For two or three minutes, the wailings of the abyss and the wind were blent; a moment later, we could hear the fast retreating currents, the hissing of the reefs, and the voice of the distant surge. Then, from the hold of the ship came sounds to set even the most intrepid sailor's heart to pounding. The ship's prow sliced the dense mass of waves with a dreadful heave, and torrents of water rushed in a maelstrom around the helm as though escaping from a floodgate. Beneath this uproar, nothing was more alarming than a certain dull murmuring sound, like the sound of a vase being filled.

Lighted by a dark-lantern and held down by lead weights, portulans, maps, and logbooks were spread over the floor of the chicken coop. A squall had already extinguished the binnacle-lamp. Everyone was arguing about the land. We had entered the Channel without knowing it, and now the ship, staggering with each wave, was adrift somewhere between the islands of Guernsey and Alderney. Shipwreck seemed inevitable, and the passengers gripped their most precious possessions in hopes of saving them.

Among the crew there were a few French sailors. One of them, in the absence of a chaplain, intoned that ancient hymn to Notre Dame de Bon-Secours which was the first song I had learned in my childhood. I would sing it again at the sight of the coast of Brittany, when I was nearly before my mother's eyes. The American Protestant sailors joined in heartily with the songs of their French Catholic comrades: danger teaches men their weakness and unites their prayers. All of us, passengers and sailors alike, were now together on the deck, clinging to the rigging, the planking, the capstans, or the flukes of the anchors, trying not to be swept away by a swell or toppled into the sea by the rolling of the ship. The captain shouted, "An ax! An ax!"

and the masts were cut down. The rudder, its tiller abandoned, swung side to side with a croaking sound.

One experiment remained to be tried. The sounding line showed us that we were no more than four fathoms over a sandbank that crossed the length of the channel; it was therefore possible that a surging wave might lift us over this sandbank and into deeper water. But who dared to seize the helm and take the safety of everyone on board in his hands? One false turn of the wheel, and we would be lost.

One of those men who burst forth from events, one of those spontaneous offspring of peril, came forward: a sailor from New York took the post deserted by the steersman. I seem to see him still, in his shirtsleeves and canvas trousers, barefooted, his hair drenched and tangled, his powerful fists gripping the tiller, while, with head turned, he watched for that wave which would save us or lay us to waste. And then there it was: a wave as wide as the channel itself, rolling high without breaking, like a sea invading another sea. Large white birds, flying calmly, preceded it like birds of death. The ship struck and heeled; there was a deep silence, and every face went pale. The surge arrived. At the moment it touched the vessel, the sailor wrenched the helm, and the ship, about to fall on her side, turned her stern, so that the swell, which looked sure to swallow us, lifted her over. The lead was heaved; a sounding was taken: the water was found to be seventeen fathoms deep. Our cheers rose up to heaven, and we all joined in a cry of *Long Live the King!* God did not hear this prayer for Louis XVI; it was for the benefit of ourselves alone.

Though we had escaped the two islands, we were not out of danger; we could not sail beyond the coast of Granville. At last, the ebbing tide carried us onward, and we doubled the cape of La Hague. I should say that I experienced no anguish during this quasi-shipwreck, and I felt no joy at being saved. It is better to clear out of life while you are young than to be evicted by time.

The next day we entered Le Havre.

All the population rushed out to see us. Our topmasts were shattered, our longboats were lost, the quarterdeck had been razed, and we shipped water at every pitch of the vessel. From this floating wreck, I stepped down onto the pier. On January 2, 1792, I was again treading my native soil. It was soon to slip from beneath my feet again. With me I brought no Eskimos from the polar regions, but two savages of an unknown race: Chactas and Atala.

BOOK NINE

I.

I VISIT MY MOTHER IN SAINT-MALO—PROGRESS OF
THE REVOLUTION—MY MARRIAGE

London, April to September 1822;
Revised in December 1846

I WROTE to my brother in Paris, relating the details of my crossing, explaining the reasons for my return, and imploring him to lend me the sum I needed to pay my passage.[1] My brother replied to me by forwarding this letter to my mother. Madame de Chateaubriand did not make me wait; she put me in a position to pay off my debts and leave Le Havre at once. She wrote to tell me that Lucile and my uncle de Bedée's family were beside her. These particulars decided me to go to Saint-Malo, where I could consult my uncle on the question of my impending emigration.

Revolutions, like rivers, widen as they flow. I found the one I had left in France enormously enlarged and overflowing its banks. I had gone away from it with Mirabeau under the Constituent, and now I found it with Danton under the Legislative.

The treaty of Pillnitz, signed August 27, 1791, had been the talk of Paris. On December 14, 1791, while I was being tossed by storms at sea, the King announced that he had written to the Princes of the Germanic Corps (notably to the elector of Trèves) about Germany's armaments. Louis XVI's brothers, the Prince de Condé, M. de Calonne, the Vicomte de Mirabeau, and M. de La Queuille were almost immediately accused of treason. On November 9, a previous decree had attacked the other émigrés. It was in these already proscribed ranks that I hastened to install myself. Others perhaps would have recoiled, but the threats of the strongest always make me take the side of the weakest; to me, the pride of victory is insupportable.

On my way from Le Havre to Saint-Malo, I had a chance to observe the divisions and misfortunes of France for myself. Houses had been burned to the ground or abandoned. Their rightful owners had been sent distaffs and were gone;[2] the women had sought refuge in the towns. Hamlets and villages groaned under the tyranny of clubs affiliated with the central Club des Cordeliers, which would later be joined with the Club des Jacobins. The opposition—the Société Monarchique and the Société des Feuillants—no longer existed. The ignoble denomination of sans-culottes had become popular. The King was never called anything but Monsieur Veto or Monsieur Capet.

I was warmly welcomed by my mother and the rest of my family, who nevertheless deplored the bad timing of my return. My uncle, the Comte de Bedée, was arranging to emigrate to Jersey with his wife, his sons, and his daughters. Now there was also the matter of finding me the money to go join the Princes. My American voyage had made a gaping hole in my inheritance. My income as a younger son had been reduced almost to nothing by the suppression of feudal rights, and the small benefices that would have devolved to me as a member of the Order of Malta had fallen, together with all the other possessions of the clergy, into the hands of the nation. This concurrence of circumstances decided the gravest act of my life: I was married off, to procure me the means to go get killed for a cause that I did not love.

There lived in Saint-Malo one M. de Lavigne, Chevalier de St. Louis, who had formerly been the Commandant of Lorient. The Comte d'Artois had once been a guest at Lavigne's house in Lorient when he visited Brittany, and the prince was so charmed by his host that he promised to grant him whatever favor he might later request.

This M. de Lavigne had two sons: one of them married Mademoiselle de La Placelière. Two daughters, the children of this marriage, were orphaned by their mother and father at a tender age. The eldest married the naval captain Comte du Plessis-Parscau, a son and grandson of admirals who today is a rear admiral and a commander at the Naval Academy in Brest; the youngest still lived with her grandfather. She was seventeen years old when, on my return from America, I arrived in Saint-Malo. She was pale, delicate, thin, and very pretty; she let her lovely blond hair hang down, like a child, in its natural curls. Her fortune was estimated to be five or six hundred thousand francs.

My sisters took it in their heads to make me marry Mademoiselle de Lavigne, who was strongly attached to Lucile. This business was conducted unbeknownst to me. I had set eyes on Mademoiselle de Lavigne no more than three or four times: I picked her out of the distant crowd on Le Sillon by her pink pelisse, her white dress, and her blond locks tangled by the wind, as I strolled along the beach, abandoning myself to the caresses of my old mistress, the sea. I did not feel myself ready to be a husband. All my illusions were vivid still; none had faded from me. If anything, my wanderings had doubled the very energy of my existence. I was tormented by the Muse. But Lucile loved Mademoiselle de Lavigne and saw the marriage as a means for me to acquire an independent fortune. "So be it!" said I. For if the public man in me is unshakable, the private man is at the mercy of whosoever wants to sway him, and in order to avoid the quarrel of an hour, I would sell myself into slavery for a century.

The consent of her grandfather, her paternal uncle, and her other principal relations was easily obtained. Only a maternal uncle, a committed democrat named M. de Vauvert, could not be convinced, for he was opposed to his niece marrying an aristocrat like me, even if I wasn't one at all. It was decided that the marriage should proceed without him, but my pious mother demanded that the religious ceremony be performed by a "non-juring" priest, which could only be done in secret. When M. de Vauvert got wind of this, he sicced the magistracy on us under the pretext of rape and violation of the law, contending that my fiancée's grandfather, M. de Lavigne, had fallen into his second childhood. Mademoiselle de Lavigne, who had become Madame de Chateaubriand without my having spoken a word to her, was taken away in the name of justice and placed in the convent of La Victoire in Saint-Malo to await the decision of the courts.

There was no rape, no violation of the law, no adventure, and no love in any of this. My marriage had nothing but the disagreeable side of a novel: the truth. The case was pleaded, and the court judged the union legally valid. Seeing that the members of the two families were in agreement, M. de Vauvert withdrew his charges. The constitutional curate, lavishly bribed, no longer made a claim against the first nuptial blessing, and so Madame de Chateaubriand left the convent, where Lucile had been locked up with her.

I now had a new acquaintance to make, and she brought me everything I could desire. I doubt whether a keener mind than my wife's has ever existed. She divines the thoughts and words of the people with whom she speaks as though these things were written on their brows. To deceive her in anything is impossible. Original and cultivated in her thinking, mordant in her writing, and a marvelous storyteller, Madame de Chateaubriand admires me without ever having read two lines of my work. She would dread finding ideas not her own in these pages, or discovering that the world has received me with less enthusiasm than I deserve. Although a passionate critic, she is learned and fair.

Madame de Chateaubriand's defects, if she has any, stem from the superabundance of her good qualities; my very real defects result from the sterility of mine. It is easy to be resigned, patient, generally obliging and serene, when you don't take to anything, you're bored by everything, and you reply to bad luck and good luck alike with a desperate and despairing: "Well, what does it matter?"

Madame de Chateaubriand is better than I am, although she is less congenial company. Have I acted blamelessly toward her? Have I granted my companion all the feelings that she deserved and that were owed to her? Has she ever complained of this? What happiness has she tasted in return for her unfailing affection? She has suffered my adversities; she was plunged into the dungeons of the Terror, the persecutions of the Empire, the disgraces of the Restoration, and she has not had the joys of motherhood to counterbalance these sorrows. Without children, which she might have had in another marriage, and which she would have loved to distraction; without those honors and affections that come to the mother of a family and console her for the loss of her best years, she has proceeded, barren and alone, toward old age. Often separated from me, and averse to literature, the pride of bearing my name is hardly a compensation. Timorous and trembling for me alone, her incessantly resurgent anxieties rob her of sleep and of the time needed to recover from her illnesses: I am her chronic infirmity and the cause of her relapses. How can I compare the few little signs of irritation she has shown me to all the worries I have caused her over the years? How can I set my good qualities, such as they are, against her many virtues? She feeds the poor; she has helped establish the Marie-Thérèse Infirmary despite every obstacle. What are my labors beside these Christian good works? When the two of us appear before God, it is I who will be condemned.

All in all, when I consider the complexion and the imperfection of my nature, is it certain that marriage has spoiled my life? No doubt I would have enjoyed more leisure and rest; I would have been better received in certain circles and by certain great men of the earth; but in politics, though Madame de Chateaubriand has contradicted me, she has never held me back, for in political matters, as in matters of honor, I make my judgments based solely on my own feelings. Would I have produced a greater number of works if I had remained independent, and would these works have been better? Have there not been circumstances, as we shall soon see, where I might have married outside of France, ceased to write, and renounced my country? Yet if I hadn't married, wouldn't my weakness have made me prey to some undignified creature? Wouldn't I have wasted and polluted my days like Lord Byron? Now that I'm sinking into old age, all my follies would be behind me; I would have nothing before me but emptiness and regrets: I would be an undignified old bachelor, deluded or undeluded, an old bird repeating his worn-out song to ears that do not hear. The full indulgence of my desires wouldn't have added another string to my lyre or a more poignant tone to my voice. The restraint of my feelings and the mystery of my thoughts may even perhaps have augmented the energy of my tongue and animated my works with an internal fever, a hidden flame that might have been blown out in the open air of love. Held fast by an indissoluble bond, I bought the sweet pleasures I taste today for the price of a short-lived bitterness:

I retain only the incurable miseries of my existence. I therefore owe a tender and eternal debt of gratitude to my wife, whose fondness for me has been as touching as it has been deep and sincere. She has made my life more serious, more noble, and more honorable, and she always inspires me with a respect for, if not always the strength to perform, my duties.

2.

PARIS—ACQUAINTANCES, OLD AND NEW—ABBÉ
BARTHÉLEMY—SAINT-ANGE—THEATER

London, April to September 1822

I was married at the end of March 1792, and on April 20 the
Legislative Assembly declared war on Francis II of Germany, who
had recently succeeded his father Leopold; on April 10, Benedict
Labre had been beatified in Rome. There you have two worlds. The
declaration of war hastened the exodus of those French nobles who
still remained at home. On the one hand, the violent persecutions
redoubled; on the other, it was no longer possible for a Royalist to
remain by his hearthside without being accused of cowardice. It was
now time for me to make my way toward the camp that I had come
so far to seek. My uncle de Bedée and his family found passage on a
boat bound for Jersey, and I set off for Paris with my wife and my
sisters Lucile and Julie.

We had secured an apartment in the Faubourg Saint-Germain,
Cul-de-Sac Férou, at the Petit Hôtel de Villette. I was eager to see
my old friends again. I went to visit the Parisian men of letters whom
I used to know. Among other new faces, I encountered the learned
Abbé Barthélemy and the poet Saint-Ange. The Abbé has modeled
his descriptions of Athenian Gynaecums too much on the salons of
Chanteloup. The translator of Ovid was not without talent; but talent is a gift, an isolate thing, which can be combined with other
mental faculties or exist by itself, and Saint-Ange furnished proof of
this. He made a concerted effort not to be stupid, but he could never
quite prevent himself. A man whose style I have admired and admire
still, Bernard de Saint-Pierre, also lacks intelligence, and unfortunately

his character is on a level with his intelligence. How many descriptions in his *Études de la nature* are spoiled by a flaw in the writer's soul!

Rulhière had died suddenly, in 1791, before my departure for America. I have since seen his little house in Saint-Denis, with the fount and the pretty statue of Love, at the foot of which one reads these verses:

> *D'Egmont avec l'Amour visita cette rive:*
> *Une image de sa beauté*
> *Se peignit un moment sur l'onde fugitive:*
> *D'Egmont a disparu; l'Amour seul est resté.*[3]

When I left France, the theaters of Paris still resounded with *The Awakening of Epimenides*:

> *J'aime la vertu guerrière*
> *De nos braves défenseurs,*
> *Mais d'un peuple sanguinaire*
> *Je déteste les fureurs.*
> *À l'Europe redoutables,*
> *Soyons libres à jamais,*
> *Mais soyons toujours aimables*
> *Et gardons l'esprit français.*[4]

By the time of my return, *The Awakening of Epimenides* was forgotten, and if these lines had been sung, they might have had terrible consequences for their author. *Charles IX* had prevailed. The play had come into vogue largely thanks to circumstance. The alarm bells, the people armed with pikes, and the hatred of kings and priests offered the audiences a reproduction, behind closed doors, of what was playing out in the streets. Talma, the debutant, continued his success.[5]

While tragedy reddened the streets, pastoral flourished in the theater. This meant not merely innocent shepherds and virginal shepherdesses. Meadows, streams, fields, sheep, doves—a whole golden age under thatch—were revived to the music of the reed-pipe played before the cooing Phillis for the naive *tricoteuses*[6] fresh from the spectacle of the guillotine.[7] If Sanson had the time, he might have played the role of Colin, and Mademoiselle Théroigne de Méricourt the role of Babet.[8] The members of the National Convention made believe they were the most benign men on earth: good fathers, good sons, good husbands, they took their small children on walks around the city; they hired nurses for them; they wept tenderly at the sight of their simple games; gently, they took these little lambs in their arms and showed them the horsie that led the cart which carried victims to their punishment. They sang of nature, peace, pity, beneficence, candor, and domestic virtues, and meanwhile these blessed philanthropists sent their neighbors to have their necks sliced, with extreme sensibility, for the greater happiness of the human race.

3.

THE CHANGING FACE OF PARIS—THE CLUB DES
CORDELIERS—MARAT

London, April to September 1822; Revised in December 1846

PARIS in 1792 no longer looked as it had in 1789 and 1790. This was no longer the Revolution in its infancy; it was a people marching drunkenly toward their destiny over the depths by twisted paths. The people themselves no longer seemed tumultuous, curious, reckless; they were outright menacing. The faces one encountered in the streets were invariably frightened or fierce: either men gliding along close to the houses to avoid being seen or men prowling openly in search of prey. They turned from you with a fearful gaze lowered, or they fixed their gaze on yours to scrutinize you and pin you.

The variety of fashions had ceased; the old world was being effaced: it had shouldered the uniform coat of the new world, a coat which was then merely the last garment of the convicts to come. The social license displayed during the rejuvenation of France, the newfound liberties of 1789—those whimsical and unregulated freedoms of an order of things that is being destroyed but that hasn't yet fallen into anarchy— were already being flattened beneath the people's scepter. One sensed the approach of a plebeian tyranny: a fecund tyranny, it's true, and one filled with hope, but also formidable in a way altogether different from the lapsed despotism of the old monarchy. For the sovereign people are everywhere, and when they become tyrants, tyranny is everywhere; it is the universal presence of a universal Tiberius.

Into the Parisian population there began to mix an alien population of cutthroats from the South. This vanguard of the Marseillais, whom Danton would lure to Paris for the Tenth of August and the

September Massacres, could be recognized by their ragged clothes, their bronzed skin, and their look of cowardice and crime, but of crime from under another sun: *in vultu vitium*, "with vice written on their faces."

At the Legislative Assembly, I recognized no one. Mirabeau and the other early idols of our troubles were either dead or had lost their altars. To pick up the historical thread broken by my travels in America, it is necessary to trace things back a bit further.

A RETROSPECTIVE VIEW

The flight of the King on June 21, 1791, had forced the Revolution to take a gigantic step. Brought back to Paris on June 25, the King had been dethroned for the first time, and the National Assembly declared that its decrees would have the force of law, without any need of royal sanction or approval. A high court of justice, heralding the Revolutionary tribunal, was established in Orléans. It was at this time that Madame Roland demanded the Queen's head, not long before the Revolution demanded hers. A mob gathered on the Champ-de-Mars to protest the decree which removed the King from his duties instead of putting him on trial. The ratification of the Constitution on September 14 settled nothing. There was then the question of deposing Louis XVI. If this deposition had taken place, the crimes of January 21 would never have been committed, and the position of the French people in relation to the monarchy and to posterity would have been completely different. The members of the Constituent Assembly who opposed the King's deposition intended to save the crown, and they laid it to waste; those who intended to lay it to waste by demanding a deposition might have saved it. As it almost always is in politics, the result was contrary to predictions.

On the last day of September 1791, the Constituent Assembly held its final session. The impudent decree of the previous May 17, forbidding the reelection of outgoing members, had given rise to the Convention. Nothing is more dangerous, nothing more insufficient, nothing more unsuitable to public affairs than resolutions directed against individuals or bodies, even when these resolutions are honorable.

The decree of September 29, regarding the regulation of popular assemblies, only served to make these assemblies more violent. This was the final act of the Constituent Assembly. The next day it dispersed and left France to a revolution.

THE LEGISLATIVE ASSEMBLY—CLUBS

The Legislative Assembly, installed on October 1, 1791, tumbled along in the whirlwind that was about to sweep away the living and the dead. Disturbances bloodied the *départements*; in Caen, they had their fill of murders and ate the heart of M. de Belzunce.[9]

The King stamped his veto on the decree against the émigrés and on another that stripped the non-juring priests of their rights. These legal acts fomented public unrest. Pétion had meanwhile become Mayor of Paris. On January 1, 1792, the deputies passed a decree demanding the prosecution of the emigrated Princes; on January 2, they resolved that this same January 1 would thenceforth be known as Year IV of Liberty. Sometime around February 13, the red caps made their appearance in the streets of Paris and the municipality began manufacturing pikes. The Émigré Manifesto was issued on March 1, and Austria assembled its arms. Paris was divided into sections more or less hostile to one another. On March 20, 1792, the Legislative Assembly adopted the sepulchral machine, without which the judgments of the Terror could never have been executed; it was first tried on corpses, so that it could learn its work. One really can speak of this machine as one speaks of an executioner, since some people, touched by its good services, donated sums of money for its upkeep. The invention of this murderous instrument, at the very moment it was needed by the spirit of crime, is memorable proof of the coordinating intelligence of events, or rather of the hidden workings of Providence, when she wishes to change the face of empires.

At the instigation of the Girondins, Roland was called to advise the King. On April 20, war was declared on the King of Hungary and Bohemia.[10] Marat went on publishing the *Ami du Peuple* despite the decree issued against him. The Royal German Guards and the Berchini Regiment deserted. Isnard spoke of treachery in the Court. Gensonné and Brissot denounced the Austrian Committee. An insurrection broke out over the Royal Guard, which was disbanded. On May 28, the Assembly proclaimed its sessions permanent. On June 20, the Tuileries Palace was stormed by crowds from the Faubourgs Saint-Antoine and Saint-Marceau; the pretext was Louis XVI's refusal to sanction the proscription of priests: in this, the King was running the risk of death. France was declared to be in danger. M. de Lafayette was burned in effigy. The confederates of the second Federation were arriving; the Marseillais, lured by Danton, were on the march. They entered Paris on July 30 and took up quarters in the Club des Cordeliers.

THE CORDELIERS

Together with the national tribunal, two other tribunals had simultaneously been established: that of the Jacobins and that of the Cordeliers, which was then the most formidable because it furnished members for the famous Paris Commune and gave this Commune the means to act. If the Commune had never been formed, Paris, for want of a point of concentration, would have been divided, and the different districts would have become rival powers.

The Club des Cordeliers was established in the Cordeliers Convent, which had been built in the year 1259, during the reign of Saint Louis, with money given in reparation for a murder;* in 1590, it became a safe haven for the most infamous of the Leaguers.

Some places seem to be laboratories of factionalism: "Notice was given to the Duc de Mayenne," says L'Estoile (on July 12, 1593), "that

*It was burned to the ground in 1580.

two hundred friars were arriving in Paris, furnished with arms and in agreement with the Sixteen, who held their daily councils in the Cordeliers of Paris.... On that day the Sixteen, assembled in the Cordeliers, laid down their arms." The fanatics of the Holy League had thus yielded the Cordeliers Convent, like a morgue, to the Revolutionary philosophers.

The pictures, the sculpted and painted images, the veils, and the curtains of the monastery had been pulled down. The basilica, gutted, was now nothing but bones and shredded sinew. In the apse of the church, where the wind and the rain poured in through the broken panes of the rose-windows, a carpenter's workbench served as the President's station whenever the tribunal was in session. The red caps were left on this bench, to be donned by each orator in turn before he mounted the rostrum: this rostrum consisted of four small beams nailed crosswise, with a plank laid across this X as on a scaffold. Behind the President, beside a statue of Liberty, one saw the old, so-called instruments of justice—those instruments that would be supplanted by a single, bloody machine, as complicated mechanisms have been replaced by the hydraulic ram. The Club des Jacobins, once it had been "purified," borrowed a few of these arrangements from the Club des Cordeliers.

ORATORS

The orators, assembled for the sake of destruction, agreed neither on the leaders to be chosen nor the means to be employed. They accosted each other like beggars, crooks, pickpockets, thieves, and murderers, to the cacophony of whistles and shouts that came from their various diabolical groups. Their metaphors were taken from the material of murder, borrowed from the filthiest objects to be found on the garbage heap and the dunghill, or drawn from places dedicated to the prostitution of men and women alike. Gestures accentuated these figures of speech, and everything was called by its name, with the cynicism of dogs, in an impious and obscene series of oaths and blasphemies.

Nothing could be gleaned from this savage argot but the stuff of destruction and production, death and generation. All the speechifiers, no matter how reedy or thunderous their voices, were disrupted by creatures other than their opponents: small black owls, who inhabited the belfry without bells in this monkless monastery, swooped through the broken windows in search of quarry. At first the birds were called to order by the tintinnabulation of a useless bell; but when they did not cease their screeching, they were silenced by rifle fire, and fell, quivering, wounded and fatidic, in the midst of this Pandemonium. The fallen ceiling beams, the broken benches, the dismantled stalls, and the shards of saints that had been rolled and pushed against the walls, formed terraces on which spectators squatted, caked in mud and dust, sweaty and drunk, wearing threadworn carmagnoles, with pikes on their shoulders, or with their bare arms crossed.

The most misshapen of this gang were the preferred speakers. All the infirmities of soul and body have played their part in our troubles: disappointed self-love has made some great revolutionaries.

MARAT AND HIS FRIENDS

Following the precedent of hideousness, a succession of Gorgon-like heads mixed with the spectral presence of the Sixteen.[11] The former physician to the bodyguard of the Comte d'Artois, the fetus-faced Swiss Marat, with his bare feet stuffed in wooden clogs or in shoes shod with iron, was the first to deliver his speech, by virtue of his incontestable rights. Awarded the office of fool in the Court of the People, he shouted through his flat-nosed physiognomy with the banal half-smile that the old order of politeness smeared on every face, "People, we are going to have cut off two hundred and seventy thousand heads!" This Caligula of the crossroads was followed by the atheist cobbler Chaumette. Next came Camille Desmoulins, the attorney-general of the lamppost, a stammering Cicero, a public counselor of murderers, always exhausted from his debauches, a lighthearted

Republican full of bons mots and puns, a connoisseur of gallows humor who said of the September Massacres: *everything was done in an orderly fashion*. He consented to become a Spartan only so long as the recipe for the black broth was left to Méot, the restaurateur.

Fouché, who had rushed up from Juilly and Nantes, took lessons from these professors of disaster. In the circle of ferocious beasts that gathered round the base of the chair, he looked like a dressed-up hyena, panting for the impending effluvium of blood. He was already on the scent of the incense drifting from the processions of idiots and executioners, and waiting for the day when, driven from the Club des Jacobins as a thief, an atheist, and a murderer, he would be appointed a minister. When Marat stepped down from his plank, this Triboulet of the people became the plaything of his masters: they mocked him, trod on his toes, jostled him, and screamed in his face—none of which stopped him from becoming a leader of the multitude, mounting the tower of the Hôtel de Ville, sounding the tocsin of wholesale massacre, and triumphing over the Revolutionary tribunal.

Marat, like Milton's Sin, was raped by Death:[12] Chénier wrote his apotheosis, David depicted him in his bloody bath, and he was many times compared to the divine author of the Gospels. A prayer was dedicated to him: "Heart of Jesus, Heart of Marat; O Sacred Heart of Jesus, O Sacred Heart of Marat!" This sacred heart had for its ciborium a precious pyxis taken from the storehouse. On a cenotaph of turf raised in the Place du Carrousel, one could visit the bust, the bathtub, the lamp, and the writing-case of this divinity. Then the winds changed, and the unclean thing, poured from its agate urn into another vase, was emptied into the gutter.[13]

4·

DANTON—CAMILLE DESMOULINS—FABRE D'ÉGLANTINE

London, April to September 1822

THE SCENES of the Club des Cordeliers, which I witnessed three or four times, were dominated and presided over by Danton. A Hun with the stature of a Goth, a squashed nose, windward nostrils, and scarred cheeks, Danton had the face of a gendarme crossed with that of a slippery and ruthless attorney. Inside the shell of his church, as though inside the carcass of the centuries, he organized the September Massacres with the help of his three male Furies: Desmoulins, Marat, and Fabre d'Églantine. Billaud de Varennes proposed setting fire to the prisons and burning everyone within; another member of the Convention suggested drowning all the detainees; Marat declared himself in favor of a general massacre. "I don't give a f—— about the prisoners," replied Danton. In his capacity as author of the Commune circular, he invited friends of Liberty to reproduce in their various *départements* the enormities perpetrated at the Carmelite Convent and L'Abbaye.

But let us take heed of history. Sixtus V said that Jacques Clément's devotion was equal, for the salvation of mankind, to the mystery of the Incarnation, just as Marat was compared to the Savior of the World.[14] Charles IX wrote to the governors of the provinces to imitate the Saint Bartholomew Massacres, just as Danton ordered patriots to copy the September Massacres. The Jacobins were plagiarists; they even plagiarized the sacrifice of Louis XVI from the execution of Charles I. As crimes have been found mixed in a great social movement, it has been imagined, quite wrongly as it happens, that these crimes yielded the Revolution's greatness, of which they are no more than a horrible pastiche. Passionate and systematic minds have admired only the convulsions of the Revolution's beautiful but sickly nature.

Danton, more frank than the English, said, "We shall not judge the King; we shall kill him." He also said, "None of these priests or nobles is guilty, but they must die because they are out of place: they are impeding the progress of events and waylaying the future." These words, under the semblance of a sort of horrible profundity, show no real understanding or genius: for they suppose that innocence is worth nothing and that the moral order may be subtracted from the political order without annihilating it, which is false.

Danton was not convinced of the principles he defended; he merely wrapped himself in the Revolutionary mantle to make his fortune. "Come and *holler* with us," he told one young man. "When you're rich, you can do whatever you please." He confessed that he had refused to go over to the Court's party only because they hadn't agreed to pay him what he asked. Such was the effrontery of a mind that understood itself and of a corruption that proclaimed itself with the sluice gates wide open.

Inferior to Mirabeau even in ugliness, Danton was superior to Robespierre, even if he did not bequeath his name to his crimes. He preserved some sense of religion: "We have not," he said, "destroyed superstition in order to institute atheism." His passions may have been good for the simple reason that they *were* passions. We should pay some mind to the role a man's character plays in his deeds. Criminals like Danton, who are guilty in imagination, seem, by reason of their exaggerated words and gestures, more perverse than cold-blooded criminals, but in fact they are less perverse. This observation applies equally well to a people. Taken collectively, the people are a poet, at once author and ardent actor of the part they play, or the part they are made to play. Their excesses come not so much from instinctual or inborn cruelty as from the unpredictable delirium of a crowd intoxicated by spectacles, especially when the spectacles are tragic: a thing so true that, in the popular horror shows, you will always find something superfluous added to the scenery and the emotion.

Danton was caught in the trap he himself had set. It did him no good to flick bread-balls at the judges' noses, or to answer their questions with nobility and courage, or to make the tribunal hesitate, or to make the Convention fear for its life. It was no use rationalizing the crimes that had given power to his enemies, or crying out, seized by a barren fit of repentance, "It was I who instituted this infamous tribunal, and now I ask pardon for the deed from God and man!"—a phrase that has been pillaged more than once. He ought to have betrayed the infamy of the tribunal long before he was called to its bar.

There was nothing left for Danton but to show himself as pitiless toward his own death as he had been toward the deaths of his victims, to hold his head higher than the suspended blade. So he did. In the open theater of the Terror, where his feet stuck to the clotted matte of yesterday's blood, he cast a look of contempt and superiority over the crowd and said to the executioner, "You shall show my head to the people; it is worth the trouble." Danton's head thus remained in the executioner's hands, even as his acephalous shade went down to join the decapitated shades of his victims. This, too, was equality.

Danton's deacon and sub-deacon, Camille Desmoulins and Fabre d'Églantine, perished in the same manner as their priest.

In those days when a pension was paid to the guillotine; when one wore in the buttonhole of his carmagnole, as he might have worn a flower, either a small gilt guillotine or a small bit of flesh from the heart of one of its victims; when one shouted *Long Live Hell!*; when one celebrated the joyous orgies of blood, steel, and rage, and drank himself to nothingness; when one danced the Bloody Waltz of the Dead all night, completely naked, to avoid the inconvenience of undressing to go and join them; in those days, sooner or later, everyone had to arrive at the last banquet, at the last sorrowful joke. When Desmoulins was summoned to Fouquier-Tinville's tribunal, the President asked him his age. "The same age as the sans-culotte Jesus," Camille said in jest. A vengeful obsession compelled these butchers of Christian throats to utter the name of Jesus Christ incessantly.

It would be unjust to forget that Camille Desmoulins dared to defy Robespierre and redeemed some of his debauchery with his courage. He gave the first signal for the wider reaction against the Terror. A young woman, charming and full of life, made him capable of love, sacrifice, and even virtue. Fierce indignation inspired the eloquent, fearless, bawdy irony he displayed before the tribunal: he openly condemned the scaffolds he had helped to raise, and he conformed his conduct to his words. He did not submit to his punishment. He grappled with the executioner in the tumbrel and arrived at the brink of the final chasm half torn to pieces.

Fabre d'Églantine, the author of a play that will last, showed himself, the very reverse of Desmoulins, to be a man of remarkable weakness. Jean Roseau, the executioner in Paris under the Holy League, was sentenced to be hanged for offering his services to the murderers of President Brisson; he could not bring himself to face the rope. It seems that no one learns how to die by killing others.

The debates I witnessed at the Club des Cordeliers made it clear to me that society was in a stage of most rapid transformation. I had seen the Constituent Assembly beginning the massacre of the royalty in 1789 and 1790; in 1792, I found the still warm carcass of the old monarchy, handed over to the gut-working legislators: they disemboweled it and dissected it under the low ceilings of their clubs, as halberdiers once dismembered and burned the body of Henri Le Balafré in the tunnels beneath the Château de Blois.[15]

Of all the men I here recall—Danton, Marat, Camille Desmoulins, Fabre d'Églantine, Robespierre—not one is alive today. I encountered them for a moment on my journey, between a nascent society in America and a dying society in Europe, between the forests of the New World and the solitudes of exile: I had been on foreign soil only a few months when these lovers of Death grew weary of her embraces. At the distance from which I gaze back at their apparitions, it seems to me that, having descended into hell in my youth, I retain a confused memory of the wraiths I glimpsed wandering along the banks of the Cocytus. They add something to the varied dreams of my life, and they are now inscribed on these tablets from beyond the grave.

5.

M. DE MALESHERBES'S OPINION OF EMIGRATION
London, April to September 1822

IT GAVE me great satisfaction to see M. de Malesherbes again and talk with him about my former projects. I mentioned my plans for a second voyage which would last nine years. I had nothing to do before this but take a short trip to Germany: I would rush to the Army of Princes, rush back to slay the Revolution, and it would all be over in two or three months. I would hoist my sail and return to the New World with one revolution the less and one marriage the more.

Even then, my zeal outstripped my faith. I felt that the emigration was a nonsensical folly: "Pummeled on every side," as Montaigne says, "a Guelph to the Ghibellines and a Ghibelline to the Guelphs."[16] My distaste for absolute monarchy left me no illusions about the side I was taking: I would maintain my scruples, and although I had resolved to sacrifice myself for the sake of honor, I would take M. de Malesherbes's opinion of emigration to heart. I found him quite animated on the subject. The crimes that he witnessed with his own eyes had dissolved the political tolerance of this friend of Rousseau. Between the cause of the victims and the cause of the executioners, M. de Malesherbes did not hesitate. He believed that anything would be better than the extant order of things, and, in my particular case, he thought that a man of the sword had a duty to join the brothers of a King who had been oppressed and betrayed to his enemies. He was also very much in favor of me returning to America, and he urged my brother to go with me.

I raised some of the usual objections regarding alliances with

367

foreigners: the interests of the homeland, etc., etc. M. de Malesherbes responded to these objections at length. Passing from general arguments to specifics, he cited me a few rather awkward examples. He put before me the case of the Guelphs and the Ghibellines lending aid to the Armies of the Pope; in England, the barons rising up against John Lackland. Finally, speaking of our own days, he cited the Republic of the United States of America asking the assistance of France.

"Thus we see," said M. de Malesherbes, "that the men most devoted to liberty and to philosophy, which is to say Republicans and Protestants, saw nothing shameful in borrowing the strength that should make them victorious. Without our gold, our ships, and our soldiers, would the New World be free today? I, Malesherbes, I who am speaking to you now—did I not, in 1776, go to greet Franklin when he came to resume the negotiations begun by Silas Deane? And was Franklin a traitor? Was American liberty less honorably won because Lafayette and the French grenadiers helped win it? A government ceases to exist when, instead of guaranteeing the fundamental laws of society, it transgresses the laws of equality and the rules of justice. It is then licit to defend oneself however one can, by whatever means best serve to overthrow tyranny and reestablish the rights of each and all."

The principles of natural rights, first put forth by the greatest polemicists, developed so eloquently by such a man as M. de Malesherbes, and supported by so many historical examples, were striking; but I remained unconvinced. In truth, I merely yielded to the impulse of my era, on a point of honor.

—Today I can add a few more recent examples to those given by M. de Malesherbes. During the Spanish War of 1823, French Republicans went to serve under the flag of Cortes without any scruples about bearing arms against their countrymen. In 1830 and 1831, the Poles and the Italian Constitutional Party asked for French support. And the Portuguese who supported the Constitutional Charter invaded their own country with the help of foreign money and soldiers. We have always two weights and two measures: we approve of an idea for one system, one interest, or one man which we condemn for another system, another interest, or another man.

6.

I GAMBLE AND LOSE—ADVENTURE OF THE CAB—MADAME ROLAND—AT THE GATE OF ROUSSEAU'S HERMITAGE—THE SECOND FEDERATION OF THE FOURTEENTH OF JULY—PREPARATIONS FOR EMIGRATION

London, April to September 1822

THESE conversations between me and the illustrious defender of the King took place at my sister-in-law's house. She had just given birth to her second son, to whom M. de Malesherbes, the child's godfather, gave the name Christian. I was present at the baptism of this boy, who would only know his mother and father at an age when life has no memories and which seems, at a distance, like a vague and shapeless dream. The preparations for my departure were meanwhile dragging on. My family had thought they were making me a wealthy marriage; they now discovered that my wife's fortune was invested in Church securities, which the nation undertook to pay in its own fashion. Madame de Chateaubriand, moreover, had lent the scrip of the larger part of these securities to her sister, the Comtesse du Plessix-Parscau, who had already emigrated. There was still no money to be had. It would thus be necessary to borrow.

A notary procured ten thousand francs for us, and I was taking them home in *assignats* to the Cul-de-Sac Férou when I bumped into my old friend from the Navarre Regiment in the rue de Richelieu. This man, the Comte Achard, was a great gambler. He proposed that we go to the rooms of Monsieur X—, where we could chat. The devil pushed me onward. I went upstairs, gambled, and lost all but fifteen hundred francs, with which, full of remorse and confusion, I climbed into the first carriage that came along. I had never gambled in my life: the game had produced a sort of painful intoxication in me. I have no doubt that, if this passion had really taken hold of me, it would have conquered my brain. As it was, my mind was still half-deranged when I left the cab at Saint-Sulpice, and I forgot my pock-etbook, which contained the residue of my former wealth. I rushed home to tell my family that I had left all 10,000 francs in the cab.

I went back out, turned down the rue Dauphine, crossed the Pont-Neuf, feeling tempted to throw myself in the Seine, and made my way to the Place du Palais-Royal, where I had climbed into the cursed vehicle. I questioned a few Savoyards busy watering the nags, described my cab to them, and was given a number seemingly at random. The *commissaire de police* of the quarter informed me that this number belonged to a coach-master who lived at the top of the Faubourg Saint-Denis. I hurried to this man's house, where I stayed all night in the stables waiting for the cabs to return. A great number of them arrived one after another, but none of them was mine. Finally, at two in the morning, I saw my chariot come rolling in. I barely had time to recognize my two white steeds before the poor beasts, whipped to pieces, let themselves collapse, spent, on the straw, their bellies dis-tended and their legs splayed out as if dead.

The coachman remembered having driven me. After me, he had picked up a citizen who had asked to be taken down to the Jacobins; after the citizen, a lady whom he had brought to rue de Cléry, no. 13; after the lady, a man whom he had let out at the Recollects in the rue Saint-Martin. I promised the coachman a tip, and there I was, the moment day began to break, setting out to discover my fifteen hundred francs as though in search of the Northwest Passage. It seemed clear to me that the citizen had confiscated them by rights of his sovereignty, for the young lady of the rue de Cléry assured me that she had seen nothing in the cab. I arrived at my third stop feeling hopeless. The coachman had given me, as best he could, a description of the man he had driven. I repeated it, and the porter exclaimed, "Oh, that's Father So-and-so!"

He led me through a series of hallways, past abandoned apartments, to the rooms of a Recollect who had stayed behind alone in order to make an inventory of the furniture of his monastery. This monk, in

his dusty frockcoat, sitting on a heap of ruins, listened to the story
that I had to tell him.

"Are you," he asked me, "the Chevalier de Chateaubriand?"

"Yes," I said.

"Here is your pocketbook," he said. "I was going to bring it to you
when the day's work was done. I found your address inside."

It was this hunted and despoiled monk, conscientiously counting
up the relics of his cloister for the sake of those that had outlawed
him, who restored me the fifteen hundred francs with which I would
make my way toward exile. Without this small sum, I would never
have emigrated, and what would have happened to me then? Everything in my life would have been different. I would be hanged today
before I'd move a single step to recover a million.

Thus passed June 16, 1792.

Loyal to my instincts, I had come back from America to offer my
sword to Louis XVI, not to involve myself in party intrigues. The
disbanding of the new Royal Guard, in which Murat had served; the
ministries of Roland, Dumouriez, and Duport du Tertre following
one after another; the minor conspiracies of the Court, and the great
popular uprisings—I was bored and contemptuous of all these events.
I heard endless gossip about Madame Roland, but I never laid eyes
on her; her *Memoirs* prove that she possessed an extraordinary strength
of mind. She was rumored to be pleasant company, but I doubt whether
she was pleasant enough to make the cynicism of her unnatural
virtues tolerable. Certainly a woman who, at the foot of the guillotine,
requests pen and ink to record the last moments of her journey, to
jot down the discoveries she has made from the Conciergerie to the
Place de la Révolution—such a woman shows a preoccupation with
the future, and a disdain for life, of which there are few examples.
But Madame Roland was a woman of character rather than of genius:
the first may grant a person the second, but the second does not
guarantee the first.

On June 19, I had gone to the valley of Montmorency, to visit J.-J. Rousseau's Hermitage, not because it pleased me to remember Madame d'Épinay and all that depraved and artificial group, but because I wanted to say goodbye to the solitary retreat of a man who, although his morals and manners were antipathetic to mine, was endowed with a talent whose outpourings had stirred my youth. The next day, June 20, I was still at the Hermitage, and there, strolling in that wild place, on that day which would be fatal to the monarchy, I saw two men indifferent, as I thought they were and ever would be, to the affairs of the world: the one was M. Maret of the Empire, the other M. Barère of the Republic.[17] The gentle Barère had come far from the noise, as befitted his sentimental philosophy, to recite little Revolutionary sonnets to the shade of Rousseau's Julie. The troubadour of the guillotine, on whose report the Convention declared that "Terror was the order of the day," escaped from this same Terror by hiding himself in a basket of heads. From the bottom of this bloody vessel, he could be heard croaking: *Death! Death!* Barère must have been of that species of tigers which Oppian said were engendered by the light breath of the wind: *velocis Zephyri proles.*[18]

Ginguené and Chamfort, my old friends the men of letters, were delighted by the events of June 20. La Harpe, in the middle of his lectures at the Lycée, shouted in stentorian voice:

"Madmen! You replied to every protest that the people made with *Bayonets! Bayonets!* Well! Here are your *bayonets!*"

Though my voyage to America had made me a less insignificant personage in Paris, I was unable to rise to such transcendent heights of principle and eloquence. Fontanes's life was in danger because of his former connection with the Société Monarchique. My brother was a member of a club of Enragés. The Prussians were on the march after an agreement made between the Cabinets of Vienna and Berlin, and already some rather heated skirmishes had taken place between the French and the Austrians, near Mons. It was high time for me to make a decision.

My brother and I procured two forged passports for Lille. We would be two wine merchants and National Guards of Paris (whose uniforms we wore) on our way to sign contracts to provision the Republican army. My brother's footman, Louis Poullain, nicknamed "Saint Louis," would be traveling under his own name: although from Lamballe, in Lower Brittany, he would be going to see relatives in Flanders. The day of our emigration was to be July 15, 1792, the day after the second Federation. We spent the Fourteenth in Tivoli Gardens with the Rosambo family, my sisters, and my wife. Tivoli then belonged to M. Boutin, whose daughter had married M. de Malesherbes. Late in the afternoon, we caught sight of a large number of Federalists wandering over the grounds, their hats chalked with the phrase "Pétion or Death!" Tivoli, the point of my departure into exile, would soon be a rendezvous for games and gatherings. Our relatives parted from us without any sad farewells; they were convinced that we were going on a pleasure trip. I was convinced that the 1,500 francs I had recovered would be more than enough to bring me back to Paris in triumph.

7.

I EMIGRATE WITH MY BROTHER—THE ADVENTURE OF SAINT LOUIS—WE CROSS THE BORDER

London, April to September 1822

ON JULY 15, at six o'clock in the morning, we climbed into the diligence. My brother and I had secured our places in the cabriolet, beside the driver; the footman, whom we were supposed not to know, ensconced himself in the carriage among the other passengers. Now, I have not yet said that Saint Louis was a sleepwalker. In Paris he used to go looking for his master at night, eyes open, but sound asleep. He would undress my brother, put him to bed, all the while dozing and replying to everything that was said to him during these attacks: *I know, I know.* There was no way to wake him except to throw cold water in his face. He was a man of about forty, nearly six feet tall, and as ugly as he was large. This poor and extremely respectful servant had never worked for any master but my brother, and he was very troubled when he sat down to supper with us at the same table. The other passengers, all great patriots, were talking about hanging aristocrats from lampposts, which made him still more anxious. The idea that, at the end of all this, he would be obliged to brave the Austrian army and go fight for the Army of Princes must have completed his derangement. He drank a great deal and climbed back into the coach. My brother and I resumed our places in the cabriolet.

In the middle of the night, we heard the passengers shouting, sticking their heads through the carriage door: "Stop, postilion, stop!"

We stopped. The carriage door was thrown open and out came a clamor of male and female voices: "Out, citizen, out! You can't stay here, you swine! Get out! He's a brigand! Out! Out!"

We got out also and saw poor befuddled Saint Louis, who had been ejected from the coach, rise to his feet, look around him with wide-open, fast asleep eyes, and then set off at full tilt, and without his hat, in the direction of Paris. We could not call to him, for we would have betrayed ourselves: he had to be abandoned to his fate. Stopped and apprehended at the first village he entered, he declared that he was the servant of M. le Comte de Chateaubriand and that he lived in Paris in the rue de Bondy. The police transferred him from one brigade to another until he reached the house of President Rosambo. The deposition of this unlucky man was enough to prove that we had emigrated and to send my brother and his wife, by and by, to the scaffold.

The next morning, when the diligence stopped for breakfast, we had to hear the story of Saint Louis twenty times over.

"The man's mind was disturbed," they said. "He dreamed aloud and said such strange things. He was without doubt a conspirator, probably a murderer fleeing justice."

The well-mannered lady citizens blushed and fluttered large green "Constitutional" fans.[19] We easily recognized in their accounts the effects of somnambulism, fear, and wine.

On arriving in Lille, we went to find the person who was to take us across the border. The Emigration had many agents of protection, who turned out in the end to be agents of perdition. The monarchical party was still powerful, the question undecided; the weak and the cowardly served it while they awaited the results.

We were gone from Lille before the gates were shut. We stopped at an isolated farmhouse and did not resume our journey until ten at night, when the sky was completely dark. We carried nothing with us except our walking sticks: it had been less than a year since I had followed my Dutchman through the American forests in this same manner.

We followed winding paths lightly traced across the wheatfields. French and Austrian patrols were scouring the countryside. At any moment, we could fall into the hands of one or the other, or find ourselves in range of a mounted sentry's pistol. We caught glimpses of solitary horsemen in the distance, motionless, shouldering a gun. We heard the tread of horses in sunken lanes. Putting our ears to the earth, we listened to the steady sound of an infantry unit on the march. After three hours, sometimes running, sometimes going slowly on tiptoe, we arrived at a crossroads deep in the woods where a few nightingales belatedly sang. All of a sudden a company of soldiers ambushed us with sabers drawn. We cried out, "Officers come to join the Princes!" We asked to be taken to Tournay and declared that we had means of proving that we were who we claimed to be. The company commander positioned us between his horsemen and led us away.

When day dawned, the men caught sight of the National Guard uniforms we wore beneath our great coats, and they insulted the colors that France would make a subjugated Europe wear.

It was in Tournaisis, the ancient kingdom of the Franks, that Clovis resided during the first years of his reign. He left Tournay with his companions, called as he was to conquer the Gauls. "Arms claim every right for themselves," Tacitus says. It was through this same city, which the first king of the first race left in 486, to found a powerful and lasting monarchy, that I passed in 1792, to join the princes of the third race on a foreign soil, and passed again in 1815, when the last King of the French abandoned the kingdom of the first King of the Franks: *omnia migrant.*[20]

On arriving in Tournay, I left my brother to contend with the authorities while I visited the cathedral in the custody of a soldier. In the old days, Odon d'Orléans, a scholastic of this cathedral, sat all night under the portal of the church, teaching his disciples the paths of the stars and pointing out the Milky Way and the constellations with his finger: I would much rather have found that simple eleventh-century astronomer in Tournay than the Pandours. I am enchanted by those days when, so the chronicles tell me, in an entry for the year 1049, a Norman man was metamorphosed into an ass: exactly what was thought to have happened to me when I was taken to the house of those hunchbacked Couppart sisters who first tried to teach me and my sister to read. In 1114, Hildebert records the existence of a girl who had wheatstalks growing from her ears: perhaps she was Ceres. The River Meuse, which I was about to cross, was seen suspended midair in 1118: Guillaume de Nangis and Albéric were there to witness it. Rigord assures us that in the year 1194, between Compiègne and Clermont-en-Beauvoisis, a storm of hail and crows fell upon the earth, dropping coals that set every thing they touched on fire. If no storm, Gervais of Tilbury tells us, was able to blow out a candle above the window of the Priory of Saint-Michel de Camissa, we also know, from the same source, that in the diocese of Uzès there was a pure and beautiful spring that changed location whenever any unclean thing was tossed into it. Consciences today are not so easily troubled.

—Reader, I swear, I'm not wasting time; I'm simply making conversation while we patiently wait for my brother to finish his negotiations. Ah! Here he is now. He has explained everything to the satisfaction of the Austrian commander, who has given us permission to travel on to Brussels. It is an exile purchased with too much care.

8.

BRUSSELS—DINNER AT THE BARON DE BRETEUIL'S—RIVAROL—DEPARTURE FOR THE ARMY OF PRINCES—ROUTE—MEETING THE PRUSSIAN ARMY—I ARRIVE IN TRÈVES

London, April to September 1822

BRUSSELS was the headquarters of the High Emigration. The most elegant women of Paris and the most fashionable men—those who wouldn't march except as aides-de-camp—were waiting in the lap of luxury for victory to arrive. The men wore handsome, newly bought uniforms and paraded them in all the rigor of their frivolity. In a matter of days they ate up considerable sums that could have sustained them for several years; but then, it wasn't worth the trouble of economizing, since any day now they would find themselves back in Paris again. These brilliant knights were preparing for success on the battlefield by success in love: just the reverse of the old chivalry. They looked down disdainfully on all of us little gentlemen from the provinces and poor officers turned soldiers, tramping around afoot with rucksacks on our backs. At the feet of their Omphales, these Herculeans twirled the distaffs that they had sent us and that we returned to them the moment we arrived, contenting ourselves with our swords.[21]

In Brussels I found my trifling baggage, which had been smuggled there before me: it consisted of my uniform from the Navarre Regiment packed in with a few changes of linen and my precious manuscripts, from which I would not be parted. My brother and I were invited to dine at the Baron de Breteuil's house, where I met the Baroness de Montmorency, then young and beautiful, and who is dying today; martyred bishops in mohair cassocks and gold crosses; young magistrates transformed into Hungarian colonels; and Rivarol, whom I saw only this once in my life. No one had mentioned his name, but I was struck by the language of this man who soliloquized at length and was listened to, with some reason, as though he were an oracle. Rivarol's wit harmed his talents, as his words harmed the works of his pen. About revolutions, he said: "The first blow carries to God's ear; the second strikes but a senseless slab of marble."

By that time, I had resumed the shabby dress of an infantry sub-lieutenant. I was to depart at the end of dinner. My rucksack was behind the door. I was still bronzed by the American sun and the sea air. I wore my hair straight and unpowdered. Both my face and my silence bothered Rivarol, and the Baron de Breteuil, seeing his vexed curiosity, made to satisfy it. "Where is your brother the Chevalier coming from?" he asked my brother.

I replied, "From Niagara."

Rivarol burst in: "From a waterfall!"

I fell silent.

He hazarded the beginning of a question: "Monsieur is going...?"

"Where men are fighting," I said, cutting him off.

We all stood up from the table.

These smug émigrés were odious to me. I couldn't wait to meet my peers: émigrés with six hundred livres in income like myself. We were quite stupid no doubt, but at least our rapiers were at the ready, and, even if we had been successful, we never would have profited from the victory.

In the end, my brother stayed behind in Brussels with the Baron de Montboissier, who appointed him his aide-de-camp, and I set off alone for Coblenz.

Nothing is more historic than the route I followed; every place along the way recalled some memory or some splendid triumph of France. I passed through Liège, one of those municipal republics that rose so many times against its bishops and against the Counts of Flanders. Louis XI, an ally of the Liégois, was once obliged to help sack their city in order to escape his ridiculous imprisonment in Péronne.[22]

I was going to join ranks with men of war who sought glory in similar things. But in 1792, the relations between Liège and France were more peaceable: every year, the Abbé de Saint-Hubert was obliged to send two hunting dogs to the successors of King Dagobert.

In Aix-la-Chapelle, another gift, but from France. The mortuary sheet used in the burial of a truly Christian monarch had been sent there, to Charlemagne's tomb, like a liege's flag sent to the ruling fief.[23] Our Kings thus lent fealty and homage by taking possession of this heirloom of Eternity; they swore an oath of loyalty between the knees of Death, their Lady, and gave her a feudal kiss on the mouth: this was the sole suzerainty to which France considered itself a vassal. The cathedral of Aix-la-Chapelle was built by Charlemagne and consecrated by Leo III. Two prelates, having gone missing from the ceremony, were replaced by two bishops from Maastricht who had been dead for centuries and resurrected expressly for this purpose. Charlemagne, having lost a beautiful mistress, held her dead body in his arms and refused to be separated from it. His passion was attributed to a charm: the young corpse was examined and a small pearl was found beneath her tongue. The pearl was thrown into a marsh. Charlemagne, now madly in love with the marsh, ordered it drained, and in its place he built a palace and a church. In the first, he would spend his life; in the second, his death. The authorities here are Archbishop Turpin and Petrarch.[24]

In Cologne, I admired the cathedral. Had it been completed, it would have been the most magnificent Gothic building in Europe. The monks were the painters, the sculptors, the architects, and the masons of their basilica; they gloried in the title of *caementarius*, or "master mason."

It is curious today to hear ignorant philosophers and blustery democrats rail against religion, as if those frocked proletarians and mendicant orders to whom we owe almost everything had been gentlemen.

Cologne put me in mind of Caligula and Saint Bruno: in my life, I have seen the remains of the dykes built by the former at Baiae and the empty cell of the second at the Grand Chartreuse.

I traveled up the Rhine as far as Coblentz (*Confluentia*), but the

Army of Princes was no longer there. I crossed those ancient empty kingdoms, *inania regna*,[25] and saw that beautiful Rhine valley, the Temple of the Barbarian Muses, where ghostly knights once loomed around the ruined castles, and where at night one heard the clash of arms, whenever wartime was at hand.

Somewhere between Coblentz and Trèves, I fell in with the Prussian Army. I was making my way along the column of soldiers when, coming near the Guards, I saw that they were marching in battle formation with cannon in line. The King and the Duke of Brunswick occupied the center of the square formed by the men who had once been Frederick's grenadiers. My white uniform caught the King's eye, and he sent for me. He and the Duke of Brunswick doffed their hats and saluted the old French Army in my person. They asked my name, my regiment, and where I was bound. Their military welcome touched me, and I replied with great emotion that, having learned in America of the King's misfortune, I had returned to shed my blood in his service. The officers and generals who surrounded Frederick William gave a general murmur of approval, and the Prussian monarch said to me, "Monsieur, one can always recognize the sentiments of the French nobility."

He doffed his hat once more, and remained that way, uncovered and unmoving, until I had disappeared behind the mass of grenadiers. People now condemn the émigrés and say we were nothing but "a pack of tigers who clawed at their mother's breast"; but in the epoch of which I am speaking, a man held fast to the old examples, and honor counted just as much as country. In 1792, loyalty to oaths was still seen as a duty; today, it has become so rare it is regarded as a virtue.

A bizarre exchange, which had already happened many times to others, almost forced me to turn back. I was refused admittance in Trèves, where the Army of Princes had already arrived: I was told I was "one of those men who wait for events to decide his future"; that I "ought to have been in camp three years ago"; that I was "arriving when victory was certain and my services were no longer needed"; that they "already had plenty of brave men ready to fight; whole cavalry squadrons were deserting every day, and even the artillery

382 · MEMOIRS FROM BEYOND THE GRAVE

was leaving en masse, and, if this exodus continued, no one would know what to do with all these new men...."

What a wonderful partisan delusion!

I found my cousin Armand de Chateaubriand, who took me under his wing and called a meeting of Bretons to plead my case. I was summoned and made to explain myself. I said that I had come back from America to have the honor of serving with my comrades, that the campaign was opened but not yet begun, and that I was still in time to face the first fire. Finally, I said that I would leave if they insisted, but only after I had been told the reasons for such an un-merited insult. The matter was soon settled. As I was a good fellow, the ranks opened to receive me, and I had nothing less than an em-barrassment of choices.

9.

ARMY OF PRINCES—ROMAN AMPHITHEATER—
ATALA—HENRI IV'S SHIRTS

THE ARMY of Princes was made up of gentlemen classed according
to province and serving together as common soldiers. The nobility
was returning to its origins and to the origin of the monarchy like
an old man returning to his infancy, at the very moment when this
nobility and this monarchy were coming to an end. There were also
brigades of émigré officers from various regiments who had gone back
to being foot soldiers. Among this number were my comrades from
the Navarre Regiment, now under the command of their colonel, the
Marquis de Mortemart. I was sorely tempted to enlist with La Martinière, even if he should still happen to be in love; but in the end
Armorican patriotism prevailed. I signed on with the Seventh Breton
Company under the command of M. Goyon-Miniac. The nobles of
my province had furnished enough men for seven companies, and an
eighth company comprised young men of the Third Estate: the iron-
gray uniform of this last differed from the royal blue and ermine
facings of the others. Men dedicated to the same cause and exposed
to the same dangers thus perpetuated their political inequality by
hateful distinctions. The true heroes were the plebeian soldiers, who
had no personal interests clouding their sacrifice.

Here is an enumeration of our little army:

An infantry of noble soldiers and officers, four companies of deserters dressed in the various uniforms of the regiments whence they
came, one artillery company, and a few high-ranking engineers, bringing with them a few cannon, howitzers, and mortars. (Artillerymen

and engineers, nearly all of whom embraced the Revolutionary cause, were also largely responsible for its success.) A very handsome cavalry of German carabiniers, musketeers under the command of the aged Comte de Montmorin, and naval officers from Brest, Rochefort, and Toulon lent support to our infantry. The ubiquitous emigration of naval officers plunged the French Navy back into that weakened condition from which Louis XVI had rescued it. Never, since Duquesne and Tourville, had our squadrons won greater glory. My comrades were cheerful, but I admit I had tears in my eyes when I saw these dragoons of the Ocean no longer navigating those ships with which they'd humiliated the English and emancipated America. Instead of sailing in search of new continents to bequeath France, these brethren of La Pérouse were sinking their boots in German mud. They mounted horses dedicated to Neptune; but they had changed their element, and the earth was not for them. In vain did their leader fly the tattered standard of the *Belle Poule*—a holy relic of the white flag, from whose tatters Honor still hung, though Victory had fallen.

We had tents, but we lacked for everything else. Our German-made rifles were rejects so dreadfully heavy they broke our shoulders, and often in no state to be fired. I went through the whole campaign with one of these muskets, whose hammer permanently refused to fall.

For two days we tarried in Trèves. It gave me great pleasure to see Roman ruins there, after having seen the nameless ruins on the Ohio, and to walk through that city so often sacked that Salvian said of it: "Fugitives of Trèves, you ask the Emperors, where is the theater? Where is the circus? But I ask of you, where is your town? Where are your people?" *Theatra igitur quaritis, circum a principus postulatis? Cui, quaeso, statui, cui populo, cui civitati?*[26]

Fugitives of France, I ask you, where were the people for whom we sought to reestablish the monuments of Saint Louis?

I sat down with my rifle among the ruins and took from my rucksack the manuscript of my travels in America. I arranged the separate sheets on the grass around me. I reread and corrected a description of the forest, a passage of *Atala*, in the ruins of a Roman amphitheater. In this way, I prepared myself to conquer France. Then I packed up my treasure, the weight of which, added to my shirts, my cape, my tin canteen, my wicker bottle, and my pocket Homer, made me spit blood. I tried to stuff *Atala* into a pouch with all my useless cartridges, but my comrades laughed at me and tore at the pages that stuck out from the leather cover. Providence soon came to my aid: one morning, after a night spent sleeping in a hayloft, I found that I no longer had any shirts in my rucksack. Only the papers had been left untouched. And I thank God! This accident, while assuring my *glory*, also saved my life, for those sixty pounds set between my shoulders would surely have made me consumptive.

"How many shirts do I have?" Henri IV asked his footman.

"Sire," he said, "there are a dozen, and all of them are torn."

"And handkerchiefs," said the King, "I have eight?"

"At present there are only five."

The Old Béarnais won the Battle of Ivry without any shirts; I was unable to restore the kingdom to his descendants by losing mine.

10.

A SOLDIER'S LIFE—LAST GLIMPSE OF THE OLD FRENCH MILITARY

London, April to September 1822

THE ORDER was given to march on Thionville. We covered five or six leagues a day in terrible weather. We trudged through rain and mud, singing "Ô Richard! ô mon Roi!" and "Pauvre Jacques!" When we arrived at our camping ground, without wagons or provisions, we took our donkeys, which had been following behind our column like an Arabian caravan, and wandered from farm to village looking for something to eat. We paid for everything quite scrupulously. Nevertheless, I was once punished for absentmindedly taking a couple of pears from the garden of a castle. A great steeple, a great river, and a great lord, sayeth the proverb, make bad neighbors.

We pitched our tents haphazardly and stayed up half the night beating their canvas to enlarge the threads and keep the rain from leaking through. We were ten soldiers to a tent, and each man in turn was charged with the cooking. One went for meat, another for bread, another for wood, and a fourth for straw. I made a wonderful soup, for which I received hearty compliments, especially when, in true Breton fashion, I added some milk and cabbage to the stock. With the Iroquois in America I had learned to tolerate smoke; now I conducted myself easily around my fire of moist green branches. Indeed, this soldier's life had many pleasures: I could often imagine myself still among the Indians. While we ate our mess under the flapping canvas, my comrades would ask me for tales of my travels and repay me with lovely tales of their own, all of us lying like a corporal in a tavern when a conscript is footing the bill.

The only thing that wearied me was having to wash my linen. But this had to be done, and often: for the obliging thieves had left me but a single shirt (borrowed from my cousin Armand) besides the one I had on me. Whenever I cleaned my boots, my handkerchiefs, and my shirt on a stream bank, with my head down and my loins in the air, I began to feel giddy; the motion of my arms caused an unbearable pain in my chest. I was then obliged to sit down among the horsetails and the watercress, and, amid the commotion of war, I passed the time gazing at the peaceful waters. Lope de Vega imagined Love's bandage washed by a shepherdess; this shepherdess would have been very useful to me if she had been there to wash the little birchbark turban I had been given by my Floridians.

An army is typically composed of soldiers more or less the same age, the same height, and the same strength. Ours was a bit different. It was a ragtag assemblage of grown men, old men, and fledglings not long out of their nests, jabbering in the dialects of Normandy, Brittany, Picardy, Auvergne, Gascony, Provence, and Languedoc. Fathers served with sons; fathers-in-law with sons-in-law; uncles with nephews; brothers with brothers; cousins with cousins. This confused *arrière-ban*, ridiculous as it appeared, had something honorable and even touching about it, for it was animated by sincere convictions; it offered a picture of the old monarchy and gave one last glimpse of a dying world. I have seen old gray-headed gentlemen with stern expressions and torn coats, packs on their backs and rifles on their shoulders, limping with the aid of a walking stick and supported by their son's arm. I have seen M. de Boishue, the father of that friend of mine murdered at the Estates of Rennes, marching sad and alone, barefoot in the mud, toting his shoes on the point of a bayonet for fear of wearing them out. I have seen wounded young men lying wide-eyed beneath a tree while a chaplain in frock and stole kneels to pray by their side, sending them to Saint Louis, whose descendants they had endeavored to defend. All these poor troops, who received not a sou from the Princes, made war at their own expense, while decrees despoiled them and threw their wives and mothers into prison.

The old men of earlier eras were less miserable and isolated than they are today. If, during their residence on earth, they had lost their friends, at least few other things changed around them. Although strangers to youth, they were no strangers to society. Today, a laggard in this world has not only seen men dying, he has seen ideas dying. Principles, manners, tastes, pleasures, pains, and feelings: nothing anymore resembles what he once knew. He finishes his days among a different species of the human race.

You, Frenchmen of the Nineteenth Century, you must learn to appreciate this old France which was worth just as much as you. You shall grow old in your turn, and you shall be accused, as we have been accused, of holding to superannuated ideas. It is your fathers you have vanquished; do not disown them: you have sprung from their blood. Had they not been so generously loyal to the old ways, you could never have drawn on that native loyalty which has led to your glory in the new ways. There is nothing between the old France and the new France but a transformation of virtue.

II.

THE SIEGE OF THIONVILLE BEGINS—THE CHEVALIER DE LA BARONNAIS

London, April to September 1822

NEXT TO our indigent and obscure camp there was another camp, brilliant and rich. Around the headquarters, one saw a crowd of wagons loaded with victuals and a mob of cooks, footmen, and aides-de-camp. Nothing could have better represented the Court and the provinces: the monarchy that perished at Versailles and the monarchy that died on Du Guesclin's heaths. The aides-de-camp had become odious to us. When there was a skirmish near Thionville, we shouted, "Forward, aides-de-camp!" as the patriots shouted, "Forward, officers!"

I felt my heart grow heavy when, one gloomy day, we came in sight of some woods that lined the horizon and were told these woods were France. Crossing the border of my own country with a musket in my hand had an indescribable effect on me: I had a kind of revelation of things to come, the more so since I did not share my comrades' illusions, either about the cause they were supporting, or about the triumphal dreams with which they deluded themselves. I was like Falkland in the army of Charles I.[27] There was not one Knight of La Mancha, sick, lame, and sporting a nightcap beneath his beaver-skin tricorn, who didn't firmly believe himself capable of putting to flight, all by himself, at least fifty vigorous young patriots. Such honorable and amusing pride, the source of prodigious feats in another era, never afflicted me: I did not feel so persuaded of the power of my invincible arm.

We clattered into Thionville on September 1 undefeated, for we had encountered no one on our way. The cavalry camped on the right and the infantry on the left of the highway that ran from the heart of town to the German border. From this campsite we could not quite see the fortress, but six hundred paces away, on the crest of a hill, the eye plunged down into the Moselle River Valley. The mounted marines linked the right flank of our infantry to the Prince of Waldeck's Austrian corps, and the left flank of this same infantry was covered by eighteen hundred horsemen of the Maison-Rouge and the Royal German Regiments. We dug a trench in front of our position along which we arranged our weapons stacks. The eight Breton companies occupied two cross-streets of camp, and below us were my old comrades, the officers of Navarre.

When, after three days, our labors were finished, *Monsieur* and the Comte d'Artois arrived. They reconnoitered the place, which was called to surrender in vain, although Wimpffen did seem inclined to yield it.[28] We would not win the Battle of Rocroi, like the Great Condé, and therefore we could not capture Thionville; but we were at least not defeated beneath its walls, like Feuquières.[29] We took up a position on the public road above a village that served as a suburb of town and beyond the outworks that defended the bridge over the Moselle. Shots were fired from house to house. Our post kept possession of what it had taken. I myself was not present at this first engagement, but my cousin Armand took part and conducted himself bravely. My company, during this skirmish in the suburbs, was ordered to build a battery at the edge of the woods that crowned the summit of a hill. Vineyards wound down the slope of this hill all the way to the plains that bordered the outer fortifications of Thionville.

The engineer who oversaw our labors made us raise a sod-covered mound on which to mount our guns. Then, in a parallel line, we dug an open trench to place us below the range of bullets and balls. The digging went slowly, for none of us, young or old, was used to the weight of mattocks and shovels. Without wheelbarrows, we had to carry the earth in our coats, which we used as sacks. Shots were fired from a lunette, which inconvenienced us all the more since we could not return fire: two eight-pound cannon and a Cohorn howitzer with a range too short to do any good formed the whole of our artillery. The first shell we launched from the Cohorn fell short even of the glacis and prompted derisive howls from the garrison. A few days later, the Austrian guns and gunners arrived. A hundred infantrymen and a picket of mounted marines relieved the battery every twenty-four hours. The besieged were preparing to counterattack. Through the telescope, we observed some activity on the ramparts. At nightfall a column marched, under the protection of a covered passage, from one of the posterns to a position behind the lunette. My company was ordered to reinforce the battery. At daybreak five or six hundred patriots launched an attack on the village from the highway above town; then, turning to the left, they crossed the vineyards and took our battery in flank. The mounted marines charged bravely, but they were routed and this left us vulnerable. We were still too poorly armed to return fire, and so we marched forward with bayonets drawn. For whatever reason, the assailants retreated. If they had kept on, they would have smashed us.

We suffered several wounded and a few dead, among them the Chevalier de La Baronnais, the captain of one of the Breton companies. I brought him bad luck. The bullet that robbed him of his life had ricocheted off the barrel of my rifle and struck him with such force that it pierced both his temples; his brains sprayed me in the face. What a useless, noble victim of a lost cause! When Marshal d'Aubeterre traveled to the Estates of Brittany, he lodged at the house of M. de La Baronnais, the dead man's father, a poor gentleman who lived in Dinard, near Saint-Malo. The Marshal, who had implored him not to invite anyone, entered the house and, seeing the table set with twenty-five covers, gently reproached his host. "But Monseigneur," said M. de La Baronnais, "I have invited only my children." M. de La Baronnais had twenty-two sons and one daughter, all by the same mother. The Revolution mowed this rich family harvest before it had time to ripen.

12.

THE SIEGE CONTINUES—CONTRASTS—FOREST SAINTS—BATTLE OF BOUVINES—PATROL—AN UNEXPECTED ENCOUNTER—THE EFFECTS OF A BULLET AND A BOMB

London, April to September 1822

WALDECK'S Austrian corps now began its operations. Our maneuvers became livelier. It was a fine sight to see at night: incendiaries lit up the outworks swarming with soldiers; abrupt flashes illuminated the clouds or the dark blue sky whenever a cannon fired; and the cannonballs, crossing in midair, described parabolas of light. In the intervals between detonations, we heard drums roll, bursts of military music, and the voices of guards on the ramparts of Thionville and at our posts. Regrettably, in both camps the words shouted were French: *Sentinelles, prenez garde à vous!*

If the battles took place at dawn, the hymn of the lark followed the noise of the musketry, while the silent cannon, having ceased fire, regarded us with open mouths through their fortified embrasures. The birdsong, recalling memories of pastoral life, seemed to heap reproaches on mankind. It was the same when I stumbled over corpses in fields of flowering clover or on the banks of flowing streams that washed the dead men's hair. In the woods, a few steps from the violence of war, I came upon little statues of the saints and the Virgin. A goatherd, a shepherd, or a beggar carrying his scrip kneeled before these peaceful figures and said their rosary to the distant sound of guns. I once saw a whole parish come with its pastor to offer flowers to the patron saint of a neighboring parish, whose shrine was in a grove that grew beside a spring. The priest was a blind man; a soldier in the army of God, he had lost his sight doing good works, as a grenadier loses his sight on the battlefield. The curate gave communion on behalf of this priest, because the latter could not see to place the sacred host on the lips of his communicants. During this ceremony, and out of the depths of darkness, this holy man blessed the light!

Our fathers believed that the patron saints of hamlets, Jean le Silentiaire, Dominique l'Encuirassé, Jacques l'Intercis, Paul le Simple, Basle l'Ermite, and so many others, were no strangers to those military triumphs that protected their harvests. On the day of the Battle of Bouvines, thieves entered a monastery in Auxerre that was under the patronage of Saint Germain and stole several sacramental vessels. When the sacristan presented himself before the blessed bishop's shrine, he groaned aloud and said, "Germain, where were you when those brigands dared violate your sanctuary?" A voice issued from the shrine, saying, "I was near Cisoing, near the bridge of Bouvines; with the other saints, I was aiding the French and their King, to whom a splendid victory has been granted with our help":

Cui fuit auxilio victoria praestita nostro.[30]

We beat a path across the plain, and we pushed them back all the way to the hamlets beneath the first entrenchments of Thionville. The village on the trans-Moselle highway was incessantly taken and retaken. Twice I took part in these attacks. The patriots called us "enemies of liberty," "aristocrats," and "Capet's henchmen"; we called them "brigands," "cutthroats," "traitors," and "revolutionaries." Sometimes everything was called to a halt, and men fought duels in the presence of the combatants, who served as impartial witnesses. —Strange quirk of the French character, which not even passion can stifle!

One day I was on patrol in a vineyard. Twenty feet in front of me was an old gentleman *chasseur* who kept striking the vines with the butt of his gun, as though he were trying to drive out a hare, then looking brusquely around him in hopes of seeing a routed patriot. Everyone had his own peculiar ways.

Another day I went to visit the Austrian camp. Between this camp and the camp of the mounted marines there lay a curtain of woods against which the enemy directed no end of useless fire. They shot far too often, believing that we were more numerous than we were, which explains the pompous bulletins issued by the Commandant of Thionville. As I was crossing this wood, I caught sight of something moving in the weeds. I approached it and saw a man stretched out facedown on the ground. All that could be seen of him was his fat back. I assumed he was wounded, and I took him by the nape of the neck and half lifted his head. He opened his frightened eyes and raised himself a little upon his hands. I burst out laughing. It was my cousin Moreau! I hadn't seen him since our visit to Madame de Chastenay!

Lying flat on his belly to avoid a falling bomb, my cousin had found it impossible to stand up again. I had all the trouble in the world getting him on his feet, for his belly had tripled in size. He informed me that he was serving in the commissary and had been on his way to offer the Prince de Waldeck a few head of cattle. What's more, he was wearing a rosary! Hugues Métel tells the story of a wolf who, around the year 1203 or 1204, resolved to embrace the monastic state; but he couldn't bear fasting, so he became a canon.[31]

I had nearly returned to camp when an officer of the engineers passed by me, leading his horse by the bridle. A cannonball struck the animal at the narrowest part of the neck and neatly severed it, so that the head and the neck remained hanging from the horseman's hand and dragged him to the ground with their weight. I had already seen a bomb fall in the middle of a circle of naval officers at their mess: instantly the mess tin vanished, and the officers, knocked down and caked with mud, cried out like the old sea captain, "Fire to starboard! Fire to larboard! Fire everywhere! Fire in my wig!"

Such unusual calamities seem to belong to Thionville. In 1558, François de Guise laid siege to this place, and Marshal Strozzi was killed there in the trench, speaking with the aforementioned Sieur de Guise, who at that moment was resting his hand on Strozzi's shoulder.

13.
THE CAMP MARKET

London, April to September 1822

BEHIND our camp a sort of market had formed. Peasants had brought casks of white Moselle wine in their wagonbeds. Unhitched horses fed at one end of these carts, while men drank at the other. Here and there, small fires glowed. Sausages were being fried in pans, puddings boiled in basins, crêpes spread over iron plates, and pancakes stacked up in baskets. You could buy aniseed cakes, penny-a-piece rye bread, corn cakes, green apples, brown and white eggs, pipes, and tobacco all under a tree whose branches were hung with coarse cloth greatcoats, bargained for by passersby. Village girls straddling wooden stools milked cows, and every man stood in line and waited his turn to present the milkmaid with his cup. Provisioners in smocks and soldiers in uniforms loitered around the ovens. Cooks went back and forth, hawking their wares in French and German. Some stood in groups and others sat at pinewood tables set unevenly on the rocky ground. A few sought shelter wherever they could find it, under a canvas sheet or a roof of branches cut from the forest, as on Palm Sunday. I believe there were even marriages performed in covered wagons, in memory of the Frankish kings. The patriots might easily have followed the example of Majorian and stolen the bride's chariot away: *Rapit esseda victor, Nubentemque nurum* (Sidonius Apollinaris).[32] Everyone sang, laughed, and smoked. It was an extremely cheerful scene at night, between the fires that lit the earth and the stars that twinkled in the sky.

Whenever I was not on guard at the batteries or on duty in the camp, I loved to go sup at this fair. Here, the camp's stories were told over again; but enlivened by booze and high spirits, they were still more wonderful.

One of our comrades, a brevet captain whose name is lost to me under that of "Dinazarde," the name we gave him, was famous for his storytelling. It may have been more correct to call him "Scheherazade," but we did not consider the matter so closely at the time. We rushed to him the moment we saw him, scrabbling to get him into our mess. A short man with long legs, a saggy face, a sad mustache, eyes like commas at their outer edges, a hollow voice, a big sword in a scabbard the color of café au lait, the rigid posture of a military poet, looking like a cross between a suicide and a jolly good fellow, that solemn wag Dinazarde never laughed, but no one could lay eyes on him without laughing. He was the obliging witness to every duel and a great lover to all the ladies of the wine cask. Everything he said, he said in a tragic manner, and he never interrupted his narratives except to drink in this same manner from his bottle, or relight his pipe, or swallow a sausage.

One night, when the sky was a mist, we made a circle around the tap of a cask tilted toward us, set on the edge of a cart with its shafts in the air. A candle fastened to this cask illuminated our faces, and a piece of cloth stretched from the shafts of the cart to two posts served us as a roof. To our great satisfaction, Dinazarde, with his sword holstered at an angle after the fashion of Frederick II, standing between the wheel of the cart and the rump of a horse, began to tell us a tale; the provisioners who had brought us our rations stayed with us to listen to our Arab: our attentive mob of Bacchantes and Silenuses accompanied the story, like an ancient chorus, with noises of surprise, approval, and disgust.

"Gentlemen," said the memorialist, "you have all heard about the Green Knight who lived in the days of King John?"

"Yes, yes," everyone replied.

Dinazarde gulped down a rolled-up crêpe and burned himself.

"This Green Knight was, as you all know, since you've heard of him, very handsome. When the wind blew his red locks against his helmet, it looked like a garland of oakum wound round a green turban."

"Bravo!" cried the chorus.

"One evening in May, he blew his horn at the drawbridge of a castle in Picardy, or Auvergne. It's not important which. In this castle lived the Lady of Great Companies. She received the knight graciously, made him disarm, led him to a bath, and later came to sit with him at a magnificent feast; but she ate nothing, and her attendants were silent."

"Oh! Oh!" said the chorus.

"The Lady, you see, was tall, flat, thin, and hunched, like the major's wife; but she had a fair-looking face and a flirtatious way about her. When she laughed, and her long teeth showed beneath her snub nose, you no longer knew where you were. Well, now, the Lady fell in love with the Green Knight, and the Green Knight fell in love with the Lady, even if he was afraid of her."

Dinazarde knocked out the ashes from his pipe on the rim of the wheel behind him. He made to refill the briar, but we forced him to go on:

"Well, the Green Knight, who was by now quite bewildered, resolved to quit the castle; but before he went, he asked the Lady to explain several strange things, and at the same time, he made her a formal offer of marriage, if she would swear that she was not a sorceress."

Dinazarde's rapier was planted straight and stiff between his feet. Motionless, and leaning forward with our pipes, we formed a garland of sparks around him like the ring of Saturn. All of a sudden Dinazarde cried out as though beside himself, "Now, gentlemen, the Lady, the Lady of Great Companies—she was Death! Death! Death!"

And the brevet captain, breaking the ranks and crying out *Death! Death!* put all the provisioners to flight. The session was ended. Our brouhaha was loud and our laughter was long. We went back to Thionville in silence, to the noise of its guns.

14.

NIGHT BY THE WEAPONS STACKS—DUTCH DOGS— MEMORY OF THE MARTYRS—MY COMPANIONS IN THE OUTPOST—EUDORUS—ULYSSES

London, April to September 1822

THE SIEGE continued, or rather there was no siege, for we dug no trenches and did not have enough troops to blockade the place. We counted on intelligence and waited for news of the Prussian Army or the Army of Clairfayt, who had with them the French corps led by the Duc de Bourbon. Our meager resources were almost exhausted, and Paris seemed to be getting further and further away. The foul weather was never-ending, and we were inundated as we worked. Several times I woke in a ditch in water up to my neck, and the next day I hobbled around camp like a cripple.

Among my fellow Bretons, I had met Ferron de la Sigonière, my old classmate at Dinan. At night we tossed and turned in our shared tent; our heads, sticking out from beneath the canvas, were drummed with rain as though beneath the spout of a gutter. Often, I used to get up and pace back and forth with Ferron before the weapons stacks, for all our nights were not as cheerful as those we spent listening to Dinazarde. We walked in silence, listening to the voices of the sentries, gazing off at the lights along the streets formed by our tents as we had once gazed at the lamps that ranged along the hallways of our school. We talked of the past and the future, the errors that we had committed and the errors that we might yet commit. We lamented the blindness of the princes who believed that they would return to their country with a handful of servants and, fortified by foreign arms, place the crown back upon their brother's head. I remember saying to my friend, in the course of these conversations, that France would like to imitate England, that the King would die on the scaffold, and that our maneuvers in Thionville would probably form one of the principal counts against Louis XVI. Ferron was struck by my predictions, which were the first I ever made. Since that time I have made many others just as true and which have gone just as unheeded. Catastrophe comes and everyone takes shelter, abandoning me to grapple with the misfortune I alone had foreseen. When the Dutch are tossed by a high gale on the open sea, they go down to the ship's cabins and drink punch, leaving a dog on deck to howl at the storm. Once the danger has passed, they send Fido back to his kennel in the hold, and the captain goes out to enjoy the fine weather on the quarter-deck. I have been the Dutch dog on the ship of the Legitimacy.

But the recollections of my military life are engraved in my memory: I have already traced them in the sixth book of *The Martyrs*.

An Armorican barbarian in the camp of the Princes, I carried Homer along with my sword; I preferred my country, poor little island of Aaron, to the hundred cities of Crete. I said, like Telemachus, "The harsh country that nourishes none but goats is lovelier to me than those that rear horses."[33] My words would have made the simple-minded Menelaus laugh, ἀγαθὸς Μενέλαος.[34]

15.

THE MOSELLE PASSAGE—COMBAT—LIBBA, DEAF AND
DUMB—ATTACK ON THIONVILLE

London, April to September 1822

RUMOR spread that finally we were going to see action. The Prince of Waldeck was to attempt a frontal assault, while we, after having crossed the river, would serve as a diversion by making a feigned attack on Thionville from the direction of France.

Five Breton companies, mine included, the company of the Picardy and Navarre officers, and the regiment of volunteers, composed of young Lorraine peasants and various deserters, were ordered up for duty. We were to be supported by the Royal German Guards, a few squadrons of musketeers, and several corps of dragoons who would cover our left flank: my brother took part in this cavalry together with the Baron de Montboissier, who had married one of M. de Malesherbes's daughters, Madame de Rosambo's sister, and therefore an aunt to my sister-in-law. We would escort three Austrian artillery companies carrying heavy guns and a battery of three mortars.

We set out at six o'clock in the evening, and by ten o'clock we were crossing the Moselle above Thionville on copper pontoons:

> *amoena fluenta*
> *Subterlabentis tacito rumore Mosellae.*[35]

At daybreak, we were in battle formation on the left bank, the heavy cavalry echeloned on both sides and the light cavalry in front. Our second maneuver was to form a column and begin to march.

About nine o'clock, we heard a volley fired to our left. A carabinier officer came riding full tilt toward us, to tell us that a detachment of Kellermann's army was about to meet us and that skirmishes were already underway. This officer's horse had been struck in the nose by a bullet; it was rearing and streaming foam from its mouth and blood from its nostrils. This carabinier, with his sword in hand, on his wounded steed, looked superb. The corps marching from Metz now maneuvered to take us in flank. They had field cannon with which they opened fire on our volunteers. I heard the screams of a few recruits touched by the ball. These last cries of youth wrenched from the sap and vigor of life made me profoundly sad. I pitied their poor mothers.

The drums beat the charge, and we rushed in disarray upon the enemy. They were so close to us that not even the smoke could prevent us from seeing all that is terrible in the face of a man prepared to spill your blood. The patriots had not yet acquired that aplomb which comes from long familiarity with combat and victory: their maneuvers were weak, they were groping in the dark. Fifty grenadiers of the old guard would have routed such a motley mass of unruly nobles, young and old; but ten or twelve hundred foot soldiers were scared off by a few shots from the Austrian heavy artillery. They retreated, and our cavalry chased them for two leagues.

A deaf and dumb German girl, named Libbe or Libba, had grown fond of my cousin Armand and had followed him. I found her sitting on the grass, which had bloodied her dress: her elbows were propped on her folded and upraised knees; her hand, tangled in her thin blond hair, supported her head. She was crying, staring at three or four dead men, new conscripts in the ranks of the deaf and the dumb, around her. She had never heard the thunderclaps whose effect she beheld or the sighs that escaped her lips whenever she looked at Armand. She had never heard the voice of the man she loved, nor would she hear the first cry of the baby she was carrying in her womb. If the grave held only silence, she would have gone down to it without knowing.

But the fields of carnage are everywhere; at Père Lachaise, in Paris, twenty-seven thousand tombs and two hundred and thirty thousand bodies tell you of the battle that death wages day and night at your door.[36]

After a rather long halt, we resumed our march and arrived at nightfall beneath the walls of Thionville.

The drums had gone silent. Orders were given in a low voice. The cavalry, in an effort to repulse all attacks, moved quietly along the roads and the hedgerows toward the gate that we were to cannonade. The Austrian artillery, protected by our infantry, took up a position fifty yards from the outworks, behind a few hastily assembled gabions. At one o'clock in the morning, on September 6, a rocket sent up from the Prince of Waldeck's camp, on the other side of town, gave the signal. The Prince launched a round of heavy fire to which the town vigorously replied. We began shooting at once.

The besieged, unaware that we had troops on that side, and not having foreseen this assault, had left the southern ramparts unprotected. They did not waste time waiting. The garrison armed a double battery which shattered our fortifications and dismounted two of our guns. The sky was on fire; we were shrouded in torrents of smoke. I behaved like a little Alexander: knocked out by fatigue, I fell sound asleep almost beneath the wheels of the gun carriage I was guarding. A shell, bursting six inches above the ground, sent a splinter into my right thigh. Awoken by the blow, but feeling no pain, I knew that I was wounded only by the wet flow of my blood. I bound up my thigh with my handkerchief. Already, in the fighting on the plain, two bullets had struck my rucksack during a wheeling maneuver. Atala, like a devoted daughter, had placed herself between her father and the enemy lead: she was yet to sustain the fire of Abbé Morellet.[37]

At four o'clock in the morning, the Prince of Waldeck's firing ceased. We believed the town had surrendered, but the gates were not opened, and we were compelled to beat a retreat. We went back to our positions, after a punishing three-day march.

The Prince of Waldeck had advanced as far as the edge of the ditches, which he had tried to cross, hoping to provoke surrender by means of simultaneous attack. Our side supposed that a few divisions were already inside the town and flattered itself in thinking that the Royalist partisans within would soon deliver the keys of the city to the Princes. The Austrians, having fired in barbette, had lost a considerable number of men. The Prince of Waldeck himself had lost an arm. But while a few drops of blood flowed beneath the walls of Thionville, blood flowed in torrents in the prisons of Paris. My wife and my sister were in far more danger than I.

16.

THE SIEGE IS RAISED—ENTRY INTO VERDUN—
DYSENTERY—RETREAT—SMALLPOX

London, April to September 1822

WE RAISED the siege of Thionville and left for Verdun, which had surrendered to our allies on September 2. Longwy, the birthplace of François de Mercy, had fallen on August 23. Wreaths and flowers everywhere attested to the passage of Frederick William.

High above these trophies of peace, I observed the Prussian eagle affixed to the fortifications of Vauban: it was not to remain there long. As for the flowers, they were soon to see the innocent creatures who had gathered them fade like themselves. One of the most atrocious murders of the Terror was the murder of the young girls of Verdun.

"Fourteen young girls of Verdun," writes Riouffe, "of unparalleled purity, and with the look of young virgins bedecked for a festival, were led together to the scaffold. They disappeared suddenly and were harvested in their springtime; the *Cour des Femmes*, the morning after their death, had the air of a garden deflowered by a storm. I have never seen among us such despair as that which followed this barbarous act."[38]

Verdun is famous for its female sacrifices. According to Gregory of Tours, Deuteric, wishing to protect his daughter from the persecutions of Théodebert I, put her in a tumbrel drawn by two untamed oxen and had her thrown into the Meuse. The instigator of the massacre of the young girls of Verdun was the regicidal poetaster Pons de Verdun, who showed himself ruthless toward his native town. That the *Almanach des Muses* furnished so many agents of the Terror is incredible. The wounded vanity of mediocre men produced as many revolutionaries as the wounded pride of legless cripples and runts: a revolting parallel between infirmities of the mind and those of the body. Pons signed his dull epigrams with the point of a dagger. Apparently faithful to the traditions of Greece, the poet wanted to offer only the blood of virgins to his gods: for the Convention decreed, on his account, that no pregnant woman could be put on trial. He was also responsible for annulling the sentence that had condemned to death Madame de Bonchamp, the widow of the famous Vendean general. Alas! We Royalists in the train of the Princes have all now reached the far side of the Vendée, but without having gone through its glory.[39]

We had nothing in Verdun to pass the time. We found no "famous Comtesse de Saint-Balmon, who, having cast aside female dress, mounted a horse and served as an escort to the ladies in her coach...." We felt no passion for the "Old Gauls," and we did not write each other "notes in the language of Amadis" (Arnauld).[40]

The Prussian malady was spreading through our little army, and I was soon stricken.[41] Our cavalry had gone to join Frederick William at Valmy. We had no idea what was transpiring. We were expecting an order to advance at any moment. Eventually, we received an order to retreat.

Sapped of strength, and with my troublesome wound making it impossible for me to walk without pain, I hobbled as best I could behind my company, which soon disbanded. Jean Balue, a miller son's from Verdun, was taken from his father's house at a very young age by a monk who made him carry his sack. On leaving Verdun, the "hill of the ford" according to Saumaise (*ver dunum*), I was carrying the sack of the monarchy; but I never did manage to become a comptroller of finances, a bishop, or a cardinal.[42]

If, in the novels I have written, I have sometimes drawn on my own history, so in the histories I have written have I sometimes drawn on memories of the living history in which I played a part. Thus, in my life of the Duc de Berry, I have sketched some of the scenes that I witnessed with my own eyes:

When an army is dismissed, the men return to their hearths; but where were the hearths of Condé's soldiers? Where would they be led by those walking sticks, which they had hardly had time to cut from the German woods, now that they had laid down the muskets that they had taken up to defend their King? . . . .

They had to go their separate ways. Brothers-in-arms said their last goodbyes and set out to follow different paths over the earth. All went, before they departed, to salute their father and their captain, the white-haired Condé, the old patriarch of glory, who gave his blessing to his children, and wept over his scattered tribe, and watched the tents of his camp dismantled with all the sadness of a man who sees his father's house crumbling into rubble.

Less than twenty years later, Bonaparte, the leader of yet another French army, would also say farewell to his companions. —So many men and empires, so swiftly passing! Not even the most extraordinary fame is safe from the most ordinary destiny.

We left Verdun. Heavy rains had wrecked the roads. Everywhere we saw wagons, gun carriages, cannon enmired, carts overturned, provisioners carrying their children on their backs, soldiers dead or dying in the mud. Crossing a plowed field, I sank into clay up to my knees. Ferron and another of my comrades dragged me out despite my protests: I was begging them to leave me there. I wanted to die.

On October 16, in a camp near Longwy, the captain of my company, M. de Goyon-Miniac, handed me a certificate of very honorable discharge. In Arlon, we saw a line of hitched wagons on the highway. The horses, some standing, some kneeling, others fallen facedown in the mud, were all dead, and their corpses had gone rigid between the shafts. You might have said they were the ghosts of a battle, bivouacking on the bank of the Styx. Ferron asked me what I intended to do, and I replied, "If I can get to Ostend, I shall sail for Jersey and find my uncle de Bedée. There I should be able to join the Royalists in Brittany."

The fever was taking its toll. It caused me great pain to hold myself upright on my swollen thigh. Then I felt myself seized by another sickness. After twenty-four hours of vomiting, an eruption broke out over my face and body: an attack of confluent smallpox,[43] which came and went according to changes in the air. In this condition, I set out on foot to make a journey of two hundred leagues, enriched by eighteen *livres tournois*: all this for the greater glory of the monarchy. Ferron, who had lent me these six small coins worth three francs each, was expected in Luxembourg. And so he left me.

BOOK TEN

I.

THE ARDENNES

London, April to September 1822;
Revised in February 1845

ON THE outskirts of Arlon, a peasant's cart picked me up for the sum of four sous and dropped me five leagues away on a heap of stones. Having hobbled a few feet with the aid of my crutch, I washed the bandages around my suppurating wound in a spring that flowed along the roadside. This did me great good. The smallpox had completely gone, and I felt soothed. I gave no thought to abandoning my sack, though its straps cut into my shoulders.

The first night I spent in a barn and ate nothing at all. The wife of the farmer who owned the barn refused payment for my bed. At sunrise, she brought me a big bowl of café au lait with a hunk of black bread, which I found delicious. I took to the road again feeling hardy, although often I stumbled and fell. I was joined by four or five of my comrades, who took turns carrying my sack. These men were also quite ill. We crossed paths with villagers, and, riding cart after cart through the Ardennes, we covered enough ground to reach Attert, Flamizoul, and Bellevue in the course of five days. On the sixth day, I found myself alone again. My smallpox had turned white and flattened.

After walking five or six miles, which cost me six hours' time, I caught sight of a family of gypsies encamped on the wayside with two goats and a donkey, on the far side of a ditch, around a fire kindled with heather. I had hardly stepped into the firelight before I let myself drop, and these singular creatures hurried to help me. A young woman in rags—vibrant, dark, audacious—sang, leapt, and spun, holding her baby aslant on her breast like the hurdy-gurdy with which she might have accompanied her dance, then crouched on her heels at my side, regarded me curiously in the gleam of the fire, and took my dying hand, to tell my fortune, asking only a *petit sou*. This was much too dear. It would be difficult to be any wiser, tenderer, or poorer than my sybil of the Ardennes. I know not when the nomads, whose worthy son I might have been, left me; when, at dawn, I emerged from my torpor, they were no longer there. My sweet fortune-teller had gone away with the secret of my future. In exchange for my *petit sou*, she had placed an apple beside my head which served to freshen my mouth. I was shivering like Jeannot Lapin in the *thyme* and the *dew*; but I could neither *nibble*, nor *scamper*, nor run *around and around*. I roused myself nevertheless, with a notion to *pay court to the Dawn*.[1] She was very beautiful, and I was very ugly; her pink face proclaimed her good health: she was feeling quite a bit better than her poor Armorican Cephalus. Although both young, we were old friends, and that morning I let myself imagine that her tears were for me.

I plunged into the forest, and felt none too sad, for the solitude had restored me to my nature. I began to sing the ballad by the doomed Cazotte:

> Deep down in the middle of the Ardennes,
> There's a castle high up on the rocks . . .[2]

Was it not in the keep of this same haunted castle that the King of Spain, Philip II, had imprisoned my countryman, Captain La Noue, whose grandmother was a Chateaubriand? Philip agreed to release his illustrious prisoner only if the latter would agree to have his eyes gouged out; La Noue was on the verge of accepting the proposition, so thirsty was he to return to his beloved Brittany. Alas! I was possessed of the same desire, and all I needed to lose my vision was the illness with which it had pleased God to afflict me. I did not meet "Sir Enguerrand riding home from Spain," as the ballad says, but only poor vagabonds and peddlers who, like me, carried the whole of their fortunes on their backs. A woodcutter wearing felt knee-patches passed me in the forest: I am surprised he did not take me for a dead branch and saw me down. A few crows, a few larks, and a few buntings (a species of large finch) scampered over the pathway, or perched unmoving on the stone wall, attentive to a hawk that was circling in the sky. From time to time, I heard a swineherd sound his horn as he watched over the sows and their little ones rooting for acorns beneath the oaks. I rested in a shepherd's wheeled hut, where I found no one home but a kitten, who gave me a thousand courteous caresses. The shepherd must have been standing somewhere far off, in the center of some pasturage, with his dogs sitting at various removes from the sheep. By day, this shepherd gathered simples, for he was an herbalist and a sorcerer; by night, he gazed at the stars, for he was a Chaldean shepherd.

I stopped again, half a league or so from the shepherd's hut, in a grazing ground frequented by tragelaphi: hunters were moving along the far edge. A spring bubbled up at my feet; at the bottom of this spring, in this very forest, Orlando *innamorato*, not *furioso*, beheld a crystal palace thronged with ladies and knights. If the paladin who went down among the glittering naiads had at least left the Golden Bridle at the water's edge, or if Shakespeare had sent me Rosalind and the exiled Duke, they might have been most helpful to me.[3]

Having caught my breath, I continued on my way. My enfeebled thoughts floated on a wave of delirium that was not without charm: my old ghosts, hardly more substantial now than an evening shadow three-quarters effaced, were gathering around me to bid me adieu. I no longer had the power of memory. At an indeterminate distance, intermingled with strange apparitions, I seemed to see the airy forms of my family and friends. When I sat down against a milestone, I believed I could see their faces smiling at me from the doorways of distant cabins, in the blue smoke that drifted from the thatched roofs of cottages, in the treetops, in the transparent edges of the clouds, in the luminous sheaves of the sun that dragged its rays over the heather like a golden rake. These visions came from the Muses, who had come to bear witness to a poet's death: my grave, dug with the lintels of their lyres beneath an Ardennes oak, would have been well suited to a soldier and a traveler. A few grouse lost in the hare's form beneath the privet, made, together with the insects, some small noise around me: lives as slight and desolate as my own. I found I was no longer able to walk; I felt sicker than ever. The smallpox had come back to suffocate me.

Toward the end of the day, I was lying supine against the earth, in a ditch, my head propped on Atala's rucksack, my crutch at my side, my eyes fixed on the sun whose gaze was going out with my own. With every sweet thought I could summon, I saluted this star that had shone upon my first youth in my father's lands. Now we were going to rest together: she, to rise in all her glory; I, in all likelihood, never to wake again. I lost consciousness in a prayerful haze. The last sounds I heard were the fall of a leaf and the whistling of a bullfinch.

2.

THE PRINCE DE LIGNE'S WAGONS—WOMEN OF NAMUR—I FIND MY BROTHER IN BRUSSELS—OUR LAST GOODBYES

IT SEEMS that I remained in this state of unconsciousness for nearly two hours before the Prince de Ligne's wagons happened past. One of the drivers, who had stopped to cut a switch from a birch tree, stumbled over my body. Supposing I was dead, he gave me a shove with his boot: I showed some sign of life. The driver called to his comrades, and, moved by an impulse of pity, they loaded me into one of the wagons. The jolts of the road revived me. I made an effort to speak to my saviors; I told them I was a soldier in the Army of Princes and that if they could get me to Brussels I would reward them for their troubles.

"Fine, comrade," one of them replied, "but you shall have to get down at Namur, for we're forbidden to pick up passengers. We shall find you again at the other end of town."

I asked for a drink and swallowed a few drops of eau-de-vie, which aggravated my symptoms but momentarily relieved the pain in my chest. Nature had endowed me with extraordinary fortitude.

At about ten o'clock in the morning, we arrived in the suburbs of Namur. I swung my feet to the ground and followed the wagons at a distance. Soon I lost sight of them. At the entrance to the city, I was stopped. While my papers were examined, I sat beneath the gate. The soldiers on guard, seeing my uniform, offered me a tear of ration bread, and the corporal presented me with a blue glass goblet brimming with pear brandywine. I pretended to drink from the cup of military hospitality, and the corporal became angry:

"Take it!" he barked, accompanying his order with a *Sacrement der Teufel*!

My progress through the town of Namur was painful. I walked leaning against the houses. The first woman to see me came out of her shop, gave me her arm with a look of deep compassion, and helped me drag myself along. I thanked her, and she replied, "No thanks are needed, soldier." Soon, other women were rushing to join us, carrying bread, wine, fruit, milk, broth, old clothes, and blankets. "He is wounded," said some, in their Flemish-French patois; "he has the smallpox," cried others, shooing their children away. "But, young man, you cannot walk: you shall die. Please, you must go to the hospital." They wanted to take me there themselves; they relayed me from door to door; and in this way they led me through the whole length of town, at the end of which I found the Prince's wagons. You have already seen a farmer's wife help me in a time of need, and I shall soon speak of another woman who took care of me on the island of Guernsey. Oh, all you women who have watched over me in my hours of distress, if you are still living, may God comfort you in your old age and your sorrows! If you have left this life, may your children partake of that happiness which heaven has so long denied me!

The women of Namur helped me climb into the wagon, commended me to the driver, and forced me to accept a wool blanket. I observed that they treated me with a certain respect and deference: there is something superior and delicate in a Frenchman's nature that other nations cannot help but recognize. The Prince de Ligne's men set me down again on the road outside the gate of Brussels and refused to take my last coin.

But no hotelkeeper in Brussels would receive me. The Wandering Jew, the Orestes of the people, whom the old ballad led through this city—

> When he was in the town of Brussels,
> In the Duchy of Brabant

—was made far more welcome there than I, for he at least had five sous in his pocket.[4] I knocked, and doors were opened; but at the sight of me everyone cried, "Go on! Get out of here!" and shut the door in my face. I was chased from a café. My hair hung down over my face, which was masked by my beard and mustache; I had plastered my thigh with mud and straw; and, over my tattered uniform, I wore the wool blanket from the women of Namur knotted around my neck like a cloak. The beggar in the *Odyssey* was more insolent, but nowhere near as poor as me.[5]

I had made my first attempt at the hotel where I'd stayed with my brother earlier in the year; I was now about to try again. But as I was approaching the door, I caught sight of the Comte de Chateaubriand himself, stepping down from a carriage with the Baron de Montboissier. My brother was scared by my spectral appearance. He went in search of a room for me outside the hotel, for the owner absolutely refused to admit me. A wigmaker offered up a hovel well suited to my wretched condition. My brother brought me a doctor and a surgeon. He told me that he had received letters from Paris, and that M. de Malesherbes had urged him to return to France. He informed me of the Tenth of August, the September Massacres, and other political news of which I had heard nothing. He approved of my plan to go to the island of Jersey and advanced me twenty-five louis d'or. My weakened eyesight barely allowed me to pick out the features of my ill-fated brother: at the time, I believed that these shadows emanated from me, but they were the shadows of Eternity spilling around him. Without knowing it, we were seeing each other for the last time. All of us, so long as we exist, have nothing but the present moment; what follows is a matter for God. Always, there are two chances that we will never see the friend we leave again: our death or his. How many men walk down a staircase never to climb up it again?

Death touches us more before than after the passing of one we love: it is a part of us that drifts away—a world of childhood memories, family intimacies, common interests and affections dissolving. My brother preceded me in my mother's womb; he was the first to sit before my father's hearth; he waited several years to receive me, give me my Christian name, and become a part of my youth. If my blood had mixed with his in the Revolutionary tub, I have no doubt that it would have had the same savor, like milk from the same mountain pasture. But if men have made my brother's head drop before its time, the years are not sparing mine. Already my brow is stripped clean, as though the Ugolino of Time were leaning over me, gnawing at my skull:

...come 'l pan per fame si manduca.[6]

3·

OSTEND—PASSAGE TO JERSEY—I LAND IN GUERNSEY
—THE PILOT'S WIFE—JERSEY—MY UNCLE DE BEDÉE
AND HIS FAMILY—DESCRIPTION OF THE ISLAND—
THE DUC DE BERRY—DISAPPEARED RELATIVES AND
FRIENDS—THE UNHAPPINESS OF AGING—I GO TO
ENGLAND—LAST MEETING WITH GESRIL

London, from April to September 1822

THE DOCTOR could not get over his astonishment. He regarded my smallpox, which broke out and disappeared at intervals yet did not develop to its usual crises and kill me, as a phenomenon of which the annals of medicine furnished no examples. Gangrene had set into my wound, and it was dressed with quinine. As soon as I received these basic ministrations, I insisted on going to Ostend. Brussels was odious to me; I was ardent to leave it. It was filling up again with armchair heroes come back from Verdun in private calashes. I did not see these men in Brussels again when I returned there, with the King, during the Hundred Days.

I had an easy trip to Ostend on a canal-barge, aboard which I found a few Bretons, my companions in arms. We chartered a decked boat and careened down the Channel, sleeping in the hold, on boulders that served as ballast. My constitutional vigor was finally exhausted. I was no longer able to speak, and the swell of the rough seas was nearly the end of me. I could hardly swallow a few drops of lemon water, and when bad weather forced us to put in to Guernsey harbor, it seemed certain that I would die. An émigré priest read me the prayers for the dying. The captain, who did not want me breathing my last on his boat, ordered me carried down to the quay: I was set in the sunlight, with my back against a wall and my face turned toward the open sea, in sight of that island of Alderney where, eight months earlier, I had confronted death in another form.

I was apparently fated to arouse pity. The wife of an English pilot happened past. Moved by the sight of me, she called for her husband who, with the aid of two or three sailors, transported me to the house of a fisherman: I, who had always been a friend of the waves. They laid me on a good bed and draped me in cool white sheets. The young pilot's wife took every possible care of her foreigner; I owe her my life. The next day, I was carried back aboard. My hostess almost wept when she was parted from her invalid. Women have a heavenly instinct to help the unfortunate. My lovely blond guardian looked as though she had stepped out of an old English engraving. When she pressed my swollen, burning hands between her long, cool fingers, I felt ashamed to be the cause of such hideousness brought so close to such beauty.

We set sail again and landed on the western point of Jersey. One of my companions, M. de Tilleul, went to Saint-Hélier to search out my uncle. The next morning, M. de Bedée sent him back in a carriage to fetch me. Together we rode across the entire island: deathly as I felt, I was charmed by its woodlands; but I could do nothing but rant and rave, having fallen deep into delirium.

For four months, I hovered between life and death. My uncle, his wife, his son, and his three daughters took turns sitting by my bed. I stayed in an apartment, in one of the houses that were then beginning to be built along the harbor. The windows of my bedroom went down to the floor, and beyond the foot of my bed I beheld the sea. My doctor, M. Delattre, had forbidden anyone to talk to me of serious things and especially of politics; but one day, late in January 1793, seeing my uncle enter my room dressed in mourning, I trembled, for I assumed we must have lost a member of the family. He told me of the death of Louis XVI. I was not surprised; I had foreseen it. I inquired if there was any news of my relatives and learned that my sisters and my wife had gone back to Brittany after the September Massacres, though they had a great deal of trouble leaving Paris. My brother, on his return to France, had taken refuge in Malesherbes.

I was beginning to leave my bed. The smallpox had gone; but my chest ached, and I would be weak and weary for a long time to come.

Jersey, the Caesarea of the Antonine Itinerary, has been subject to English dominion since the death of Robert, Duc de Normandie. Several times we have tried to take it back, but always without success. This island is a piece of wreckage from our ancient history. The saints who traveled from Hibernia and Albion to Armorica stopped over on Jersey. Saint Hélier, the hermit, lived among the rocks of Caesarea until the Vandals murdered him. And one discovers a sampling of the ancient Normans here: you can almost fancy that you are hearing the language of William the Bastard or the author of the *Roman de Rou*.

The island is fertile. It has two towns and twelve parishes, and it is covered over with country houses and herds of cattle and sheep. The ocean breezes, which on Jersey seem to belie their severity, give the island its exquisite honey, its extraordinarily sweet cream, and its dark yellow butter, which smells of violets. Bernardin de Saint-Pierre supposes that the apple tree came to us from Jersey, but in this he is deceived: we owe the apple and the pear to Greece, as we owe the peach to Persia, the lemon to Media, the plum to Syria, the cherry to Turkey, the chestnut to Castano, the quince to Crete, and the pomegranate to Cyprus.

I took great pleasure going out for walks in the first days of May. Spring preserves all its youthfulness on Jersey. There, it can still be called *primavera*, as in former times: a name that, having grown old, it has left to its daughter, the first flower in her crown.[7]

Here, I will transcribe for you two pages from my life of the Duc de Berry, for they tell you something of my own life also:

After twenty-two years of combat, the brazen barrier that enclosed France was broken; the hour of the Restoration was

422 · MEMOIRS FROM BEYOND THE GRAVE

approaching, and our Princes left their retreats. Each of them
made for a different point of the border, like travelers who, at
the risk of their lives, seek to enter a country that is rumored
to be rife with marvels. *Monsieur* left for Switzerland, the Duc
d'Angoulême for Spain, and the Duc's brother for Jersey. On
this island, where some of Charles I's judges died in obscurity,
the Duc de Berry found French Royalists grown old in exile
and as forgotten for their virtues as the English regicides had
been for their crimes. He met with old priests, now dedicated
to solitude, and at the sight of them realized the fiction of the
poet who imagined a Bourbon landing on the island of Jersey,
after a storm. One of these confessors and martyrs might have
said to the heir of Henri IV, like the hermit of Jersey to the
great king himself:

> Far from the Court to this obscure cave
> Have I come to mourn the slander of my faith.
> (*Henriade*)[8]

The Duc de Berry spent several months on Jersey; seas, winds,
and policy kept him prisoner there. Everything thwarted his
impatience, and he was on the point of renouncing his enterprise
and setting sail for Bordeaux. A letter written by him to Madame
la Maréchale Moreau gives a clear idea of his occupations on
Jersey:

8 February, 1814

Here I am like Tantalus, in sight of ill-fated France, which has
struggled so long to burst its chains. You whose soul is so lovely,
so French, can imagine what my feelings are—how much it
would cost me to distance myself from that shore which it
would take me but two hours to reach! When the sun lights it,
I climb the highest rocks and I scan the whole coast through
my spyglass: I contemplate the rocks of Coutances. My imagination soars, I see myself leaping ashore, surrounded by French-

men wearing white cockades in their hats. I hear the cry of *Long Live the King!*—that cry which no Frenchman has ever heard with indifference. The most beautiful woman of the province throws a white scarf around my neck, for love and glory always go together. We march on Cherbourg, a wretched fort, which a garrison of foreigners vainly attempts to defend. We take it by storm, and a vessel puts out to fetch the King sporting a white flag that recalls the days of France's glory and happiness! Ah, madame, when one is no more than a few hours from such a likely dream, how can one think of leaving it?

It was three years ago that I wrote these pages in Paris; I had landed on Jersey, the city of exile, twenty-two years before the Duc de Berry. I was to leave my name on the island: Armand de Chateaubriand was married there and his son Frédéric was born there.

The spirit of joy had not abandoned my uncle de Bedée's family. My aunt still doted on a large dog (a descendant of one of those whose virtues I have already extolled); but, as he bit everyone and was often mangy, my cousins had him secretly hanged, despite his nobility. Madame de Bedée was persuaded that some English officers, charmed by the beauty of Azor, had stolen him, and that now he lived a life of honors and banquets in the richest castle of the three kingdoms. Alas! Our present laughter was prompted only by our past gaiety: by telling old stories from Monchoix, we found the means to laugh on Jersey. The case is unusual, for in the human heart pleasures do not preserve the same intimate relations that sorrows do; new joys do not renew the springtime feeling of old joys, though recent sorrows revive even those which are long past.

At least the émigrés then excited general sympathy. Our cause seemed to be the cause of European order; and a misfortune honored, as ours was, is a rare thing.

M. de Bouillon was the protector of the French refugees in Jersey. He dissuaded me from my plans to go to Brittany: I was in no state, he said, to endure a life lived in forests and caves. He advised me to go to England and look for an opportunity to enter the regular service. My uncle, who had very little money to his name, was beginning to feel ill at ease on account of his large family. He had already been forced to send one of his sons to London to survive on misery and hopes. Fearing that I was a burden on M. de Bedée, I made up my mind to relieve him of my presence.

Thirty louis d'or, delivered to me by a Saint-Malo smuggler, put me in a position to execute my plan, and I booked passage on a packet boat bound for Southampton. Saying goodbye to my uncle, I was deeply moved: he had cared for me as a father cares for his son; with him, I associated the few happy moments of my childhood; he knew everyone I loved. I rediscovered the close resemblance between his and my mother's face: I had left behind this excellent mother, whom I would never see again; I had left behind my sister Julie and my brother, and I was condemned never to see them again either. Now I was leaving my uncle, whose openhearted countenance would never more gladden my eyes. A few months had been enough to bring about all these losses: for the death of our friends is not to be reckoned from the moment they die, but from the moment when we cease to live beside them.

If we could say to Time, "Hold on!" we would stop it in our hours of delight; but since we cannot, let us not tarry here below. Let us depart before we have seen all our friends disappear, together with those years which the poet says are uniquely worthy of life: *Vita dignior aetas.*[9] What is enchanting in the days of connection becomes an object of suffering and regret in these days of isolation. A man no longer wishes for the smiling months to return to earth; he dreads them. The birds, the flowers, the beautiful evenings at the end of April, the beautiful nights that begin with the dusk's first nightingale and end with the dawn's first swallow, these things that make you need and crave happiness—you snuff them out. You still feel their charm, but they are no longer for you. Youth tastes them at your side and you gaze at her disdainfully; you feel jealous, and are made better to understand the depths of your desolation. The freshening grace of nature, which reminds you of your past joys, makes your miseries uglier. You are nothing but a stain upon the earth. You spoil nature's harmony and sweetness with your presence, your words, and even with the feelings that you dare express. You may love, but you can no longer be loved. The vernal spring has renewed its waters without giving you back your youth, and the sight of everything that has been reborn, everything that is blessed, reduces you to the painful memory of your pleasures.

The packet boat on which I embarked for England was crowded with émigré families. On board I made the acquaintance of M. Hingant, a former colleague of my brother's in the High Court of Brittany, a man of taste and intelligence of whom I shall soon have much to say. In the captain's cabin I caught sight of a naval officer at a game of chess: I was so altered in appearance that he did not recognize me, but I recognized Gesril straightaway. We had not seen each other since my days in Brest, and we would take our leave again in Southampton. But as we crossed the waters, I told him of my travels and he told me of his. This young man, born so near to me among the waves, would embrace his first friend for the last time among those waves that would soon bear witness to his glorious death. Lamba Doria, the Genoese admiral, having outmaneuvered the Venetian fleet, learned that his son had been killed in battle: "Let him be thrown into the sea," said this father, like an ancient Roman. It was as though he had said: "Let him be thrown into victory." Gesril was willing to leave the waves into which he had hurled himself only the better to show them his "victory" on their shore.

At the beginning of the sixth book of these *Memoirs*, I have already given the certificate of my disembarkation in Southampton. There I landed in 1793, after my excursions through the forests of America and the camps of Germany, a poor émigré, alone in the same country where, in 1822, I am writing all this, and where today I am the magnificent ambassador.

4.

LITERARY FUND—A GARRET IN HOLBORN—MY HEALTH FAILS—VISITS TO PHYSICIANS—ÉMIGRÉS IN LONDON

London, April to September 1822

A SOCIETY has recently been formed in London to give aid to men of letters, both English and foreign. When this society invited me to its annual meeting, I considered it my duty to attend and pay my subscription. His Royal Highness the Duke of York occupied the president's chair; to his right were the Duke of Somerset, Lord Torrington, and Lord Bolton; I was seated to his left. At the meeting, I also saw my friend Mr. Canning. This poet, orator, and illustrious minister made a speech, a certain passage of which was far too respectful toward me and was printed in all the newspapers the next day: "Although the person of my noble friend, the French Ambassador, is but little known in England, his character and writings are well known in Europe. He began his career by uncovering the principles of Christianity; he continued by defending the principles of the Monarchy; and now he has come again to England, to help unite our two States with the common bonds of monarchical principles and Christian virtues."

It has been many years since Mr. Canning, the man of letters, was schooled in London politics by Mr. Pitt: almost the same number of years that have passed since I began to write, in total obscurity, in this same English capital. Both of us have come into high regard, and we are now members of a society dedicated to the relief of destitute writers. But is it the affinity of our accomplishments or the harmony of our sufferings which has united us? What are a Governor of the East Indies and a French ambassador doing together at a banquet for

the stricken Muses? It is only George Canning and François de Chateaubriand sitting there, talking over their past adversity and, perhaps,
their past happiness: they drink to the memory of Homer, who recited
his verses for a morsel of bread.

If the Literary Fund had existed when I arrived in London from
Southampton on May 21, 1793, it might have paid for the doctor who
came to see me in my garret in Holborn, where my cousin La Bouëtardais, my uncle de Bedée's son, had found me lodgings. Everybody
spoke of the change of air as though it would perform miracles and
restore me a soldier's strength; but my health, instead of improving,
declined. My chest was afflicted; I became thin and pale; I coughed
frequently; I breathed with difficulty; I broke into sweats and coughed
up blood. My friends, who were all as poor as I, dragged me from
physician to physician. These disciples of Hippocrates made my band
of beggars stand outside their door and then announced to me, for
the price of a guinea, that I must endure my illness with patience,
adding, "*'Tis done, dear sir.*" Doctor Godwin, famous for those ex-
periments in drowning he had performed, according to careful instructions, on his own person, was more generous: he offered me his
opinion free of charge, but told me, with the same austerity that he
turned upon himself, that I might *last* a few months, perhaps a year
or two, provided that I give up everything that fatigued me. "Do not
count on a long career." Such was the gist of his consultations.

The certainty that my end was fast approaching, while intensifying the native gloominess of my imagination, gave me an incredible
sense of calm. My state of mind explains the note printed in my *Essai
historique*,[10] and also this passage in the *Essai* itself: "Attacked by an
illness which leaves me little hope, I look upon the things of this
world with a tranquil eye; the calm air of the tomb brushes the face
of a traveler who is no more than a few days distant." The bitterness
of the reflections scattered throughout the *Essai* should come as no
surprise to anyone: the work was composed under the stunning blow
of a death sentence, between the judgment and the execution. A writer
who thinks he has come to the end, who lives in a state of penury and
exile, can hardly cast a smiling eye on the world.

The question was how to spend the grace days accorded me. I could either live or die without delay by the sword; but the sword was forbidden me. What remained? A pen? But the pen was unknown and untried: I was ignorant of its power. Could my inborn taste for letters, the poems of my childhood, the rough sketches of my travels, command the attention of the public? The idea of writing a work comparing revolutions had occurred to me; it had stuck in my mind as a subject suited to the interests of the day. But who would burden himself printing a manuscript with no one to praise or promote it? And while I composed this manuscript, who would support me? Even if I had only a few days left to live on earth, it was nonetheless necessary to have some sustenance for those days. My thirty louis d'or, already seriously depleted, would not go much further, and, beyond my private afflictions, I felt it my duty to help alleviate the common distress of my fellow émigrés. My companions in London had all taken up occupations. Some had gone into the coal trade; some helped their wives make straw hats; others taught the French that they hardly knew. Yet they were all very cheerful. Flippancy, the great defect of our national character, was at that time changed into a virtue. We laughed in the face of Fortune—that thief who had sheepishly carried off what no one would ask her to return.

5.

PELLETIER—LITERARY LABORS—MY FRIENDSHIP WITH HINGANT—OUR WALKS—A NIGHT IN WESTMINSTER ABBEY

London, April to September 1822

PELLETIER, the author of *Domine salvum fac Regem* and chief editor of the *Actes des Apôtres*, continued in London the enterprise he had started in Paris. He was not exactly a vicious man; but he was gnawed at by a verminous horde of little defects of which he could not be cleansed. He was a libertine and a rogue, who made a great deal of money and then ate it all up; he was at the same time a slave to the Legitimacy and an ambassador of the Negro King Christophe to George III, a diplomatic correspondent of the Comte de Limonade and a man who drank in champagne whatever was paid to him in sugar. This specious M. Violet, playing the grand airs of the Revolution on a pocket fiddle, came to me as a Breton, offering his services. I mentioned my plan for the *Essai* to him, and he loudly approved. "This shall be *superb*!" he cried, and immediately proposed that I take a room with his printer, Baylis, who would put the work to press piece by piece as I composed it. Deboffe's bookshop would manage its sale, and he, Pelletier, would blow its horn in his paper, *l'Ambigu*; it might also be introduced to the *Courrier de Londres*, whose editorship was about to pass to M. de Montlosier. Pelletier was not a man for doubts: he used to talk about having me given the Cross of St. Louis for my part in the Siege of Thionville. My Gil Blas: tall, thin, rambunctious, with his powdered hair and balding brow, forever shouting and guffawing, he pulled his round hat over one ear, took me by the arm, and led me to Baylis the printer, who rented me a room above his shop without any fuss, for the price of one guinea a month.

I could see my golden future; but by what plank was I to cross the present abyss? Pelletier procured me some work translating Latin and English. I labored by day over these translations, and by night I turned to the *Essai historique*, into which I inscribed a part of my travels and my dreams. Baylis furnished me with books, and I squandered a few shillings buying others on display in the shops.

Hingant, whom I had met on the packet boat from Jersey, became my close friend in London. He was devoted to literature; he was well read, and secretly wrote novels from whose pages he read aloud to me. His rooms were not far from Baylis's print shop, at the bottom of a street that gave onto Holborn. Every morning at ten o'clock I breakfasted with him; we talked of politics and above all of my work. I told him how much I had built of my nocturnal edifice, the *Essai*, and then I returned to my daytime toil of translation. We met again for dinner, in a tavern where the meal cost a shilling a head; from there, we often went to walk together in the fields. Just as often, though, we would go it alone, for we both loved to lose ourselves in dreams.

On these evenings, I would wend my way toward Kensington or Westminster. Kensington pleased me: I could wander in the empty part of the garden even while the part bordering Hyde Park teemed with the glittering crowd. The contrast between my poverty and their wealth, my isolation and their multitude, was agreeable to me. I would gaze at the young English girls going by in the distance with the same desirous confusion that I had in former times felt for my sylph, after I had dressed her to suit my follies and hardly dared raise my eyes to my work. Death, which I believed I was fast approaching, added mystery to this vision of the world I was about to abandon. Did anyone ever cast a glance at the foreigner sitting at the foot of a pine? Did some beautiful woman divine the invisible presence of René?

In Westminster, I had another pastime. In its labyrinth of tombs, I thought of mine ready to be opened. The bust of an unknown man like me would never take its place among all those illustrious effigies! I meditated on the sepulchers of the monarchs: Cromwell was no longer there, and Charles I was not there either. Yet the ashes of a traitor, Robert d'Artois, rested below the flagstones that I trod with my loyal feet. In those days, the fate of Charles I had only recently been extended to Louis XVI, and every day the iron blade was reaping its harvest in France, where my family's graves had already been dug.

The songs of the chapel-masters and the chatter of strangers disrupted my solitary reflections. I could not multiply my visits, for I was obliged to give the guardians of those who were no longer living the shilling that I needed to survive. At times, I would take my turns outside the abbey with the crows, or I would pause to contemplate the towers, those twins of unequal size, which the fires of the setting sun streaked blood red against the black backdrop of the city's smoke.

One evening, however, it happened that, wishing to see the interior of the basilica in the fading light, I forgot myself in marveling at its spirited and whimsical architecture. Overcome by a feeling for the "somber immensity of Christian churches" (Montaigne),[11] I wandered around by slow steps and was benighted. When I went to leave, I discovered the doors were locked. I looked for an exit; I called for the usher and rattled the gates; but all this noise, spreading and thinning into silence, was wasted. I had to resign myself to lying down with the dead.

After hesitating a few minutes over the choice of my burrow, I paused beside the tomb of Lord Chatham, at the base of the rood-loft and the double staircase to the Chapel of the Knights and Henry VII. At the foot of these stairs leading up to those aisles enclosed by railings, a sarcophagus, built into the wall opposite a marble figure of Death armed with her scythe, offered me shelter. The fold of a winding-sheet, likewise made of marble, served me for a nook. Following the example of Charles V, I reconciled myself to my interment.

Now I found myself in the ideal position to see the world as it is. What a heap of grandeur is shut up beneath those domes! And what remains of it? Sufferings are no less vain than joys. What is the difference between the unfortunate Jane Grey and the fortunate Alys of Salisbury? Lady Jane's skeleton is the less horrible because it is headless; her carcass was beautified by her execution and by the deprivation of that which gave her beauty. The tournaments of the victor of Crécy and the games of Henry VIII on the Field of the

Golden Cloth shall never be renewed in this theater of funereal pomp. Bacon, Newton, and Milton are as deeply buried and as fully passed as the most obscure of their contemporaries. Would I, an exile, a vagabond, a pauper, have traded being the sad little forgotten thing I was for the glory of being one of those famous dead men, powerful and sated with pleasures? Oh, but there is more to life than that! If, from the shores of this world, we do not discern divine things clearly, we should not be surprised. Time is a veil between ourselves and God, as our eyelids are a veil between our pupils and the light.

Hidden beneath my marble sheet, my mind redescended from these lofty thoughts to the simple impressions of time and place. My disquiet, mixed with rapture, recalled what I felt in my turret at Combourg when I listened to the howling of winter winds. A gust of air and a shadow are of the same nature.

Little by little, my eyes adjusting to the dark, I distinguished the figures on the tombs. Inside that Cathédral St. Denis of England I studied the corbels, from which one might have said that past events and vanished years hung down like Gothic lamps. The entire edifice was like a monolithic temple of petrified centuries.

I had counted ten hours, then eleven by the clock. The hammer that rose and fell upon the old bronze was the only thing living, besides me, in those regions. Outside, a carriage happened past, a watchman cried; and that was all. The distant noises of the earth reached me as if in a world within a world. Fog from the Thames and smoke from the coal-fires infiltrated the church and spread through it like a second darkness.

At last, a pane of twilight appeared in a corner of the deepest shadow, and I watched the quickening progress of the morning light transfixed, as though it emanated from Edward IV's sons, murdered by their uncle. "Thus lay the gentle babes," the great tragedian writes,

> girdling one another
> Within their alabaster innocent arms:
> Their lips were four red roses on a stalk,
> Which in their summer beauty kiss'd each other.[12]

God did not send me these sad and charming souls; but the slender phantom of a barely adolescent girl appeared, carrying a candle sheathed in a sheet of paper which had been folded into the shape of a shell: the little one had come to ring the bells. I heard the sound of a kiss, and the clocks rang out the break of day. The bell-ringer was quite terrified as I went out with her through the abbey door. I told her of my adventure, and she told me that she had come to fulfill the duties of her sick father. We did not speak of the kiss.

6.

**DESTITUTION—UNFORESEEN ASSISTANCE—ROOMS
OVERLOOKING A CEMETERY—NEW COMRADES IN
MISFORTUNE—OUR PLEASURES—MY COUSIN LA
BOUËTARDAIS**

London, April to September 1822

I AMUSED Hingant with the story of my adventure, and we made
plans to have ourselves shut up in Westminster Abbey together, but
our poverty soon forced us to call on the dead in a less poetical fashion.

My funds were exhausted. Baylis and Deboffe had ventured, once
they had received a note promising reimbursement in case of non-sale,
to begin printing the *Essai*. Here, their generosity reached its end, as
was only natural; indeed, I am still amazed by their daring. No more
translations were forthcoming, for Pelletier, a man of pleasure, was
bored by prolonged charity. He would gladly have given me what he
had, if he had not preferred eating it up himself, but searching for
work here and there, and patiently doing good deeds: such tasks could
not hold his attention. Hingant, too, saw his savings shrinking day
by day. Between the two of us, we soon possessed sixty francs. Like
sailors on a voyage that had lasted longer than foreseen, we cut our
rations. Instead of a shilling a head, we spent half a shilling on our
dinners. In the mornings, with our tea, we halved the bread and
eliminated butter. This abstinence frayed Hingant's nerves. His mind
began to wander. Out of nowhere he would prick up his ears as though
listening to someone; then, in reply, he would burst into laughter or
tears. Hingant believed in magnetism; he had clouded his brain with
Swedenborg's blather. Every morning, he would tell me about the
noises that had stirred around him in the dark, and he would become
furious whenever I dismissed his hallucinations. The anxiety he caused
me kept me from dwelling on my own sufferings.

These sufferings were great, however. Our rigorous diet, combined with my work, aggravated the pain in my chest. I began to have difficulty walking, but still I went on spending my days and part of my nights outdoors, so that no one would suspect my destitution. One morning, down to our last shilling, Hingant and I agreed to keep the coin and merely make believe that we were breakfasting. We decided that we would buy a two-penny roll; we would have the hot water and the tea-kettle brought up as usual; but we would not eat any bread or take any tea: we would drink the hot water with some of the little crumbs of sugar stuck to the bottom of the sugar bowl.

Five days went by in this manner. I was devoured by hunger; my body was on fire; sleep had forsaken me. I sucked on pieces of linen that I had soaked in water, and I chewed on grass and paper. Whenever I passed a bakery, the torment was horrible. I remember one blustery winter evening I stood outside a shop that sold dried fruits and smoked meats, swallowing everything I saw with my eyes. At that moment, I would have eaten not only the food but also the boxes, the baskets, and the wooden bins.

On the morning of the fifth day, ready to collapse from inanition, I dragged myself to Hingant's room. I knocked on the door and found it locked. I called for him, but Hingant was a long time responding. At last, he got up and opened the door. He had a demented smile on his face and his frock coat was buttoned to the throat. He went and sat down at the tea table. "Our breakfast is coming soon," he said to me, in an extraordinary voice. I thought I saw blood stains on his shirt and brusquely unbuttoned his coat: he had stabbed himself with his pen knife, leaving a wound two inches deep in the lower part of his left breast. I called for help. The maid ran for a surgeon. The wound was dangerous.

This new misfortune forced me to take action. Hingant, who had been a councilor in the Parliament of Brittany, had been refusing to accept the payment which the English government accorded to former French magistrats, just as I had not wanted to accept the shilling a day doled out to every émigré in town. Now I wrote to M. de Barentin explaining my friend's situation, and Hingant's relations hastened

436 · MEMOIRS FROM BEYOND THE GRAVE

to take him away to the country. At this same moment, my uncle de Bedée sent me one hundred and twenty livres d'or: a moving sacrifice from my persecuted family which seemed like all the gold of Peru to me. The donations of those prisoners of France helped keep the French in exile alive.

My poverty had by now become an obstacle to my work. As I was no longer providing manuscript, printing had been suspended. Deprived of Hingant's company, I gave up my guinea-a-month lodging above Baylis's shop, paid my rent to the expiry, and went away. Below the indigent émigrés who had been my first protectors in London, there were others even more in need. There are degrees of poverty as there are degrees of wealth. One can go from the man who survives the winter sleeping beside his dog to the man who shivers alone in torn rags. My friends found me a room more appropriate to my dwindling fortune (one is not always at the height of prosperity), and I was soon installed in the vicinity of Marylebone Street, in a garret with windows overlooking a graveyard. Every night, the watchman's rattle told me that men had come to steal cadavers. At least I had the consolation of knowing that Hingant was out of danger.

My countrymen came to see me in my studio. Given our independence and our poverty, we might have been taken for painters seated on the ruins of Rome. In fact we were artists in misery seated on the ruins of France. My face served as a model and my bed as a seat for my pupils. This bed consisted of a mattress and a blanket. I had no sheets. My clothes and a chair, which I laid atop the blanket, kept me warm when nights were cold. Too weak to bother with my linens, they remained always as the Good Lord arranged them.

When my cousin La Bouëtardais was turned out from an Irish boarding house for failing to pay his rent, despite having pawned his violin, he came to me seeking shelter from the constable. Fortunately, a curate from Lower Brittany had loaned him a cot. Like Hingant, La Bouëtardais had been a councilor in the Parliament of Brittany, and like Hingant he did not have so much as a handkerchief to his name. But he had deserted with arms and baggage, which is to say that he had taken his black square cap and his red robe, and he slept *beneath* the purple at my side. He was a rascal, La Bouëtardais, and a good musician with a fine voice. On nights when neither of us could sleep, he would sit for hours completely naked on his cot, wearing his square cap and singing ballads while he strummed a guitar that was down to its last three strings. One night, as the poor man was singing Metastasio's "Hymn to Venus," *Scendi propizia*,[13] he was stricken by a draft, his mouth became twisted, and he died, but not right away, for I rubbed his cheeks with all my might. We held council in our high chamber, debated politics, and entertained ourselves with émigré gossip. In the evenings, we went to dance with our aunts and cousins, after the dresses had been trimmed with ribbons and the hats had been made.

7.

A SUMPTUOUS BANQUET—THE END OF MY 120 FRANCS—FURTHER DESTITUTION—TABLE D'HÔTE— BISHOPS—DINNER AT THE LONDON TAVERN— CAMDEN'S MANUSCRIPTS

London, April to September 1822

THOSE who read this part of my *Memoirs* will not notice that I have interrupted them twice: once, to give a grand dinner for the Duke of York, the King of England's brother, and once again to give a banquet celebrating the anniversary of the King of France's return to Paris on July 8, 1822. This banquet cost me forty thousand francs. Peers and peeresses of the British Empire, ambassadors, and distinguished foreigners filled my magnificently decorated rooms. My tables glittered with London crystal and the gold of Sèvres porcelain. The most delectable dishes, wines, and flowers were laid out in abundance. Portland Place was packed with brilliant carriages. Collinet and Almack's orchestra charmed the fashionably melancholy dandies and the dreamily elegant ladies dancing pensively across my floors. The Opposition and the Ministerial majority declared a truce: Lady Canning chatted with Lord Londonderry, and Lady Jersey laughed with the Duke of Wellington. *Monsieur*, who lavished me with compliments for my sumptuous hospitality in 1822, was unaware that, in 1793, a future minister subsisted not far from him, awaiting his future grandeur, fasting for the sin of his fidelity in a room above a graveyard. I congratulate myself today for having been shipwrecked, having had a glimpse of war, and having shared in the suffering of the humblest class of society, even as I am pleased, in my days of prosperity, to have encountered injustice and slander. I have made the most of these lessons. Life, without the misfortunes that give it weight, is nothing but a baby's rattle.

*

I was the man with one hundred and twenty louis d'or, but equality of wealth had not yet been established, and commodities were not less expensive. There was nothing to counterbalance my rapidly emptying purse. I could not count on further assistance from my family in Brittany, exposed as they were to the double scourge of the Chouannerie and the Terror, and I saw nothing before me except the poorhouse or the Thames.

Some of the émigrés' servants, whom their masters could no longer feed, had transformed themselves into restaurateurs in order to feed their masters. God knows what merriment was made at those tables! And God knows what politics were heard there! All the victories of the Republic were changed into defeats, and if by chance someone doubted an immediate restoration he was declared a Jacobin. Two old bishops, who looked like animate corpses, were out walking one spring morning in Saint James Park.

"Monseigneur," said the one, "do you think we shall be in France in the month of June?"

"But, Monseigneur," replied the other, after ripe reflection, "I don't see why not!"

Pelletier, the man of resources, came to disinter me, or rather to pluck me down from my eyrie. He had read in a Yarmouth paper that an antiquarian society was about to undertake a history of Suffolk: they were advertising for a Frenchman capable of deciphering some twelfth-century French manuscripts in the Camden collection. The parson of Beccles was in charge of this historical enterprise, and it was he to whom I needed to apply.

"This is *perfect* for you," Pelletier told me. "Go, decipher some old papers! You can keep on sending copy to Baylis, and I shall force the coward to start printing it again. Then you'll come back to London with two hundred guineas and your work finished—and let the chips fall where they may!"

I started to stammer my objections.

"Ah, go to the devil, why don't you?" said Pelletier. "Do you count on staying here in this *palace* where I've already frozen half to death? If Rivarol, Champcenetz, Mirabeau-Tonneau, and I had been such simpering simpletons, we'd have made *fine* work of the *Actes des Apôtres*! Do you know that this story about you and Hingant made a hell of a racket? You would have liked to let yourselves die of hunger? Ha! Ha! Ha! Poof!...Ha! Ha!..."

Pelletier was doubled over and holding onto his knees, he was laughing so hard. He had recently sold a hundred copies of his paper in the colonies, and the guineas he had received in payment jingled in his pocket. He carried me away by force, together with the apoplectic La Bouëtardais and two other ragged émigrés we happened across, to dine at the London Tavern. He made us drink port wine and eat roast beef and plum pudding until we were fit to burst.

"Tell me, Monsieur le Comte," Pelletier said to my cousin, "how did your muzzle get so twisted?"

La Bouëtardais, half shocked and half flattered, explained the thing as best he could. He told him how he had been stricken suddenly while singing the words: *O bella Venere*! My poor paralyzed cousin burbled these words in such a dead, numb, exhausted tone that Pelletier, overcome by a fit of deranged laughter, overturned the table by kicking it from below with both feet.

On reflection, the advice of my countryman (truly a character out of my other countryman Le Sage) did not seem so bad. Over the next three days I made inquiries, had myself clothed by Pelletier's tailor, and left for Beccles with some money Deboffe lent me on the assurance that I would soon resume the *Essai*. I changed my name, which no Englishman could pronounce, to *Combourg*, which my brother had already adopted and which brought to mind both the pains and pleasures of my earliest youth. Alighting at an inn, I presented the village parson with a letter from Deboffe, who was highly regarded in the English book trade: the letter recommended me as a scholar of the first order. Made perfectly welcome, I was introduced to all the gentlemen of the county, and met two officers from our Royal Navy who were giving French lessons in the region.

8.

MY PASTIMES IN THE PROVINCES—THE DEATH OF MY BROTHER—MY FAMILY'S MISFORTUNES—THE TWO FRANCES—LETTERS FROM HINGANT

London, April to September 1822

I WAS BEGINNING to regain my strength. The rides that I took on horseback restored me a degree of health. The landscape of England, seen thus in detail, was melancholy, but charming; every place I went, it was the same thing and the same view. M. de Combourg was invited to every gathering. I owed the softening of my hard lot at this time to study: Cicero was right to recommend the camaraderie of letters as a balm for the sorrows of life. All the women were delighted to meet a Frenchman with whom to speak French.

My family's misfortunes, which I learned from the newspapers, and which revealed my true name (for I could not hide my grief), made me all the more sympathetic to my neighbors. The public pages announced the death of M. de Malesherbes; the death of his daughter, Madame de Rosambo; the death of his granddaughter, Madame la Comtesse de Chateaubriand; and the death of his grandson-in-law, the Comte de Chateaubriand, my brother, all massacred together, on the same day, in the same hour, on the same scaffold. M. de Malesherbes was an object of admiration and veneration among the English, and my family connection with this defender of Louis XVI redoubled the benevolence of my hosts.

At this same time, my uncle de Bedée wrote to tell me of the persecutions experienced by the rest of my family. My aged and incomparable mother had been thrown in a cart with other victims of the Terror and taken from the heart of Brittany to the jails of Paris, where she was sentenced to share the fate of the son whom she had loved so well. My wife and my sister Lucile were in the dungeons of Rennes awaiting sentence; there had been some talk of imprisoning them in the Château de Combourg, which had become a fortress of the State. Despite their innocence, they were both accused of the crime of my emigration. What were our sufferings in a foreign land compared to the sufferings of the French who had remained at home? And yet how miserable it was to know that our exile itself was a pretext for persecuting our dear ones!

Two years ago, my sister-in-law's wedding ring was picked up from the gutter of the rue Cassette and brought to me. It was broken: the two hoops of the ring had separated and hung loosely embracing each other, but the names engraved there were still perfectly legible. How was it that this ring had been retrieved? In what place and at what time was it lost? Had the victim, imprisoned in the Luxembourg, passed through the rue Cassette on the way to her punishment? Had she let the ring fall from the tumbrel? Or had it been tugged from her finger after the execution? The sight of this broken emblem, with its clear inscription, overwhelmed me; it called to mind unimaginable cruelties. Something mysterious and fateful clung to this ring, which my sister-in-law seemed to have sent me from the land of the dead, in memory of her and of my brother. I have handed it down to her son. May it not bring him misfortune!

> Dear orphan, image of your mother,
> From here below I ask the Lord
> To give you the happy days denied your father
> And the children that your uncle shall never have.

This bad stanza and two or three others were the only wedding gift I was able to give my nephew when he married.

One other token of these old misfortunes remains to me. Here is what M. de Contencin wrote me when, combing through the city archives, he discovered the order of the Revolutionary Tribunal which sent my brother and his family to the scaffold:

Monsieur le Vicomte,

There is a sort of cruelty in reawakening the memory of evils which have caused so much grief to a soul that has suffered as deeply as yours. This thought made me hesitate before offering to send you a very sad document which has fallen into my hands in the course of my research. It is a death warrant signed before execution, by a man who always showed himself as implacable as Death herself, whenever he found exemplary virtue and goodness together in the same head.

I hope, M. le Vicomte, that you shall not think too poorly of me if I add to your family archives a document which recalls such cruel memories. I supposed it would be of interest to you, since it had some value in my eyes, and this is why I thought to offer it to you. If I have not been indiscreet in doing so, I would be doubly pleased with myself, as this letter gives me occasion to express the feelings of profound respect and sincere admiration which you have long inspired in me, and with which I am, Monsieur le Vicomte,

> Your very humble and obedient servant,
> A. De Contencin
> *Hôtel de la Préfecture de la Seine*
> *Paris, March 23, 1835*

Here is my reply to this letter:

Monsieur,

I once had Saint-Chapelle scoured for the documents that record my poor brother's trial, but nobody was able to find the order that you have had the kindness to send me. This order, along with so many others, with their erasures and their misspelled names, must be presented to Fouquier at God's Tribunal: there, he will surely have to acknowledge his signature. Here is a relic of those times that people regret, and about which they write volumes in admiration! Yet I envy my brother: for many long years now, he has been out of this sad world. I owe you infinite thanks, Monsieur, for the esteem you show me in your good and noble letter, and I beg you to accept my assurance of the very distinguished consideration with which I have the honor of being, etc.

This death warrant is especially remarkable as evidence of the frivolity with which the murders were committed: names are wrongly spelled and others half-erased. These formal defects, which should have been enough to annul the simplest sentence, did not stop the executioners. They were concerned only with the exact hour of death: *at precisely five o'clock*. Here is the authentic document, which I copy faithfully:

EXECUTOR OF CRIMINAL SENTENCES
REVOLUTIONARY TRIBUNAL

The executor of criminal sentences shall not fail to betake himself to the house of justice of the Conciergerie, where he shall execute the sentence condemning Mousset d'Esprémenil, Chapelier, Thouret, Hell, Lamoignon Malsherbes, the wife of Lepelletier Rosambo, Chateau Brian and his wife (the name itself is smudged, illegible), the widow Duchatelet, the wife of Grammont, formerly a Duke, the woman Rochechuart (Rochechouart), and Parmentier: —14, to the penalty of death. The execution shall take place today, at precisely five o'clock, in the Place de la Révolution, in this city.

The Public Prosecutor,
H.Q. Fouquier
Given at the Tribunal, Year III Floréal,
in the second year of the French Republic
—Two Carts

The Ninth of Thermidor saved my mother's life; but she would be left forgotten in the Conciergerie. The commissaire under the National Convention found her there and asked her, "What are you doing here, *citoyenne*? Who are you and why are you still here?" My mother replied that, having lost her son, she gave no thought to the future, that she was indifferent whether she died in prison or out of it. "But perhaps you have other children?" said the commissaire. My mother gave the names of my wife and my sisters, who had been detained in Rennes. An order was sent to set them free, and my mother was constrained to leave the prison.

In histories of the Revolution, writers forget to set the picture of outer France beside the picture of inner France—to depict that great colony of émigrés who varied their labors and their sorrows according to diverse climates and different national customs.

Outside France, everything was brought about by individuals, altered conditions, obscure sufferings, soundless and unrewarded sacrifices; and in this plethora of individuals of every rank, age, and sex, one idea held fast: Old France traveled abroad with all its prejudices and loyalties intact, as in former times the Church of God wandered the earth with its virtues and martyrs.

Inside France, everything was brought about en masse: Barère announcing murders and conquests, civil wars and foreign wars; the colossal battles of the Vendée and the Rhine; thrones crumbling to the sound of our armies on the march; our fleets engulfed by the waves; the people disinterring the monarchs at Saint-Denis and throwing the dust of dead Kings in the face of living Kings, to blind them; the new France, glorious in its new liberties, proud even of its crimes, standing firm on its own soil, and all the while extending its frontiers, doubly armed with the executioner's blade and the soldier's sword.

In the midst of my family sorrows, some letters from my friend Hingant arrived, reassuring me of his fate, letters that were really quite remarkable. He wrote to me in September 1795:

> Your letter of August 23 is full of the most moving sentiments. The few people to whom I have shown it were moved to tears as they read. I am almost tempted to say what Diderot said the day that J.-J. Rousseau came to weep for him in his cell at Vincennes: "See, how my friends do love me!"[14] My illness is

nothing, in truth, but one of those nervous fevers which cause one a great deal of suffering and for which time and patience are the best remedies. During the fever, I was reading some extracts from the *Phaedo* and *Timaeus*. Those books make one yearn for death, and I said to myself, like Cato:

It must be so, Plato; thou reason'st so well![15]

I imagined my voyage as one might imagine a voyage to the Indies. I believed I would see a profusion of unfamiliar new sights in the "world of the spirits" (as Swedenborg calls it) and, above all, that I would be exempt from the torpor and the danger of the voyage.

9.

CHARLOTTE

London, April to September 1822

ABOUT four leagues from Beccles, in a small village called Bungay, there lived an English clergyman, the reverend Mr. Ives, a great Hellenist and mathematician. He had a still young wife, charming in her person, her mind, and her manner, and an only daughter, who was fifteen.[16] Having been introduced into this household, I was more warmly welcomed there than anywhere else. We drank together in the old English fashion, Mr. Ives and I, staying at table for two hours after the women had withdrawn. This man, who had seen America, loved telling tales of his travels, hearing the story of mine, and talking about Newton and Homer. His daughter, who had studied hard to please him, was an excellent musician, and she sang as well as Madame Pasta sings today.[17] She would reappear at teatime and charm away the old parson's infectious drowsiness. Leaning on the end of the piano, I would listen to Miss Ives in silence.

When the music was over, the young lady questioned me about France and literature; she asked me to draw up courses of study. She especially wanted to acquaint herself with the Italian authors, and begged me to give her some notes on the *Divina Commedia* and the *Gerusalemme*. Little by little, I began to feel the timid charm of an affection that springs from the soul. I had bedecked the Floridians with flowers, but I would not have dared to pick up Miss Ives's glove. I felt embarrassed when I tried to translate a few passages of Tasso: I was more at ease when I turned my hand to Dante, a genius more masculine and chaste.

Charlotte Ives's age and mine were in concord. Something melancholy enters into relationships not formed until the middle of our lives. If two people do not meet in the prime of youth, the memories of the beloved are not mixed in the portion of days when we breathed without knowing her, and these days, which belong to other companions, are painful to recall and, as it were, severed from our present existence. Is there a disproportion of age? Then the drawbacks increase. The older one began his life before the younger one was born, and the younger one, in turn, is destined to live on alone; the one walked in solitude on the far side of the cradle, and the other shall walk in solitude on the near side of the grave. The past was a desert for the first, and the future shall be a desert for the second. It is difficult to love with all the conditions of happiness, youth, beauty, and opportunity, and with a harmony of heart, taste, character, graces, and years.

Having taken a fall from my horse, I stayed some time in Mr. Ives's house. It was winter, and the dreams of my life began to flee in the face of reality. Miss Ives became more reserved. She stopped bringing me flowers, and she no longer wanted to sing.

If someone had told me that I would spend the rest of my life in obscurity at the hearth of this isolated family, I would have died of joy. Love needs nothing but continuance to be at once Eden before the Fall and a Hosanna without end. Make beauty stay, youth last, and the heart never grow weary, and you shall re-create heaven on earth. Love is so much the supreme happiness, it is haunted always by the illusion of infinitude. It wishes to make only irrevocable promises. In the absence of its joys, it attempts to eternalize its sorrows. A fallen angel, it still speaks the language it spoke in the incorruptible abode, and its hope is never to die. In its double nature and its double illusion here below, it aspires to perpetuate itself by immortal thoughts and unending generations.

I foresaw with some dismay the moment when I would be obliged to leave. On the eve of my departure, dinner was a gloomy affair. To my great surprise, Mr. Ives withdrew after dessert, taking his daughter with him, and I remained alone with Mrs. Ives. She was extremely embarrassed. I suspected she was going to reproach me for an inclination that she must have long since guessed, but of which I had never spoken a word. She looked at me, lowered her eyes, and blushed. She herself was, in her discomfort, quite seductive: there was no feeling she could have failed to inspire in me. At long last, making an effort to overcome the obstacle that prevented her from speech, she said to me, in English: "Sir, you have seen my confusion: I do not know if Charlotte pleases you, but it is impossible to deceive a mother. My daughter has certainly become attached to you. Mr. Ives and I have discussed the matter. You suit us in every respect and we believe you would make our daughter happy. You no longer have a native country, you have just lost your family, and your property has been sold. What could possibly take you back to France? Until you inherit from us, you can live with us, here."

Of all the painful things that I had endured, this was the greatest and most wounding. I threw myself on my knees at Mrs. Ives's feet and covered her hands with kisses and tears. She thought I was weeping with happiness and started sobbing with joy. She stretched out her arm to pull the bell-rope and called out to her husband and her daughter.

"Stop!" I cried. "I am married!"

Mrs. Ives fell back in a faint.

I left and set out on foot without returning to my room. When I reached Beccles, I caught the mail coach for London, after having written a letter to Mrs. Ives. I regret I did not keep a copy.

I have retained the sweetest, most tender, and most grateful recollection of these events. Before my name was known far and wide, Mr. Ives's family were the only people to take an interest in me and the only ones to welcome me with sincere affection. When I was poor, unknown, outcast, without beauty or allure, they offered me a definite future, a country, an enchanting wife to draw me out of my shell, a mother almost equal to her daughter in beauty to take the place of my own aged mother, and a well-educated father who loved and cultivated literature to replace the father whom Heaven had taken from me. What did I have to offer in recompense for all that? No illusions could have entered into their choice of me; I had a right to believe myself loved. Since that time, I have met with only one attachment lofty enough to inspire me with the same confidence.[18] As for the interest which was shown in me later, I have never been able to sort out whether external causes—the fracas of fame and the prestige of parties, the glamour of high literary and political status— were not a cloak that drew such eagerness around me.

I see now that, had I married Charlotte Ives, my role on earth would have changed. Buried in a county of Great Britain, I would have become a gentleman *chasseur* and not a single line would have issued from my pen. I might even have forgotten my language, for I could write in English and even the thoughts in my head were beginning to take form in English. Would my country have lost so much by my disappearance? If I could set aside what has consoled me, I would say that I might already have counted up many days of calm, instead of the many troubled days fallen to my lot. What would the Empire, the Restoration, and all the other divisions and quarrels of France have meant to me? I wouldn't have had to palliate failings and combat errors every morning of my life. Is it even certain that I have real talent: a talent worth all the sacrifices of my life? Will I survive my tomb? And if I do live beyond the grave, given the transformations that are even now taking place, in a world changed and occupied by entirely different things, will there be a public there to hear me? Will I not be a man of another time, unintelligible to the new generations? Will my ideas, my feelings, my very style not seem boring and old-fashioned to a sneering posterity? Will my shade be able to say, as Virgil's did to Dante: *Poeta fui e cantai*? "I was a poet and I sang."[19]

10.
RETURN TO LONDON

BACK IN London, I found no peace. I had fled before my destiny like a malefactor before his crime. How painful it must have been for a family so worthy of my respect and gratitude to have suffered this rejection by a poor unknown, a man whom they had welcomed into their house with a simplicity, an absence of suspicion and precaution, that seemed to have been handed down from the ancients! I imagined Charlotte's grief and all the well-deserved reproaches that could and should be heaped on my head: for the fact was that I had complacently abandoned myself to an inclination whose insurmountable illegality I well understood. Was it true then that I had vaguely attempted to seduce Charlotte without holding myself accountable for this culpable conduct? But whether I stopped myself, as I did, in order to remain an honest man, or overcame all obstacles in order to surrender to a desire blighted in advance by my conduct, I could only have plunged the object of this seduction into regret or sorrow.

From these bitter reflections, I let my mind wander to no less bitter feelings: I cursed my marriage, which, according to the false perceptions of my mind, then quite disturbed, had thrown me off course and deprived me of happiness. I did not give any thought to the possibility that, because of the melancholy nature with which I am afflicted and the romantic notions of liberty by which I lived, a marriage with Miss Ives might have been as painful for me as a more independent union.

One thing remained pure and enchanting to my mind, although

the thought of it made me profoundly sad: the image of Charlotte. This image would finally subjugate my rebellions against fate. A hundred times I was tempted to return to Bungay, going not to present myself to the baffled family but to hide by the roadside and watch Charlotte walk past; to follow her to the temple where we had the same God, if not the same altar, in common; to offer this woman, through the medium of heaven, the inexpressible ardor of my vows; to pronounce, at least in thought, that nuptial blessing which, if life had led me otherwise, I might have heard from the mouth of a pastor in this same temple.

Wandering from resolution to resolution, I wrote Charlotte long letters that I tore to shreds. The few insignificant notes I had received from her served me as talismans; conjured to my side by my thoughts, Charlotte, gracious and tender, followed me, purifying my every step, along the paths of my sylph. She absorbed my faculties; she was the center through which all my thoughts passed, as all the blood passes through the heart. She made me disgusted with everything, for I was constantly drawing comparisons to her advantage. A genuine and unhappy passion is a poisonous leaven that lingers in the depths of the soul and would spoil the bread of the angels.

The places where I had walked and the hours and words I had exchanged with Charlotte were engraved in my memory. I gazed at the smile of the woman who had been destined for me; I respectfully touched her black hair; I pressed her lovely arms to my chest like a chain of lilies that I might have worn around my neck. No sooner was I in a secluded spot than Charlotte, with her fair hands, would come sit by my side: I divined her presence, as at night one breathes the fragrance of flowers which he does not see.

Deprived of Hingant's company, my strolls, more solitary than ever, left me quite free to carry with me the image of Charlotte. There is not a heath, a road, or a church within thirty miles of London which I have not visited. The most forsaken places, a nettle patch, a ditch planted with thistles—anywhere that had been neglected by men—became the places I preferred: the same places where Byron had already breathed. With my head in my hand, I contemplated these sites that men had scorned, and when their painful impression became too much to bear, the memory of Charlotte came to ravish me. I was then like the pilgrim who, after wandering many days in the desert, beheld the rocks of Sinai and heard the nightingale's song.

In London, my manners aroused surprise. I looked at no one; I did not reply to anyone; I did not understand what was being said to me. My old friends suspected I had gone mad.

11.

AN EXTRAORDINARY ENCOUNTER

But what happened in Bungay after my departure? What became of that family whom I brought such joy and such grief?

You must bear in mind that I am an ambassador to George IV and that I am writing in London in 1822 of what transpired in London in 1795.

Eight days ago, some business affairs obliged me to drop the thread of the narrative that I am picking up again today. One afternoon during this interval, my footman came to tell me that a carriage had stopped outside the door, and that an English lady was asking to speak with me. As I have made it a rule, considering my public position, never to turn anyone away, I said that the lady should be shown upstairs.

I was in my study when Lady Sutton was announced. I turned and saw a woman dressed in mourning, accompanied by two handsome boys also in mourning: one was about sixteen and the other about fourteen. I rose to meet the stranger and perceived that she was so overcome by emotion that she had difficulty walking. She said to me in a broken voice, "My Lord, do you recognize me?"

Yes, I recognized Miss Ives. The years that had passed over her head had left only their springtime behind. I took her hand, offered her a seat, and sat down beside her. I found myself unable to utter a word; my eyes welled up with tears, and through these tears I looked at her in silence. I felt, by the strength of what I was experiencing, just how deeply I had loved her. Finally I was able to say to her in turn, "And you, Madame, do you recognize me?"

She raised her eyes, which she had kept lowered, and appealed to me with a smiling and melancholy look that lingered like a long memory. Her hand was still between mine. Charlotte said to me: "I am in mourning for my mother. My father died several years ago. These young men are my children."

At these words, she withdrew her hand and fell back into the armchair, covering her face with her handkerchief.

After a moment, she continued: "My Lord, I am speaking to you now in the language that I used to attempt with you in Bungay. I am nervous: forgive me. My children are the sons of Admiral Sutton, whom I married three years after you left England. But today I have no mind to go into details. Please, allow me to come again soon."

I asked for her address, and I gave her my arm, leading her downstairs to her carriage. She was trembling, and I pressed her hand against my heart.

The next day I went to Lady Sutton's house and found her alone. There then began between us a back and forth of *Do you remember?* that reanimated a whole lifetime. With each *Do you remember?* we gazed at one another, searching the other's face for those marks of time that so cruelly measure our distance from the moment of parting and the length of the road we have traveled.

"How did your mother let you know—" I said to Charlotte.

Charlotte blushed and brusquely interrupted me: "I have come to London to beg that you intercede for Admiral Sutton's children. The eldest wishes to go to Bombay. Mr. Canning, who has been named Governor-General of India, is your friend. He could take my son there with him. I would be very grateful, and I would love to owe my first child's happiness to you." She lingered on these last words.

"Ah, Madame," I said to her. "You have recalled so many things to my mind. And this is such an extraordinary reversal of destinies! You, who received me so hospitably at your father's table, when I was but a poor exile; you, who sympathized with that man's sufferings; you, who perhaps may have thought of raising him to a glorious and unhoped-for rank: it is you who now come asking him for his protection in your own country! Of course I will go see Mr. Canning. Your son, much as it pains me to call him that—your son, if it is within my power, shall go to India. But please, tell me, Madame, what do you make of my changed fortune? How do you see me now? This phrase *My Lord* you keep repeating, it seems rather cold."

Charlotte answered: "I find you unchanged, not even aged. When I used to talk about you with my parents during your absence, it was always by the title *My Lord*. It seemed to me you deserved to bear it. Were you not like a husband to me, *my lord and master*?"

As she uttered these words, this graceful woman had something of Milton's Eve about her. Surely, I thought, she was not born of woman, for her beauty bore the imprint of the divine hand that had formed it.

I hastened to call on Mr. Canning and Lord Londonderry, who made as many difficulties about securing this little post as they would have made in France; but in the end they swore to help as men swear to tell the truth in court. I kept Lady Sutton abreast of my progress; I went to visit her three more times. On my fourth visit, she told me that she was going back to Bungay. This last conversation was sorrowful. Charlotte spoke to me once more of the past, our hidden life, our readings, our strolls, the music, the flowers of yesteryear, and the hopes of bygone times.

"When I knew you," she said to me, "no one could pronounce your name. But who has not heard it today? Do you know that I have a work and several letters written in your hand? Here—"

And she placed a packet in my hand.

"Please, do not take offense if I want to keep nothing of you," she told me, and she began to weep. "Farewell! Farewell!" she said to me, "and remember my son. I shall never see you again, for you shall not come calling on me in Bungay."

"But I shall," I cried. "I shall bring you your son's commission!"

She shook her head doubtfully and withdrew.

When I returned to the embassy in Portland Place, I shut myself in my room and opened the packet. Inside were only a few insignificant notes and a course of study with remarks on English and Italian poets. I had hoped to find a letter from Charlotte, but there was no such thing. In the margins of the manuscripts, however, I did discover a few notes in English, French, and Latin, whose faded ink and youthful handwriting verified that they had been scratched in those margins long ago.

That is the story of Miss Ives and me. As I finish committing the tale to paper, it seems as if I am losing Charlotte a second time, on the same island where I first lost her. But between what I feel for her in this moment and what I experienced in the tender hours I have just recalled, there lies the whole expanse of innocence: the passions have interposed themselves between Miss Ives and Lady Sutton. No longer would I be bringing an ingenuous young woman all the naive desires and sweet ignorance of a love that remained within the realm of dreams. I wrote then on waves of sadness; but I am no longer tossed on the waves of life. In truth, if I had taken a wife and mother in my arms, a woman who was once destined to be my virgin bride, I would have done so with a sort of rage, a desire to undo, to fill with sorrow, to smother those twenty-seven years given over to another after having been offered to me.

I must regard the feelings that I have just recalled as the first such feelings that entered my heart. They were not at all suited, however, to my tempestuous nature, which would have corrupted them and have made me incapable of savoring any blessed delight for long. It was in those days, embittered by misfortunes, already a pilgrim overseas, and having already begun my solitary voyage—it was in those days that the mad ideas described in the mystery of René obsessed me and made me the most tormented being on earth. However that may be, the chaste image of Charlotte, by allowing a few rays of genuine light to penetrate the depths of my soul, had begun to dissipate my cloud of phantoms. My daemon, like an evil spirit, plunged again into the abyss, and lay there in wait, letting time do its work, until she made her next appearance.

BOOK ELEVEN

I.

A DEFECT OF MY CHARACTER

London, April to September 1822;
Revised in December 1846

MY RELATIONS with Deboffe regarding the *Essai historique* had never been completely broken off, and it was important, on my return to London, that I renew them as soon as possible to sustain my material life. But what had brought about my latest misfortune? My obstinate silence. To make sense of this, it is necessary to examine my character.

At no time has it been possible for me to overcome the spirit of restraint and inward solitude that prevents me from discussing what moves me. No one could attest without lying that I have ever uttered words such as most men utter in moments of pain, pleasure, or vanity. A name or a confession of any seriousness never, or almost never, escapes my lips. I do not talk with casual acquaintances about my interests, my plans, my works, my ideas, my friendships, my joys, or my sorrows, being persuaded of the profound boredom that we cause others by speaking of ourselves. I am sincere and truthful, but I am lacking in openness of heart. My soul tends constantly to close up. I stop in the middle of saying a thing, and I have never let on about my whole life except in these *Memoirs*. If I venture to begin a story, suddenly the thought of its length frightens me; after three or four words, the sound of my voice becomes intolerable to me and I hold my tongue. As I believe in nothing, outside of religion, I am leery of everything. Spite and disparagement are two distinctive qualities of the French mind; mockery and slander, the sure result of any confidence.

But what have I gained by my reserved disposition? Often, because

I am so impenetrable, I have become for others a sort of fantastic being with no relation to my reality. Even my friends are wrong about me when, out of affection for me, they think to promote and embellish my reputation. All the mediocrities of antechambers, offices, newspapers, and cafés suppose I am rife with ambitions, yet I have none. Cold and dry in everyday matters, I have nothing of the enthusiast or the sentimentalist about me: my swift and exact perceptions cut to the heart of men and events and strip them of all importance. Far from dragging me away, or idealizing practical truths, my imagination swallows up the biggest events and perplexes even me. The petty and ridiculous side of things is always the first to strike me. Real genius and real greatness hardly exist in my eyes. Polite, congratulatory, and respectful toward pretenders who proclaim their superior intelligence, my hidden contempt smiles and places Callot's masks on every one of those incense-wreathed faces.[1] In politics, the warmth of my opinions has never outlasted the length of my speech or my pamphlet. In my inward and theoretical life, I am the man of dreams; in my outward and practical life, I am the man of realities. Adventurous yet disciplined, passionate yet methodical, there has never been a being more visionary and more positive, more ardent and more frozen than I: a bizarre androgyne forged by the divergent bloods of my mother and my father.

The portraits that have been made of me bear me no resemblance, and this is chiefly due to my reticence. The crowd is too frivolous, too inattentive to give themselves the time, unless they've been warned beforehand, to see individuals as they are. Whenever, by chance, I attempt to redress some of these false judgments in my prefaces, no one believes me. The result, all things being equal, is that I have never insisted; an *as you wish* has always relieved me of the boredom of persuading anyone or of trying to assert a truth. I retreat into my heart like a hare into its form, and there I set myself to contemplating the motion of a leaf or the bending of a blade of grass.

I do not make a virtue of my invincible and quite involuntary circumspection. It is not duplicity, however it may appear, and it is inharmonious with happier, friendlier, more easygoing and naive natures. Often, it has injured me in matters of feeling and business, for I have never been able to suffer explanations, reconcilements brought about by clarifications and protests, verbosity and accusations, details and apology.

In the case of the Ives family, my obstinate silence about myself proved fatal to me in the extreme. Twenty times Charlotte's mother had inquired after my relatives and put me on the road to revelation. Not foreseeing where my muteness would lead me, I contented myself as usual with a few vague words. If I had not been subject to this odious mental oddity, any misunderstanding would have been impossible, and I would not have seemed as though I had intentionally abused the most generous hospitality. The truth, spoken by me at the decisive moment, does not excuse me: real harm had been done.

I resumed my work in the midst of my grief and my well-deserved self-reproach. I even came to like my labors, for it had occurred to me that by acquiring some renown, I might make the Ives family less repentant of the interest they had shown me. Charlotte, with whom I thus sought to be reconciled through glory, came to preside over my studies. Her image sat before me as I wrote. When I raised my eyes from my paper, I fixed them on her venerable image as though the original were there in fact. The inhabitants of Ceylon were watching the sun rise in extraordinary splendor one morning when suddenly its orb divided, and out came a brilliant creature saying to the Ceylonese, "I come to reign over you." Charlotte had come forth from a ray of light to reign over me.

But let us forsake these memories; memories grow old and fade like hopes. My life is about to change its course, to flow through other valleys, under other skies. First love of my youth, you vanish from me with all your charms! I have just seen Charlotte again, it's true, but after how many years apart?[2] Sweet gleam of the past—pale rose of twilight edging into night—when the sun has set so long ago!

2.

THE *ESSAI HISTORIQUE SUR LES RÉVOLUTIONS*— ITS EFFECT—A LETTER FROM LEMIÈRE, THE POET'S NEPHEW

London, April to September 1822

LIFE HAS often been represented (by me first of all) as a mountain which we climb on one side and rush down on the other. It would be equally valid to compare it to one of the Alps—one of those bald summits crowned in ice which has no other side. To pursue this image further: the traveler is perpetually ascending and never descends. He therefore has a better view of the expanse he has crossed: the paths that he has not chosen and by the aid of which he might have come up some less arduous slope. He gazes back with regret and sorrow at the spot where he went astray. So it is with the publication of the *Essai historique*, which marks my first step off the path of peace. I finished the first part of the great work I had sketched; I wrote the last word of it hovering between the thought of death (I had fallen ill again) and a vanished dream: *In somnis venit imago conjugis.* "In my dream there came the image of a bride."[3] The *Essai* was printed by Baylis and published by Deboffe in 1797. This date marks one of the turning points of my life. There are moments when our destiny, whether it yields to society, or obeys the laws of nature, or begins to mold us into the form we are to take, abruptly changes direction, like a river that changes course around a sudden bend.

The *Essai* offers a compendium of my existence, as a poet, a moralist, a polemicist, and a political thinker. That I hoped, to the extent that I was able to hope, that the work would be a great success, goes without saying. We authors, petty prodigies of a prodigious era, wish to commune with future generations; but we are ignorant, I think, of posterity's dwelling place. We put down the wrong address. When we are numb in the grave, death will freeze our words, written or sung, so hard that they will never melt again like the "frozen words" of Rabelais.[4]

The *Essai* was to be a sort of historical encyclopedia. The single volume published is already a large enough undertaking. I had the rest of it in manuscript. Next would come, to complement the research and annotations of the archivist, the lays and virelays of the poet, *The Natchez*, and so on. It is difficult for me today to understand how I could give myself over to such considerable studies amid a life so active, so errant, and subject to so many reversals. My tenacious working habits explain this: in my youth, I often wrote for twelve or fifteen hours without leaving the table where I sat, crossing out and rewriting the same page ten times over. Age has not robbed me of this assiduity. Today, my diplomatic correspondence, which never interferes with my literary labors, is written entirely in my own hand.

The *Essai* made a stir among the émigrés. It was at odds with the feelings of my companions in misfortune. In the varied social positions I have occupied, my independence has almost always wounded the men with whom I've marched. I have by turns been the leader of various armies in which the soldiers were not of my party: I have led old Royalists in the fight for public freedoms, and particularly the freedom of the press, which they detested; I have rallied liberals in the name of this same freedom, under the flag of the Bourbons, whom they held in horror. It happened that émigré opinion became attached, through self-love, to my person: the English reviews wrote in praise of me, and this praise reflected on all *the faithful*.

I had sent copies of the *Essai* to La Harpe, Ginguené, and de Sales. Lemière, the nephew of the poet of that name and a translator of Gray's poetry, wrote to me from Paris on July 15, 1797, telling me that my *Essai* was a great success. There is no doubt that the *Essai* was famous for a moment, but it was almost immediately forgotten. A sudden shadow engulfed the first ray of my glory.

Having become almost a personage, I was sought out by the well-to-do émigrés of London. I made my way from street to street, moving from my garret on Tottenham Court and proceeding as far as Hampstead Road. There, I stayed a few months in the house of one Mrs. O'Larry, an Irish widow, the mother of a very pretty daughter of fourteen with a tender love of cats. United by this common passion, we commiserated over the loss of two elegant kittens, white all over, like two ermines, but with black-tipped tails.

Mrs. O'Larry's house was frequented by the old women of the neighborhood, with whom I was obliged to drink tea in the old English fashion. Madame de Staël has depicted this scene in *Corinne* at Lady Edgermond's house: "My dear, do you think the water has boiled long enough to pour it over the tea?"

"My dear, I do believe it's just a *bit* too early."

There also came to these soirées a tall and beautiful young Irishwoman, named Mary Neale, in the custody of a tutor. She perceived some wound in the depths of my gaze, for she said to me, "You carry your heart in a sling."[5]

I carried my heart I know not how.

After Mrs. O'Larry left for Dublin, I moved still farther away from the colony of poor émigrés in the East End and arrived, lodging by lodging, in the quarter of the rich émigrés in the West End, where I lived among bishops, Court families, and colonists from Martinique. Pelletier had come back to me. He had got married on a lark. The same old braggart as ever, he still squandered his kindness and visited his neighbors for their money rather than for their company. At this same time, I made several new acquaintances, particularly in the circle in which I had some family connections. I befriended Christian de Lamoignon, whose leg had been seriously wounded in the Quiberon affair and who today is my colleague in the Chamber of Peers. He introduced me to Mrs. Lindsay, who was attached to his brother, Auguste de Lamoignon. President Guillaume was not better installed at Basville among Boileau, Madame de Sévigné, and Bourdaloue.[6]

Mrs. Lindsay, of Irish ancestry, with her dry wit, her somewhat curt temperament, her elegant height, and her charming face, had a noble soul and a lofty character. Worthy émigrés spent their evenings at the hearth of this last of the Ninons.[7] The old monarchy was dying out with all its abuses and its graces. It will be disinterred one day, like those skeletal queens, adorned with necklaces, bracelets, and earrings, who were exhumed in Etruria. At Mrs. Lindsay's, I met M. Malouët, Madame du Belloy (a woman deserving of affection), the Comte de Montlosier, and the Chevalier de Panat. The last had a well-merited reputation for wit, uncleanliness, and gourmandism. He was one of those "men of taste," who used to sit with arms crossed before the spectacle of French society: one of those idlers whose mission was to see all and judge all. These men exercised the function now exercised by the newspapers, but without their asperity or their great popular influence.

As for Montlosier, he had ridden the crest of his famous phrase, "the wooden cross," a phrase that I neatened up a bit when I quoted it, but true enough at the core.[8] On leaving France, he had gone to Coblentz, where he was poorly received by the Princes. He had a quarrel, fought a duel one night on the banks of the Rhine, and was run through. Unable to move, and unable to see so much as a drop of blood, he asked the witnesses whether the point of the sword had passed through his back.

"By three inches," they told him, after feeling around for it.

"Then it's nothing," said Montlosier. "Monsieur, withdraw your thrust."

Montlosier, having been thus repaid for his royalism, traveled on to England and took refuge in literature, that great émigré workhouse in which I pulled up my pallet next to his. He obtained the editorship of the *Courrier de Londres*. In addition to his newspaper, he wrote physico-politico-philosophical works, in one of which he proved that blue was the color of life, for the veins turn blue after death: evidence that life was coming to the body's surface to evaporate and return to the blue sky. As I am very fond of the color blue, I was quite charmed.

A liberal feudalist, an aristocrat, and a democrat, with a variegated, patchwork mind, Montlosier is a long time giving birth to his disparate ideas; but once he has disengaged them from their difficult delivery, they are sometimes beautiful, and always energetic. Anti-priest and anti-noble, a Christian by sophistry and an enthusiast of ancient history, in pagan days he would have been a fervent partisan of emancipation in theory and slavery in practice: the sort of man who would throw a slave to the sharks in the name of liberty for the human race. A babbler, a quibbler, implacable and hirsute, this former deputy of the Riom nobility doesn't mind paying court to power. He has always known how to take care of his interests, but he lets no one see him doing it; he hides his weakness as a man behind his honor as a gentleman. I do not wish to say anything against my smoky Auvernat, with his novels of Mont-d'Or and his polemics of the Plaine. I am partial to his heteroclite nature. The long, obscure development and contortion of his ideas, with all their parentheses and throat noises and quavering *oh! oh!* has bored me (anything dark, tangled, misty, or tiresome is abhorrent to me); but I am nevertheless fond of this naturalist of volcanoes, this Pascal manqué, this orator from the mountains who speechifies to the gallery as his little compatriots sing from the chimney tops; I love this gazetteer of peat bogs, this self-proclaimed liberal explaining the Charter through a Gothic window, this gentleman shepherd half-married to his milkmaid, scattering his barley among the snow in his little field of pebbles. I will be forever grateful to him for having dedicated to me, in his chalet in the Puy-de-Dôme, an ancient black rock taken from a Gaulish burial-ground which he himself had discovered.

Abbé Delille (another compatriot of Sidonius Apollinaris, the Chancelier de L'Hôpital, Lafayette, Thomas, and Chamfort),[9] driven from the continent by the torrent of Republic victories, had also recently established himself in London. The émigrés were proud to count him among their ranks: he sang of our misfortunes, which was only one more reason to love his muse. He toiled and toiled; but then he had little choice in the matter, for Madame Delille locked him up and would not let him out until he had earned his keep by completing a certain number of verses. One day I went to see him. He kept me waiting a long time, then appeared with very red cheeks. It is rumored that Madame Delille used to slap him around, but I know nothing of it. I say only what I saw.

Who hasn't heard Abbé Delille recite his poems? He also told a very good story. His ugly and wrinkled face, animated by his imagination, went marvelously with his coquettish speech, his peculiar talent, and his priestly profession. Abbé Delille's masterpiece is his translation of the *Georgics*, apart from the sentimental parts; but it's as if you were reading Racine translated into the language of Louis XV.

The literature of the eighteenth century, apart from the few great geniuses who dominate it, situated as it is between the classical literature of the seventeenth century and the romantic literature of the nineteenth, is not out of touch with naturalness, but it is out of touch with nature. Devoted to the arrangement of words, it is neither as original as the new school nor as pure as the old school. Abbé Delille was a poet of modern castles, as the troubadour was the poet of the old ones. The verses of the one and the ballads of the other point up the difference between the aristocracy in the prime of its life and the aristocracy in its decrepitude: the Abbé describes readings and chess parties in the same houses where the troubadours sang of crusades and tournaments.

The distinguished personages of our Church militant were also in England at that time: Abbé Carron, of whom I've already spoken, when I borrowed from his biography of my sister Julie; the Bishop of Saint-Pol-de-Léon, a stern and narrow-minded prelate who helped make the Comte d'Artois more and more a stranger to his century; the Archbishop of Aux, who was slandered, perhaps because of his success in society; and another learned and pious bishop so avaricious that, if he'd had the bad luck to lose his soul, he would never have bought it back. Nearly all misers are men of intelligence: it must be that I am very stupid.

Among the Frenchwomen of the West End was Madame de Boigne. She was amiable, clever, talented, extremely pretty, and very young. She has since, together with her father, the Marquis d'Osmond, represented the French Court in England much better than a savage like me could have done. She is writing now, and her talents will no doubt marvelously reproduce what she has seen.

Mesdames de Caumont, de Gontaut, and du Cluzel also lived in the quarter of the felicitous émigrés, although I may be wrong about

Madame de Caumont and Madame du Cluzel, whom I had briefly met in Brussels.

I am quite certain, however, that Madame la Duchesse de Duras was in London in those days: I would not make her acquaintance until ten years later. How many times in life do we pass by what would give us pleasure, like a sailor crossing the waters of a land favored by the heavens which he has missed by no more than one horizon and one day's sail! I write this on the bank of the Thames, and tomorrow a letter will go by post to Madame de Duras, on the bank of the Seine, letting her know that I have encountered my first memory of her.[10]

3.

FONTANES

London, April to September 1822

FROM TIME to time, the Revolution sent us émigrés of a new type and of a new opinion. Various strata of exiles were forming in London: the earth contains strata of sand and of clay, deposited there by the waves of the Flood. One of these waves brought me a man whose loss I still mourn today, a man who was my guide in the world of letters and whose friendship was one of the honors, and one of the consolations, of my life.

You have seen, in Book Four of these *Memoirs*, that I had met M. Fontanes in 1789; it was in Berlin last year that I heard news of his death. He was born in Niort, to a noble Protestant family. His father had had the horrible misfortune to kill his brother-in-law in a duel. The young Fontanes, raised by a very commendable brother, was sent to Paris. There he met the dying Voltaire, and that great representative of the eighteenth century inspired him to write his first verse; La Harpe took notice of these early poetic attempts. Fontanes undertook some works for the theater and made the acquaintance of a charming actress named Mademoiselle Desgarcins. Residing near the Odéon, wandering around the Chartreuse, he celebrated the neighborhood's solitude. Already he had met a man destined also to become a friend of mine: M. Joubert.[11] When the Revolution arrived, the young poet involved himself in one of those static parties that always perish, torn in two by the party of progress that drags it forward and by the retrograde party that pulls it from behind. The Monarchists made M. Fontanes the editor of the *Modérateur*. When the bad days came, he sought refuge in Lyon, where he married. His wife gave birth to a son. During the siege of Lyon, which the Revolutionaries had declared a Freed Commune, as Louis XI had once declared Arras, by banishing its citizens, a Free City, Madame Fontanes was obliged to depart with the infant's cradle to keep the child safe from the bombs. Returned to Paris on the 9th of Thermidor, M. Fontanes founded the *Mémorial* with M. La Harpe and Abbé de Vauxelles. Outlawed on the 18th of Fructidor, England became his safe haven.

M. Fontanes was, together with Chénier, the last writer of the classical school in the elder line. His prose and verse resemble one another and have similar merit. Yet his thoughts and images exhibit a melancholy unknown to the age of Louis XIV, which knew only the austere and holy sadness of religious eloquence. This melancholia mingled among the works of the bard of the *Jour des Morts* is, as it were, the imprint of the epoch in which he lived: it fixes the date of his arrival; it shows him to have been born after J.-J. Rousseau and to be connected, by his tastes, with Fénelon. Were someone to condense M. Fontanes's writings into two very slender volumes (one of prose, the other of verse), they would form the most elegant funeral monument that could ever be placed on the tomb of the classical school.*

Among the papers that my friend left are several cantos of a poem called *La Grèce Sauvée*, a few books of odes, miscellaneous poems, etc. He never published anything else himself: for this critic, so fine, so perceptive, and, when not blinded by his political opinions, so impartial, was dreadfully afraid of criticism. He was supremely unjust toward Madame de Staël. An envious article by Garat on the *Forêt de Navarre* almost stopped him short at the start of his poetical career. Fontanes, as soon as he appeared, destroyed the artificial school of Dorat; but he was unable to reestablish the classical school, which was coming to an end together with the language of Racine.

---

*This monument was recently raised by the filial piety of Madame Christine Fontanes; M. Saint-Beuve has adorned its base with an ingenious introduction. (Paris, 1839)

If anything in the world was sure to be antipathetic to M. Fontanes, it was my style of writing. In my person, with the so-called Romantic school, there began a revolution in French literature. And yet my friend, instead of being revolted by my barbarity, became its passionate defender. I saw a look of amazement on his face when I read fragments from *The Natchez*, *Atala*, and *René*. He found it impossible to reduce these productions to the established critical rules, but he sensed that he was entering a new world; he beheld a new nature; he comprehended a language that he did not speak. I had some excellent advice from him, and I owe him whatever is correct in my style. He taught me to respect the ear, and he prevented me from falling prey to the extravagant inventions and uneven executions of my disciples.

It made me very happy to see him again in London, fêted by émigrés who crowded around him asking him to recite cantos from *La Grèce Sauvée*. His rooms were near mine, and there was a period when we never left each other's company. We were present together at a scene worthy of that ill-fated epoch: Cléry, having recently landed in London, read to us from the manuscripts of his *Memoirs*. Let yourself imagine the emotion elicited from an audience of exiles listening to Louis XVI's footman recounting, as an eyewitness, the sufferings and death of the prisoner of the Temple! The Directory, fearing the effects of Cléry's *Memoirs*, later published an interpolated edition which had the author speaking like a lackey and Louis like a porter. Among all the Revolutionary turpitudes, this is perhaps one of the filthiest.

A VENDEAN PEASANT

The Comte d'Artois's London chargé d'affaires, M. du Theil, had hastened to seek out Fontanes, who in turn implored me to introduce him to this agent of the Princes. We found M. du Theil surrounded by all the defenders of the throne and the altar who loitered on the pavements of Piccadilly; by a crowd of parasites and spies who had escaped Paris under various names and disguises, together with swarms of Belgian, German, and Irish counter-revolutionary swindlers. At the edge of this crowd was a man of about thirty or thirty-two who locked eyes with no one, and who had fixed his gaze on an engraving depicting the death of General Wolfe. Struck by his appearance, I inquired after his name. "That's no one," someone said; "just a Vendean peasant, delivering a letter for his superiors."

This man, "who was no one," had witnessed the deaths of Cathelineau, the commander-in-chief of the Vendean Army; Bonchamp, in whom the spirit of Bayard lived again; Lescure, armored in a hair shirt that was no match for the ball; d'Elbée, shot in an armchair because his wounds did not permit him to face the firing squad on his feet; La Rochejaquelein, whose corpse the patriots had ordered "verified" in order to reassure the Convention, which was then at the height of its triumph.

This man, "who was no one," had been present at the taking and retaking of two hundred towns, villages, and redoubts, seven hundred skirmishes, and seventeen pitched battles; he had fought against three hundred thousand regular troops and six or seven hundred thousand conscripts and National Guards; he had helped carry off five hundred cannon and fifty thousand rifles; he had passed through the "infernal columns" (those companies of arsonists commanded by members of the Convention); he had braved the ocean of fire which, on three separate occasions, rolled its waves over the woods of the Vendée. Finally, he had seen the death of three hundred thousand Hercules of the plough, his companions in labor, and five hundred thousand acres of fertile country changed into a desert of ashes.

The two Frances met on that soil which they themselves had razed. All that remained of the blood and the memory of the Crusades struggled, in the Vendée, against what there was of the new blood and hopes of Revolutionary France. The victor felt the greatness of the vanquished. Thureau, the Republican general, declared that "the Vendeans would go down in history as soldiering men of the first rank." Another general wrote to Merlin de Thionville: "Troops who have conquered Frenchmen such as these can flatter themselves of being able to conquer all other nations." The legions of Probus, in their song, said as much of our fathers.[12] Bonaparte called the battles of the Vendée "the battles of giants."

In the crush of the parlor, I was the only one to gaze with admiration and respect at this representative of the ancient peasants who, under Charles V, repulsed a foreign invasion even as they broke free from the yoke of their Lords. I seemed to behold a child of the communes from the time of Charles VII which, in league with the provincial nobility, won back the soil of France foot by foot and furrow by furrow. This man, "who was no one," wore the impassive expression of a savage; his eyes were as gray and unbending as an iron rod; his lower lip trembled over his clenched teeth; his hair curled down from his head like so many torpid serpents, ready to rise up and strike; his arms, hanging at his sides, gave his huge saber-scarred wrists a nervous tremor. One might have taken him for a sawyer. His physiognomy expressed a common rustic nature put to the service of interests and ideals contrary to that nature. In him, the native loyalty of the vassal and the simple faith of the Christian had been mixed with the crude independence of a plebeian accustomed to judging and meting out justice for himself. The feeling of liberty in him seemed merely the consciousness of the strength of his hands and the valor of his heart. He spoke no more than a lion; he scratched himself like a lion, yawned like a lion, lay down on his side like a bored lion, and appeared to be dreaming of blood and forests.

What men the French of all parties were in those days—and what a race we are today! But the Republicans had their principle within themselves, in the midst of themselves, whereas the principle of the Royalists lay outside of France. Vendeans sent deputies to the exiles like giants going to look for leaders among pygmies. The rustic messenger that I beheld had seized the Revolution by the throat and cried, "Come on, men, stand behind me! It shall do you no harm! It won't so much as budge; I've got it." But nobody wanted to move. Thus Jacques Bonhomme let the Revolution go, and Charette broke his sword.[13]

MY WALKS WITH FONTANES

While I was lost in these reflections on this man of the soil, as I had previously been lost in reflections of another sort on Danton and Mirabeau, Fontanes had obtained a private audience with the man he jokingly called the Comptroller-General of Finances. He emerged very satisfied, for M. du Theil had promised him he would encourage the publication of my works, and Fontanes thought only of me. It would be impossible to find a better man. Timid in everything that concerned himself, he became brazen in defense of his friends. He proved this to me at the time of my resignation after the death of the Duc d'Enghien. In conversation, he would burst into ridiculous fits of literary anger. In politics, he was unreasonable. The crimes of the Convention had given him a horror of liberty. He hated newspapers, philosophizing, and ideologies, and he communicated this hatred to Bonaparte when he became close to the master of Europe.

We used to go for walks together in the country and rest side by side under one of those large elms that dotted the meadows. Leaning against the trunk of one of these elms, my friend told me about his travels in England many years before the Revolution and recited a few lines of verse that he had addressed to two young ladies who had since grown old in the shadows of Westminster's towers. The towers he found standing as he had left them, but the hours and the illusions of his youth had long ago been buried at their base.

Often we dined in some solitary tavern in Chelsea, by the Thames, talking for hours of Milton and Shakespeare. They had seen what we were seeing; they had sat like us on the bank of this river: for us a foreign river, for them a native stream. At night, we would go back to London by the faint light of the stars, which were submerged one after another in the city's fog; we reached our lodgings, guided by uncertain glimmers that scarcely showed the way through the coal smoke hovering red around every lamp. In this way, the poet's life rolls by.

We saw London in detail. As a seasoned exile, I served as cicerone to the new recruits of banishment which the Revolution demanded.

Some were young and some were old: there is no legal age for misfortune. In the middle of one of these excursions through the city, Fontanes and I were surprised by a violent thunderstorm and took refuge in an alley behind a wretched house, the door of which just happened to be open. There we met the Duc de Bourbon: it was the first time I laid eyes on this prince who was not yet the last of the Condés.

To think of it: the Duc de Bourbon, Fontanes, and I, all three outlawed, seeking shelter from the same storm, in a foreign land, under the same humble roof! *Fata viam invenient.*[14]

When Fontanes was called back to France, he embraced me and promised we would soon see each other again. On arriving in Germany, he wrote me the following letter:

July 28, 1798

If you have felt some regrets at my departure from London, I swear to you that mine have not been less real. You are the second person in whom, during the whole course of my life, I have found an imagination and a heart similar to my own. I shall never forget the consolation I have had in knowing you during my exile in a foreign land. My tenderest and most constant thoughts since I took leave of you have turned upon *The Natchez*. What you read to me, especially in the very last days, is admirable, and will not leave my memory. But the charm of the poetical ideas with which you impressed me immediately disappeared on my arrival in Germany. There has been most frightful news from France. I have spent the last five or six days in the cruelest perplexities: I have lived in fear that my family might be persecuted. My terrors have been allayed somewhat today. The evil has been very slight (the threat greater than the blow), and anyhow it is not against people of my birth date that the executioners want. The last courier has just brought me assurances of peace and goodwill. I can continue my journey, and should be traveling by the beginning of next month. I will be staying in a house near the forest of Saint-Germain, holing

478 · MEMOIRS FROM BEYOND THE GRAVE

up with my family, my *Grèce*, and my books—would I could say with *The Natchez*!

The unexpected storm that has just taken place in Paris was the result, I am sure, of the blunders of agents and leaders whom you already know. I have very clear proof of this in my hands. Being now certain, I am writing to Great Pulteney Street (where M. du Theil lived) with all possible politeness, but also with all the caution that prudence demands. I am trying to avoid correspondence in the coming month, and I leave it in the deepest doubt whom I am taking with me, and the dwelling place I shall select.

But I speak to you in a tone of friendship, and I wish from the bottom of my heart that you will know that I am honored to be of any use to such a fine person with such distinguished talents. Work—work, my dear friend, and became illustrious. It is in your power; the future is yours. I hope the promise so often made by the Comptroller-General of Finances will be fulfilled, at least in part. This consoles me, for I can't stand the idea that a fine work might be stopped for lack of some assistance.

Write to me. Let us communicate our hearts. Let our muses always be friends. Have no doubt that, so long as I can go about freely in my native land, I shall be making ready a beehive and a bed of flowers beside my own. My affection is unalterable. I will be lonely so long as I am not with you. Tell me of your labors. I wish you the joy of completing them. I have done half of a new poem here on the banks of the Elbe and am more satisfied with it than with all the rest.

Adieu—I embrace you tenderly, and am always your friend,

Fontanes

Fontanes lets me know that he is writing verse even as he changes his place of exile. A poet can never be robbed of everything: he carries his lyre with him. Leave the swan his wings, and every evening, from whatever distant river, he shall chant those melodious lamentations that would be better understood on the banks of the Eurotas.[15]

"The future is yours," Fontanes writes; but did he speak the truth? Should I congratulate myself on having fulfilled his prophecy? Alas! The future of which he spoke is already past. Will I have another? This first affectionate letter I received from one of my first friends, a man who for twenty-three years walked side by side with me on the earth, serves as a sad reminder of my progressive isolation. Fontanes is gone. A profound grief, following his son's death, sent him to an early grave. Almost everyone I mention in these *Memoirs* has vanished; it is a Registry of Deaths. A few more years, and I, who have been condemned to catalogue the dead, shall leave no one to inscribe my name in the Book of the Absent.

But if I must remain alone, and if no being who loved me shall survive me and lead me to my final sanctuary, perhaps I have less need of a guide than others: I have inquired about the way, I have studied the places through which I must pass, I have desired to see what transpires in the last moment. Often, standing at the edge of a grave into which the coffin is being lowered with ropes, I have listened to the death-rattle of these ropes. Next, I have heard the sound of the first shovelful of earth falling on the coffin. With each successive shovelful, the hollow noise diminishes, and the earth, filling the burial ground, raises eternal silence up to the surface of the grave.

Fontanes! You wrote me: Let our muses always be friends.

You have not written me in vain.

4.

DEATH OF MY MOTHER—RETURN TO RELIGION

London, April to September 1822

Alloquar? audiero nunquam tua verba loquentem?
Nunquam ego te, vita frater amabilior,
Aspiciam posthac? at, certe, semper amabo![16]

"AM I NEVER to speak to you again? Never to hear you speak? Am I never to see you again, oh my brother more dear to me than life itself? Oh, but I shall love you forever!"

I have just lost a friend and I am about to lose a mother: it falls to me to repeat these lines that Catullus addressed to his dead brother. In our valley of tears, as in hell, there is an eternal lamentation, impossible to describe, which forms the groundwork, or the presiding note, of human grief; the sound is endless, and it would continue even if all the pains of Creation fell silent.

A letter from Julie, which I received not long after the letter from Fontanes, confirmed my sad remark about my progressive isolation. Fontanes urged me to "work, and become illustrious"; my sister entreated me to "renounce writing altogether": the one proposed glory and the other oblivion. You have seen, in my account of Madame de Farcy, that she tended toward such thoughts. She had taken a dislike to literature because she regarded it as one of the temptations of her life.

Saint-Servan, July 1, 1798

My dear brother, we have just lost the best of mothers; it is with deep sorrow that I write to you of this mortal blow. When you cease to be the object of our solicitude, we shall have ceased to live. If you know how many tears your errant ways have caused our honorable mother to weep, and how deplorable they appear to anyone of a thoughtful mind, to anyone who lays claim, not only to piety, but to reason; if you knew this, it would perhaps persuade you to open your eyes and make you renounce writing altogether; and if Heaven, touched by our prayers, permits us to meet again, you shall find among us all the happiness that is to be had here on earth; you would give us this happiness, for there is nothing but sorrow for us so long as you are absent, and so long as we have so many reasons to be anxious about your fate.

Ah! Why didn't I follow my sister's advice? Why did I keep writing? Subtract my writings from my century, and would there have been any difference in the events or the spirit of that century?

So it was that I had lost my mother; so it was that I had distressed her in the final hours of her life! When she was breathing her last sigh, far from her last surviving son, when she was praying for him, what was I doing in London? I was taking a walk perhaps in the fresh morning dew, at the very moment when the death-sweat drenched my mother's brow, without my hand there to wipe it away!

The filial tenderness I felt for Madame de Chateaubriand was profound. My childhood and youth were intimately linked with the memory of my mother: everything I knew I had learned from her. The thought of having poisoned the last days of the woman who carried me in her womb cast me into despair. I flung my copies of the *Essai* into the fire, for it was the instrument of my crime. If it had been possible to erase the work from existence, I would have done so without hesitation. I did not recover from this disturbance until the thought came to me of expiating my first work by composing a religious work. Such were the origins of *The Genius of Christianity*.

"My mother," I wrote in the first preface to this book, "after being thrown, at the age of seventy-two, into dungeons where she saw her children perish, at last came to die on the pallet to which her misfortunes had consigned her. The memory of my errors embittered her final days, and on her deathbed she charged one of my sisters with calling me back to the religion in which I had been raised. My sister communicated my mother's last wish to me. But when the letter arrived from across the sea, the sister who had written it was no more; she too had died from the effects of her imprisonment. These two voices issuing from the grave, the dead serving as interpreter of the dead, made a deep impression on me. I became a Christian. I did not yield, I admit, to any great supernatural light: my conviction issued from the heart. I wept and I believed."

I exaggerated my faults. The *Essai* was not an impious book but a book of doubt and desolation. Through the gloom of that book there glides a ray of the Christian light that shone upon my cradle. No great effort was needed to return from the skepticism of the *Essai* to the certitude of *The Genius of Christianity*.

5.

THE GENIUS OF CHRISTIANITY—LETTER FROM THE
CHEVALIER DE PANAT

London, April to September 1822

WHEN, after the sad news of my mother's death, I suddenly resolved
to change my course, the title *The Genius of Christianity*, which came
to me on the spot, inspired me. I set myself to work, and I toiled with
the ardor of a son building a mausoleum for his mother. My materials had long been roughed out and assembled by my previous studies.
I knew the works of the Church Fathers better than they are known
today. I had studied them in order to combat them, but having started
down that road with wicked intentions, I left it not as the victor but
as the vanquished.

As for history properly so called, I had been particularly occupied
by it when composing the *Essai historique*. The Camden manuscripts
I had recently examined had made me familiar with the manners and
institutions of the Middle Ages. Finally, the terrific manuscript of
The Natchez (all two thousand three hundred and ninety-three folio
pages) contained everything that *The Genius of Christianity* could
need in the way of descriptions of nature. I would draw largely from
this source, as I had already done in the *Essai*.

When I finished the first part of *The Genius of Christianity*, the
Dulau brothers, who had become the preferred booksellers of the
émigré French clergy, agreed to publish it. The first sheets of the first
volume were printed. The work thus begun in London in 1799 was
finished in Paris in 1802, as one can see by the different prefaces to
The Genius of Christianity. A kind of fever consumed me during the
whole of its composition: no one shall ever know what it was to carry

483

Atala and *René* simultaneously in his brain, in his blood, in his soul, and to combine with the painful birthing of those ardent twins the labor of conceiving the other parts of *The Genius of Christianity*. The memory of Charlotte warmed and governed all my thoughts, and, to finish me off, the first desire for fame and glory inflamed my feverish imagination. This desire came to me out of filial affection; I wanted to make such a stir that it would rise up to my mother's dwelling place and inspire the angels to sing of my holy expiation.

As one course of study leads to another, I could not occupy myself with French scholia without taking note of the literature and the men of the country in which I was living: I was soon drawn into this new line of research. I spent my days and nights reading, writing, and taking Hebrew lessons from a learned priest called Abbé Caperan; I consulted libraries and educated men, roamed the fields lost in my implacable reveries, and paid and received visits. If future events had retroactive and symptomatic effects, I should have been able to prophesy the commotion to be caused by this work which would make my name by the turmoil in my mind and the throbbing of my muse.

Some readings of my first sketches served to enlighten me. Readings are excellent means of instruction, so long as one doesn't take the obligatory flattery for genuine coin. An author who reads aloud in good faith will quickly discover, through an instinctive impression of others, the weak places in his work, and especially if this work is too long or too short—whether he has achieved, undershot, or exceeded the proper measure. I have a letter from the Chevalier de Panat, giving his opinion of the readings of a work that was then unknown. The letter is charming: the dirty Chevalier's droll and scornful wit had never seemed susceptible to getting so involved with poetry. I do not hesitate to give this letter as a document of my history, although it is so smeared from one end to the other with my praise it may seem as if the caddish author had taken pleasure in pouring his inkwell over the page:

This Monday

Mon Dieu! What an interesting reading you have given this

morning! Our religion has counted some great geniuses among its defenders: those great athletes, the illustrious Fathers of the Church, vigorously wielded all the weapons of reason; unbelief was vanquished. But it was not enough. It was necessary to show all of this admirable religion's charms; to show how well fitted it is to the human heart; to reveal the magnificent images it offers the imagination. You are not a theologian but a great painter—a man of feeling opening up a new horizon. Your work was missing from the landscape, and you were, I believe, called to do it. Nature has endowed you with all the eminently fine qualities that she requires: you belong to another century...

Ah! If the truths of feeling are first in the order of nature, no one can communicate the feelings of our religion better than you. You will confuse the impious at the temple gate and lead the delicate minds and sensitive hearts straight to the inner sanctum. You put me in mind of those ancient philosophers who gave their lessons with their heads crowned with flowers and their hands bathed in sweet perfumes. Yet this is but a weak image of your spirit—so sweet, so pure, and so ancient.

I find myself more pleased each day by the happy circumstances that brought me close to you. I cannot forget that this kindness was done me by Fontanes, whom I love all the more for it. My heart shall never separate these two names, which should be united in the same glory, if Providence should elect to open our country's gates to us again!

Chevalier de Panat

Abbé Delille also came to hear me read several fragments of *The Genius of Christianity* in London. He seemed surprised, and he did me the honor, shortly after, of versifying the prose that had pleased him. He naturalized my wild American flowers in his various French gardens and put my rather overheated wine to cool in the frigid water of his clear spring.

The unfinished edition of *The Genius of Christianity*, begun in

London, differed a bit from the order of materials as published in France. Consular censorship, soon to become imperial censorship, showed itself to be sensitive on the subject of kings; their persons, their honor, and their virtue were dear to it a priori. Already Fouché's police saw the white pigeon, the symbol of Bonaparte's candor and Revolutionary innocence, descending from heaven with its sacred vial. The sincere believers in the Republican processions of Lyon forced me to cut out a chapter titled "The Atheist Kings" and to disperse its paragraphs here and there throughout the body of the work.

6.

MY UNCLE M. DE BEDÉE: HIS ELDEST DAUGHTER
London, April to September 1822

BEFORE going on with these literary investigations, I must interrupt them a moment to take leave of my uncle de Bedée. Alas! It is to take leave of one of the first joys of my life: *freno non remorante dies,* "no rein can curb the flight of days."[17] See the old sepulchers in the old crypts. Conquered by time, decrepit and without memory, having lost their epitaphs, they have forgotten even the names of the men they contain.

I had written to my uncle on the subject of my mother's death. He had written back a long letter, in which there were mingled some moving words of grief; but three-quarters of those double folio sheets were dedicated to my genealogy. He especially recommended that, when I returned to France, I look into the titles of the "Bedée quartering" which had been conferred on my brother. Neither exile, nor ruin, nor the massacre of his closest friends, nor the murder of Louis XVI, could alert this venerable émigré to the Revolution. For him, nothing had happened and nothing had changed; he was still in the Estates of Brittany and the Assembly of Nobles. This fixity of ideas in a man's mind is quite striking in the midst and, as it were, in the presence of the decay of his body, the flight of his years, and the loss of his relatives and friends.

On returning from exile, my uncle de Bedée retired to Dinan, where he died, six leagues from Monchoix, without having seen it again. My cousin Caroline, the eldest of my three cousins, is still alive. She was endowed with lovely dark brown eyes and a pretty waist; she could dance like La Camargo, and she believes she remembers me being secretly in love with her. She has stayed an old maid, despite the respectable proposals she received in her bygone youth. She writes me misspelled letters in which she addresses me as *tu*, calls me *Chevalier*, and reminisces about the good old days: *in illo tempore*. I reply to her in the same tone, setting aside, as she does, my age, my honors, and my fame: "Yes, *dear Caroline*, your Chevalier," and so on. At least thirty years have gone by since last we met, and Heaven be praised for that! If we ever did come to embrace each other, God knows what a figure we would cut!

Sweet, patriarchal, innocent, honorable family friendship, your century has passed! We no longer hold to the soil by a multitude of flowers, reeds, and roots; we are born and we die now one by one. The living are in a hurry to cast the dead into Eternity and free themselves from the burden of a corpse. Of the dead man's friends, a few sit by the coffin at the church, grumbling about the inconvenient interruption of their daily habits; a few others carry their devotion so far as to follow the convoy to the cemetery; but once the grave is filled, all memory is effaced. You shall never return, days of religion and tenderness, when the son died in the same house, in the same armchair beside the same hearth where his father and grandfather had died before him, surrounded, as they were, by tearful children and grandchildren gathered to receive one last paternal blessing.

Goodbye, my dear uncle! Goodbye to my mother's family, disappearing now like all the rest! Goodbye, my cousin of old—you who still love me as you loved me when we listened together to our great-aunt Boisteilleul sing about "the sparrow hawk," or when you were there in the Abbey of Nazareth to see the lifting of my nurse's vow! If you outlive me, please accept the share of gratitude and affection I bequeath you here. Do not believe the false smile forming on my lips as I speak of you. My eyes, I assure you, are filled with tears.

BOOK TWELVE

I.

ENGLISH LITERATURE—THE FADING OF THE OLD SCHOOL—HISTORIANS—POETS—CIVILIANS—SHAKESPEARE

London, April to September 1822;
Revised in February 1845

MY READINGS correlative to *The Genius of Christianity* had little by little (as I have said) led me to a more thorough consideration of English literature. When I took refuge in England in 1792, I had to reform most of the judgments that I had gathered from critics. As regards historians, Hume had a reputation as a Tory and a reactionary: he was accused, as was Gibbon, of having overburdened the English language with Gallicisms; his proponent, Smollett, was preferred. A philosopher all his life who became a Christian at his death, Gibbon remained, as such, impeached and convicted of being a no-good man. Robertson was still discussed, because he was dry.

Where poets were concerned, the *Elegant Extracts* served to introduce the exile to a few pieces by Dryden. Pope's rhymes were unpardonable, but everyone paid a visit to his house in Twickenham and cut twigs from the weeping willow which he had planted, and which was now withering, like his reputation.

Blair was regarded as a tedious critic in the French style and ranked far below Johnson. As for the old *Spectator*, it was stacked up and gathering dust in the attic.

The English political works were of little interest to us. Economic treatises were somewhat less circumscribed, since calculations of the wealth of nations, the employment of capital, and the balance of trade were equally applicable to European societies.

Burke emerged as a spokesman for the nation's politics; by declaring himself opposed to the French Revolution, he drew his country into that long campaign of hostilities which ended on the fields of Waterloo.

Still, a few great figures remained. One stumbled across Milton and Shakespeare everywhere. Did Montmorency, Biron, or Sully (by turns the ambassadors of France to Elizabeth and James I) ever hear of a strolling player who acted in his own plays and in those of others? Did they ever pronounce the name, so barbarous in French, of Shakespeare? Did they suspect that in this name there was a glory before which their honors, their pomp, and their rank would sink into insignificance? Who knows! The actor who took on the role of the ghost in *Hamlet* was the great phantom, the shade of the Middle Ages who rose over the world like a star in the night at the very moment when those ages went down among the dead: enormous centuries that Dante opened and that Shakespeare sealed.

In the *Précis historique* by Whitelock, a contemporary of the bard of *Paradise Lost*, one reads of "a certain blind man, named Milton, Latin Secretary to the Parliament." Molière, the buffoon, played Pourceaugnac, just as Shakespeare, the mountebank, pulled faces as Falstaff.

These veiled travelers who come to sit at our table from time to time are treated like common guests. We are ignorant of their real nature until the day they disappear. When they leave the earth, they are transfigured, and they say to us, as the angel said to Tobit, "I am one of the seven who stand continually in the presence of the Lord."[1] But if, in their passage, they are misunderstood by men, these divinities never misunderstand one another. "What needs my Shakespeare," Milton writes,

> for his honour'd bones,
> the labour of an age in piled stones?

Michelangelo, envying Dante's fate and genius, exclaims:

> *Pur fuss'io tal ...*
> *Per l'aspro esilio suo con sua virtute*
> *Darei del mondo più felice stato.*[2]

"Had I been such as he! For his bitter exile, together with his talent, I would give up all the happiness in the world!"

Tasso celebrated Camões when the latter was almost unknown and thereby garnered him a "reputation." Is there anything more admirable than this society of illustrious equals, revealing themselves to one another by signs, hailing one another, and conversing in a language understood by themselves alone?

Was Shakespeare lame like Lord Byron, Walter Scott, and Homer's Prayers, the daughters of Jupiter?[3] If in fact he was, the boy from Stratford was far from being ashamed of his infirmity and, like Childe Harold, was unafraid to speak of it to one of his mistresses:

> ... lame by fortune's dearest spite.[4]

Shakespeare would have had a great number of lovers if we reckoned them one per sonnet. The creator of Desdemona and Juliet grew old without losing his taste for love. Was the unnamed woman addressed in such charming verse proud or happy to be the object of Shakespeare's sonnets? One might doubt it, for an old man's fame is like an old woman's diamonds: they may adorn her, but they cannot make her pretty.

The tragic Englishman wrote his mistress:

> No longer mourn for me when I am dead:
> Then you shall hear the surly sullen bell
> Give warning to the world that I am fled
> From this vile world, with vilest worms to dwell:
> Nay, if you read this line, remember not
> The hand that writ it; for I love you so,
> That I in your sweet thoughts would be forgot,
> If thinking on me then should make you woe.
> O, if, I say, you look upon this verse,
> When I, perhaps, compounded am with clay;
> Do not so much as my poor name rehearse,
> But let your love ever with my life decay;

> Lest the wise world should look into your moan,
> And mock you with me after I am gone.[5]

Shakespeare loved, but he gave no more credence to love than to other things. A woman for him was a bird, a breeze, a flower: some charming thing that happens past. Owing to his insouciance, or to his ignorance of his fame, or to the accident of his birth, which kept him far from high society, and far from conditions he could not hope to attain, he seems to have taken life as a light and unoccupied hour—a swift, sweet leisure-time.

Shakespeare, in his youth, met with aged monks who had been driven from their cloisters, monks who had seen the reforms, the destruction of the monasteries, the fools, wives, mistresses, and headsmen of Henry VIII. When the poet left this world, Charles I was sixteen years old.

Thus, with one hand, Shakespeare could have touched the gray-haired heads threatened by the blade of the second-to-last of the Tudors; with the other, he could have touched the brown-haired head of the second of the Stuarts, which the Parliamentarian ax would fell. Leaning on these tragic brows, the great tragedian sank into the grave. He filled the interval of days when he lived with his ghosts and his blind kings, his punished pretenders and his ill-fated women, attempting, by analogous fictions, to connect the realities of the past with the realities of the future.

Shakespeare is one of five or six writers who have everything needed to nourish the mind. These mother-geniuses seem to have birthed and brought up all the others. Homer impregnated Antiquity; Aeschylus, Sophocles, Euripides, Aristophanes, Horace, and Virgil are his sons. Dante gave rise to modern Italy, from Petrarch to Tasso. Rabelais created French letters; Montaigne, La Fontaine, and Molière are his descendants. And England is all Shakespeare, even down to the latest times; he has lent his language to Byron, his dialogue to Walter Scott.

These supreme masters are often disowned. We rebel against them and tally up their faults; we accuse them of being boring, tedious,

bizarre, tasteless, and all the while we deplume them we adorn ourselves with their feathers; but we struggle in vain under their yoke.
Everything takes on their colors. Every place is imprinted with their
traces. They invented the words and the names that have gone to swell
the vocabularies of whole populations; their expressions have become
proverbs; their imagined characters have changed into real characters
with heirs and lineage. They open up horizons from which rays of
light shine forth like honey; they sow ideas that yield a thousand
others; they furnish images, subjects, and styles for every art. Their
works are the mines, or the wombs, of the human spirit.

Such geniuses occupy the first rank. Their immensity, their variety,
their fecundity, their originality: these things cause them to be regarded
from the first as laws, examples, molds, types of the various forms of
intelligence, as there are four or five races of men issuing from a single
trunk, of which the rest are merely branches. Let us beware of deni-
grating the disorder into which these mighty beings sometimes fall;
let us not imitate Ham; not laugh if we encounter, naked and asleep,
in the shadow of the ark stranded in the mountains of Armenia, the
solitary boatman of the abyss. Let us respect this diluvian navigator
who began creation anew after heaven's downpour. Pious children,
blessed by our father, let us cover him chastely with our cloak.

Shakespeare, when he lived, gave no thought to whether he would
live after death. What does my canticle of admiration matter to him
today? Making all these suppositions, examining the truth or error
with which the human mind is penetrated or imbued, what can fame
mean to Shakespeare? Its noise will never rise to his ear. If a Christian,
in the bliss of eternal happiness, would he trouble himself with the
nothingness of the world? If a Deist, free from the shades of matter,
and lost among the splendors of God, would he lower his eyes to the
grain of sand where he passed his days? If an atheist, he sleeps a sleep
without breath or reawakening, which is called death. Nothing is
more vain than glory from the other side of the grave, unless it has
given life to friendship, been useful to virtue, lent a hand to the
unfortunate—unless it be granted to us to enjoy in heaven the consol-
ing, generous, and liberating idea left by us on earth.

2.

OLD NOVELS—NEW NOVELS—RICHARDSON—WALTER SCOTT

London, April to September 1822

NOVELS, at the end of the last century, were included in the general proscription. Richardson slept forgotten; his countrymen saw traces in his style of the inferior society in the heart of which he had lived. Fielding maintained his reputation. Sterne, the impresario of originality, was passé. *The Vicar of Wakefield* was still read.

If Richardson lacks style (which we foreigners are in no position to judge), he will not survive, for we live only by means of style. It is useless to rebel against this truth: the best-composed work, adorned with verisimilar description and filled with a thousand other perfections, is stillborn without style. Style, and there are a thousand kinds, is not to be learned; it is a gift from heaven; it is talent itself. But if Richardson has been abandoned merely because of certain bourgeois turns of phrase, intolerable to elegant society, he may live again. The Revolution underway, by abasing the aristocracy and lifting up the middle classes, will make the traces of household customs and inferior language less remarkable, or make them disappear.

From *Clarissa* and *Tom Jones* sprang the two principal branches of the family of modern English novels: the novels of family life and domestic drama, and the novels of adventure and social description. With Richardson, the manners of the West End erupted into fiction's domain: novels were suddenly full of castles, Lords and Ladies, water-parties, adventures on the race-course, at balls, at the opera, and at Ranelagh, complete with plenty of "chit-chat" and endless prattle. It was never long before the scene shifted to Italy, where lovers crossed the Alps amid dreadful perils and sorrows of the soul fit to melt the heart of a lion. "A lion would shed tears!" was common parlance in good society.

Among the thousands of novels that have flooded England for half a century, two have held their ground: *Caleb Williams* and *The Monk*. I never did meet Godwin during my exile in London, but I saw Lewis twice. He was then a young member of Parliament, an amiable man with the look and manners of a Frenchman. The works of Anne Radcliffe were a type unto themselves. Those of Mrs. Barbauld, Miss Edgeworth, Miss Burney, and so on, have, as they say, a chance of survival. "There ought to be laws," Montaigne says, "against inept and useless *scribblers*, as there are against vagabonds and idlers. They should ban the use of people's hands, including mine and a hundred others. Scribbling seems to be a symptom of an inundated age."[6]

But these diverse schools of sedentary novelists, novelists traveling by stagecoach or carriage, novelists of lakes and mountains, of ruins and ghosts, cities and drawing rooms, have all been lost in the new school of Walter Scott, just as poetry has hurried to follow in the footsteps of Lord Byron.

The illustrious Scots writer made his debut in the theater of letters, during my exile in London, with a translation of Goethe's *Götz von Berlichingen*. He went on to make his name as a poet, and the bent of his genius finally led him to the novel. It seems to me that he created a false genre, perverting novel and history alike, so that novelists are trying now to write historical novels and historians are novelizing their histories. If, in Walter Scott, I sometimes have to pass over the interminable conversations, no doubt it is my own fault; but, in my eyes, one of Walter Scott's great merits is that everyone can read him. It demands much greater efforts of talent to interest the reader by keeping within limits than to please him by exceeding all measure; it is more difficult to regulate the heart than to disturb it.

Burke may have rooted English politics in the past, but Walter Scott pushed the English back to the Middle Ages. Everything that he wrote, made, and built was Gothic: books, furniture, churches, castles. But the lords of the Magna Carta are today the "fashionables" of Bond Street: a frivolous tribe pitching camp in ancient manors, awaiting the arrival of the new generations who are preparing to drive them out.

3.

RECENT POETRY—BEATTIE

London, April to September 1822

AT THE same time that the novel was becoming "romantic," poetry was undergoing a similar transformation. Cowper abandoned the French school and revived the national school; Burns started a similar revolution in Scotland. After them came the restorers of the ballads. Several of these poets of 1792 to 1800 belonged to what was called the "Lake School" (the name has survived) because these romantics dwelled on the lakeshores of Cumberland and Westmoreland, and they sang of them sometimes.

Thomas Moore, Campbell, Rogers, Crabbe, Wordsworth, Southey, Hunt, Knowles, Lord Holland, Canning, and Croker are still alive, to the honor of English letters; but a man must be born English to appreciate the merit of such an intimate style of composition, which comes home particularly to natives of the soil.

No one, in a living literature, can be a competent judge except of works written in his own language. It is vain to believe you possess a foreign idiom in all its depths. You did not swallow it with your nurse's milk; you did not hear the first words of it at her breast, and taste them on your tongue. Certain accents belong only to the homeland. About our men of letters, the English and the Germans have the most baroque notions: they adore what we scorn and scorn what we adore. They do not understand Racine, or La Fontaine, or even most of Molière. It makes one laugh to learn the names of our great writers in London, Vienna, Berlin, Petersburg, Munich, Leipzig,

Göttingen, and Cologne—to learn whom they read with fervor and whom they do not read at all.

When an author's chief merit is his diction, a foreigner will never fully comprehend this merit. The more intimate, individual, and national a talent, the more its mysteries escape the mind which is not, so to speak, a "compatriot" of this talent. We admire the Greeks and Romans by hearsay. Our admiration comes to us from tradition, and the Greeks and Romans are not here to mock our Barbarian judgments. Who among us can form any idea of the harmonies of Demosthenes or Cicero, the cadences of Alcaeus or Horace, as they must have sounded to a Greek or Latin ear? It has been claimed that true beauty is for all time and all countries: yes, if we are speaking of the beauties of feeling and thought, but no, not the beauties of style. Style is not, like thought, cosmopolitan: it has a native soil, sky, and sun of its own.

Burns, Mason, and Cowper died during my London exile, either before or in the year 1800. They ended one century, and I began another. Erasmus Darwin and Beattie died two years after my return from exile.

Beattie had heralded the new era of lyric poetry. *The Minstrel; or, The Progress of Genius* is a description of the Muse's earliest effects on a young bard who is still ignorant of the breath that torments him. Sometimes, the future poet goes to sit by the seashore during a tempest; sometimes, he leaves the games of the village behind him to listen, lonesomely, to the music of the bagpipes in the distance.

Beattie has gone through the whole series of reveries and melancholy ideas of which a hundred other poets have believed themselves "discoverers." He was planning to continue with his poem and in fact wrote a second canto. One evening Edwin hears a solemn voice issuing from the depths of a valley. It is the voice of a hermit who, having comprehended the illusions of the world, has buried himself in this retreat in order to collect his thoughts and sing the wonders of the Creator. The hermit instructs the young minstrel and reveals the secret of his genius to him. The idea was a happy one, but the execution wasn't quite equal to the idea. Beattie was destined to shed tears; his son's death broke his heart. Like Ossian after the loss of Oscar, Beattie hung up his harp in the branches of an oak. Perhaps Beattie's son was that young minstrel of whom the father had sung and whose footsteps he no longer saw on the mountain.

4 ·
LORD BYRON

London, April to September 1822

ONE FINDS striking imitations of *The Minstrel* in Lord Byron's verse. At the time of my exile in England, Lord Byron was still in school at Harrow, a village ten miles from London. He was a child, and I was young and as unknown as he; he was brought up on the moors of Scotland, beside the sea, as I was brought up on the heaths of Brittany, beside the sea; he loved the Bible and Ossian as I loved them; he sang his childhood memories in Newstead Abbey as I sang of my childhood memories in the Château de Combourg.

> When I rov'd a young Highlander o'er the dark heath,
>   And climb'd thy steep summit, oh Morven of snow!
> To gaze on the torrent that thunder'd beneath,
>   Or the mist of the tempest that gather'd below…

On my walks around the city of London, when I was so miserably poor, I passed through the village of Harrow twenty times without knowing what genius it contained. I sat in the graveyard at the foot of the elm under which, in 1807, at the moment I was returning from Palestine, Lord Byron was writing these verses:

> Spot of my youth! whose hoary branches sigh,
> Swept by the breeze that fans thy cloudless sky;
> Where now alone I muse, who oft have trod,
> With those I loved, thy soft and verdant sod
>
> . . . .

When fate shall chill, at length, this fevered breast,
And calm its cares and passions into rest

. . . .

And here it lingered, here my heart might lie;
Here might I sleep, where all my hopes arose

. . . .

Blest by the tongues that charmed my youthful ear,
Mourned by the few my soul acknowledged here;
Deplored by those in early days allied,
And unremember'd by the world beside.

And I say: *Hail! ancient elm*, at whose foot Byron abandoned himself to the whims of his youth, as I had dreamed of *René* under that same elm's shade, and where the poet, a few years later, came to dream of *Childe Harold*! Byron asked of this graveyard, the witness of his first childhood games, a humble grave—a useless request that fame denied him. Yet Byron is no longer what he used to be. When I first visited Venice, I had discovered him everywhere; a few years later, in this same city, I found his name blotted from memory and everywhere unknown. The echoes of the Lido no longer resounded with it, and if you ask the Venetians now, they have no idea whom you mean. Lord Byron is entirely dead for them; they no longer hear the neighing of his horse. It is the same in London, where his memory is fading fast. This is what becomes of us.

If I went to Harrow without knowing that the child Lord Byron breathed the air, so an Englishman went to Combourg without suspecting that a little vagabond, perched up in those woods, would ever leave a trace behind him. The traveler Arthur Young, passing through Combourg, wrote:

To Combourg, the country has a savage aspect, husbandry not much further advanced, at least in skill, than among the Hurons, which appears incredible amidst inclosures; the people almost as wild as their country, and their town of Combourg one of the most brutal, filthy places that can be seen; mud houses, no windows, and a pavement so broken as to impede all passengers, but ease none. Yet here is a château, and inhabited; who is this M. de Chateaubriand, the owner, that has nerves strung for a residence amongst such filth and poverty? Below this hideous heap of wretchedness is a fine lake, surrounded by well-wooded inclosures.[7]

This M. de Chateaubriand was my father. The retreat that seemed so hideous to the ill-humored agriculturalist was nonetheless a fine and noble dwelling, albeit somewhat somber and grave. As for me, I was but a feeble stalk of ivy just beginning to climb the foot of those savage towers. How could Mr. Young have seen me, occupied as he was with his review of our harvests?

Here let me add to these pages written in England in 1822 the following pages written in 1834 and 1840: they complete this fragment on Lord Byron, or rather this fragment which will be more complete if the reader seeks out what I have said about the great poet when I passed through Venice.

There may be, perhaps, some interest in commenting later on the affinities between the two leaders of the new French and English schools, who have a similar fund of ideas, and similar destinies, although slightly less similar morals and manners. One was a Peer of England, the other a Peer of France; both travelers in the Orient; often close to one another without ever having seen each other. Only the life of the English poet was mixed up in events of far less importance than mine.

Lord Byron went to visit the ruins of Greeks years after me. In *Childe Harold*, he seems to embellish my descriptions in the *Itinerary* with his own colors. At the start of my pilgrimage, I reproduced Sire de Joinville's farewell to his castle; Byron addressed a similar farewell to his Gothic abode.

In *The Martyrs*, Eudore sets out from Messenia to go to Rome. "Our voyage was long," he says; "we saw all the promontories marked by temples or tombs.... My young companions had never heard of the metamorphoses of Jupiter and understood nothing of the ruins before their eyes. Alone, I had already sat with the Prophet, on the ruins of desolate cities, and Babylon taught me the fate of Corinth."

The English poet, like the French prose writer, follows Sulpicius's letter to Cicero. Such a perfect affinity is, to my mind, singularly glorious, since I preceded the immortal bard on the shores where both of us cherished the same memories and commemorated the same ruins.

I have the further honor of being in accord with Lord Byron in my description of Rome: *The Martyrs* and my *Letter on the Roman Countryside* have, for me, the inestimable virtue of having anticipated the inspirations of a great genius.

Lord Byron's first translators, commentators, and admirers have been careful not to mention certain pages of mine which may have lingered a moment in the memory of the author of *Childe Harold*; they may have thought that mentioning them would subtract something from Byron's genius. Now that enthusiasm has calmed a bit, they do not refuse me this honor. Our immortal songster, Béranger, in the last volume of his *Chansons*, has said: "In one of the foregoing stanzas, I speak of the 'lyres' that France owes M. de Chateaubriand. I have no fear of this being disputed by the new poetic school, which, being born under the wings of the eagle, has often, and for good reason, gloried in such an origin. The influence of the author of *The Genius of Christianity* has also made itself felt abroad, and it would perhaps be just to recognize that the bard of *Childe Harold* belongs to the family of *René*."

In an excellent article on Lord Byron, M. Villemain has repeated Béranger's observation. "A few incomparable pages of *René*," he says, "had, it is true, already exhausted this poetical character. I know not whether Byron imitated them, or reproduced them by his own genius."

Whatever I say here about the affinities of imagination and destiny that subsist between the chronicler of *René* and the poet of *Childe Harold* does not pluck a single hair from the immortal bard's head. How could my pedestrian, luteless muse hold a candle to the Muse of the River Dee, with its lyre and its wings? Lord Byron will survive, whether or not he, as a child of his century like me, has expressed its passions and its sadness, like Goethe before us; whether or not the rhumb and rushlight of my Gaulish barque showed the ship from Albion the way over uncharted seas.

Besides, two minds of a similar nature may very well have analogous ideas without there being any reason to reproach one of having marched obsequiously behind the other. It is permissible to profit from ideas and images expressed in a foreign tongue in order to enrich our own: this has been the case in every century and every era. I am the first to admit that in my early youth Ossian, *Werther*, *Les Rêveries d'un Promeneur Solitaire*, and *Les Études de la Nature* may have aligned themselves with my ideas; but I have hidden nothing, concealed nothing of the pleasure given me by these works in which I delighted.

If it were true that *René* helped form the basis of that single character introduced under the various names of Childe Harold, Conrad, Lara, Manfred, and the Giaour; if, by chance, Lord Byron had given me life by his own, would he then have had the weakness never to name me? Was I one of those fathers whom a man disowns as soon as he has come to power? Can Lord Byron have been completely unaware of me, when he quotes almost every other contemporary French author? Did he never hear of me, when the English papers, like the French papers, had for twenty years been rife with the controversies surrounding my work—when even the *New Times* drew a parallel between the author of *The Genius of Christianity* and the author of *Childe Harold*?

No mind, however favored it may be, is without susceptibilities and suspicions. One man wants to hold onto the scepter; another fears sharing it; still another is irritated by all comparisons. So it was that another superior talent omitted my name in her work on *Literature*.[8] Thank God, I have valued myself for what I'm worth, and never laid claim to absolute power. As I believe in nothing except religious truth, of which freedom is one form, I have no more faith in myself than in anything else here below. But I have never felt the need to keep silent when I have admired something, and that is why I proclaim my enthusiasm for both Madame de Staël and Byron.

What is sweeter than admiration? It is heavenly love; it is affection raised to adoration. We feel ourselves filled with gratitude for the divinity who thus extends the roots of our intelligence, who opens up new vistas for our soul to contemplate, who grants us a happiness so great and so pure that it is without any taint of fear or envy.

In the end, the little dispute I have in these *Memoirs* with the greatest poet England has produced since Milton proves only one thing: the high value I would have attached to being remembered by his muse.

Lord Byron has opened the doors to a deplorable school: I assume that he is as distressed by all the Childe Harolds to whom he has given birth as I am by all the Renés that I find daydreaming around me.

His life has been the subject of much investigation and defamation. Young men have taken his magic words seriously; women have felt disposed to letting themselves be fearfully seduced by this "monster," to console this lonely and unhappy Satan. Who knows? Perhaps he could never find the woman he sought, a woman beautiful enough, with a heart as vast as his own. Byron, according to the phantasmagoria of public opinion, is the ancient serpent of the Garden, a seducer, and a corrupter, because he sees the corruption of the human race. He is a doomed and suffering genius, seated between the mysteries of matter and the mysteries of mind, who discovers no word for the enigma of the universe, and who regards life as nothing more than a terrible irony without cause, like a perverse smile of evil. He is the son of despair who despises and denies, who, bearing within him an incurable wound, takes vengeance by leading everyone who comes near him through hedonism to sorrow. He is a man who has never passed through the age of innocence, who has never had the privilege to be rejected and cursed by God—a man who, having come forth debauched from nature's womb, is the damned soul of nothingness itself.

Such is the Byron imagined by heated imaginations: he is by no means, to my mind, the Byron of reality.

Two different beings, as it is with most men, are joined in Lord Byron: the man of *nature* and the man of *structure*. The poet, seeing the role that the public gave him to play, accepted it and began cursing the world which at first he had only viewed dreamily. This progression is evident in the chronological order of his works. His genius, far from having the range attributed to it, is rather modest; his poetical thought is no more than a groan, a lament, an imprecation. In this capacity, however, it is admirable. One should not ask the lyre what it thinks, but what it sings. As for his wit, it is sarcastic and uneven, but of a troubled nature and a deadly influence: the writer has read Voltaire, and he imitates him.

Lord Byron, endowed with every advantage, had little reason to reproach his birth. The same accident that made him unhappy and linked his lofty superiorities to human infirmity should not have tormented him, since it did not prevent him from being loved. The immortal bard knew, from his own experience, the truth of Zeno's maxim: "The voice is the flower of beauty."[9]

A deplorable thing is the rapidity with which reputations crumble these days. After a few years—what am I saying? After a few months, infatuation disappears and denigration ensues. Already Lord Byron's glory has grown pale; his genius is better understood among us: his altars will stand longer in France than in England. As *Childe Harold* excels chiefly by describing sentiments particular to the individual, the English, who prefer sentiments common to all, will end by washing their hands of a poet whose cry is so heartfelt and so sad. They should be wary: if they shatter the image of the man who has given them new life, what will remain to them?

When I was noting down my feelings about Lord Byron, during my sojourn in London in 1822, the man had only two years left to live. He died in 1824, when the wave of disenchantment and disgust was about to rise against him. I preceded him in life; he has preceded me in death. He was summoned before his turn. My number was ahead of his, yet his was called first. *Childe Harold* ought to have stayed; the world could lose me without noticing my disappearance. I have met, as I continue on my way, Madame Guiccioli in Rome and Lady Byron in Paris. Frailty and virtue thus appeared to me: the first had perhaps too much substance; the second, too few dreams.

5.

ENGLAND, FROM RICHMOND TO GREENWICH—A
TRIP WITH PELLETIER—BLEINHEIM—STOWE—
HAMPTON COURT—OXFORD—ETON—MANNERS,
PRIVATE AND POLITICAL—FOX—PITT—BURKE—
GEORGE III

London, April to September 1822

NOW THAT I have yammered on to you about English writers at
the time when England gave me asylum, there is nothing left but to
say something of England itself at that time, something of its appearance, its sites, its houses, its private and political manners.

The whole of England can be seen in the space of four leagues,
from Richmond, above London, down to Greenwich and below.

Below London is industrial and commercial England, with its
docks, warehouses, customhouses, arsenals, breweries, factories,
foundries, and ships. At each tide, these ships sail up the Thames in
three divisions: first the smallest, then the middle-sized, and lastly,
the great vessels so large that their sails graze the columns of the Old
Sailors Home and the tavern where foreigners dine.

Above London is agricultural and pastoral England, with its
meadows, herds, country houses, and parks, where the waters of the
Thames, driven back by the tide, bathe the shrubs and grasses twice
a day. In the middle of these two opposing points, Richmond and
Greenwich, London mixes all of this double England together: the
aristocracy to the West, the democracy to the East, the Tower of
London and Westminster, boundaries between which the whole
history of Great Britain has taken place.

I spent part of the summer of 1799 in Richmond with Christian
de Lamoignon, occupying myself with *The Genius of Christianity*. I
went out in a rowboat on the Thames or for walks in Richmond Park.
I might well have wished that Richmond-near-London were the

Richmond of the treaty *Honor Richemundiae*, for then I would have found myself in my native land, and here's how: William the Bastard made a present to his son-in-law Alain, a duke of Brittany, of four hundred and forty-two English lordships, which would later form the County of Richmond.* The Dukes of Brittany, Alain's successors, enfeoffed these lordships to a few Breton knights, the younger sons of the families of Rohan, Tinteniac, Chateaubriand, Goyon, and Montboucher. But, despite my goodwill, I have to look in Yorkshire for the County of Richmond established as a Duchy of Brittany by Charles II for the benefit of his bastard son: Richmond on the Thames was formerly the town of Sheen.

It was there, in 1377, that Edward III died after being robbed by his mistress, Alice Pearce; not the same Alice, or Catherine, of Salisbury,[10] from the days when the victor of Crécy was young: you should not love at an age when you can no longer be loved. Henry VIII and Elizabeth also died in Richmond; but then, where can one not die? Henry took pleasure in this residence. English historians are quite embarrassed by this abominable man. On one hand, they cannot disguise his tyranny or the servility of the Parliament; on the other, if they were to speak too harshly against the leader of the Reformation, they would condemn themselves by condemning him:

The viler the oppressor, the viler the slave.[11]

You can still see the hill in Richmond Park that served Henry VIII as an observatory when he watched for news of Anne Boleyn's execution. Henry must have shivered with pleasure when the signal was fired from the Tower of London. What delectation! To think of the ax cutting through the woman's fragile neck, bloodying the lovely hair that the poet-king had only recently clasped in his fatal embrace.

Alone in empty Richmond Park, I awaited no homicidal signals

* See the *Domesday Book*.

and would not even have wished the slightest harm on whomever might have betrayed me. I took my strolls with a few peaceful deer. They were accustomed to running before a pack of hounds, stopping when they were tired, and then being carried back, quite cheerful and well pleased by the game, in a cart filled with straw. Several times, I went to Kew Gardens to see the kangaroos, ridiculous creatures, just the inverse of giraffes. These innocent quadruped-hoppers must have peopled Australia better than the old Duke of Queensbury's prostitutes peopled the backstreets of Richmond. The Thames here bordered the lawn of a cottage, half hidden beneath a Lebanese cedar and among the weeping willows: a newly married couple had come to spend their honeymoon in this paradise.

One evening, as I was strolling quietly over the swards of Twickenham, Pelletier appeared out of nowhere, holding his handkerchief over his mouth: "What perpetual miscreant fog!" he cried, as soon as he was in earshot. "How in hell can you stay out here? Look, I have drawn up a list: Stowe, Blenheim, Hampton Court, Oxford. You go around drunk on dreams: you would live here in John Bull's land *in vitam aeternam* and see *nothing*."

I begged in vain to be excused, but I had to go. In the carriage, Pelletier enumerated his hopes to me. He had relays of hopes. If one died under him, he bestrode another, and so on, one leg here, one leg there, until the end of his days. One of his hopes, the most robust of them, eventually led him to Bonaparte, whom he took by the collar: Napoleon had the naiveté to cross swords with him. Pelletier had James Mackintosh as a second. Condemned before the tribunals, he made a new fortune (which he squandered directly) by selling the narrative of his trial.

Blenheim was odious to me. I found it the more painful to be reminded of my country's old defeat because I had recently suffered a personal affront. A boat rowing up the Thames caught sight of me on shore, and the oarsmen, perceiving that I was French, began huzzahing. News of the naval battle at Aboukir had just reached town. These foreign successes, though they reopened the gates of France to me, were nonetheless odious in my eyes. Admiral Nelson, whom I had seen several times in Hyde Park, dragged his victories to Naples in Lady Hamilton's shawl, while the *lazzaroni* played boules with human heads. Nelson died gloriously at Trafalgar; his mistress died miserably in Calais, having lost her beauty, her youth, and her fortune. And I, so outraged on the Thames by the English triumph of Aboukir, have seen the palm trees of Libya beside the calm and vacant sea that once was reddened by my countrymen's blood.

The park in Stowe is famous for its buildings; but I prefer its shade. The cicerone of the place showed us, in a shadowy ravine, a copy of an Eastern temple whose original I would later admire in the bright valley of the Cephissus. A few lovely pictures done by the Italian school were pining away at the back of some uninhabited rooms where the shutters were always closed: poor Raphael, a prisoner in an old English castle, far from the sky of the Villa Farnesina!

Hampton Court still had its collection of portraits of Charles II's mistresses: this was how the prince had done things after escaping a revolution that had felled his father's head and that was destined to banish his race.

We went to Slough, where Herschel lived with his learned sister and his forty-foot telescope. He was looking for new planets; this made Pelletier, who held fast to the seven old ones, quite amused.

We stopped for two days in Oxford. I enjoyed my time in that republic of Alfred the Great; it represented, to my mind, the privileged freedoms and manners of literary institutions of the Middle Ages. We combed through the twenty-five colleges, the libraries, the museum, and the botanical garden. Among the manuscripts of Worcester College, I leafed through the pages of a life of the Black Prince, written in French verse by the Prince's herald, with the utmost pleasure.

Oxford did not resemble the modest schools of Dol, Rennes, or Dinan, but it recalled them to my memory. I had translated Gray's "Elegy Written in a Country Churchyard."

The curfew tolls the knell of parting day,

An imitation of these lines by Dante:

> ... *squilla di lontano,*
> *Che paia 'l giorno pianger che si more*[12]

Pelletier had hastened to publish my translation in his paper. Now, at the sight of Oxford, I remembered the same poet's "Ode on a Distant Prospect of Eton College":

> Ah, happy hills, ah, pleasing shade,
>   Ah, fields beloved in vain,
> Where once my careless childhood strayed,
>   A stranger yet to pain!
> I feel the gales that from ye blow,
> A momentary bliss bestow,
>   As waving fresh their gladsome wing,
> My weary soul they seem to soothe,
> And, redolent of joy and youth,
>   To breathe a second spring.
>
> Say, Father Thames ...
> . . . .
> What idle progeny succeed
> To chase the rolling circle's speed,
>   Or urge the flying ball?
> . . . .
> Alas, regardless of their doom,
>   The little victims play!
> No sense have they of ills to come,
>   Nor care beyond to-day.

Who has not experienced the feelings and regrets expressed here with all the sweetness of the Muse? Who has not been moved by the re-membrance of the games, the studies, and the loves of past years? But can we bring them back to life? The pleasures of youth reproduced by memory are like ruins seen by torchlight.

THE PRIVATE LIFE OF THE ENGLISH

Separated from the Continent by a long war, the English still preserved, at the last century's end, their national character and manners. They were still a people, in whose name an aristocratic government exercised authority. Only two great classes existed, amiably united by common interests: the patrons and the clients. The jealous class which is called the "bourgeoisie" in France, and which has since begun to develop in England, did not yet exist. Nothing came between the rich landowners and the men who lived by their labor. All was not yet machinery in the manufacturing professions or folly in the privileged ranks. On the same sidewalks where today you see nothing but filthy faces and men in frockcoats, there used to be little girls in white cloaks, straw hats tied under their chins with ribbon, carrying a basket in which there were fruits or a book. They all kept their eyes lowered and blushed when anyone looked at them. "England," says Shakespeare, "is a nest of swans amid the waters."[13] Frockcoats were so rarely worn in the London of 1793 that a woman, weeping hot tears over the death of Louis XVI, paused to ask me, "But, my dear sir, is it true that the poor King was dressed in a *frockcoat* when he was beheaded?"

The "gentleman farmers" had not yet sold their patrimonies to take up residence in London. They still formed an independent faction in the House of Commons that, sometimes supporting the opposition and other times the government, maintained the ideas of liberty, order, and propriety. They hunted foxes and pheasants in the autumn, ate fatted geese at Christmas, shouted *vivat roast beef,* groused about the present, aggrandized the past, cursed Pitt and the war (which had raised the price of port wine), and went to bed drunk to start this same life again the next day. They were sure that the glory of Great Britain would never fade so long as they sang "God Save the King," so long as the rottener boroughs were kept in check, so long as the game laws were enforced, so long as they were allowed to go on surreptitiously selling hares and partridges to the markets under the name of "lions" and "ostriches."

The Anglican clergy were erudite, hospitable, and generous. They had received the French clergy with a charity worthy of Christians. Oxford University had printed, and freely distributed copies to foreign priests, of a New Testament according to the Roman Catholic text, with these words on the title page: *A l'usage du clergé catholique exilé pour la Religion*. As for English high society, I was a wretched exile and saw it only from the outside. When there were receptions at Court or in the drawing rooms of the Prince of Wales, ladies went past me seated sideways in sedan chairs, their enormous hoops projecting from the doors like the cloth-hangings of an altar. The ladies, seated on their petticoat altars, looked like Madonnas or pagodas. These fair women were the daughters of others just as fair, whom the Duc de Guiche and the Duc de Lauzun once worshipped; the same daughters who are today, in 1822, the mothers and grandmothers of the little girls who dance across my floor in short dresses, to the sound of Collinet's flute—another swiftly passing generation of flowers.

THE POLITICAL LIFE OF THE ENGLISH

Toward the end of the last century, the England of 1688 was at the height of its glory. A poor émigré living in London from 1792 to 1800, I listened to the speeches of Pitt, Fox, Sheridan, Wilberforce, Grenville, Whitebread, Lauderdale, and Erskine. A magnificent ambassador in London today, in 1822, I cannot begin to say how shocked I am when, instead of the great orators that I used to admire, I see men rising to the podium who were once their subordinates. The students are truly taking the place of the masters. *Public* ideas have penetrated this formerly *private* society. But the enlightened aristocracy that stood at the helm of English affairs for a hundred and forty years showed the world one of the finest and greatest societies to have honored mankind since the Roman patriciate. Perhaps some old family in the depths of one of the English counties will recognize the society I have just described, and will mourn the times whose loss I am here lamenting.

In 1792, Mr. Burke cut ties with Mr. Fox. The cause was the French Revolution, which Mr. Burke attacked and Mr. Fox defended. Never had the two orators, who were until then the best of friends, deployed such eloquence. The whole House was moved, and Fox's eyes were wet, when Mr. Burke recapitulated the political questions upon which he had differed with "the right honorable gentleman" on former occasions, and concluded with these words: "The right honorable gentleman, in the speech which he has just made, has treated me in every sentence with uncommon harshness. He has brought down the whole strength and heavy artillery of his judgment, eloquence, and abilities upon me, to crush me at once by a censure upon my whole life, conduct, and opinions. Notwithstanding this great and serious, though on my part unmerited, attack and attempt to crush me, I will not be dismayed. I am not yet afraid to state my sentiments in this House or anywhere else, and I will tell all the world that the constitution is in danger. It certainly is an indiscretion at any period, but especially at my time of life, to provoke enemies, or give my friends occasion to desert me; yet, if my firm and steady adherence to the British constitution placed me in such a dilemma, I will risk all; and, as public duty and public prudence teach me, with my last words exclaim, *Fly from the French Constitution!*"[14]

Mr. Fox having whispered that *there was no loss of friendship*, Burke cried out: "Yes, I regret to say there is. I know the price of my line of conduct: *I have done my duty at the price of my friend; our friendship is at an end*. I would warn the right honourable gentlemen who were the great rivals in that House, that whether they should in future move in the political hemisphere as two flaming meteors, or walk together as brethren, that they should preserve and cherish the British constitution; that they should guard against innovation, and save it *from the danger of these new theories*." A memorable epoch of the world!

Mr. Burke, whom I knew toward the end of his life, was overwhelmed with grief after the death of his only son. He had founded a school dedicated to the children of impoverished émigrés. I went to see what he called his "nursery." He was pleased by the vivacity of this foreign race growing up under his paternal genius. Watching the carefree little exiles hopping about, he said to me, "Our boys could not do that," and his eyes were wet with tears. No doubt he was thinking of his own son, gone into a longer exile.

Pitt, Fox, and Burke are no more, and the English Constitution has suffered the influence of the "new theories." One would need to have experienced the seriousness of the old Parliamentary debates, to have heard those orators whose prophetic voices seemed to proclaim an impending revolution, in order to form an idea of the scenes I recall. Liberty, contained within the limits of order, seemed to do battle at Westminster under the influence of anarchical liberty, which spoke to a rostrum still bloody from the Convention.

Mr. Pitt was tall and thin, and wore a sadly sneering expression. His speech was cold, his intonation monotonous, his gestures spiritless. Yet the lucidity and fluidity of his thought, together with the logic of his arguments, which would suddenly be lit by flashes of eloquence, made him somehow extraordinary.

I saw Mr. Pitt fairly often, as he went on foot across St. James's Park from his house to the King's palace. George III, for his part, had perhaps just come home from Windsor, where he had drunk beer from a pewter pot with the local farmers: he would cross the ugly court of his ugly palace in a gray carriage, followed by a scattering of equestrian guards. This was the master of the Kings of Europe, in the sense that five or six city merchants are the masters of India. Mr. Pitt, dressed all in black, with a steel-hilted sword at his side and a hat beneath his arm, would climb the stairs, taking two or three steps at a time. Along his way he found only three or four idling émigrés: favoring us with a disdainful gaze, he walked on, with his nose in the air, and his face very pale.

This great financier kept no order at home: he had no regular hours for meals or sleep. Riddled with debts, he repaid nothing and could never bring himself to draw up a memorandum of the sum owed. A footman ran his house. Badly dressed, without passions or pleasures, avid only for power, he held honorifics in contempt and wished to be called nothing but "William Pitt."

Lord Liverpool, in the month of June 1822, took me to dine at his country house. As we crossed Putney Heath, he pointed out to me the tiny house where the son of the Earl of Chatham, the statesman who had all of Europe on his balances and who distributed all the earth's billions with his own hands, died insolvent.

George III outlived Mr. Pitt, but he had lost his reason and his sight. At the opening of each session of Parliament, the ministers read out a Report on the King's Health to the silent and commiserating members. One day, I went to visit Windsor. For a few shillings I obtained the obliging services of a doorman who hid me so that I could see the King. The monarch appeared, white-haired and blind, wandering his palace like King Lear, groping his way along the walls of the rooms. He sat down before an old piano, whose place he knew, and played a few fragments of a sonata by Handel. It was a beautiful end to *Old England*!

6.

THE ÉMIGRÉS RETURN TO FRANCE—THE PRUSSIAN
MINISTRY ISSUES ME A FALSE PASSPORT UNDER
THE NAME "LASSAGNE" OF NEUFCHÂTEL,
SWITZERLAND—THE CLOSE OF MY CAREER AS A
SOLDIER AND A TRAVELER—I SAIL FOR CALAIS

London, April to September 1822

I WAS BEGINNING to turn my eyes toward my native land. A great revolution had taken place. Bonaparte, become First Consul, was restoring order through despotism. Many exiles were returning. The wealthy émigrés especially wasted no time in going home to gather up the debris of their fortunes: loyalty was dying at the head, while its heart went on beating in the breasts of a few half-naked provincial gentlemen. Mrs. Lindsay had gone. She wrote to Messrs. de Lamoignon, urging them to return, and she invited their sister, Madame d'Aguesseau, to cross the Channel. Fontanes appealed to me to finish the printing of *The Genius of Christianity* in Paris. Although I remembered my country, I felt no desire to see it again: gods more powerful than the paternal *lares* held me back. I no longer had possessions or a place to live in France. The country had become for me a stone bosom, a breast without milk. I would not find my mother there, or my brother, or my sister Julie. Lucile was still alive, but she had married M. de Caud and no longer shared my name. My young "widow" knew me only through a union of a few months and through the unhappiness and absence of eight years.

Had it been left up to me alone, I do not think I would have had the strength to leave; but I saw my little circle dissolving around me. When Madame d'Aguesseau offered to take me to Paris, I let myself go. The Prussian Minister procured me a false passport under the name of Lassagne, an inhabitant of Neufchâtel. Messrs. Dulau interrupted the pressing of *The Genius of Christianity* and gave me the sheets that had already been composed. I removed the sketches of *Atala* and *René* from *The Natchez*, locked the rest of the manuscript in a trunk which I entrusted to the care of my hosts in London,[15] and set out for Dover with Madame d'Aguesseau: Mrs. Lindsay would be waiting for us in Calais.

That was how I went away from England in 1800. My heart was taken up with different things than it is now, as I write these words, in 1822. I brought back nothing from the land of exile but regrets and dreams. Today my head reels with scenes of ambition, politics, grandeur, and royal courts: it is all so unbecoming to my nature. How many events have heaped up in my present existence! Pass on, men, pass on; my turn is coming. I have unfolded only a third of my story before your eyes. If the sufferings that I have endured weighed on my springtime serenity, now, as I enter a more fruitful age, the germ of *René* is about to develop and another kind of bitterness will be blended in my tale. What shall I not have to say when I speak of my country and her revolutions, which I have already begun to sketch; of the Empire and the giant man whose fall I have witnessed; of that Restoration in which I played such a part, so glorious today in 1822, but which I nevertheless seem to see only through a funereal mist?

I end this book here, having brought myself up to the spring of 1800. Having arrived at the close of my first career, *the career of a writer* is opening before me. Having been a private man, I am about to become a public man; I am leaving the hushed and virginal refuge of solitude for the dirt and clamor of the world, and broad daylight is going to illuminate my dreamy life with light enough to penetrate a kingdom of shadows. I cast a tender glance over these books that contain my immemorial hours. I seem to be saying a last goodbye to my father's house, abandoning the thoughts and illusions of my youth like sisters or sweethearts whom I leave beside the family hearth and shall never see again.

We took four hours going from Dover to Calais. I slipped into my country under cover of a foreign name. Doubly hidden beneath the obscurity of the Swiss Lassagne and my own obscurity, I landed in France with the century.

TRANSLATOR'S ACKNOWLEDGMENTS

WHAT YOU have in your hands is the first of the four parts of François-René de Chateaubriand's *Mémoires d'Outre-Tombe*—a behemoth of history, mythography, and autobiography which, in the two-volume Pléiade edition of 1946, runs to over two thousand pages.

This edition, annotated by Maurice Levaillant and Georges Moulinier, was my first source, though I have also consulted the text and notes of the Flammarion edition (1982) compiled by Levaillant, the Gallimard Quarto edition (1997) compiled by Jean-Paul Clément, and the G.P. Putnam edition of 1903, translated into English by Alexander Teixeira de Mattos, with annotations by Teixeira de Mattos and Edmond Biré.

As a reader, I owe a great debt to Paul Auster, whose novel *The Book of Illusions* first introduced me to Chateaubriand. As a translator, I am especially grateful to Rosanna Warren, Edwin Frank, William Boyle, Jane Eblen Keller, and my father, Stevan Edward Shakespeare. Their encouragement has meant the world to me.

My deepest thanks go to Oona, who has listened to every word.

—A.A.

NOTES

PREFACE

1. In Latin, in Chateaubriand's hand: "*Sicut nubes... quasi naves... velut umbra.*" These three quotations are from three non-consecutive chapters of the Book of Job, 30:15 ("Terrors are turned upon me: they pursue my soul as the wind: and my welfare passeth away as a cloud"), 9:26 ("They are passed away as the swift ships: as the eagle that hasteth to the prey"), and 14:2 ("He cometh forth like a flower, and is cut down: he fleeth also as a shadow, and continueth not").

2. In the 1830s, Chateaubriand fell deeply in debt. Knowing that he did not want the *Memoirs* published until fifty years after his death, no publisher would offer him an advance. Then, in February–March 1834, Chateaubriand's longtime mistress and ally, Madame Récamier, organized three weeks of private readings, which were held in her rooms in the Abbaye-aux-Bois, near the rue de Sèvres, in Paris. A small group of carefully selected guests had been invited. These readings were so well received that Chateaubriand soon after agreed to let several chapters of the *Memoirs* appear in journals and reviews. But the money earned from these pieces was not enough to sustain him.

   In 1836, again with Madame de Récamier's help, a society of shareholders was formed around the booksellers H.-L. Delloye and Adolphe Sala. This society sold shares in Chateaubriand's *Memoirs*, providing him with an immediate payment of 155,000 francs and a lifetime annuity of 12,000 francs, which was raised to 25,000 francs after the publication of his successful *Congrès de Vérone*. "In effect," as Paul Auster sums up this bizarre situation in his novel *The Book of Illusions*, "Chateaubriand mortgaged his autobiography to finance his old age."

3. The word translated as "troubles" here is *ennuis*, a sort of keyword in Chateaubriand's writing (and life). "*Ennui* is my element," Chateaubriand once wrote his friend the Comte de Marcellus; "I began to be bored

[*m'ennuyer*] in my mother's womb, and since then I have never been anything but bored [*désennuyé*]."

BOOK ONE

1. "Cut your long hopes down to the brief space of life." Horace's *Odes*, Book 1, Poem 11.

2. Literally, "I scatter gold" or "I sow gold," though also, in a sense probably unintended in the eleventh century, "I squander gold."

3. Red, as one of the heraldic colors.

4. "To him and his heirs, Saint Louis, King of the French, for his valor in battle, conferred golden fleurs-de-lys placed beside the golden pinecones."

5. In other words, the members of Chateaubriand's immediate family.

6. Malesherbes (b. 1721), a lawyer, a statesman, and a correspondent of J.-J. Rousseau, was a mentor to the young Chateaubriand, whom he encouraged to travel to America. In the 1750s and '60s, he advocated for the publication of Diderot and d'Alembert's *Encyclopedia*. As Secretary of State of the Maison du Roi, he rallied for the freedom of the press and the emancipation of Protestants and Jews. In 1792, he had the misfortune to defend Louis XVI at his trial. All Malesherbes's Republican sympathies and Enlightenment credentials couldn't save him from the Terror. On April 23, 1794, he was guillotined along with several members of his family, including his daughter and her husband, Chateaubriand's brother, Jean-Baptiste.

7. "No stranger to misfortune, I have learned to help the wretched," Virgil's *Aeneid*, Book 1, line 630.

8. *Commentarii de Bello Gallico* (*Commentaries on the Gallic War*), Book 3, Chapter 7.

9. Cedron, a ravine east of the Old City of Jerusalem, between the Temple Mount and the Mount of Olives, is the site of one of the earliest Christian monasteries, founded by Saint Sabbas in 483 CE.

10. La Chatolais (1701–1785), a French nobleman and jurist, was arrested in 1765 for conspiring against Louis XV. During the La Chatolais affair (now usually called "the Brittany Affair") he was imprisoned in the Château de Saint-Malo, where he wrote his *Memoirs* with a toothpick dipped in a mixture of water and soot.

11. "I would like to speak with you, my mind: / You have some faults I cannot hide." Nicolas Boileau's "À Mon Esprit."

12. Monsieur Després's insult in the original is *tête d'achôcre*. This phrase is still used in parts of Brittany and Normandy to describe a klutz, a know-nothing, a boor, a brute. It probably has no etymological connection with the quasi-homophonic Greek word Ἀχώρ, meaning dandruff, as Chateaubriand seems to think, nor with the French word *gourme*, which most immediately refers to "strangles" or "equine distemper" (a bacterial disease that affects young horses) but has various other connotations: a snot-nosed kid, a scab-picker, a dunderhead.

13. In English, "the Furrow."

14. Dante's *Paradiso* Canto 17, lines 58–65, 67–69.

15. The *Notitia Imperii*, or *Notitia dignitatum imperii Romani*, is a Roman government document of the fourth or fifth century CE, containing detailed information about the empire's provinces, officials, and the locations of its military forces.

16. "in sight of Tenedos." Virgil's *Aeneid*, Book 2, lines 21–22.

17. "on the lands of Machutis."

18. "Asylum, which in this city is most inviolable."

19. *Minihi* is a Breton word meaning "sanctified." The *minihis* of Brittany were places consecrated by a saint and therefore considered beyond the reach of human law. Criminals who sought asylum within them could not be arrested. Some of these places were quite large: the city of Saint-Malo, which had been visited by several saints, was considered one long *minihi*.

20. Gilles de Bretagne, a Baron de Chateaubriand and a Prince of Brittany, was the son of Jean V of Brittany and Jeanne de France, the daughter of King Charles VII of France. When, in 1444, his brother, François I of Brittany, denied his claim to a larger share of the family inheritance, Gilles made an alliance with King Henry VI of England. In July 1445, his brother intercepted a letter from Gilles to Henry. Accused of treason, he was captured in 1446. After several years of intrigue and incarceration, on April 25, 1450, in the Château de Moncontour, Gilles's jailers strangled him to death in his cell.

21. *Coutumes* (literally, customs) were regional laws established during the medieval era which continued to form the basis of many French judicial procedures under the Ancien Régime.

22. The Falkland Islands.

23. Delos, a Greek island, was the birthplace of Apollo and the site of the meetings of the Delian League, an assembly of city-states founded in the fifth century BCE.

24. Book 6, Chapter 1 of Aulus Gellius's *Attic Nights* (*Noctes Atticae*): "It is worth mentioning that Scipio Africanus did very frequently, at the end of the night, before the break of day, go to the Capitol and order the shrine of Jupiter opened. There he would remain a long time alone, consulting with Jupiter about the state of the republic. The guardians of the temple were greatly astonished that, despite his coming to the Capitol by himself, and at that early hour, the dogs, who were always ferocious toward other people, neither barked nor bit at Scipio."

25. Saint Augustine's *Confessions*, Book 9.

26. "I place my faith, Virgin, in your aid; / Serve as my defense and watch over my days; / And when my final hour / Comes to seal my fate, / Grant that I die / A good death." This hymn, which is still sung today, is called "Notre-Dame de Bons Secours."

27. In July 1795, more than ten thousand Royalist émigrés, led by Charles Eugène Gabriel de Sombreuil, landed on the Quiberon peninsula in an attempt to invade Brittany. At least half of these men were killed in battle or, like Gesril and Sombreuil, captured and executed by Republican troops.

28. Armorica was the Gallo-Roman name for Brittany. Its roots seem to be the Celtic *ar* (on or before) and the Latin *mare* (the sea). Hence: the Land beside the Sea.

29. Wace's *Roman de Rou*, lines 6395–6420. "The forest of Brécheliant, about which the Bretons tell many tales, is a deep, wide forest, famous throughout Brittany. In one part of the forest, the fountain of Barenton springs up from beneath a stone, and the hunters go there in sultry weather, and draw water with their horns, and douse the stone to summon the rain, which is then wont to fall, they say, over the whole forest; but I know not why. Here, too, fairies are to be seen, if the Bretons are to be believed, and many other wonders besides. Once there were many hawk-nests and huge herds of stag in this forest, but the peasants have destroyed them all. I went there in search of marvels. I saw the forest and the countryside and looked for marvels everywhere, but I found none. A fool I went, and a fool I returned. I sought folly, and was taken for a fool."

30. Pliny's *Natural History* Volume 1, Book 4. "Gallia Lugdunensis has … a celebrated river, the Loire, and also a very remarkable peninsula (*Paeninsulam spectatiorem*) which extends into the ocean."

31. In a letter sent September 2, 1671, Madame de Sévigné wrote her daughter: "I'm dying to be alone again. I find solitude very beautiful. Combourg is not so beautiful."

BOOK TWO

1. Étienne Bézout (1730–1783) was a gifted mathematician whose textbooks were widely taught in late eighteenth-century France.

2. The Saut des Poissonniers was a Maundy Thursday tradition in which every man who had sold fish during Lent had to jump in the pond.

3. Du Cange (1610–1688) was a French philologist who compiled the *Glossarium mediae et infimae Latinitatis*. This glossary traces the origins of the Quintaine to the thirteenth century, when jousters first began lancing a Turk, named Quintain, in effigy.

4. Most gladly and gallantly did he go
   Into the woods and over the river;
   For no men take to the woods so
   Gladly or so gallantly as the French.

   These lines are from a thirteenth-century historical poem called the *Chroniques rimée*, by Philippe Mouskes (d. 1282), which Chateaubriand would have come across in Du Cange's *Glossarium*. (See book two, note 3.)

5. Michel de Montaigne's "Of Liars."

6. The first line of Lucretius's *De Rerum Natura*.

7. Elegies of Tibullus, Book 1, line 45.

8. Synderesis is a scholastic term that Chateaubriand derives from Plato, via Saint Jerome, used to refer to the innate human impulse toward the good.

9. "Have courage, boy of noble birth!" A quotation from a line of Statius's *Silvae* (*macte animo, generose puer; sic itur ad astra*, "Have courage, boy of noble birth; it is thus that you shall reach the stars"), which is itself a recasting of Virgil's *Aeneid*, Book 9, line 641 (*macte nova virtute, puer*, "be proud, boy, in your newfound manhood").

10. Montaigne's "Of War Horses." "[The Romans] also had *desultorios equos*, horses trained in such a way that, while they were galloping at top speed, yoked side by side, without bridle or saddle, the Roman nobles, even fully armed, could launch themselves back and forth from one to the other."

11. Quoted from Racine's Spiritual Canticle 4, "On the Vain Occupations of Men in this Century":
    The bread I offer you
    Serves as food for the angels;

> God himself has made it
> From the finest of his wheat.

12. Charles Rollin (1661–1741) was a teacher, and a historian well known for his books about ancient Egypt and Rome.

13. "O Terpsichore, O Polyhymnia, / Come, come fill up our voices; / Reason Herself invites you here!"

14. Limoëlan (1768–1826), a French military officer, conspired to assassinate Napoleon in 1799. This assassination attempt, which involved an explosive device consisting of a barrel loaded with gunpowder, was referred to as *la Machine Infernale*.

15. La Fontaine Book 9, Fable 16, "The Monkey and the Cat."

16. An allusion to the mystical hymns of Orpheus, which were called "perfumes" (*thymiamata*).

17. Suetonius's *Lives of the Caesars*, Chapter 2, Section 16.

18. Job 38:11.

BOOK THREE

1. Montaigne's "Of Diversion."

2. The Abbé de Marolles (1600–1681) was a monk, a translator, and a memoirist. Chateaubriand here refers to a passage in his *Memoirs* in which Marolles recalls how his father, while away in Hungary during the Long War of 1591–1606, sent home four horses and a light chariot, in which he and his mother used to ride to church.

3. Following this passage in the manuscript of 1826, Chateaubriand wrote two paragraphs that he subsequently deleted:

> A single occurrence varied these evenings which might otherwise figure in a romance of the eleventh century. Sometimes, it happened that my father would interrupt his stroll and come sit down beside us at the hearth, telling us stories about the trials of his childhood and the travails of his life. He spoke of storms and dangers, a journey to Italy, a shipwreck on the coast of Spain.
>
> He had seen Paris, and he spoke of it as a place of abomination and as a foreign country: Bretons felt that China was in their neighborhood, but Paris seemed to them the end of the world. I listened attentively to my father. When I heard this man, who was so hard on himself, regret not having done enough for his family, and complain in curt, bitter words of his destiny; when I saw him, at the end of his account, rise abruptly, wrap himself in his cloak,

and resume his stroll, at first hastening his steps, then slowing them to match the movements of his heart, filial love brought tears to my eyes. In my mind, I went over my father's sorrows again, and it seemed to me that the sufferings undergone by the author of my days should have fallen on me and me alone.

4. Montaigne's "Of the Education of Children."

5. *Laures* in Chateaubriand's hand, but typically spelled *lares*: local deities of ancient Rome, their shrines were housed at crossroads.

6. On August 10, 1792, a riot inaugurated the downfall of the constitutional monarchy. The September massacres followed. One hundred and seventy-two priests and other residents of the Carmelite convent were killed.

7. "A dream appearing and wandering by day," Aeschylus's *Oresteia* (trans. Christopher Collard).

8. Book of Job 10:1, 14:1; Lucretius's *De Rerum Natura*, Book 5, line 223.

9. Ismen, a Saracen sorcerer, and Armida, a Saracen sorceress, are characters in Torquato Tasso's *Jerusalem Delivered*.

10. Tavernier (1605–1689), a Huguenot merchant and frequent traveler to the East, published a very popular account of his travels, *The Six Voyages of Jean-Baptiste Tavernier*, in 1675.

11. "The fields where Troy once stood," Virgil's *Aeneid*, Book 3, line 11.

12. "Unto the waves on the horizon," paraphrased from Abelard's *Historia Calamitatum*: "*ad horrisoni undas oceani.*" Remembering the beaches of Brittany, Abelard writes: "I went from danger to danger with eyes wide open, and there, by the waves of the dread-sounding ocean where no spit of land now could offer me flight, I called out in my prayers again and again" (trans. William Levitan).

13. Milton's *Paradise Lost*, Book 12, line 646: "and the world was all before them."

BOOK FOUR

1. On February 13, 1820, Charles-Ferdinand, Duc de Berry, was stabbed to death on the steps of the Opéra by a Bonapartist named Louis Pierre Louvel. Later that same year, Chateaubriand would compile a biography of the murdered man, titled *Mémoires, lettres et pièces authentiques touchant la vie et la mort de S. A. R. Monseigneur Charles-Ferdinand d'Artois, fils de France, duc de Berry.*

2. The "false Julian" is King Frederick the Great (1740–1786), who built his summer palace, the Schloss Sanssouci, in Potsdam, a "false Athens."

3. Martin Luther (1483–1546) is the "defrocked schismatic." Frederick II (1712–1786) is "the sophist to the crown."

4. "Editha Swanes-Hales, which is to say, the Swan-necked." The first two words are Old English. Chateaubriand borrows this line from Augustin Thierry's *History of the Conquest of England by the Normans*, Book 3. "They went to the heap of dead bodies," Thierry writes, "and examined them carefully one after another, but that which they sought was so much disfigured by wounds that they could not recognize it. Sorrowful, and despairing of succeeding in their search by themselves, they applied to a woman whom Harold, before he was king, had kept as his mistress, and entreated her to assist them. She was called Edith *Swanes-Hales*, which is to say, the *Swan-necked*. She consented to follow the two monks, and succeeded better than they had done, in discovering the corpse of the man whom she had loved" (trans. Charles Claude Hamilton).

5. An apocryphal story told by Abbé Maury about an episode in the life of the writer François Fénelon (1651–1715). Fénelon sits down one day beside a young Cambrai farmer who tells him that his cow has been commandeered by soldiers and taken to the next town over. Hearing this, he goes to fetch the cow himself and leads it back to the poor peasant (quoted in La Harpe's *Cours de littérature*, Volume 13).

6. This passage from Marshal de Montluc's *Memoirs* is quoted in Montaigne's "Of the Affection of Fathers to Their Children."

7. Rabelais's *Gargantua*, Book One.

8. In January 1815, Chateaubriand was present at the exhumation of Louis XVI and Marie-Antoinette, which took place in the Cimetière de la Madeleine.

9. François-Henri de Franquetot, Duc de Coigny (1737–1821), was one of Marie-Antoinette's most favored male companions. In the early years of the Revolution, he was rumored to have fathered the Queen's sons.

10. This is a slight exaggeration on Chateaubriand's part. In 1645, a woman named Anne Cauchie, a native of Dieppe, was reported to be one hundred and five years old and still "of very sound mind." Chateaubriand would probably have encountered this report either in Ludovic Vitet's *Histoire des anciennes villes de France* (1833) or his *Histoire de Dieppe* (1838).

11. Madame de Motteville's *Mémoires sur Anne d'Autriche et sa cour* (1723), Volume 1, Chapter 16.

12. Évariste de Parny, *Poésies érotiques*, 1778, lines from "Le Raccommodement":

> Oh, let our happy, well-appointed life
> Run in secret, beneath the wing of love,
> Like a brook that, just barely murmuring,
> And guarding all the ripples within its bed,
> Cautiously searches out the willow's shade,
> And doesn't dare appear upon the plains.

13. "Je l'ai planté, je l'ai vu naître" ("I have planted it, I have watched it grow") was a love song by Alexandre Deleyre; the tune was attributed, though the attribution is questionable, to Jean-Jacques Rousseau. Many songs of the Revolution were set to this tune, including Ginguené's "L'Arbre de la Liberté" ("The Tree of Liberty"). The Cadran-Bleu was a café on the boulevard du Temple frequented by the men behind the insurrection of August 10, 1792.

14. "in a short jacket." Ginguené, appointed in 1798 as ambassador to Turin, was quickly ordered back to France by Talleyrand, then Minister of Foreign Affairs, after his wife caused a scandal at the Court of Turin by appearing in this liberated Republican attire.

15. The Chénier mentioned here is not André Chénier but his younger brother, Marie-Joseph Chénier. When the latter died in January 1811, Chateaubriand's friends nominated him to inherit his seat in the Académie française (which had been incorporated into the Republican Institut de France in 1795). Despite paying his ceremonial visits to the other members of the Academy flippantly, often without dismounting from his horse, Chateaubriand was elected by a narrow margin on February 20. He wrote a very long speech. It wisely ended with several paragraphs praising Napoleon, but only after many pages obliquely but vigorously criticizing Marie-Joseph Chénier, not only as a poet but as a man. ("What! After a revolution that caused us to live through the events of several centuries in a few brief years, shall the writer be forbidden to consider all lofty moral considerations? Should he be forbidden from examining the serious side of things? Should he fritter away a frivolous life with grammatical quibbles, rules of taste, petty literary judgments?") Napoleon, outraged, returned the speech to Chateaubriand "marked *ab irato* with parentheses and pencil marks," but Chateaubriand refused to

rewrite it. He was consequently refused entrance to the Academy and fell further out of favor with the Emperor.

16. Rabelais's *Pantagruel*, Book 2, Chapter 6 (trans. Urquhart and Motteux).

17. In ancient Roman religion, *manes* are the deified souls of dead ancestors.

BOOK FIVE

1. Madame de Sévigné's Letter to Madame de Grignan, August 5, 1671 (trans. Leonard Tancock).

2. *Ker* is a slur or sobriquet for a Breton. A number of old Breton names begin with "Ker."

3. In this elusively allusive paragraph, Chateaubriand refers to a duel which took place about the year 1735 between two gentlemen: Jean François de Kératry (a younger son, or *cadet*, from La Cornuaille, not Morbihan as Chateaubriand says) and the Marquis de Sabran. Saint Corentin was appointed the first Bishop of Quimper sometime late in the fifth century CE. While it is possible that "three hundred years before Christ" is a misprint on Chateaubriand's part, more likely it is a parody of the ridiculous braggadocio under discussion.

4. "Now the baying waves of Scylla." A Latin line attributed to Virgil by some commentators, but probably apocryphal. Chateaubriand may be remembering the *Aeneid*, Book 1, line 200: "*Vos et Scyllaeam rabiem penitusque sonantis*," "You sailed by Scylla's rage, her echoing crags."

5. Valkyries are powerful female figures in Norse mythology who decide the fate of warriors and lead the dead to Valhalla. Canephori (literally, "basket bearers") were those virginal young noblewomen of ancient Athens charged with carrying the implements of ritual sacrifice in baskets atop their heads. They are often depicted in procession on vases and the entablatures of temples.

6. *Monsieur*, the Comte de Provence, was one of Louis XVI's brothers. Under the Restoration, he would become Louis XVIII.

7. Foulon was the Comptroller of Finances under Louis XVI. He and his son-in-law Bertier, a civil servant, were beheaded in front of the Hôtel de Ville on July 22, 1789.

8. The Marquis de Favras (b. 1744) was hanged for conspiring against the Revolution on February 19, 1790.

9. An allusion to *Paradise Lost*, Book 2, lines 894–897.

10. Sabots, wooden clogs worn by the peasants of northern France, came to be associated with working-class insurrection. It's from this association that we get the words *saboteur* and *sabotage*.

11. The word *calotin* is used to refer to anyone sporting a *calotte*, the black skullcap worn by Catholic ecclesiastics.

12. "The holy candle of Arras, / The torch of Provence, / Though they do not shed their light for us, / They set fire to France; / They cannot be touched, / But they may be snuffed." *The holy candle of Arras* refers to Robespierre, who was born in Arras; *the torch of Provence* to Mirabeau, whose family had roots in Marseilles.

13. Pierre L'Estoile (1546–1611) was a royal secretary and a diarist who lived during the reigns of Henri III and IV.

14. The royal family were imprisoned in the Tuileries, but at this stage they still went to the theater and threw parties. "This evening we are going to have another illumination," wrote Madame Elisabeth on September 25, 1789: "The garden will be superb, all hung with lamps and those little glass things which for two hundred years no one has been able to name without horror" (Imbert de Saint-Amand's *Marie-Antoinette at the Tuileries, 1789–1791*, trans. Elizabeth Gilbert Martin).

15. "Equality" is a reference to the Duc d'Orléans, who, in 1792, renamed himself "Phillippe-Égalité." He was guillotined in 1793.

16. Madame du Barry (1743–1793) had been Louis XV's *maîtresse-en-titre* (that is, his official mistress). She died under the guillotine.

17. "She gave up her life to heaven, / And softly went to sleep, / Without a murmur against its laws; / So it was her smile faded, / So she died, leaving no more trace / Than birdsong in the woods." Évariste de Parny's "Sur la mort d'une jeune fille."

18. "Whether it rains, or snows, or blows / It makes the long nights shorter." From Jean Cazotte's comic opera *Sabot perdu*.

19. This letter, dated March 22, 1791, reads as follows: "Mr. le Chevalier de Combourg, a nobleman of the State of Brittany and a neighbourg [*sic*] of mine, is going over to North America. The purpose of that journey, I presume, is to inrich [*sic*] his mind by the active contemplation of such a moving and happy country and to satisfy his soul by seeing the extraordinary man and thoses [*sic*] respectable citizens who, led by the hand of virtue through the most difficult contest, have made their chief counsellor of her in establishing and enjoying their liberty—his relations, for whom I have a very high regard, desire me to recommend him to the notice of your excellency. I do it with pleasure, because that gentleman has always appeared to me to have a good right to the commendable reputation which he does enjoy—he is a man of wit and much of his time is taken up by the cultivation of that natural gift."

20. A translation and a paraphrase of Lord Byron's *Childe Harold's Pilgrimage*, Canto 3, Part 2, line 1: "Once more upon the waters! yet once more!"

BOOK SIX

1. Chateaubriand alters this description slightly. The original document apparently reads: "brown hair and fritted with the small Pox."

2. Voltaire's "Epistle to Phillis":

    Ah, *Your Grace*, how your life today,

    Marked by honors and great cachet,

    Differs from those happy times!

3. An image that Chateaubriand revisits in Book 29, Chapter 5: "Madame Récamier went to Kensington Gardens with Marquess Douglas, later the Duke of Hamilton, who has since entertained Charles X at Holy Rood, and with his sister the Duchess of Somerset. The crowd followed behind the beautiful foreigner. This effect was repeated every time she showed herself in public. The newspapers rang with her name; her image, engraved by Bartollozi, spread over all of England. The author of *Antigone*, M. Ballanche, reports that ships carried it as far as the islands of Greece: beauty was returning to the places where its image had been invented. There is a sketch of Madame Récamier by David, a full-length portrait by Gérard, and a bust by Canova. The portrait is Gérard's masterpiece; but it doesn't satisfy me, because in it I recognize the model's features without recognizing her expression."

4. "The first glimmer of M. de Chateaubriand's love of cats," his friend the Comte de Marcellus writes in his eccentric book *Chateaubriand et son temps*: "'I love the cat,' he once told me, 'for his independent and almost ingrate character. I love the indifference with which he descends from salons to his native gutters. He lets himself be pet; he arches his back; but what he feels is pure physical pleasure—not, like the dog, a silly satisfaction to adore and be loyal to his master, who thanks the beast with a kick. The cat lives alone, obeys when he feels like it, goes to sleep to get a better view, and claws at everything he can claw.'" The affinity between Chateaubriand and cats was both spiritual and semiotic: his wife, in her letters, often referred to her husband as "the Cat" (*le Chat*).

5. A verse from Stephen Storace's comic-opera *Pirates* (1792). As can be seen throughout the *Memoirs*, Chateaubriand cherished the lyrics of popular songs at least as much as the *Divine Comedy* and *Paradise Lost*.

6. Captain Cook (1728–1779), killed in Hawaii, and Captain La Pérouse

(1741–1788), lost in the South Seas, were dead men by the time of Chateaubriand's voyage to America.

7. Shakuntala, the daughter of the sage Vishvamitra, is celebrated in the Sanskrit epic the *Mahābhārata*.

8. "All the water was silent." A scrambled quotation of Virgil's *Aeneid*, Book 1, line 164: *Aequora tuta silent.*

9. Genesis 1:31 "And God saw every thing that he had made, and, behold, *it was* very good."

10. Psalms 19:1 "The heavens declare the glory of God."

11. Psalms 19:5 "as a bridegroom coming out of his chamber, *and* rejoiceth as a strong man to run a race."

12. Guillaume Le Breton's *Philippide*, Book 1, line 30: "Muse, help me show that I know the sea on which I now spread my sails."

13. Psalms 107:27 "They reel to and fro, and stagger like a drunken man, and are at their wits' end."

14. The *Aeneid*, Book 5, lines 614–615.

15. "Though my ardor burns immortal / Yet my love's for God alone."

16. "Now you see before you the Fortunate Isles," Torquato Tasso's *Jerusalem Delivered*, Canto 15, Stanza 35.

17. The Delaware River runs along Philadelphia's east bank. A case in which Chateaubriand relies on his memory even for an easily verifiable fact.

18. In 1791, there were at least ten thousand French émigrés in Philadelphia, some of them priests and aristocrats fleeing the Revolution in France, some of them colonists fleeing the revolutions in Santo Domingo and other French colonies. Many of these people were planning to join the colony of French aristocrats centered around the town of Gallipolis, on the banks of the Ohio River, which had been settled by some eight hundred (predominantly aristocratic) families only a few months earlier.

19. It is unclear whether Chateaubriand ever met Washington. Several historians have argued that the two men missed each other by a day. In July 1791, when he first arrived in Philadelphia, Chateaubriand was eager to get to Niagara Falls, and Washington, who had just come home after a tour of the southern states, was laid up in bed, as George D. Painter records, "by a recurrence of the carbuncle on his left buttock that had made the physicians despair of his life at New York two years before."

Painter for one is convinced that Chateaubriand *did* meet Washington, despite the many Chateaubriandists who "have rashly concluded...

that the interview and dinner which he describes so vividly never happened. On the contrary there can be no doubt that they did occur," he contends, not in July, as Chateaubriand remembered it, but in late November or early December 1791, when he returned to Philadelphia from the wilderness.

20. Alonso d'Ercilla (1533–1596) was a Spanish soldier and the author of the epic poem *La Araucana*. In Cantos 32 and 33, the poet entertains his fellow soldiers with the "true story" of Dido.

21. Corneille's *Attila*, Act 1, Scene 1.

BOOK SEVEN

1. Inscription on the tomb of Leonidas and his companions. In a footnote to the *Itinerary from Paris to Jerusalem* appended to a long account of his fruitless search for Leonidas's tomb in Sparta, Chateaubriand confesses that he had forgotten this tomb is not in Sparta but Thermopylae.

2. Charles Asgill was not arrested along the Hudson, nor was he executed. The ballad that the Quaker girl sings is most likely "Major André's Complaint," in which each verse ends with the refrain "But who can tell if thou, my dear, wilt e'er remember me?," and which tells the tale of Major John André, hanged for treason in 1780, in Tappan, New York. Curiously, Chateaubriand does not make the same mistake the first time he records this story, in a footnote to his *Essai historique* (1797). In this earlier remembrance, a passenger calls out, "Over there is the place that Major André was executed." Then "a very pretty American girl" sings the ballad of the doomed young man in a "timidly voluptuous and emotional voice."

3. The Erie Canal.

4. Antar (525–608 CE) was an Arab warrior and poet; but Chateaubriand here is alluding to the poem *Antar*, believed to have been written down by Al-Asma'i (c. 740–828 CE), which recounts Antar's heroic life. *Antar* was first translated into French, from an English translation of the Arabic, in 1819. The horse is described in Job 39:19–25.

5. The story of Phocion's ashes is from Plutarch, *The Life of Phocion*, Book 11. Phocion, an Athenian statesman, was sentenced to death for treason: he drank hemlock, but his corpse was banished from Attica. A poor man took the body away and burned it in Megara, whereupon a local woman collected the bones, carried them in her apron to her house, and buried them beneath the hearth.

6. Homer's *Odyssey*, Book 7, lines 146–147.

7. "And the swift Anio and the sacred grove of Tibur." Horace's *Carmen Saeculare*, Book 7, line 13.

8. Montaigne's "Of Cannibals."

9. Pliny the Elder's *Natural History*, Book 10, Chapter 59. "Agrippina, the wife of Claudius, had a thrush that could imitate human speech, a thing that was then unheard of. Today, the young Caesars have a starling and some nightingales that are being taught words of Greek and Latin."

10. Chateaubriand's riff on Bossuet's once famous funeral oration for the Prince de Condé: "Accept these last efforts of a voice that you once knew well. You put all my orations to an end."

11. Lady Conyngham, Francis Conyngham's mother, was King George IV's mistress. She was fifty-two years old in 1822.

BOOK EIGHT

1. Lucretius's *De Rerum Natura*, Book 2, line 578.

2. Ximena, the wife of El Cid, was the subject of many Spanish ballads.

3. Pierre Ronsard, "To Mary Stewart":

> In such garb were you appareled
> The day you left this beauteous land
> (Whose scepter you once held in hand),
> When you strolled, o'erburdened with cares,
> Bathing thy breast with crystal tears,
> In the gardens of that royal house
> That bears the name of a fountain.

4. Julie and Saint-Preux are the fictional lovers whose letters make up J.-J. Rousseau's epistolary novel *Julie, or the New Héloïse* (1761). (The old Héloïse is Héloïse d'Argenteuil, who exchanged letters of love with Pierre Abelard.)

5. Tasso's *Jerusalem Delivered*, Canto 7, Stanza 68.

6. "Beside a brook, thin replica of Simois, Andromache made an offering to the ashes [of Hector]," Virgil's *Aeneid*, Book 3, lines 302–303 (trans. Robert Fitzgerald).

7. In the text you have my rendition of Chateaubriand's own very free prose translation of George Hill's *Ruins of Athens*, Cantos 2 and 17. Here are the lines in the original:

> Alas! for her, the beautiful, but lone,

> Dethroned queen!
>
> .   .   .   .
>
> There sits the queen of temples—grey and lone.
> She, like the last of an imperial line,
> Has seen her sister structures, one by one,
> To time their gods and worshippers resign.

8. La Fontaine, Book 11, Fable 8, "The Old Man and the Three Young Men." Chateaubriand is probably remembering that, of the three young men that the old man outlives, one drowns near the harbor on his way to America.

9. Herodotus, in Book 3 of the *Histories*, speaks of a species of ant "smaller in size than dogs but larger than foxes" which brings up gold from its underground burrows. The story about Hercules and the golden vessel (the golden cup, in most translations) is told in Book 2 of Athenaeus's *Deipnosophistae*.

10. Farid ud-Din (1173–1266) was a Persian poet, dervish, and Sufi saint, murdered by Mongols invading Persia. Chateaubriand would likely have encountered Farid ud-Din's mystical poem *Pend-Nameh* in Silvestre de Sacy's translation, *Le Livre des Conseils*, published in 1819.

BOOK NINE

1. An allusion to La Fontaine's Book 1, Fable 1, "The Ant and the Grasshopper": "He went crying famine / To his neighbor the ant, / Imploring him to lend him / Some wheat to sustain him / Until the next spring."

2. Emigrated French aristocrats sent distaffs to aristocrats at home in an attempt to shame them into defending their honor abroad in the Royalist armies. Thomas Carlyle writes of this practice in Book 3, Chapter 1 of his *History of the French Revolution*: "Captain after Captain, in Royalist mustachioes, mounts his war-horse or his Rozinante war-garron, and rides minatory across the Rhine; till all have ridden. Neither does civic Emigration cease; Seigneur after Seigneur must, in like manner, ride or roll; impelled to it, and even compelled. For the very Peasants despise him, in that he dare not join his order and fight. Can he bear to have a Distaff, a *Quenouille* sent to him: say in copper-plate shadow, by post; or fixed up in wooden reality over his gate-lintel: as if he were no Hercules, but an Omphale?"

3. These lines were composed by Claude-Carloman de Rulhière (1735–1791):
   D'Egmont and Love once visited this shore:
   An emblem of its beauty
   Shone a moment on its fleeting waters.
   Now D'Egmont is gone; Love alone remains.
4. Lyrics from Flins des Oliviers's verse-comedy *Le Réveil d'Épiménide*:
   Our brave defenders' glory
   No foreign foes can rob,
   But I detest the fury
   Of a sanguinary mob!
   Let Europe be almighty,
   Let us stay forever free,
   But let us stay forever righteous
   Defending France's unity!
5. François-Joseph Talma (1763–1826) was a famous French actor much admired by Chateaubriand, who devotes most of Book 13, Chapter 9 of the *Memoirs* to singing his praises. Why was Chateaubriand fascinated by Talma? Because, he says, Talma "was a man of his century and of ancient times"; he had taken on the "deranged spirit of the Revolution through which he had lived"; and, without him, "certain marvels in the work of Corneille and Racine would have remained unknown forever."
6. *Tricoteuses* were women who knitted while the tribunals and the guillotine went about their work.
7. An allusion to La Fontaine's Book 8, Fable 13, "Damon and Phillis."
8. Sanson (1739–1806) was the Royal Executioner under Louis XVI and the High Executioner under the Republic. Apparently, his only loyalty was to his métier. Mademoiselle Théroigne de Méricourt (1762–1817) was a popular entertainer first celebrated by the Revolutionary crowds and then abused by them. She died insane in the Hospice de la Salpêtrière. "Colin" and "Babet" were stock names for lovers in French pastoral poems and plays.
9. Chateaubriand here refers to an oft-repeated, apparently factual episode recounted in Jules Michelet's *History of the French Revolution*, Book 2, Chapter 2: "Major Belzunce was a handsome, witty officer, but also impertinent, violent, haughty. He made no secret of his contempt for the National Assembly, for the people, the *rabble*; he used to walk through town armed to the teeth with a ferocious-looking servant. His looks were provoking. The people lost patience and threatened and besieged the

barracks; an officer had the impudence to fire, and then the crowd went to get the cannon; Belzunce surrendered or was surrendered to be taken to prison, but he was not allowed to reach it; he was fired upon and killed, his body torn to pieces: a woman ate his heart."

10. Francis II, to whom Chateaubriand earlier refers as "Francis II of Germany," was king of Hungary, Croatia, and Bohemia. He was elected Holy Roman Emperor on July 5, 1792.

11. The Sixteen was a sort of Committee of Public Safety avant la lettre, representing each of the sixteen neighborhoods of Paris and established by a group of priests and middle-class Parisian Catholics in 1588.

12. An allusion to *Paradise Lost*, Book 2, lines 790–798.

13. According to Chateaubriand's source (Michaud's *Biographie Universelle* of 1820), Marat's ashes were deposited in a chamber pot and dumped in the gutter of the rue Montmartre shortly after the Ninth of Thermidor (July 1794).

14. Jacques Clément was the Leaguer who assassinated King Henry III—an act Pope Sixtus V praised as proof of Clément's devotion to the true faith.

15. A reference to the killing of Henry I of France, sometimes called Henry the Scarface, or *Le Balfré*, who was murdered by the King's Bodyguard, according to Chateaubriand's source, the diaries of Pierre L'Éstoile, in the "lower courtyard" (not "an upper room") of the Château de Blois in 1588.

16. Montaigne's "Of Physiognomy."

17. "M. Maret of the Empire," or the Duc de Bassano, served as Secretary of State and, later, Minister of Foreign Affairs under Napoleon Bonaparte. "M. Barère of the Republic," who later became a member of the Committee for Public Safety, escaped execution as Chateaubriand says, and lived (in prison, in exile, and finally in Paris under the July Monarchy) until 1841.

18. "[Swift-footed tigers,] the offspring of rapid Zephyrs." Oppian's *Cynegetica*, Book 1. Although he here refers to the ancient notion that there were no male tigers and that all tigers were fathered by the West Wind, Oppian himself gave this notion no credence, as the *Cynegetica* itself lets us know.

19. In the 1790s, some *citoyennes* took to sporting green fans printed with articles of the new Constitution; the slogan *Liberté, Égalité, Fraternité*; or portraits of famous Republican heroes.

20. "Everything changes." Lucretius's *De Rerum Natura*, Book 5, line 830.

21. Omphale was the queen of the ancient kingdom of Lydia, in Asia Minor. According to myth, the Delphic Oracle punished Hercules for having murdered Iphitus, King Eurytus's son, by making him Omphale's slave for a year. In depictions of the myth, Hercules (dressed in women's clothes and often performing traditionally feminine tasks such as spinning or weaving) is shown at the feet of Omphale (dressed in manly Herculean garb: typically a lionskin).

22. Louis was negotiating with Charles the Bold in the town of Péronne in 1468 when news came that the Liégeois, who were under Louis' secret protection, had assassinated several of Charles's Burgundian allies in Liège. Louis XI, now imprisoned in the Château de Peronne, avoided execution only by signing a humiliating treaty which required him to travel with Charles and help put down the Liégeois rebellion.

23. A reference to Louis XI, who propagated the Charlemagne legend in France. In 1483, Louis presented the cathedral at Aix-la-Chapelle with a gold reliquary to hold the bones of Charlemagne's right arm. He also instituted an annual rent of 4,000 livres, which every French king thereafter would pay to the Chapter of Aix-la-Chapelle. In return, every time a new French king was coronated, the previous king's mortuary sheet was sent to Aix-la-Chapelle to be draped over Charlemagne's tomb.

24. Chateaubriand's own source here seems to be Étienne Pasquier's *Recherches de la France*, Book 5, Chapter 16, which adapts the tale of Charlemagne and the Corpse first related in Petrarch's *Familiar Letters*.

25. "Vacant kingdoms," Virgil's *Aeneid*, Book 6, line 269. A description of the underworld.

26. Salvian's *De Gubernatione Dei*, Book 6. After Trèves was ravaged by barbarian invaders, the few nobles left alive petitioned Rome to reestablish the theater and the circus. Said Salvian: "Do you then ask for theaters, and demand a circus from our emperors? For what condition, I ask, what people and what city? A city burned and destroyed, a people captive and killed, who have perished, or mourn their dead; a city of which nothing survives but sheer calamity.... So great are the miseries of the survivors that they surpass the ill fortune of the dead" (trans. Eva M. Sanford).

27. Lucius Cary, the Viscount Falkland (1610–1643), felt duty-bound to serve in Charles I's army during the first English Civil Wars, though he was a staunch believer in liberty. "Endowed with a threefold genius for literature, arms, and policy; faithful to the Muses, even in the tent, and

to Liberty, even in a palace; devoted to an ill-fated monarch, although by no means blind to his faults," Chateaubriand wrote in his study of English literature and history, "Falkland should be remembered with a mixture of melancholy and admiration."

28. General Georges Félix de Wimpffen (1744–1814), the Commandant of Thionville.

29. This sentence, as confusing in French as it is in English, seems to suggest that even if the Army of Princes did not triumph at Thionville, like the Great Condé (1621–1686) at the Battle of Rocroi, at least it was not annihilated, like Feuquières (b. 1590), who was killed during the Siege of Thionville of 1640.

30. "To whom a glorious victory has been granted with our help," Guillaume Le Breton's *Philippide*, Book 12, line 782.

31. Hugues Métel (1080–1157) was a French priest and poet. The allusion is to his apologue "Of the Wolf Who Became a Hermit."

32. "The victor seized the chariots and a new wife." These words, which Chateaubriand had previously quoted in his *Études historiques*, come from the fifth-century Gaulish writer Sidonius Apollinaris's *Panegyrics*. Apollinaris here is recounting how the Roman Emperor Majorian's troops successfully attacked the Franks while the latter were celebrating the marriage of one of their chieftains.

33. Homer's *Odyssey*, Book 4, line 606.

34. "Menelaus, lord of the great war-cry," Homer's *Iliad*, Book 17, line 656.

35. "the beautiful waters / of the Moselle, gliding by in quiet murmurings," from the Roman writer Ausonius's poem *Mosella*, line 21.

36. The Cimetière du Père Lachaise was established under Napoleon in 1804. In a notebook, Chateaubriand made the following entry: "Père Lachaise: / 27 thousand tombstones / 230 thousand bodies / Battlefields are everywhere / 'And the worm in the grave has alone found his heart' / Talma, Abbé Delille, Fontanes at Père Lachaise / Centralization of death."

37. Morellet was a virulent critic of *Atala*. In a review published in May 1801, he would say that the book violated the rules of classical art and modern decorum alike.

38. Honoré Jean Riouffe was the author of *Mémoires d'un détenu, pour servir à l'histoire de la tyrannie de Robespierre* (Memoirs of a Prisoner, Being a History of the Tyranny of Robespierre), from which this passage is taken.

39. The Vendean general is Charles de Bonchamps, one of the leaders of the Royalist Insurrection in the Vendée. "Old France made no appearance during the Revolution," Chateaubriand wrote in an article published in September 1819, "except in Condé's Army and in the western provinces."

40. A reference to the *Memoirs* of Antoine Arnauld (1616–1698), who was in Verdun in 1639, during the same Siege of Thionville at which Feuquières was killed.

41. Dysentery.

42. Allusion to a passage in Volume 12 of Piganiol de La Force's *Nouvelle Description géographique et historique de la France*: "Jean Balue was the son of a Miller in Verdun. A wandering Monk took him away very young from his father's house, & made him carry his sack. In return for this service, Jean learned some scraps of bad Latin & some seeds of guile that did not fall on barren ground. He was cunning, rough, anxious, full of a thousand kinds of ruses & tricks; in a word, he was capable of doing anything & of saying anything. He became, by and by, the Comptroller General of Finances & Secretary of State; in 1464 the Bishop of Évreux; & on June fifth, 1467, was made a Cardinal, & Bishop of Angers the eighteenth of the same year. Louis XI, having discovered his disloyalty, had him arrested and imprisoned him for fourteen years in the Château de Montbazon or in that of the Bastille."

43. According to the *Dictionnaire de l'Académie française* of 1789, "Doctors say *confluent smallpox* to indicate smallpox that are extremely widespread, as opposed to *discrete smallpox*, which indicates that the spots do not overlap." George D. Painter, in *The Longed-for Tempests*, suggests that, though Chateaubriand "naturally assumed he had smallpox, as did all who saw him ... from his symptoms it seems more likely to have been a typical case of chicken-pox, aggravated by his wound and by weakness from dysentery and hardship."

BOOK TEN

1. The italicized imagery of this passage is taken from La Fontaine, Book 7, Fable 17, "The Cat, the Weasel, and the Little Rabbit."

2. The opening lines of Jacques Cazotte's "Ballad of Sir Enguerrand," which tells the story of a wandering knight who dares to stay from dusk till dawn in a castle haunted by the ghost of a Lady, murdered by her jealous husband. When the Lady appears, Sir Enguerrand makes the sign of the cross, and the ghost vanishes.

3. A reference to Book Two of Matteo Maria Boiardo's *Orlando Innamorato* (rather than Ariosto's quixotic sequel, *Orlando Furioso*), in which Orlando, tricked into the Ardennes forest by wicked magic, sees a crystal palace at the bottom of a spring. He is so excited by the sight of the ladies dancing underwater that he dives in, armor and all. Rosalind and "the exiled Duke" are from Shakespeare's *As You Like It*.

4. A reference to the legend of the Wandering Jew, common all over Europe from the thirteenth century on, and more specifically to the Wandering Jew's last appearance, in Brussels, in the Duchy of Brabant, on April 22, 1774. The ballad Chateaubriand quotes was penned by Pierre-Jean de Béranger (1780–1857).

5. Allusion to Book 18 of the *Odyssey*, in which, before slaughtering the suitors, Odysseus returns to Ithaca in a beggar's guise.

6. "as a starving man chews bread," Dante's *Inferno*, Canto 32, line 127.

7. The primrose.

8. Voltaire's *Henriade*, Canto 1.

9. Nisus speaks these words to Euryalus in Virgil's *Aeneid*, Book 9, 212: "Your age is more deserving of life."

10. "… my health, disturbed by long voyages and many cares, vigils, and studies, is so deplorable I fear I shall not be able to fulfill the promise that I made, concerning the other volumes of the *Essai historique*."

11. Montaigne's "Apology for Raymond Sebond."

12. Shakespeare's *Richard III*, Act 4, Scene 3.

13. "Come down from propitious [skies]." A line from the Italian poet Pietro Metastasio's "Epithalamium."

14. Quoted from Rousseau's *Confessions*, Book 8. Diderot had been imprisoned in the Vincennes for having published his *Lettre sur les aveugles* (1749).

15. Addison's *Cato*, Act 5. These are the first lines of a monologue spoken directly before Cato kills himself.

16. Charlotte, born March 9, 1781, was sixteen or seventeen years old at the time.

17. Madame (Giuditta) Pasta (1797–1865) was an Italian opera singer.

18. Madame Récamier.

19. Dante's *Inferno*, Canto 1, line 74.

BOOK ELEVEN

1. Jacques Callot (1592–1663), a printmaker, was well known for his images of masked grotesque figures.

2. This is not the last time Charlotte appears in the *Memoirs*. In Book 27, Chapter 11, Chateaubriand recounts her visit to France in 1823, when Chateaubriand was Minister of Foreign Affairs under the Restoration:

   By one of those inexplicable miseries of man, I was then preoccupied by a war on which the fate of the French monarchy depended, and something was no doubt missing from my voice, for Charlotte, on returning to England, sent me a letter in which she showed herself wounded by the coolness with which I received her. I did not dare either to respond to her or to send her back the literary fragments that she had given me and to which I had promised to make some additions. If it is true that she had good reason to complain of my behavior, I should burn what I told of my first sojourn overseas in the fire [...]. The desire to burn that which regards Charlotte, although I may have treated her with religious respect, is at one with my desire to destroy these *Memoirs*. If they still belonged to me, or if I were in a position to buy them back, I might well yield to the temptation. I have such a disgust for everything, such scorn for the present and the immediate future—such a firm conviction that from now on men, taken together as the public (this shall go on for several centuries), will be pathetic—that I blush to use my final moments on earth writing about things past, describing a ruined world of which they will no longer know either the language or the name.

3. An abbreviated quotation of Virgil's *Aeneid*, Book 1, lines 353–354, *in somnis inhumati venit imago / Conjugis*: "in a dream came the image of her unburied / spouse." The dreamer here is Dido; the unburied spouse her husband, Sychaeus, who was murdered by her brother, Pygmalion.

4. Book Four of Rabelais's *Pantagruel*.

5. In Act 5, Scene 2 of *As You Like It*, Rosalind, disguised as Ganymede, says to Orlando: "O, my dear Orlando, how it grieves me to see thee wear thy heart in a scarf!"

6. Guillaume de Lamoignon (1617–1677), Christian's ancestor, was the first President of the Paris Parliament.

7. In the days of Louis XIV, Ninon de Lenclos (1616–1706) was, like Mrs. Lindsay, a *demi-mondaine*. In London, Mrs. Lindsay, whose French husband had died shortly after their marriage, had become Christian de Lamoignon's mistress.

8. In defense of the endowment of Catholic bishops, Montlosier had addressed the Constituent Assembly, saying: "Drive them from their palaces and they will seek refuge in the huts of those indigents whom they

have fed; rob them of their golden crosses, and they will take up wooden ones in their stead. It was a wooden cross which saved the world!"

9. All these men, like Montlosier, hailed from the province of Auvergne.

10. Claire de Duras (1777–1820) was the author of several novels, including *Ourika* (1823). In 1809, she became Chateaubriand's close friend, faithful correspondent, and eventually his political ally under the Restoration.

11. Joseph Joubert (1754–1824) was one of Chateaubriand's closest literary friends. In 1802, when he was first contemplating the *Memoirs*, he outlined his plan in a letter to Joubert, who encouraged him to pursue the project. In Book 13, Chapter 7, Chateaubriand memorializes him as follows:

> Full of crazes and originality, M. Joubert will be forever missed by those who knew him. He had an extraordinary hold on the mind and the heart, and once he had taken possession of you his image was there like a fact, like a fixed idea, like an obsession that you could not shake. His great pretension was to tranquility, and yet no one could have been more anxious: he kept an eye on himself, hoping to guard against those soulful emotions that he believed harmful to his health, but his friends were always disrupting the precautions he took to stay well, for he could not help being moved by their sadness or joy: he was an egotist who occupied himself only with others. To regain his strength, he deemed it necessary to close his eyes as often as possible and to go without speaking for hours at a stretch: God knows what noise and commotion went on inside him during these periods of self-prescribed silence. M. Joubert also changed his diet and his regimen from one moment to the next, so that one day he'd be living on milk and the next on ground beef; one day he'd go bounding at a grand trot over the roughest roads, and the next he'd be dawdling with short steps on freshly paved avenues. When he read a book, he would tear out the pages that displeased him and consequently came to possess a private library composed of cored works bound in overlarge covers.
>
> A profound metaphysician, his philosophy, following an elaboration all its own, became painting or poetry. A Plato with the heart of a La Fontaine, he had adopted an idea of perfection that prevented him from finishing anything. In the manuscripts discovered after his death, he says: "I am like an Aeolian harp that

makes beautiful sounds and plays no tune." Madame Victorine de Chastenay claimed that "he had the look of a soul that has encountered a body by accident and was muddling through as best it could." A true and charming statement.

12. According to Chateaubriand in *The Martyrs*, this song began: "When we have conquered a thousand Frankish warriors, how could we fail to conquer a thousand Persians!"

13. Jacques Bonhomme was the moniker that fourteenth-century aristocrats gave Guillaume Cale and other peasants who participated in the violent uprising known as the Jacquerie (1358). François de Charette (1763–1796) was a Royalist leader in the Vendée who commanded a troop of peasants in battles against the Republicans: he was forced to surrender in 1796 and was executed by firing squad.

14. "The Fates find their way." Virgil's *Aeneid*, Book 3, line 395.

15. Virgil's *Eclogues*, 6, lines 82–83: "[Silenus] sings all the airs heard on the fortunate banks of the Eurotas, when old Apollo mused upon the lyre."

16. Catullus's Poem 65, lines 9–12.

17. Ovid's *Fasti*, Book 6, line 772.

BOOK TWELVE

1. Book of Tobit 12:15.

2. Michelangelo Buonarroti's "On Dante."

3. Homer's *Iliad*, Book 9.

4. Shakespeare's Sonnet 37.

5. Shakespeare's Sonnet 71.

6. Montaigne's "Of Vanity."

7. Arthur Young's *Farmer's Tour through France, Spain, and Italy*.

8. Madame de Staël, in her study, *De la littérature considérée dans ses rapports avec les institutions sociales* (1800).

9. Quoted in Montaigne's "Apology for Raymond Sebond."

10. Toward the end of his life, Edward III abandoned his former mistress, the Countess of Salisbury, for Alice Pearce, a woman of wit and beauty who is said to have exercised great influence over the King. She was banished from England shortly after Edward's death.

11. Jean-François de La Harpe's *The Triumph of Religion, or the Martyred King*, Canto 1.

12. Dante's *Purgatorio*, Canto 8, lines 5–6: "when he has heard the distant bell / that seems to mourn the dying day."

13. A reference to *Cymbeline*, Act 3, Scene 4: "I' the world's volume / Our Britain seems as of it, but not in't; / In a great pool a swan's nest."

14. The confrontation between Edmund Burke and William Pitt described by Chateaubriand took place in May 1791 (when he was in America). The quotations that Chateaubriand incorporates into the *Memoirs* are taken from the Parliamentary Register.

15. The manuscript that Chateaubriand calls *The Natchez*, which he had begun in America and brought with him to Prussia, consisted of 2,393 folio pages. He would not be reunited with these pages until September 20, 1816. Eventually, he would revise portions of this manuscript into two separate works: *The Natchez: An Indian Romance* (1826) and *Voyage en Amérique* (1827).

OTHER NEW YORK REVIEW CLASSICS

For a complete list of titles, visit www.nyrb.com or write to:
Catalog Requests, NYRB, 435 Hudson Street, New York, NY 10014

J.R. ACKERLEY My Dog Tulip*
J.R. ACKERLEY My Father and Myself*
RENATA ADLER Pitch Dark*
RENATA ADLER Speedboat*
AESCHYLUS Prometheus Bound; translated by Joel Agee*
LEOPOLDO ALAS His Only Son *with* Doña Berta*
CÉLESTE ALBARET Monsieur Proust
DANTE ALIGHIERI The Inferno
KINGSLEY AMIS Dear Illusion: Collected Stories*
KINGSLEY AMIS Ending Up*
KINGSLEY AMIS Girl, 20*
KINGSLEY AMIS Lucky Jim*
KINGSLEY AMIS The Old Devils*
ROBERTO ARLT The Seven Madmen*
U.R. ANANTHAMURTHY Samskara: A Rite for a Dead Man*
WILLIAM ATTAWAY Blood on the Forge
W.H. AUDEN (EDITOR) The Living Thoughts of Kierkegaard
W.H. AUDEN W.H. Auden's Book of Light Verse
ERICH AUERBACH Dante: Poet of the Secular World
EVE BABITZ Eve's Hollywood*
EVE BABITZ Slow Days, Fast Company: The World, the Flesh, and L.A.*
DOROTHY BAKER Cassandra at the Wedding*
DOROTHY BAKER Young Man with a Horn*
J.A. BAKER The Peregrine
S. JOSEPHINE BAKER Fighting for Life*
HONORÉ DE BALZAC The Human Comedy: Selected Stories*
HONORÉ DE BALZAC The Memoirs of Two Young Wives*
HONORÉ DE BALZAC The Unknown Masterpiece *and* Gambara*
VICKI BAUM Grand Hotel*
SYBILLE BEDFORD A Favorite of the Gods *and* A Compass Error*
SYBILLE BEDFORD A Legacy*
SYBILLE BEDFORD A Visit to Don Otavio: A Mexican Journey*
MAX BEERBOHM The Prince of Minor Writers: The Selected Essays of Max Beerbohm*
STEPHEN BENATAR Wish Her Safe at Home*
FRANS G. BENGTSSON The Long Ships*
ALEXANDER BERKMAN Prison Memoirs of an Anarchist
GEORGES BERNANOS Mouchette
MIRON BIAŁOSZEWSKI A Memoir of the Warsaw Uprising*
ADOLFO BIOY CASARES The Invention of Morel
PAUL BLACKBURN (TRANSLATOR) Proensa*
CAROLINE BLACKWOOD Great Granny Webster*
RONALD BLYTHE Akenfield: Portrait of an English Village*
NICOLAS BOUVIER The Way of the World
EMMANUEL BOVE Henri Duchemin and His Shadows*
MALCOLM BRALY On the Yard*
MILLEN BRAND The Outward Room*
ROBERT BRESSON Notes on the Cinematograph*

* *Also available as an electronic book.*